Praise for *G*

"A lively and compelling narrative, 1[...]
the siege, from the grinding everyday [...]
the numbing terror of incessant bombardment . . . In their fine book,
such indelible episodes go far to explain why Gibraltar's long ordeal
captured the imagination of contemporaries—and why the Rock's
future continues to matter to Britons and Spaniards today."
—Stephen Brumwell, *The Wall Street Journal*

"A page-turning tale of one of the era's longest and most significant
sieges . . . This well organized, fast-paced book is a worthwhile addition to the literature on a still-neglected subject."
—*Publishers Weekly*

"The husband-and-wife historian team once again exhibit their talent
for enlivening British history. . . . Many readers will wonder why this
episode hasn't been made into a movie, with all the heroics of soldiers,
civilians, and, especially, families. Thankfully, the authors had a vast
trove of letters and diaries of those who lived through the siege, and
they use them to great effect. . . . The story is as compelling as it is
fantastic—page-turning history of one of the most important eras of
Western civilization."
—*Kirkus Reviews*

"One of those finely researched, richly detailed, seemingly narrow
histories that opens surprising vistas in our understanding of great
events. . . . A true epic, and one that would make a terrific miniseries.
The Adkinses . . . know how to extract some nugget of interest from
even the bleakest of topics."   —David Walton, *Dallas Morning News*

"This intense account portrays the heroism and sufferings of the
defenders while offering interesting vignettes that cover intriguing
personalities on both sides. The Adkinses have created an absorbing
examination of an important episode in British and European history."
—Jay Freeman, *Booklist*

"Gripping, dramatically paced and thoroughly researched history of the dogged defense of Gibraltar."

—Aram Bakshian, *Washington Times*

"Well researched and briskly written . . . The Adkinses point out, some [British] politicians believed that 'the possession of America has been sacrificed to the retention of Gibraltar.' . . . Worthy of the most melodramatic Hollywood blockbuster."

—Dominic Sandbrook, *The Sunday Times* (London)

"Fascinating . . . Timely."　　　—Tony Rennell, *Daily Mail* (London)

"This book is a fascinating, well-crafted account of a siege that defined Britishness, and shaped the strategy of the next four major wars."

—Andrew Lambert, *BBC History Magazine*

"This new book . . . breaks new ground in almost every page. . . . Most importantly, the authors set the events of the siege squarely in the larger picture of the War of American Independence. . . . They do not deal only with the triumphs and tragedies of the siege itself, but interspersed with the military events is a harrowing account of the miseries suffered both by civilians and soldiers. Because of all this, the book is difficult to put down. It reads like a thriller . . . which you will read and read again."

—Sam Benady, *Gibraltar Heritage Journal*

"*Gibraltar* is one of the few works of popular history that can truly claim to bring an untold story to the attention of modern audiences. For fans of eighteenth-century warfare or the American Revolution, I cannot recommend it highly enough. For others, *Gibraltar* provides a fascinating introduction to the diplomacy, warfare, and world that existed at the time of America's war for independence, and may even have led directly to its success."　　　—*Concerning History*

"The authors give a superb social history dimension to the official military archives. . . . This book is thoroughly recommended."

—Martin Hazell, *South West Soundings*

"This book is fascinating. . . . One of those superbly done factual books where you know how the end plays out, but you wish it were different as you turn page after page for the story unfolding."
—Nicky Moxey, *Historical Novels Review*

"Draw[s] heavily on primary sources and provid[es] a meticulous look at the military and civilian experiences of what became known as the Great Siege of Gibraltar."
—Kathleen McCallister, *Library Journal*

"Well-written history, excitedly told. Why not get yourself a copy?"
—J. J. Alcantara, *Gibraltar Chronicle*

"Daring sea battles, flaming shipwrecks, and an attempted invasion of England: all feature in this spirited retelling of the late-eighteenth-century Siege of Gibraltar. . . . Roy and Lesley Adkins' account never loses sight of the human story at the heart of an extraordinary international incident."
—*History Revealed*

"An enthralling and colorful history told with human stories at its heart, providing insight into a little-discussed period of Britain's past. The repercussions of which we are still experiencing today."
—*Family Tree*

"Another epic and illuminating look at Britain's past from Roy and Lesley Adkins, masters of the historical narrative. Ordinary mortals in extraordinary circumstances leap off the pages."
—George D. Jepson, *Quarterdeck*

"With plenty of drama to draw upon and an impressive commitment to research, this is a book to delight the military history enthusiast."
—*History of War*

"The Adkins's page-turning account makes you feel as if you were there amid the smoke, blood and gunpowder."
—*Catholic Herald* (UK)

PENGUIN BOOKS

# GIBRALTAR

Roy and Leslie Adkins are husband-and-wife historians and archae-
ologists and the bestselling authors of *Jane Austen's England*, *Nelson's
Trafalgar*, *Jack Tar*, and *The Keys of Egypt*, among other books. They
are fellows of the Society of Antiquaries of London and fellows of
the Royal Historical Society.

*Also by Roy and Lesley Adkins*

THE KEYS OF EGYPT
EMPIRES OF THE PLAIN
NELSON'S TRAFALGAR
THE WAR FOR ALL THE OCEANS
JACK TAR
JANE AUSTEN'S ENGLAND

See adkinshistory.com

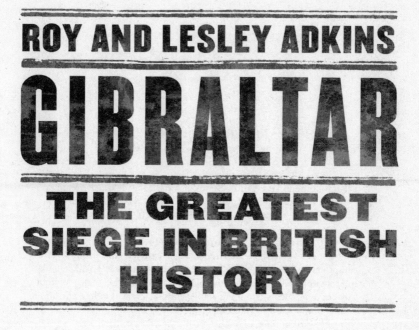

# ROY AND LESLEY ADKINS

# GIBRALTAR

## THE GREATEST SIEGE IN BRITISH HISTORY

PENGUIN BOOKS

PENGUIN BOOKS
An imprint of Penguin Random House LLC
penguinrandomhouse.com

First published in the United States of America by Viking Penguin,
an imprint of Penguin Random House LLC, 2018
Published in Penguin Books 2019

Copyright © 2017 by Roy Adkins and Lesley Adkins
Penguin supports copyright. Copyright fuels creativity, encourages diverse
voices, promotes free speech, and creates a vibrant culture. Thank you for
buying an authorized edition of this book and for complying with copyright
laws by not reproducing, scanning, or distributing any part of it in any form
without permission. You are supporting writers and allowing Penguin
to continue to publish books for every reader.

Published by arrangement with Little, Brown Book Group Ltd.
First published in the United Kingdom in 2017.

Map illustrations by John Gilkes

ISBN: 9780735221628 (hardcover)
ISBN: 9780735221642 (paperback)
ISBN: 9780735221635 (ebook)

Printed in the United States of America
1   3   5   7   9   10   8   6   4   2

Set in Caslon 540 LT Std

*To our friends*
*Charlie Rosado and Pepe Rosado in Gibraltar*
*and Peter N. Lockyer in Gosport*

# CONTENTS

———•◆•———

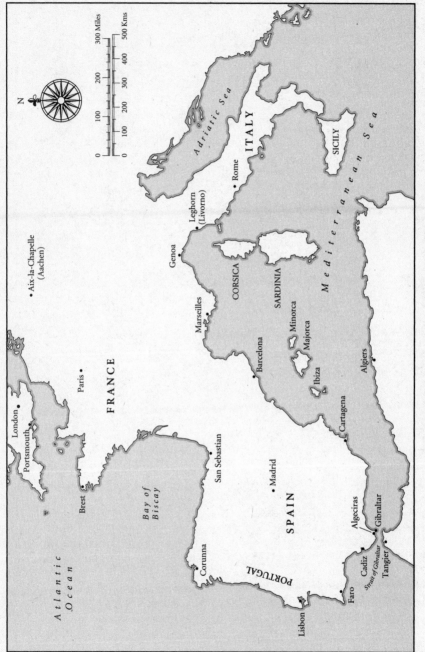

Location of Gibraltar within western Europe and north Africa

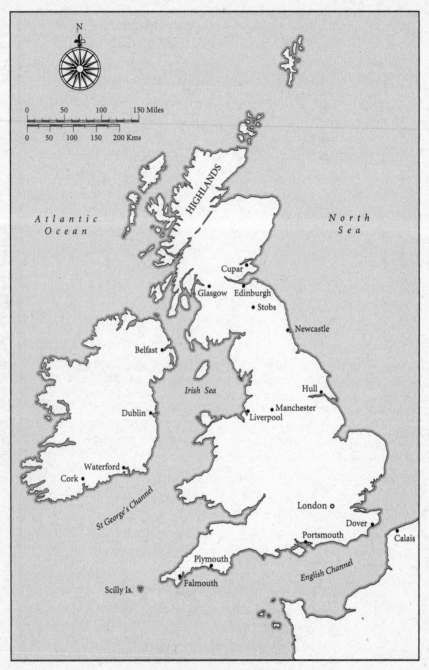

Main place-names within the British Isles

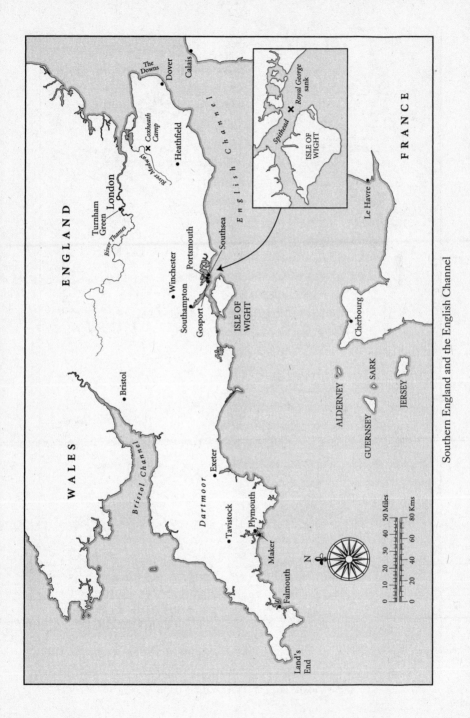

Southern England and the English Channel

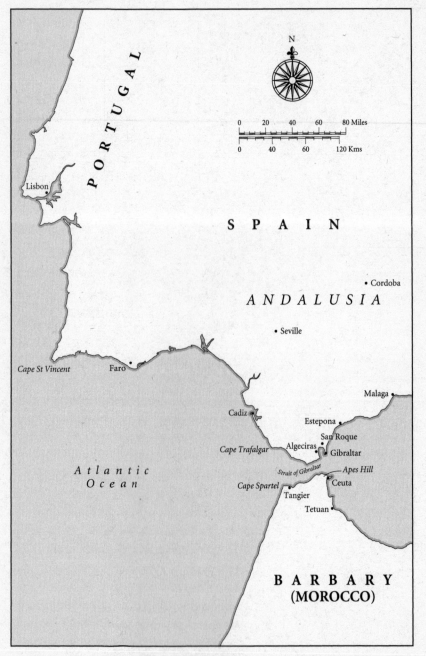

Andalusia, Gibraltar and the Strait of Gibraltar (from Cape Trafalgar to Gibraltar)

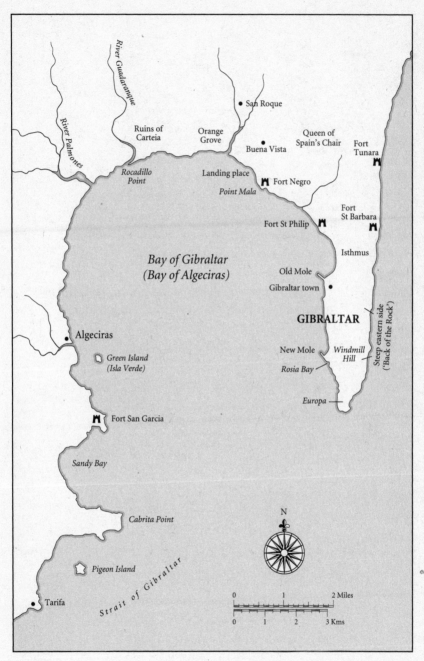

Main locations within the Bay of Gibraltar

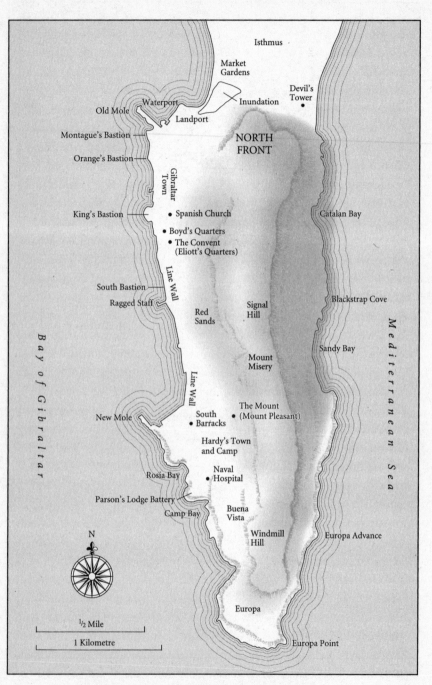

Main locations within Gibraltar and the isthmus

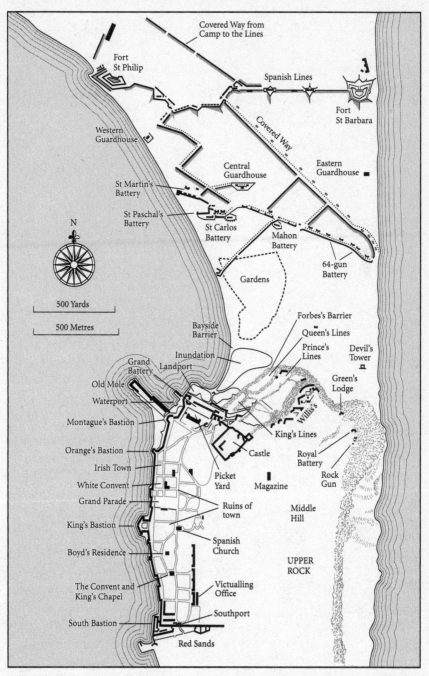

Main locations within Gibraltar town (in ruins), the northern part of the Rock, the Spanish Lines and the advance works across the isthmus by September 1782. Willis's comprised several batteries, including Princess Amelia's, Princess Anne's and Princess Caroline's.

# PROLOGUE

———— ◆ ————

# DISASTER

After three years of relentless siege, everyone on Gibraltar was starving, war-weary and desperate for the relief convoy to arrive, not realising that it was yet to set sail on the 1500-mile journey. The convoy was still at Spithead, between the Isle of Wight and Portsmouth, though with the newspapers in England full of stories about an imminent assault on the Rock, fears were growing that it was already too late to save Gibraltar. Even so, urgent preparations were being carried out on board a multitude of vessels, including the Royal Navy's greatest wooden warship, HMS *Royal George* – a formidable three-decker with more than 100 cannons and a crew of around 850 seamen, officers and marines.[1]

On board this particular warship, the final consignment of stores needed to be loaded, as well as some last-minute repairs done, but being a fine morning, the vessel would soon be ready to sail. In nearby Southsea, a woman glanced out towards the *Royal George*, taking in the idyllic scene, before starting on a letter to a distant relative. 'The day is calm and pleasant,' she wrote, 'and as I sit at the open window, the great vessel in the offing, betwixt me and the Fair Island [Isle of Wight] seems to sway not a hand-breadth, nor to flutter a single pennant.' Her shock as she looked out to sea once more was betrayed by the shaky handwriting:

A dreadful thing has happened. When I had written that beginning of my letter, Dorothy, I looked again southward; the sea was waveless as before, and the Fair Island sparkled in the sun, but betwixt us and it I saw no trace of the great three-decker. I thought my brain had gone wrong, and rang the bell for Agnes; but when she too could see nothing of her, a terrible apprehension took hold of me; and when the alarm-guns from the fort [Southsea Castle] began to thunder, I knew the vessel had gone down. I hear near a thousand men were aboard of her.[2]

In the time taken to write a few sentences with a quill pen, the *Royal George* had sunk so rapidly that hundreds of people were trapped and drowned. Men in nearby ships were equally stunned. One eyewitness related that they all rushed on deck: 'What an altered scene in a few short moments! ... She was not in the spot she so lately occupied – no vestige of her was to be seen; but as soon as the commotion of the water was stilled (for some minutes it was very great), all the boats ... put off for the spot, which seemed as though a hive of bees had been cast on the waves, so thick with boats and human beings struggling for life ... Long, long, will the 29th of August, 1782, be remembered!'[3]

One of the few lucky survivors was the seaman James Ingram, who had been on the upper deck heaving massive wooden barrels of rum on to the deck as they were hauled up in a sling. 'The last lighter [the *Lark* sloop], with rum on board had come alongside,' he later wrote,

> this vessel was a sloop of about fifty tons, and belonged to three brothers, who used her to carry things on board the men-of-war. She was lashed to the larboard [port] side of the Royal George, and we were piped to clear the lighter and get the rum out of her, and stow it in the hold of the Royal George. I was in the waist of our ship [middle part of the upper deck], on the larboard side, bearing the rum-casks [barrels] over, as some men of the Royal George were aboard the sloop to sling them.[4]

Although the warship had been tilted to one side to carry out a repair just below the waterline, the angle was so slight that those on board took little notice, and from nearby ships everything looked normal. With barely a breath of wind and a flat calm on the sea, conditions for repairs and loading supplies were ideal, but suddenly Ingram heard an urgent order to bring the ship upright: 'I ran down to my station, and, by the time I had got there, the men were tumbling down the hatchways one over another to get to their stations as quick as possible to right [the] ship. My station was at the third gun from the head of the ship on the starboard side of the lower gun-deck.' Before anything could be done, the warship began to tip over sideways, and Ingram managed to escape by following his friend Ned Carrell through a gunport: 'I immediately got out at the same port-hole, which was the third from the head of the ship on the starboard side of the lower gun-deck, and when I had done so, I saw the port-hole as full of heads as it could cram, all trying to get out.'[5] Even as he scrambled to safety, the ship was falling sideways, so that the gunports were now facing upwards, towards the sky:

I caught hold of the best bower-anchor, which was just above me, to prevent falling back into the port-hole, and seized hold of a woman who was trying to get out at that same port-hole – I dragged her out. The ship was full of Jews, women, and people selling all sorts of things. I threw the woman from me – and saw all the heads drop back again in at the port-hole, for the ship had got so much on her larboard side, that the starboard port-holes were as upright as if the men had tried to get out of the top of a chimney with nothing for their legs and feet to act upon.[6]

He was just in time, because the huge vessel went straight to the bottom:

I threw the woman from me, and just after that moment the air that was between decks drafted out at the port-holes very swiftly. It was quite a huff of wind, and it blew my hat off, for

I had all my clothes on, including my hat. The ship then sunk in a moment. I tried to swim, but I could not swim a morsel, although I plunged as hard as I could both hands and feet. The sinking of the ship drew me down so – indeed I think I must have gone down within a yard as low as the ship did. When the ship touched the bottom, the water boiled up a great deal, and then I felt that I could swim, and began to rise.[7]

The vortex caused by the sinking of the ship sucked Ingram down almost to the seabed, but he managed to struggle to the surface and found that the masts of the *Royal George* had risen up above the water. 'In going down,' he explained, 'the main yard of the Royal George caught the boom of the rum-lighter and sunk her, and there is no doubt that this made the Royal George more upright in the water when sunk than she otherwise would have been, as she did not lie much more on her beam ends than small vessels often do when left dry on a bank of mud.' These masts proved a blessing for the survivors, and Ingram swam to the main mast where he tried to save the woman he had previously rescued. He called to another seaman, a baker, who managed to grab her unconscious body as she floated past: 'He caught hold of the woman and hung her head over one of the ratlins of the mizen shrouds, and there she hung by her chin, which was hitched over the ratlin, but a surf came and knocked her backwards, and away she went rolling over and over.'[8]

On shore a mile-and-a-half away, thirty-year-old Richard Dennison Cumberland, vicar of Driffield in Gloucestershire, was strolling to Southsea Castle with his cousin John Balchen. The pair had come to Portsmouth to see the Grand Fleet before it sailed, and the previous afternoon they had taken advantage of the custom of respectable sightseers being permitted to visit warships, as Cumberland described in a letter to his brother George in London: '[we] took a wherry and went aboard the Royal George at Spithead – as being one of the finest ships in the fleet. We met with the most civil behaviour from the officers, who shewed us every part worth seeing ... We took notice of the number of women on board and they assured us there were above 400 and near double the number of men.'[9]

Once they reached Southsea, the two men found everyone peering out to sea: 'They told us, a large ship had just foundered, and shewed us the mizen and main masts lying sloping out of the water and a crowd of boats busy about them. With the help of a glass I distinguished a blue flag at the mizen mast, yet we flattered ourselves it was only a transport.' While walking back to Portsmouth, they heard the dreadful news that this was in fact the *Royal George*, and the blue pennant indicated that it was the flagship of the sixty-four-year-old Rear-Admiral Richard Kempenfelt. An extremely experienced seaman and brilliant tactician, Kempenfelt had radically changed the system of naval signalling and was one of the most highly regarded officers of the Royal Navy. 'You cannot think how much we were affected,' Cumberland wrote. 'It was the identical ship in which we had begun to take an interest. The genteel treatment we had met with the preceding evening, the more than possibility of our having delayed our visit till this morning or perhaps renewed it and the recollection of every face we had seen on board, struck us at once.'[10]

Attempts were already being made to rescue survivors, though Ingram, still clinging to the main mast, was more concerned about the woman who was being washed away:

A captain of a frigate which was lying at Spithead came up in a boat as fast as he could. I dashed out my left hand in a direction towards the woman as a sign to him. He saw it, and saw the woman. His men left off rowing, and they pulled the woman aboard their boat and laid her on one of the thwarts. The captain of the frigate called out to me, 'My man, I must take care of those that are in more danger than you.' I said 'I am safely moored now, sir.'[11]

Before too long, it was Ingram's turn to be taken off: 'The captain of the frigate then got all the men that were in the different parts of the rigging, including myself and the baker, into his boat

and took us on board the Victory, where the doctors recovered
the woman, but she was very ill for three or four days.' In order
to resuscitate victims, it was the practice to rub their bodies and
warm them up, though not always with success: 'I saw the body
of the carpenter, lying on the hearth before the galley fire; some
women were trying to recover him, but he was quite dead.'[12] The
woman who survived was twenty-six-year-old Elizabeth ('Betty')
Horn, and she owed her life to Ingram. Betty was one of a hand-
ful of wives who had been due to sail in the *Royal George*, some
of them with their children. She was married to the seaman John
Horn, who also survived.[13]

Bodies were now being brought ashore at Portsmouth Point,
and Cumberland and his cousin did what they could to help:

> We walked to the Point and came up just as they had brought
> one of the poor fellows on shore and were rolling him over
> a barrel [to get water from his lungs] in his wet cloaths and
> in the rain. We thrust ourselves among the mob and made
> them carry him to the next tavern, assisted in pulling off his
> cloaths, procured warm blankets and pursued the methods
> recommended by the Society [for the Recovery of Persons
> Apparently Drowned] but they were applied too late. Finding
> him in good hands and hearing other bodies were brought
> ashore, we went out and found a woman in the same condition
> on the shore and no one attempting to do any thing to save
> her.[14]

They now separated, with Cumberland later admitting that 'after
the greatest exertion I ever made for two hours I had the mortification of only leaving the bodies in a more decent situation than
I found them. After making the people amends for their trouble
I returned to our inn, and found Balchen there as much fatigued
as myself.'[15]

The number of survivors and dead brought on shore in the first
few hours was relatively small, because the *Royal George* had sunk
so rapidly that the majority of those on board were trapped. The

warship had been badly overcrowded with crew members, prostitutes, wives of seamen, children, craftsmen from the dockyard, tourists and many traders – well in excess of a thousand people. In the wars of the eighteenth and early nineteenth centuries, the Royal Navy was constantly short of seamen and resorted to conscription by press-gangs. Once in a ship, the unwilling men might be at sea for months on end, with no shore leave in case they deserted. Warships anchored well away from land, as at Spithead, to prevent the men from swimming to freedom, and all supplies and visitors were instead taken out by boat to the ship. Traders in small boats, many of them Jewish, were also permitted to bring all manner of goods to sell, including so-called wives – prostitutes.[16]

Warships effectively became floating brothels when moored at Spithead. Hundreds of prostitutes, at times outnumbering the men, remained for several days, selling sex and liquor, drinking, swearing and joining in the general raucous revelry. Francis Vernon, a young Irish midshipman who had taken part in an earlier relief convoy of Gibraltar, described what happened when his ship, HMS *Terrible*, was at Portsmouth:

> Our ship's company could now revel in the delights of Portsmouth, and filled the ship with hundreds of those obliging females, who desert the capital during the war, and reside in the genteel recesses of Portsmouth, and other naval towns. The back of the point at Portsmouth has been famous [for] some centuries, and the appearance of its inhabitants serves as a barometer, whereby our success against the enemy can in some degree be ascertained, for captures produce money, and this circulating, passes from the seaman to his lass, who being lavish in expence, gives room by the flash of her appearance and dress, to point out the strength of Jack's purse.[17]

Exactly how many people were on board the *Royal George* that day will never be known, as Ingram explained: 'The number of persons who lost their lives I cannot state with any degree of accuracy, because of there being many Jews, women, and other persons on board who did not belong to the ship. The complement of the ship was nominally 1000 men, but it was not full. Some were ashore, and sixty marines had gone ashore that morning.'[18] Although Cumberland had been told the previous day that more than four hundred women were present, the real number may have been greater, most of whom would have been prostitutes from Portsmouth and Gosport. While relatively good records of the officers and sailors were kept, there was no record of the prostitutes and other civilians, and it was left to the newspapers to speculate:

> There was also a body of carpenters from the Dock, to assist in careening the ship; and, as usual on board all ships of war in harbour, a very large number of women, probably near 400. Of these the bulk were the lowest order of prostitutes, but not a few were the wives of the warrant and petty officers. A most poignant scene of anguish and distress was exhibited by a respectable looking old woman, whose daughter and five children had gone on board the same morning to see their father.[19]

At Portsmouth, attempts at resuscitation changed rapidly to dealing with the corpses that were being washed ashore or picked up in boats. Cumberland was struck by the reaction of the Portsmouth Point prostitutes:

> I cannot help mentioning a circumstance that has since made us smile. It was the false delicacy of the Point Ladies at the publick houses we were in who could not be persuaded to strip and rub the bodies till a clean shift had been procured and then their lamentations over them were curious indeed. One of the poor creatures left two children at Gosport, the other lost one from her arms. Very few of the women were saved, being below decks – many of them sailors wives who kept a little market on board.[20]

After all hope of survivors had faded, preparing the fleet to relieve Gibraltar was once more the priority, though corpses continued to emerge from the wreck, as Ingram described: 'In a few days after the Royal George sunk, bodies would come up, thirty or forty nearly at a time. A body would rise, and come up so suddenly as to frighten any one.'[21] Another seaman, Samuel Kelly, arrived at Spithead some days later on board the packet boat *Grenville* and moored nearby:

> the dead bodies belonging to the *Royal George* floated and passed our ship both with ebb and flood tide ... the rigging of the *Royal George* was decorated, not with colours, but with dead bodies, who were hung up by arms, legs etc., which presented a horrid spectacle. These men had floated at high water, and to prevent the tide carrying them away, had been tied fast to the shrouds and mainstay, and at low water ... they were suspended several feet above the water. Some people searched the pockets of the dead while [they] floated on the tide. 'Tis more than probable that as this crew had just been paid their wages, that they had been the day before rioting in drunkenness and debauchery.[22]

Once the corpses were stripped of their possessions, they had little chance of being identified. Because no authority had responsibility for burying bodies washed ashore, they were dealt with in a haphazard way, in spite of protests voiced in the newspapers. At least nine hundred people had drowned in a matter of minutes. Only a few women, a couple of children and around two hundred seamen and officers were saved. A fund was set up at Lloyd's Coffee House in London to help the widows and orphans of the seamen who lost their lives. This was the start of the Lloyd's Patriotic Fund that has, over the centuries, provided assistance to the families of sailors and continues to help former service personnel and their dependants. With predictable parsimony, some of the money was subverted to deal with the corpses that continued to break free from the wreck: 'The bodies that have been found were heretofore carried in carts to be buried, but the Committee have now directed that those which may be found shall be conveyed in hearses, and decently interred, the expense to be paid out of the subscription money.'[23] No support was given to the families of the prostitutes and other civilians.

The sudden, shocking loss of such a formidable battleship in a flat calm and at a safe anchorage, within sight of land, was an incomprehensible tragedy that affected everyone – not just in Portsmouth, but throughout the country and across Europe. The *Royal George* was a prestigious warship, one of only three that were constructed specifically to carry a hundred guns and destined to be flagships. The others were the *Victory* and the *Britannia*, both of which were also at Spithead ready to escort the convoy. The *Royal George* was named after George II, the grandfather of the present King George III, but many people regarded the warship as a symbol of the monarchy. Until eclipsed by the *Titanic*, the sinking of the *Royal George* remained the most famous shipping tragedy. For the Grand Fleet, which the king and his government hoped would break the blockade of Gibraltar, it felt like a disaster. The additional delay caused by the aftermath of the loss of the ship made it even more likely that the convoy would not be in time to save Gibraltar from falling to the French and Spaniards.

# CHAPTER ONE

——— ·◆· ———

## BEGINNINGS

*We on salt pork and beef are fed,*
*A stone supports each wearied head,*
*A horn of water is our drink,*
*Pleasures forgot, on War we think.*
*We cry 'Alls well', count shell and shot,*
*Who'd envy our happy lot?*
*Come here and learn the Ways of War.*

Written by a soldier in Gibraltar
during the Great Siege[1]

Spain desperately wanted Gibraltar. This strange rocky peninsula fortress, protruding from the southern shore of Andalusia and dominating the landscape, had proved a constant source of irritation ever since its capture by the British in 1704. The Spanish king and his government insisted on regarding Gibraltar as a plundered possession that had to be reclaimed, but the inhabitants of Andalusia were more relaxed, content to enjoy plentiful trade and friendly relations with their neighbours. So there was nothing unusual about the morning of Saturday 19 June 1779, when the British governor of Gibraltar, Lieutenant-General George Augustus Eliott, rode across the border into Spain at the head of a splendid procession of officers and aides-de-camp. Their destination was the hilltop town of San Roque, 5 miles away, where they intended to congratulate Joaquin de Mendoza, the Spanish governor, on his recent promotion to lieutenant-general.

Reciprocal social events between the people of Spain and Gibraltar were frequent, and the normal courtesies were dutifully observed, as had happened only two weeks earlier when the British and Spaniards celebrated the birthday of King George III at a gala ball – though with hindsight it was perhaps odd that Mendoza's wife attended the event when he himself was absent.[2] Life was exceptionally pleasant for those posted to the military garrison of Gibraltar, and several officers had sent their families to spend the summer at San Roque and in the small Andalusian villages around the picturesque Bay of Gibraltar. They themselves could indulge in fishing or perhaps go on hunting trips further inland, and according to John Drinkwater, an ensign in the 72nd Regiment,

> the strictest intimacy subsisted between the military, and the Spaniards resident in the adjacent villages. Parties were reciprocally visiting each other, and the officers constantly making excursions into the country. These excursions, with others to the coast of Barbary [Morocco], (which in the season superabounds with various species of game) were pleasing relaxations from the duties of the garrison, and rendered Gibraltar as eligible a station as any to which a soldier could be ordered.[3]

Private letters often mentioned local wine being shipped to England, and only a few weeks earlier, on 12 April, Eliott had written to his brother-in-law Sir Francis Drake (a descendant of the famous Elizabethan seafarer) that a shipment of wine was on its way to him at Nutwell Court near Exeter in Devon. No payment was required, Eliott said, only Devon cider in return, and he urged Sir Francis to join him at Gibraltar: 'I am sure it would delight you; travelling in Spain is full as commodious as in Wales. I don't despair of seeing you when the war [with France] is over. The French I should think have nearly enough.'[4] Eliott's assessment was wrong, because on the very day he wrote this letter, France and Spain signed a treaty that would change the lives of everyone on Gibraltar.

When Eliott and his officers reached San Roque, instead of their normal welcome, Governor Mendoza was noticeably embarrassed, and their visit was awkward and brief. Something was obviously wrong. Later on that day, back in Gibraltar, the reason for his manner became startlingly clear when Charles Logie, the British consul at Tangier, sailed across the Straits to bring Eliott the news that war between Britain and Spain looked highly likely.[5] Such a war had long been the subject of speculation, and just forty-eight hours later Mendoza wrote officially to Eliott that he had received orders from Madrid to cut off all contact with Gibraltar by land and sea. Every British subject living at San Roque, he said, should return immediately to Gibraltar, even some young girls sick with smallpox, while British residents further afield were instructed to travel to Portugal.

Lieutenant-Colonel Charles Ross and Captain John Vignoles, both of the 39th Regiment, were on leave in Spain and found themselves unable to return. From Malaga, they rode to San Roque, but on being refused entry were forced to make a long journey to the port of Faro in Portugal. They only reached Gibraltar a month later, after rowing back in disguise in an open boat.[6] Others failed in their escape attempts and were taken prisoner. Britain and Spain were now at war, and with cool diplomatic courtesy, Gibraltar was cut off from the world. The Great Siege had begun.

Already one of the most bitterly contested territories on earth, this was Gibraltar's fourteenth siege. Siege warfare was the process of capturing a fortified place, such as a castle, city or fortress, usually by setting up a blockade to stop supplies getting in, which meant deploying a sizeable army. Especially in the ancient world and during medieval times, before the invention of gunpowder, sieges were commonplace and could drag on for years. The aim was to wear down the defenders so that starvation, thirst and disease would force them to surrender. The besiegers would also attack the defensive walls to weaken and breach them, perhaps using battering rams or weapons such as catapults that fired huge stones. One such siege took place at Harlech Castle.

Following his conquest of Wales in 1283, the English King Edward I built the castle right on the coast (though it is land-locked now). From 1460, during the Wars of the Roses, it was held by the Lancastrians against the Yorkists and became a base for operations. Edward IV chose not to attack Harlech as it was too costly, but finally decided to capture the castle when Jasper Tudor, the Earl of Pembroke, landed near Harlech in June 1468 and led raids into Wales. A large army was mobilised, and after a siege lasting a few weeks, the garrison surrendered. Claims are made that Harlech was the longest siege in British history, but the siege itself lasted only a very short time.[7] The longest siege was the Great Siege of Gibraltar, lasting 1323 days, from 21 June 1779 to 2 February 1783 and far exceeding the duration of other notable sieges such as Leningrad and Malta in World War Two.

Although known as the Great Siege, this fourteenth siege of Gibraltar is arguably the greatest ever siege, with its extraordinary events, innovations and massive artillery bombardments exchanged between the British and Spaniards. When it started in 1779, Spain was unable to spare large numbers of troops to capture Gibraltar, and in any case previous sieges had shown the futility of relying on infantry and cavalry attacks. Instead, the plan was to prevent all provisions reaching Gibraltar. It was relatively straightforward to stop communication by land, and Spanish war-ships would try to prevent vessels sailing to and from the Rock. While the garrison was being starved into submission, France and Spain also planned to invade Britain in order to force everyone to the negotiating table.

The strategic importance of Gibraltar was well known from Classical times, when it was regarded as one of the Pillars of Hercules, an awe-inspiring sight that warned sailors they had reached the edge of civilisation. Beyond was the perilous 'Ocean', thought to be a vast river that encircled the earth. Gibraltar ('Calpe') was one of the pillars that the god Hercules had set up, and the other one was Ceuta ('Abyla'), a similar-shaped rock on the opposite African coast. Originating with the ancient Greeks, the myth of the pillars was subsequently adopted by the Romans.

It explained how Hercules had cut a channel – the Straits – to separate Africa and Europe, though another version said that he actually pulled the two continents together to prevent Atlantic sea monsters from bursting into the Mediterranean. With the limitations of their sailing vessels, only the most intrepid sailors would have ventured westwards into the Ocean. The rest would have been deterred by fears of the unknown and the real dangers of difficult tides, currents and winds at the meeting point of the Mediterranean and Atlantic.

In the fifth century AD, Roman Spain fell to Visigothic invaders. Three centuries later the daughter of Count Julian, the governor of Ceuta, was raped by the Visigothic King Roderick, provoking Julian to persuade the Moors – the Muslim inhabitants of Morocco and Algeria – to invade Spain. At least, that is how legend explained why, in 711, an invasion and conquest of Spain by Muslim Arabs began when Tarik ibn Ziyad sailed with his army from Tangier, some 30 miles west of Ceuta. He landed near (or possibly on) Gibraltar, a name that derives from the Arabic Djabal Tarik – Tarik's Mountain.

The subsequent Christian 'Reconquest' (Reconquista) to recover the lost lands across the Iberian peninsula lasted nearly eight centuries, and during this struggle Ferdinand IV of Castile took control of Gibraltar in 1309 after its very first siege. It was a brief Christian interlude, because during a fourth siege twenty-four years later, the fortress reverted to Muslim control. On the other side of the Straits, Ceuta was captured from the Moors in 1415 by Portugal, which was that country's first overseas conquest. Gibraltar itself did not again surrender to Christian control until the eighth siege, on 20 August 1462 – the feast day of St Bernard of Clairvaux, who became Gibraltar's patron saint. This ended seven centuries of Muslim rule, and although further sieges followed, they were between warring Christian factions.

Ferdinand II of Aragon and his cousin Isabella of Castile were married in 1469, and their joint rule as the 'Catholic Monarchs' led to the unification of Spain as a single nation. Granada was the last Muslim kingdom to surrender, in January 1492, marking the end of the Reconquest, and Ferdinand and Isabella then gave their blessing for Christopher Columbus to embark on his voyage of exploration across the Atlantic – well beyond the Pillars of Hercules. That same year also saw religious persecution escalate across Spain, with the expulsion of thousands of Jews who refused to convert to Christianity, followed shortly afterwards by Muslims being given the same choice of conversion or expulsion.

By now, the Duke of Medina Sidonia held Gibraltar, but he eventually complied with an order from Isabella to surrender it to the Spanish Crown, and in July 1502 a new coat-of-arms was granted to Gibraltar that included a castle linked by a chain to a key. The accompanying Royal Warrant explained that Gibraltar 'is very strong and, by virtue of its position, is the key to those kingdoms between the eastern and western seas, and the guardian and defender of the Straits between these same seas, such that no ships or people passing from one sea to the other can fail to see it or call in'.[8] Isabella died two years later, and her last will and testament decreed: 'I charge the Princess [her daughter Joanna] and the Prince, her husband [Philip of Burgundy], and the Kings who shall succeed me in these Realms, ever to hold as inalienably of the Crown and Royal Patrimony, the City of Gibraltar and all that belongs to it; never to give it away, or alienate it or suffer it to be given away or alienated, nor anything that belongs to it.'[9] Contrary to her will, Gibraltar was lost two centuries later, but before then Spain gained Ceuta when, in 1580, Philip II of Spain also became Portugal's king. Ceuta has remained in Spanish hands ever since, even after Portugal became independent.

With an improvement in sailing ships, the seventeenth century saw power shift from the central Mediterranean to countries on Europe's western seaboard, notably Britain, Spain, Portugal and Holland. In the middle of the century, England decided to keep a permanent naval squadron in the Mediterranean, though Oliver Cromwell thought a few frigates would be sufficient if Gibraltar was taken. Without a suitable invasion force, nothing came of this plan, but after the restoration of the monarchy Charles II obtained Tangier in 1662 as part of the dowry of his wife, Catherine of Braganza, daughter of the king of Portugal. A vast amount was spent on a mole to create a sheltered harbour, but Tangier was deemed too costly to maintain, especially after being constantly attacked and besieged by the Moors under their ruler Muley Ismail. Samuel Pepys was brought from London to advise on Tangier's destruction, which was then reduced to rubble and abandoned. The Moors partly rebuilt Tangier, and from 1694 thousands of Muley Ismail's troops turned their attention to taking Spanish-held Ceuta.[10]

When Carlos II of Spain died childless in November 1700, Philip, Duke of Anjou, succeeded to the throne as Philip V of Spain. Because he was the grandson of Louis XIV of France, the Sun King, it was feared that France would dominate worldwide trade, and so the War of the Spanish Succession was triggered, with Britain, Austria and the Netherlands supporting the rival Habsburg claimant – the Archduke Charles of Austria. On the Continent, the Duke of Marlborough commanded Anglo-Dutch forces against the French, with notable victories at Blenheim and Ramillies, while Admiral Sir George Rooke was in charge of an Anglo-Dutch fleet. A naval base was urgently needed between the French and Spanish Atlantic and Mediterranean ports, and so in 1703 Rooke was ordered to seize the Spanish port of Cadiz. He failed in the attempt, but shortly afterwards Portugal signed the Methuen Treaty with England, and the allied fleet was able to make use of Lisbon instead.[11]

The following year, Rooke attempted to take Barcelona, but the attack was soon called off. At a council of war on board his flagship, it was decided – almost as an afterthought – to attack Gibraltar. Manned by a weak Spanish garrison, the Rock was captured with relative ease in the name of Archduke Charles on 24 July 1704 (according to the calendar still used in England; it was 4 August elsewhere in Europe). Just three months later, the Spaniards tried to regain Gibraltar in what was its twelfth siege, but gave up in April 1705. The War of the Spanish Succession dragged on with enormous costs to both sides, but peace negotiations finally began in 1712, and the Treaty of Utrecht was signed in March 1713.

Part of the settlement confirmed Philip V as king of Spain, so the intended purpose of the war had failed, though Great Britain (Scotland and England having formally established a union in 1707) did gain Gibraltar, which was granted in perpetuity, along with the Mediterranean island of Minorca that had been captured from Spain in 1708. The treaty did not deter Spain from mounting yet another siege of Gibraltar in 1727, the thirteenth, but the attempt was abandoned four months later. The Spaniards fared better at Ceuta, because on the death of Muley Ismail in the same year, the siege that had lasted intermittently for so long was finally lifted.[12]

At the outbreak of the Seven Years' War in 1756, rumours were heard that Minorca was under threat, and so in early April Vice-Admiral John Byng's squadron was ordered to sail there from Portsmouth. On reaching Gibraltar four weeks later, Byng learned that it was too late – the French had already landed thousands of troops without opposition and were besieging the formidable Fort St Philip at Port Mahon, into which the weak British garrison had retreated. He headed for Minorca and engaged with the French fleet, but after suffering damage and casualties he decided to retreat in order to safeguard Gibraltar. Fort St Philip surrendered two months later – news that was met with hysterical consternation in Britain.

In a court-martial at Portsmouth, Byng was found guilty of failing to do his utmost to take or destroy the French ships. He was shot by firing squad on 14 March 1757 and is best remembered through Voltaire's 1759 novel *Candide* in which the hero witnesses Byng's execution and is told that 'in this country it is good to kill an admiral from time to time in order to encourage the others' ('pour encourager les autres'). In France, jubilation at the victory was expressed in songs and plays, as well as in the creation of a new culinary treat named after Port Mahon – Mahonaise sauce, now spelled mayonnaise.[13] The celebration was short-lived, because at the end of the war, under the Treaty of Paris, France lost a great deal of territory, including Minorca, which was returned to Britain.

Just over a decade later, America became the focus of attention when the struggle for freedom from Britain broke out at Lexington in 1775. In an attempt to gain revenge for their losses in the Seven Years' War, Louis XVI's France soon sided with the rebel American colonies and agreed to supply ships, men and weapons, but once the French intervened a new wave of patriotism spread through Britain. Many militia regiments were formed as a home guard, since there was a genuine fear of Britain being invaded, while new regiments were enthusiastically recruited by private subscription, including the 72nd Regiment of Foot at Manchester. It was originally intended for America, but was actually diverted to Gibraltar, with recruiting posters boasting that this was 'the best garrison in His Majesty's Dominion'.[14] The recruits included fifteen-year-old John Drinkwater from Latchford in Cheshire, a former pupil of Manchester Grammar School, who became an ensign. His father, also known as John Drinkwater, was a surgeon and man-midwife who practised in Salford and was one of the committee responsible for raising this regiment. All the recruits were young, and Joseph Budworth, another former pupil, wrote of his company: 'I never saw so *fine* a body of men, or more undaunted soldiers ... I was the oldest man but one ... at twenty-one.'[15]

Although hostilities had already started, France only officially declared war on Britain in July 1778, but they needed Spanish naval ships to achieve overwhelming superiority.[16] The Spaniards under Carlos III, who had become king in 1759, were initially reluctant to help the American colonists gain independence. Because Carlos III wished to regain Minorca and Gibraltar, for which an invasion of Britain was part of the strategy, they were finally persuaded by the French to unite against Britain, their common enemy. The French promised to fulfil their wishes and pledged not to sign any peace treaty with Britain or enter into a truce until everything was achieved. In April 1779 France and Spain signed a treaty at the royal palace of Aranjuez that set out the aims of both sides, and in June, after various delays, Spain declared war on Britain, marking the start of the siege of Gibraltar.

Drinkwater kept a detailed journal of events throughout the conflict, and he summarised the situation with the words 'the Fortress of Gibraltar was now become a little world of itself'.[17]

Although the Great Siege has no other name, it was in reality part of the American War of Independence. The actions and ambitions of France and Spain had caused that war to spill across the Atlantic into Europe, and the war zone would extend from Britain to Gibraltar, Spain and Minorca. Britain found herself virtually alone, at war with most countries in western Europe as well as America, with the Great Siege forming one of the most neglected events within the American War of Independence. No major study of the Great Siege has been published since 1965, when (coincidentally) two books were published, by Jack Russell and T.H. McGuffie.[18] If France and Spain had not become entangled in this conflict, Britain would have had thousands more troops and many more warships to deploy in America, and so the outcome of the War of Independence might have been very different. As it is, the Great Siege became one of the most amazing military events in history.

# CHAPTER TWO

————— ·◆· —————

# BLOCKADE

The start of the Great Siege in 1779 was not marked by any spectacular event. There was no sudden bombardment or Spanish ground assault. Nor did a vast Spanish fleet sail into Gibraltar Bay with all guns firing. Instead, the frontier between Spain and Gibraltar was politely but firmly closed, and on either side hasty measures were taken to put the defences on a wartime footing, while engineers considered how the fortifications could be strengthened. As communications with the outside world became more difficult or were cut altogether, everyone on the Rock lost their peacetime idyll and wondered what lay ahead.

The commander of the tiny British Mediterranean fleet, Vice-Admiral Robert Duff, was based on Gibraltar. He had arrived eighteen months earlier, in January 1778, with his wife Lady Helen Duff, who described her impressions of the town to her younger brother Arthur: 'It is the most uncommon place I ever saw and has a very striking appearance to a stranger, from the tremendous rock that hangs over it. In the streets you would think you was at a masquerade for you see people of all nations in different dresses and speaking different languages.'[1] The soldiers of the garrison were largely Protestant, but children born on Gibraltar to parents of any nationality or religion became British subjects. The population was divided more by religion than race, with Protestants, Roman Catholics and Jews forming a mainly harmonious, cosmopolitan society. Ignacio Lopez de

Ayala, a Spanish historian writing around this time, explained
how military rule kept in check racial and religious hostility
within the town itself, which measured less than a mile long and
a quarter of a mile wide:

> It was apprehended that amid such diversity of persons of dif-
> ferent religions, customs, and interests, quarrels and atrocities
> would prevail in Gibraltar similar to those existing in other
> cities in Spain. But the severity of a military Government has
> prevented such disorders; for individuals resorting thither,
> being aware of the certainty of punishment awaiting offences,
> and that the magistrates and those in authority cannot be
> corrupted, find their own security best guaranteed by not dis-
> turbing that of others.[2]

Apart from the military presence, the Rock functioned as a
trading port, greatly benefiting from its location between the
Mediterranean and the Atlantic, yet close to the north African
shore. A small civilian population of Genoese families, originally
from the Italian port of Genoa, had lived on the Rock since
before the British arrived in 1704, and in the decades leading up
to the Great Siege their numbers had been increased by Jews,
Portuguese, Minorcans, Spaniards and British – over three thousand individuals in all, most of them crammed together inside the
town. Ayala highlighted their great variety:

> Almost all the maritime powers maintain Consuls at Gibraltar,
> commerce being there the principal occupation. The richest
> mercantile houses are the English; and besides the military and
> civil officers of the Government, there are other Englishmen,
> who keep inns and pursue various occupations. The Jews, for
> the most part, are shopkeepers and brokers ... The Genoese
> are traders, but the greater part of them are fishermen, sailors,
> and gardeners; and these, as well as the Jews, speak a language
> compounded of Spanish and English dialect, or jargon, common
> to all southern nations, not excluding the Africans.[3]

What is missing are references to people of colour, though there are occasional glimpses, such as forty-year-old 'Bumper, a Negroe' who came from Guinea and appeared in the 1777 census, as did three female 'negroe servants'. They were Jane, thirty years old, from America, and two girls who were born on Gibraltar – Nancy, aged nine, and Betty, aged four. They were all listed as Jewish, which was a catch-all category.[4]

Some 5400 military men were stationed on Gibraltar, along with 1500 military wives and children, far outnumbering the civilians. At the outset of the siege, five British regiments were present – the 12th, 39th, 56th, 58th and 72nd, supplemented by three Hanoverian German regiments, men from the Royal Artillery, Royal Engineers and Soldier-Artificers, as well as a naval contingent. The rank-and-file soldiers were housed with their families in overcrowded barracks and lodgings within the fortified town or in the substantial South Barracks close to the naval hospital.[5] Officers and their families could rent houses from the inhabitants, while those more fortunate had villas with gardens on the hillside overlooking the bay. Life before the siege was tranquil and uneventful. Numerous officers who would play a prominent role in the siege had already been in Gibraltar for years. Some had their wives and children with them, while others were separated from their families or had suffered bereavement. It was a close-knit and constantly evolving world of complex lives and personalities, not always harmonious, where many of the officers were interconnected through marriage and military service.

Lieutenant-Colonel William Green was the chief military engineer responsible for the fortifications and who for years had been designing and implementing changes to the walls, gun batteries and even the natural defences, such as the steep cliff faces and the inundation, in order to prevent infantry assaults. He was a highly able officer who had been in the army since the age of twelve and had come to Gibraltar in 1760 after previous service in Newfoundland and Quebec. His wife Miriam constantly accompanied him to his various postings.[6] She had spent nearly half her life on Gibraltar with him and had grown up in a family with a long tradition of military service. Her grandfather Jonas Watson had commanded the artillery at the last siege of Gibraltar in 1727 and was killed at the siege of Cartagena in South America at the advanced age of seventy-eight. Her father Justly Watson had served as a cadet engineer with his father Jonas during that same Gibraltar siege, then pursued a distinguished career as a military engineer until he was murdered in 1757 at St John's in Newfoundland.

The Green family felt settled in Gibraltar and belonged there. They had an impressive residence in town and a beautiful new house, which they called 'Mount Pleasant' or simply 'The Mount', on the hillside south of the town. It had glorious views and, as Ayala noted, a substantial garden that Colonel Green had laid out at his own expense two years earlier, 'well stocked with a variety of exquisite plants, shrubs, and fruit-trees'.[7] Mrs Green had given birth to eight children, most of whom were raised on Gibraltar and where two had died – the toddler William-Smith and his sister Louisa-Anne who survived only three weeks. Both of them were buried inside the King's Chapel.[8] Their last child, four-year-old Charlotte, was the only one still with them on Gibraltar.

At the outbreak of hostilities in June 1779, Mrs Green was particularly upset by the sudden separation from Spain, because many of the people had been her friends. She decided to record her experiences in a journal, but could no longer bring herself to refer to the Spaniards by name:

I shall therefore from this time call them — The Enemy — whenever I have occasion to speak of them, which I shall do, as long as circumstances enables me to continue this uncon- nected, rough journal – and much I fear I should fall short of any style or method, were it intended for any person's informa- tion except such of my family [and] friends who perhaps will not dislike to pass an idle hour in looking over these pages. God only knows who may have the sight of this book or who may ever see the person who now writes this, however I go on. Miriam Green.[9]

Gibraltar, the place that Mrs Green looked on as home, is an isolated and mountainous crag of rock, a natural fortress jutting incongruously into the sea from the coast of southern Spain. Separated from north Africa by the narrow Strait of Gibraltar (also referred to as the Straits, Streights or Gut), it is strategically located between the Bay of Gibraltar (also known as the Bay of Algeciras) and the Mediterranean Sea and is close to the Atlantic Ocean. In recent decades its shape has been altered by land reclamation and other works, but two centuries ago it measured barely ¾ mile wide and 3 miles long, with the steep, inaccessible limestone cliffs on the eastern side (the 'back of the Rock') rising treacherously from the Mediterranean, ruling out settlements, harbours, roads and even paths to the summit.

In the south, the peaks fell away sharply to the rugged and windswept plateaus of Windmill Hill and Europa, where the cliffs around the coast made a close approach by shipping impossible until Rosia Bay was reached on the western side. This side of the Rock, facing the Bay of Gibraltar, was much less severe in profile than the Mediterranean side, and rough paths led up the steep slopes, past fissures and caves, to the perilous knife-edge ridge that was almost 1400 feet in height.[10] The traveller and antiquarian Francis Carter was a resident just before the siege: 'The shape and face of Gibraltar rock is neither promising nor pleasing, and it is as barren as uncouth, not a tree or a shrub hardly to be seen on it above the town ... On casting an eye up this barren hill, one would not imagine any living creature could exist upon it.'[11] In fact, barely two-fifths of Gibraltar was habitable, and its sole town – also known as Gibraltar – developed in the more sheltered north-western part of the promontory.

At the northern end, mountainous vertical cliffs overlooked the low and narrow sandy isthmus, much of which was transformed into an airfield in the Second World War. While the eastern and northern faces of the Rock were impossible to attack from the Mediterranean, more vulnerable parts had over the centuries been encased in fortifications, most recently by William Green and his engineers. The main defences were in the north-west, where the town faced the Spanish fortifications, with massive brick and stone walls and gun batteries, as well as ditches and a single entrance out of the town – the Landport Gate. The nearby sea gateway of Waterport led to the Old Mole and the port, which was originally the main anchorage for shipping. A mile-and-a-half to the south of the Old Mole was the New Mole (nowadays called the South Mole), just north of Rosia Bay. A monumental wall ('Line Wall') ran along the coastline from the town as far as Europa, with forti-fied outposts – bastions – protruding into the sea to give more scope for directing gun fire at different angles. At the southern end of the town, further defensive walls snaked uphill to the top of the Rock. Heavy guns were mounted not only along the walls and on the bastions, but also up the west-facing slope of the Rock and even on the very ridge.

For those who scrambled up the flights of steps and paths to the ridge, the dramatic views emphasised their isolation – assuming that the visibility was not impeded by dense cloud or sea mist. They were surrounded by water, while vast tantalising swathes of Andalusia lay before them, with the coast of Morocco and the Atlas Mountains to the south, on the other side of the Straits. Gazing towards the west, the Bay of Gibraltar was defined by the coast of Spain and the hills beyond, while the small Spanish town of Algeciras, 5 miles across the bay, was clearly visible, as was San Roque to the north, the town that housed the Spanish governor. Turning to the north-east, the Mediterranean coast of Andalusian Spain curved gently towards Estepona and Marbella, with the snow-capped Sierra Nevada mountains beyond, though access by land was difficult, as Francis Carter noted: 'The coast from Gibraltar to Estepona, and for two leagues beyond it, is extremely barren, the Sierra continuing about a league from the shore: this road is not to be travelled in the winter, on account of the many rivers and arroyos [streams] you cross, which are so impestuous after the rains, as to carry loaded beasts and horses into the sea.'[12] To the east, nothing but the Mediterranean Sea was visible, stretching beyond the horizon for hundreds of miles.

The 1713 Treaty of Utrecht declared that Gibraltar was ceded permanently to Great Britain with its town, castle and port, but without any territory and with no access to the adjoining countryside.[13] Viewed from afar, it was easy to mistake Gibraltar for an island, but it was actually linked to Spain by a sandy isthmus between the Mediterranean and the Bay of Gibraltar – only 900 to 1700 yards wide and a few feet above sea level. After the failed thirteenth siege of 1727, the Spaniards had embarked on building a fixed barrier known as 'the Lines' across the northern isthmus, some 1500 yards from the Rock, leaving the legal status of the rest of the isthmus uncertain. It was supposedly neutral territory, but some of the land close to the Rock was utilised as market gardens, a cemetery and an 'inundation' – a salt marsh that was deliberately flooded to enhance the British fortifications. One inhabitant described it as 'about 200 yards in length, and 60 in breadth. It is always kept filled with water, nearly man-height, from sluices made to let in the sea from the bay; chevaux de frize, iron hoops, and many other articles to entangle and obstruct an enemy, are also heaped in this canal.'[14]

The Spanish Lines comprised a curtain wall with gun emplacements at intervals and a fort at each end, designed to stop people crossing the isthmus and to prevent trade. It also posed a significant threat, as explained by Lieutenant-Colonel Thomas James of the Royal Artillery, who had lived in Gibraltar two decades before the Great Siege:

> The Spaniards ... have run a line from the Mediterranean to the bay [of Gibraltar], and at each end have erected strong forts under the fire [within range] of our own cannon. The above line will be of infinite service to the Spaniards, should they ever attempt to break ground [construct attacking earthworks] against the place, as likewise the fort of the bay side [Fort St Philip], which does totally interrupt the freedom of the port, and commands it so well, that no ships can ride in the proper anchorage ... so will the fort on the Mediterranean side [Fort St Barbara] prevent our ships from enfilading their approaches.[15]

Guns high up on the Rock could reach the Lines, though the Spanish guns were too far away to bombard the town or fortifications with ease, because at this stage they were mounted on ordinary gun carriages and were incapable of being elevated sufficiently to reach far into Gibraltar. The nearest guns at Fort St Barbara on the Mediterranean faced the highest part of the north face of the Rock, while on the opposite shore, Fort St Philip could fire over the low-lying defences on the north-west side and reach the town. For a bombardment to be more effective, the Spaniards needed to enhance the Lines and establish gun batteries on the isthmus itself, much closer to Gibraltar. They now embarked on spending vast sums of money working towards that objective.

At the outbreak of hostilities, Lieutenant-General George Augustus Eliott was quick to display blunt orders in the Grand Parade (now John Mackintosh Square), directed at the civilians:

> All male inhabitants of whatever country or class, who are not willing to take arms, or perform such office as shall be required, in defence of this Fortress, are forthwith to depart with their families ... All inhabitants are to send a return in writing on the first of every month, under cover to the Secretary, specifying their number in each family, and stock of provisions laid in ... Any inhabitant of, or dependant upon this Garrison who is suspected of acting contrary to this order, will be proceeded against by Military Law.[16]

In a letter sent to London, Eliott revealed his distrust of the population, saying that Gibraltar was 'now filled with a number of inhabitants to the amount of about three thousand six hundred, of all countries, and all religions, amongst which many [are] of suspicious character'. Martial law was now declared, and anyone communicating with the enemy was to be treated as a spy.[17]

One of the first tasks was to put some of the inhabitants to work levelling the isthmus close to the Rock, as Captain Rice Price of the 56th Regiment described: 'This morning at five o'clock two hundred Jews and Genoese sent under the inspection of the Engineers to level the hedges and ditches with the tumps of sand on the neutral ground to prevent the enemy's concealed approaches and to allow the fairer range to our cannon.'[18] The men were required to do any work that was needed, and as far as Eliott was concerned, those refusing to take part would be turned out. The military garrison took precedence over all else.

On Eliott's appointment as governor of Gibraltar three years earlier, Lieutenant-Governor Robert Boyd had sent him a letter of congratulation: 'After the loss of my friend Cornwallis, with whom I have lived in the most perfect agreement, I am happy to find that his successor is my very old acquaintance.'[19] Some two decades earlier Boyd was serving on Minorca with Lieutenant-General Edward Cornwallis until, in 1756, the island fell to the French. Cornwallis was on leave in England at the time, but returned to Minorca with Admiral Byng's fleet and was one of those who advised the ill-fated admiral to give up and sail away. At that very moment, Boyd had been making a heroic but unsuccessful effort to row to the fleet in a small boat with a message from the garrison commander. He subsequently fought in the German campaign, including the famous Battle of Minden against the French on 1 August 1759, during which he encountered Eliott.

In 1766, Boyd became the colonel of the 39th Regiment, and two years later, at the age of fifty-eight, he took up the post of second-in-command to Cornwallis, who was then the governor of Gibraltar. The following year, in 1769, Boyd's own regiment, the 39th, was also posted to Gibraltar.[20] In decades past, regiments carried the name of their colonel, but this had been replaced by a system of numbering regiments. A colonel was the head or proprietor of his regiment, responsible for the men's clothing and for dealing with contractors and government departments to supply everything the regiment needed. These matters were usually organised through an agent, offering opportunities for making money.

Captain James Horsbrugh, from Cupar in Scotland, was one of Boyd's officers. Born in about 1730, he had joined the 39th in 1755, initially serving in India as an ensign. He married Margaret

('Peggy') Bell in 1762, and she accompanied him to Gibraltar when the regiment was posted there. In all, his wife would give birth to four children – Madge, Betsy (who died in 1774) and another daughter named after Boyd's wife Arabella, as well as a son who was given the name Boyd, such were the close ties that developed between the Horsbrughs and the Boyds.[21]

There were no cavalry regiments in the Gibraltar garrison, so the lowest level of commissioned officer was the ensign or second lieutenant, from which an officer would hope to work his way up to become a lieutenant, then a captain, a major and finally a lieutenant-colonel. It was the lieutenant-colonel who normally commanded a regiment in the field. Under Governor Cornwallis, Horsbrugh had taken on the role of town-major and also aide-de-camp to Boyd, and by the end of 1770 he was appointed to the rank of captain.[22] The highly stratified social order in Britain drew a sharp distinction between the common soldiers, who had a dubious reputation, and the higher-class officers, who were regarded as gentlemen and mostly bought their commissions, except for the artillery and engineer officers who had technical training and were appointed on merit. All other officers were untrained, relying on their social class to command respect and buying subsequent promotions within their regiment. Below the lowest rank of commissioned officers were the non-commissioned officers, who did not buy their ranks but were appointed. At the top was the sergeant major, then the quartermaster sergeant, sergeant, corporal and drummer. At the very bottom of the hierarchy was the mass of private soldiers – the rank-and-file or common soldiers.

From 1773, Colonel Boyd was in sole command as acting governor of Gibraltar, because Cornwallis was absent, too ill ever to return, and that same year Charles Ross from north-east Scotland purchased the lieutenant-colonelcy of the 39th Regiment. About twenty years younger than Boyd and unmarried, he had been unemployed for several years, and his arrival at Gibraltar established a highly unusual and stressful situation in which the colonel and lieutenant-colonel of the same regiment were serving in the same location.[23] Having served as acting governor for some years,

Boyd may have expected promotion when Cornwallis died and so was probably disappointed that Eliott was chosen. Instead, he and Arabella decided to apply for a period of leave, but they had to wait more than a year for Eliott to arrive. Finally, at the end of May 1777, Horsbrugh wrote to his wife Peggy in Scotland to say that the new governor had at last come to Gibraltar:

> General Eliott arrived here on Sunday last, he has received me as well as I could wish, and insists on my continuing to live at the Convent [the governor's official residence]. The character he bears of being a remarkable strict Commanding Officer has put us on our mettle; nothing however has as yet appeared to confirm this. On the contrary he seems much pleased with us, but I know for a certainty that great alterations are intended, which I am afraid will fall heavy on my shoulders. He appears polite and affable to all while at same time he expects a very particular attention from those immediately under him that will require a constant attendance, which however irksome such a confinement will be, I am determined to conform myself to it, and give up every little amusement with the view of making myself useful to him.[24]

Peggy had returned to Scotland after ending up in a wretched state of health the previous year. Having given birth to Arabella in February 1776, she then nearly lost the other two children in a scarlet fever epidemic. A few weeks later, towards the end of May, Horsbrugh had accompanied her back to Britain, ostensibly for the sake of the children's education, but in reality because she could no longer cope and dreaded the prospect of another summer in Gibraltar.[25] He returned to Gibraltar alone, though the few surviving letters show his absolute love and anxiety for Peggy and the children, mingled with financial worries now that he had a household in Scotland to maintain. Horsbrugh longed for her to return, though once the siege started in 1779, his emotions must have changed to immense relief that his family was already safe. He need not have worried about Eliott's opinion of him, because he rated Horsbrugh highly, and instead of his role as town-major, he appointed him adjutant-general and would later describe him as 'so perfectly intelligent ... *a very good soldier* ... He has no riches but his integrity.'[26]

One of Eliott's first orders of the siege was that anyone staying in Gibraltar should have sufficient provisions to last six months, so that they could withstand the blockade. Many inhabitants were compelled to leave, because they were too poor to lay in such a quantity of stores. Gibraltar was not self-sufficient. Market gardens and vineyards supplied some of their needs, various animals were raised, and the seas all round teemed with fish, as did the inundation, but most provisions were imported by sea. The strategic military aim of Spain was therefore simple – to starve the garrison into an early capitulation by establishing a blockade to prevent food and other supplies reaching Gibraltar. Only a week after the siege was announced, Captain Price commented: 'Fairly blockaded by sea and land. The Enemy have two ships of the line in the Bay, three frigates and as many xebeques. These they have ranged along the opposite coast at due distances to intercept all supplies to the Garrison. I hope to live to see these ships on fire yet, if the old English spirit for enterprise still subsists.'[27]

Fifty-eight-year-old Vice-Admiral Robert Duff from Fife in Scotland had only three warships at his disposal – his flagship HMS *Panther* (a 60-gun battleship), HMS *Enterprise* (a 28-gun frigate) and HMS *Childers* (a 14-gun sloop). Before his appointment to the Mediterranean, he had been commander-in-chief at Newfoundland, after a long naval career. When his wife Helen accompanied him to Gibraltar the previous year, three of their children came with them – Jean then aged thirteen, Robert aged eleven and Adam aged three. Only a few months later, in September 1778, tragedy struck when Helen died. They had been married fourteen years, and being widowed may well have affected his outlook, exacerbated by ill health, which was attributed to gout.[28]

Duff's warships were supplemented by several privateers – these were ships and occasionally smaller boats that were privately owned and fitted out, operating as warships under licence from the government. Their main aim was to capture enemy shipping and those cargoes carried by neutral vessels intended to benefit the enemy, in return for a reward ('prize-money'). Often dubbed 'legalised pirates', privateers would prove especially useful for supplying the besieged fortress with cargoes of food and drink. In early July, Mrs Green noted the arrival of three new privateers: '3 fine cutters came in from England fitted out as privateers to take either French or Americans. They were stout vessels indeed.' Built at the port of Dover in Kent, they were capable of carrying sixteen to twenty guns each and soon made their presence felt, with Horsbrugh recording in his diary less than a week later: 'the cutters sent in a Dutch vessel loaded with wine for Cadiz, and a Spanish prize.'[29]

That same day, 11 July 1779, the *Childers* sloop was sent out into the Mediterranean to look for similar prizes, which provoked the very first shot of the siege. Drinkwater described how it came to be fired from Fort St Barbara: 'Admiral Duff having intelligence that a large fleet of small vessels was to sail from Malaga, with wine and provisions for the Spanish grand fleet, ordered the Childers, on the 11th, to cruise to the eastward, and give information, by signal, when they appeared, with the strength of their convoy. Whilst she was on the look-out, her boat gave chase to a settee, and was fired at from Fort St. Barbara, which was the first hostile shot from the enemy.'[30]

Later in the day, a substantial Spanish convoy of about thirty polacres, settees, feluccas and other vessels appeared from the east, escorted by a fairly weak naval squadron of five xebecs. These were all traditional Mediterranean craft that the Spaniards frequently used. Onlookers assumed that Duff would send out the two larger warships to try to take further prizes, but when he failed to act immediately Mrs Green was one of those who felt great disappointment at this lost opportunity: 'It was now eagerly wished, and expected, that the Admiral [in the *Panther*] and the only frigate viz. the Enterprize, Sir Thomas Rich, would hasten out, as it was pretty certain this was a fleet intended for Algezira.

At last Admiral Duff did make a signal. The Enterprize got ready, as soon as possible, but it was 5 o'clock before the Admiral got out. It was by [then] much too late! and the fleet got through that night. This occasioned great discontent.'[31]

Captain Thomas Paterson of the Royal Artillery took a more generous view, saying that Duff had waited until the Spanish convoy came close to the Rock, in case they fled south towards Ceuta, which is exactly what did happen when the *Panther* and *Enterprise* showed signs of sailing.[32] The motley assemblage of British warships and privateers made chase and returned the next morning with a few more prizes. Duff ensured that his official report portrayed this operation in the best possible light: 'The prizes are all laden with useful articles for this garrison, their cargoes consisting chiefly of wines, brandies, and some small quantities of bread, and other like provisions; of which commodities are also the cargoes of eight other Spanish prizes taken by his Majesty's vessels and the privateers from this place.' Prisoners-of-war were also captured, but they were returned to Spain straightaway, as Horsbrugh described: 'Most of the Spaniards belonging to the vessels we had taken were sent round in boats from the New Mole, landed opposite the gardens on the neutral ground and permitted to pass into Spain.'[33]

The sixty-two-year-old Spanish Admiral Don Antonio Barcelo, famous for his campaigns against Algerian pirates, was now in command of the blockade, and more ships soon arrived to enlarge his fleet, as Lieutenant Holloway recorded in mid-July: 'A Spanish squadron came into the Bay, and anchored off Algeziras between 1 and 2 o'clock. It consisted of 1 ship of 70 guns, 1 of 60, two large frigates, 3 xebeques and several small armed vessels.'[34] It was crucial to keep on good terms with Morocco, which supplied so many provisions, and Charles Logie, the British consul at Tangier, was a valuable intermediary who kept Gibraltar informed of any news and forwarded newspapers and letters. He managed to slip through the blockade in a Moorish galley to try to persuade Admiral Duff to assist with the repair of a ship belonging to the Emperor. On his return, Logie's vessel was stopped and searched for several hours by one of Barcelo's squadron, as Mrs Green heard: 'It was ... reported that Mr Logie was taken in going over (but it was not true as we heard afterwards). The vessel was certainly boarded by the Spaniards, and he was in the dress of a Moor, not only so but hid himself under some sails, and by that means escaped. Otherwise he would most likely have been taken either to Ceuta or to Algezira.'[35] Algeciras, across the bay from Gibraltar, was being used as the local base for Barcelo's squadron that was blockading the Rock. It was a small port that was protected by a fort on an island just offshore, called Green Island or Isla Verde, with its Arabic name of el Gezira el-Khadra having been corrupted to Algeciras.

With the increased blockade, it did not take long for shortages to be noticed, and despite friendly relations with Morocco, supplies were becoming less frequent. Mrs Green observed that 'the whole Garrison seems displeased and uneasy. Not any vessels of late has come from Barbary [Morocco], and our livestock is but little.'[36] In order to conserve flour for bread, Drinkwater remarked, one of Eliott's initial orders was for troops to 'mount guard with their hair unpowdered; a circumstance trifling in appearance, but which our situation afterwards proved to be of great importance'.[37] This was a significant cultural shift, because it was customary for soldiers to have shoulder-length hair, which was scraped back and plaited at the neck into a queue that was tied with leather strips, greased and covered in hair powder – usually flour. This time-consuming and pointless task would often fall to the soldiers' wives.

Towards the end of July, restrictions were imposed on the keeping of animals. 'Orders issued by the Governor,' said Price,

that no horses or mules are to remain in the Garrison after Saturday next whose owners have not one thousand weight of straw or other forage in proportion for them, except those belonging to the staff or to Field Officers. I gave my old English horse away sooner than shoot him, and some very good horses [of] Captain Tuite's of the 39th in particular sold for fifteen reals

Gibraltar currency (about five shillings and eight pence sterling). All dogs wandering about the street ordered to be killed.
NB no animals who can eat (except ourselves) privileged.[38]

Although there was no cavalry, most officers owned horses, and
as a cavalryman it would have been unpalatable for Eliott to take
such measures, but he needed to reduce the number of useless
mouths and ensure that the horses and mules did not starve. In
order to lead by example, he had one of his own horses shot. He
himself was known to favour cats, and cartoons were produced of
him with cats, including one caricature years later 'surrounded by
cats gambolling and playing many antics, to the great delight of
the General'.[39] Cats escaped his cull, and they did have their uses
in keeping down the numbers of rodents.

At the same time, he allowed several native-born Spanish
inhabitants to leave through the Landport Gate and cross the
isthmus into Spain. 'The Spaniards by some means,' Price said,
'have caused it to be signified to those inhabitants of the Garrison
who are natural born subjects of Spain that they will allow them
a free passage through the Lines until Sunday next, in case they
choose to remove with their families and effects. In consequence
of this, several have removed, terrified at the thoughts of a siege.'
Another soldier heard that the Spanish sentries at the Lines
refused to let any of them pass until they had served a period of
quarantine: 'The Spaniards keep them under quarantine on the
isthmus, six, eight, and ten days, and supply each person with a
loaf daily.' It was actually a fortnight before they were allowed to
pass into Spain.[40]

Before too long, many more inhabitants left for other desti-
nations. As Drinkwater said, they were 'apprehensive that the
garrison would be besieged, [and] thought … to seek an asylum
in time. Indeed about this time scarcely a boat or vessel left the
port without being crowded with Jews or Genoese, who preferred
a residence in Barbary, or Portugal, to remaining in Gibraltar,
where the necessaries of life became every day more scarce.'[41]
Many others went to England. Not all those who remained were

enthusiastic about undertaking the labouring duties required of them. Price heard that 'Some refractory Jews for refusing to work [were] turned out at Land Port by the Governor but readmitted on submission.' Less than a week later, Genoese inhabitants were rounded up after attending a service at the church (now the cathedral) of St Mary the Crowned in Main Street, usually referred to as the Spanish church because it was Roman Catholic: 'The Spanish church [was] surrounded by parties from the Main Guard, and several refractory Genoese who, under pretence of a Saint's day had refused to work in levelling the sands outside Land Port, [were] nabbed in coming out of church and compelled to work. A pretty set of fair weather sparks truly who, when the skies look lowering and dangers encompass us around, sneaks off and shrink from the storm.' They may have been reluctant workers, but there was no doubt of the loyalty of the Jews who, remembering their past persecution by Spain, dreaded Gibraltar being captured and were now 'fasting and praying in their synagogues for the success of his Majesty's arms the whole night long'.[42]

The next few weeks were in reality a phoney war, with Spanish ships firing at, and occasionally chasing, vessels that tried to evade the blockade, while on land both sides worked hard on their fortifications. In sieges, the besieging forces tended to win in the end, and so the key considerations were: how long would it take? and how much would it cost (both financially and in manpower)? The Spaniards were confident that by maintaining the blockade and building up considerable forces for an attack, it was inevitable that the Rock would be theirs. Gibraltar's more limited options were focused on withstanding the siege and wearing down the Spanish forces to such a degree that they might give up or be forced eventually to move to another more pressing theatre of war. All through July and August 1779, guns were shifted about and new ones mounted, the fortifications were reinforced and improved, new batteries constructed, a communication line dug from the Moorish castle to the Prince's Lines, the rock face cut back at the north end to prevent an infantry attack and stores moved to safety. All this activity was summarised by Drinkwater:

The engineers were busily employed in putting the works at
Willis's [batteries high up on the north front] in the best repair,
and in erecting new batteries on the heights of the North
front. A considerable extent of ground above the Town was
cleared and levelled, to encamp the different regiments in case
the enemy should fire upon the Town. Parties were likewise
detached to collect shrubs, &c. from the face of the hill, for
fascines; and the artillery were daily engaged in completing
the expence magazines with powder, ranging the different
ordnance, and preparing everything for immediate use in their
department.[43]

A rapid way of shoring up and repairing fortifications in siege
warfare was with sandbags and with wooden barrels and gabions
(cylindrical wicker baskets) filled with sand, soil, stones or rocks.
Also used were fascines, which were long bundles of brushwood
tightly bound with pliable wood or rope.[44] Brushwood began to
be cut for the never-ending task of making fascines, and early on
General Orders were displayed to prohibit the wasteful cutting of
materials: 'To preserve firing [fuel] for our ovens in case of necessity, strict orders were given to prevent soldiers or others cutting
down the Palmeto bushes, brushwood or grass on any part of the
Garrison without leave from the Governor.' Boats were even taken
round the back of the Rock so that brushwood could be cut in
that inaccessible location. Another order affected the inhabitants
in particular – much of the Rock was declared out of bounds: 'No
person without a permit, except belonging to the Navy or Army,
in their uniform, to be suffered to go upon the Hill above the New
Road.'[45]

While the engineers were responsible for constructing defensive works and batteries in which guns were placed, it was the
role of the Royal Artillery to fire the guns, but they had too few
men, and so about 180 men were ordered to be taken from the
regiments and attached to the artillery. Paterson noticed that
two inhabitants also stepped forward to join: 'Mr. A. Webber &
Mr. J. Grumly have joined the R. Artillery with the Governor's

approbation to serve as Volunteers during the investiture of this place by the Enemy. Are to be attested and receive each Mattrosses cloathing.' In the 1777 census, both men were listed as Protestants. John Grumley was now twenty years old and Arthur Webber was a thirty-seven-year-old merchant, and they were both joining the Royal Artillery as matrosses, who were assistants to the gunners. Many inhabitants were already employed in the King's service, though it was rare for any of them to join the armed forces. Grumley would later become a second lieutenant, but was killed in action before the end of the siege.[46]

Because insufficient men were highly skilled in the use of the musket, another order was given to recruit marksmen:

A Corps of Marksmen to consist of a lieutenant, one British serjeant and corporal, one Hanoverian serjeant and corporal, and one private man from each battalion company of the line to be formed immediately, care to be taken that the men fixed upon for this service are expert at firing at a mark. Lieutenant Burleigh of the 39th Regiment is appointed to command this Corps. The non-commissioned officers and one half the private men to attend the drill twice a day and fire ball at a mark. From the time they begin to be employed upon actual service they will receive an addition to their pay equal to what has been ordered for the men attached to the Royal Artillery.[47]

All the soldiers were armed with a smooth-bore musket of the 'Brown Bess' type that had been standard issue for decades. It was fired by a flintlock, a mechanism powered by a strong spring, which was 'cocked' by drawing back a lever with a flint attached. When the trigger was pulled, the spring brought this lever down on to a steel striking plate. Sparks flew into a small pan of gunpowder, and the resulting flame travelled through a touch-hole and set off the gunpowder charge inside the barrel.

By the time of the siege, prepared cartridges containing gunpowder and a round lead bullet (usually called a 'ball') were issued. To load the musket with a cartridge, the soldier first pulled back the cock to the first notch, 'half-cock', allowing the cover ('friz-zen') of the pan to be raised. This cover was attached to the steel striking plate. The soldier then bit the end off the cartridge and held the ball in his mouth, while he tipped a little gunpowder into the pan of the flintlock. Once he had replaced the cover on the pan to stop the gunpowder spilling out, he tipped the rest down the barrel, spat in the ball and rammed the paper casing of the cartridge on top to hold it in place. The musket was now ready to fire. Muskets were most effective and accurate at ranges of less than 100 yards; beyond this distance they became increasingly inaccurate. The main advantage of the musket was that well-trained soldiers could load and fire one every twelve seconds, giving a rate of fire of five shots per minute. For close combat, muskets also had detachable bayonets.

The Spaniards were also busy, and an ominous development occurred when a camp started to form some 3 to 4 miles away on the common of San Roque, with streets of white canvas bell tents. After only two days, Mrs Green wrote: 'the Enemy increasing their encampment and making great preparation ... unloading stores, pitching more tents, &c, &c, and thus ended the month of July. Various were the opinions, though it seemed most probable that the Enemy's intentions were to make every possible and effectual trial to establish a stronger blockade.' She had to admit that Barcelo was an extremely good naval officer, as his squadron was managing to stop virtually every vessel heading their way.[48]

In her diary, Mrs Green jotted down her own observations and also fragments of information shared with her. She was sure they could 'be depended upon, as they are from our own Corps [Engineers], and mostly from the Gentleman that is in the Colonel's family, who would hardly bring a false account'. She meant thirty-year-old Lieutenant Charles Holloway, an engineer, who had arrived in Gibraltar in 1777. Colonel Green had appointed him as his aide-de-camp, and so Holloway was one of his close circle, or military 'family'. Several officers, she said, also kept journals: 'The Engineers all do, for the Chief Engineer's inspections, and <u>he</u> keeps a very separate one, which I believe is not intended to be shown to anyone in this Garrison.' Until now, nobody knew what Spain had in mind, apart from the blockade, but Mrs Green concluded that 'it is not to be doubted but the intention of the Spaniards is to attack this Garrison'.[49]

From high up on the Rock, it was possible for the officers to look across to Spain with the aid of portable telescopes or spy glasses and spot much of what was going on. Gibraltar towered above everything, so that the Spanish positions were laid out below them like a map. The Spaniards were at a huge disadvantage, looking upwards at the Rock and unable to gain a clear picture of the fortress. Even their highest positions at San Roque and the adjacent hill known as the Queen of Spain's Chair (or Sierra Carbonera) were too low and too distant to yield much helpful information, even with the assistance of telescopes. In Britain, John Dollond had developed a telescope that included an achromatic lens which produced a clearer image, and his firm had a virtual monopoly on telescopes used by naval officers on board ship and by army officers on land. It amused Mrs Green to see the young officers competing with each other for information:

> It now became quite fashionable to get all the news each one could collect; and by way of gaining all that, everybody was using spy glasses from morning to night. All those that affected great cleverness were ever ready with a pencil and paper, and it was really laughable enough to see with what a jealous eye each aid de camp looked at the other, fearing he should be the first to communicate his ideas of what he supposed the Enemy was about! Various therefore was the reports, and could not always agree.[50]

Officers from the navy, artillery and engineers were frequently accomplished artists and draughtsmen, which were valuable skills in reconnaissance and espionage, and so pencil and paper were not just for jotting down ideas, but for sketching details. One of those officers was Captain Paterson: 'Took a sketch of the enemy camp consisting of 2 battalions of foot, 2 regiments of horse and about 400 artillery. Discovered from the top of the Rock about 26 heavy guns mounted on travelling carriages drawn up in two lines behind Fort Negro.'[51]

More and more Spanish troops and cavalry came into their camp, and by the first week in August, Holloway thought there were 4500 men all told. Prodigious quantities of equipment were also being landed from boats and ships, including guns, gun carriages, mortars, shot, shells, tents, bedding, vast quantities of brushwood for fascines, wool, straw, planks and timber piles. The guns along the entire stretch of the Lines were dismantled and then gradually remounted, with considerable structural work done to improve the fortifications, particularly in the forts at each end. Much of the work took place at night, out of view, and Drinkwater said that 'at night we generally observed a number of lights, and frequently heard a noise like that of men employed on some laborious duty; this might be that of dragging cannon'.[52] Each day the scene changed for those officers watching intently. 'Saw from the top of the Rock 18 guns laying dismounted in Fort Barbara,' wrote Paterson in mid-August, 'likewise tracks of carriages into Fort St. Philips, and 4 guns supposed to be brought from their camp last night and the night before. Behind Fort Negro the enemy appear to have 6 brass mortars, 26 battering cannon, a great quantity of shot, shells, ammunition boxes etc.'[53] More than forty ox teams were hauling materials to the forts, along with numerous waggons.

By the end of August, five large laboratory tents had been erected for the preparation of ammunition, and the garrison realised that a huge mortar battery was being constructed next to Fort St Philip.[54] Everyone feared that the bombardment of the Rock was about to begin. They were completely unaware that Spain's attention was in fact focused far more on invading Britain at that moment.

# CHAPTER THREE

———·◆·———

# INVASION

France had joined America as an ally in the war against Britain in 1778, still feeling humiliated by the loss of territories after the Seven Years' War. With this opportunity to avenge their defeat and adjust the balance of power within Europe, the old plans for an invasion of Britain were revised. Although the last war had drained the resources of both countries, in France there had been a determined effort to improve the armed forces, especially the navy. This was not the case in Britain, and by the time the two countries were at war once more, many ships in the Royal Navy were facing repair or replacement. Even so, the French navy was not strong enough to send ships to help the Americans, defend French overseas territories and provide protection for an invasion of Britain. What France also needed was the Spanish navy.[1]

Both France and Spain agreed on the idea of an invasion of Britain, yet it took months to settle the details. France thought that Britain's strength lay in its control of the English Channel, the anchorage at Spithead and the nearby naval base at Portsmouth, and so wanted to seize those key places. Spain, perhaps more realistically, believed that any invasion of southern England would force Britain to relinquish Gibraltar in return for a withdrawal of the invading forces. In the final version of the invasion plan, it was decided that the French and Spanish fleets would meet up no later than mid-May 1779 off the port of Corunna in north-west Spain. Together, they would head for the English Channel, and, with the protection of this combined fleet, a French invasion force would cross the Channel from France and capture the Isle of Wight, Gosport and Portsmouth. Various alternative targets, such as Plymouth and the Channel Islands, were also chosen in case of unforeseen events.

Without a common language or signalling system, there was plenty of scope for confusion, while a string of last-minute changes added to the problems of the two navies working together. From the outset, delays occurred because the Spaniards insisted on a formal statement of their grievances with Britain and a declaration of war, which they would only undertake after the French fleet had left the port of Brest in north-west France and was heading for the rendezvous. Under this additional pressure, the French commander Admiral d'Orvilliers set sail in early June, already a month late, with insufficient food, water and medicine, no lemons to combat scurvy and unsuitable recruits as sailors and soldiers. A week later, the rendezvous was reached, and a vessel went into Corunna to inform the Spanish fleet.

The British government was well aware of events in France and Spain, including the preparations of the invasion fleet, because it assembled intelligence from a variety of sources, such as captains of naval and merchant ships, smugglers, friends of Britain in neutral countries, British residents still living in France and, of course, spies. Most nations had their own intelligence network, and those of Britain and France were particularly active. In every major port, spies were observing the movements of shipping, and in Britain there was a constant watch for potential spies and saboteurs. The General Post Office had a specific department dedicated to the interception and copying of dispatches and correspondence to and from foreign countries, which often operated similar systems themselves. To combat this, letters were sent in code, and the Post Office had a cipher department that decoded letters for government and official bodies before passing them on, as well as attempting to decipher foreign letters written in code. Another source of information was the network of consuls and ambassadors in neutral countries, which had included Spain until the official declaration of war.[2]

Detailed intelligence about the preparations of the Franco-Spanish fleet had already found its way to Britain. When part of the Spanish fleet was being fitted out in the port of Cadiz, the British consul there, Josiah Hardy, was well placed to pass on reports. On 25 May he wrote in code to Lord Grantham, who was the British ambassador at Madrid: 'Orders came yesterday to get the whole fleet now here completely equipt for sea on the first of next month, the ships are to come down into the bay in order to be ready for sailing. They are to be formed into three divisions, one of which is to sail immediately under the command of Vice Admiral [Don Antonio] Ulloa and will be eight ships of the line & two frigates.'[3] The actual coded passage began 'kwnbwr. mlyb. dbrxbwnld. ak. &bx. azb. ezkso. gsbbx.', representing the words 'Orders came yesterday to get the whole fleet'. This is a substitution code, where k = o, w = r, d = n, e = b, r = s, and so on, but such codes are relatively simple and easy to break. Hardy's letters are unusual in this respect, because most letters were written in a numerical code, constructed from a table where each word was represented by a specific group of numbers. Surviving letters to and from Eliott on Gibraltar used a stronger, numerical code, not a simple substitution code like Hardy's.

As a result of all the intelligence flowing back to London, preparations were being made for a defence against invasion. The biggest problem was a shortage of men for both the army and navy. They were all – technically – volunteers, but countless rank-and-file volunteers ('privates') were lured into the army by dubious recruiting methods, while the navy frequently resorted to forcible recruitment by press-gangs. The army units assigned to the defence of Britain were greatly under strength, but were bolstered by the militia and fencibles. The militia was the army reserve, raised locally by ballot and, despite any training, largely inexperienced. Coxheath Camp near Maidstone in Kent became the biggest camp for training completely raw militia conscripts from all over the country, forming a strategically placed reserve against invasion. The fencibles were similar forces, but their service was strictly limited in duration and confined to a particular area. Taken together, the army, militia and fencibles appeared to be a strong defensive force, but the quality of these troops varied enormously, and many were barely fit for any military service.[4]

Units of fencibles were being hastily recruited and trained all over Britain, and John Macdonald, an unmarried teacher of about twenty-six years of age, was one of many who joined a regiment in Scotland, enlisting in the North Fencibles during the summer of 1778. A few months later at Inverness, he was persuaded to join the second battalion of the 73rd Highland Regiment by its colonel, George Mackenzie, who had heard him play the Highland bagpipes. The 73rd was originally raised for the war in America, mostly from the remote Scottish Highlands of Ross-shire and Cromarty, but the first battalion would be sent to Africa and India and this second battalion to Gibraltar. Being too late to travel on board the transports, Macdonald made his own way to Portsmouth, the first time he had ever left the Highlands, and in June 1779 he sailed with the rest of the troops to the naval base of Plymouth.[5]

After almost a month, on 24 July, Macdonald said that they 'received an order to remove from Dock Barracks and encamp a little beyond Maker Church, on Lord Edgecomb's estate in Cornwall. The troops which composed this camp were the 1st battalion of the Royal Scots on the right, the Leicester and North Hampshire militia regiments in the centre, and the 2nd battalion of the 73rd regiment on the left.'[6] Although soldiers like him may have been unaware of why they were shifting position, regiments were being strategically placed in vulnerable areas, and in their case it was to strengthen the defences of Plymouth in the light of the intelligence about the invasion fleet. The Edgecumbe estate, where Macdonald was camped, was on the west side of Plymouth Sound, separated from the town of Plymouth and the naval base by a narrow stretch of water. Troops were stationed here to prevent any invaders from coming ashore and bombarding the town and dockyard.

Although the French fleet arrived off Corunna by 10 June, six weeks passed while Don Antonio d'Arce, the admiral in charge of the Spanish fleet, stalled and wasted time until finally ordered by

his government to sail. By now, Spain had officially declared war
on Britain and the siege of Gibraltar had begun. After all this waiting, the French fleet found that their inadequate supplies were
rapidly dwindling, and sickness had also taken hold, with seamen
falling ill with smallpox and fevers. It was not until the end of July
that the combined fleet finally set sail for Britain and was almost
immediately caught by adverse winds that delayed them reaching
the English Channel. It was not an auspicious start to the invasion.

In mid-August, close to Falmouth in Cornwall, the 74-gun
battleship HMS *Marlborough*, accompanied by the *Ramillies*, *Isis*
and *Cormorant* sloop, came across the invasion fleet. Believing the
ships to be British, they only just avoided capture. For speed, the
*Marlborough*'s first lieutenant, Sir Jacob Wheate, travelled in the
*Cormorant* to Plymouth, from where he used a relay of horses to
rush to London with the news that a huge French and Spanish
fleet of over sixty warships had arrived. Before long, it was spotted from the Cornish coast, creating sheer panic, as newspapers
reported:

> Extract of a letter from Falmouth ... On the 15th inst. about
> twelve at noon, we were much alarmed by seeing a great fleet.
> On their near approach they appeared to be the French and
> Spanish fleets, consisting to the best of our knowledge of 62 sail
> of the line, and about 40 inferior sail. They remained here till
> three this afternoon, and then steered to the eastward. Most of
> the inhabitants on their approach sent their families and effects
> away to different parts. We have about eight companies of
> militia, and a great number of miners [mainly tin miners], who
> paraded the town and harbours all night and day. This place is
> in confusion, everything is at a stand. We illuminated all our
> windows, and no person was in bed the whole night.[7]

While Lieutenant Wheate headed for London, the *Hampshire
Chronicle* related that the invasion fleet was next seen off Plymouth:
'Monday, August 16. This morning at break of day the Cormorant
arrived and put on shore Sir J. Wheate, with intelligence of the

combined fleet having entered the channel ... At one o'clock the flags were hoisted on the Maker [church tower], being the signal for seeing the enemy's fleet. The garrison was immediately put under arms, the avenues into the town and dock secured, and the troops sent for from the adjacent camps.'[8] By now, the 73rd Regiment had been in their camp near Maker church for three weeks, and Macdonald recalled their initial sighting of the enemy fleet:

> During our stay in this camp, the French fleet, which was so much dreaded, appeared off the Ram-head [south-west end of Plymouth Sound]; some of them sailed close by the Sound and had a fair view of the garrison of Plymouth, the shipping, &c. The formidable appearance of this fleet, and the nearness of their approach, struck such terror into the breasts of the inhabitants of that coast, that the most part of them left their houses and fled to the interior of the country, taking their cash and most valuable effects with them.[9]

According to the *Hampshire Chronicle*, vessels were immediately sent from Falmouth and Plymouth to alert Sir Charles Hardy, Vice-Admiral of the Channel Fleet, 'and the vessel was promised a reward of one hundred guineas, that first reached Sir Charles with this intelligence'.[10] Previously governor of Greenwich Hospital, Hardy had earlier in the year been put in charge of the Channel Fleet, in what was a political rather than a military appointment. He was sixty-four years old, in poor health (he would die the following year) and had not served at sea for twenty years. The Channel Fleet was seriously undermanned, and many seamen were suffering from infectious diseases such as typhus, largely due to press-gangs being used to augment the crews. These gangs took anyone they could find, including those already ill, and when disease spread through the crews, depleting their numbers, the press-gangs were forced to supply even more men. Hardy had struggled to get his ships and crews fit for sea and take on sufficient stores. Repeatedly criticised for tardiness, he was now on his appointed station, west of the Scilly Isles, trapped by contrary winds that made it impossible to sail eastwards to engage the invasion fleet.[11]

Early on the 17th, when the French and Spanish ships were still off Plymouth, another alarm was sounded: 'At four o'clock the alarm guns on the citadel were fired, on discovering a number of ships entering the Sound, which were at first taken for transports belonging to the enemy, but afterwards proved to be coasters brought in under convoy of the Ardent man of war, which immediately after seeing them safe into port, stood out to sea in order to join Sir Charles Hardy.' After successfully escorting this convoy, the *Ardent*, a 64-gun battleship, left Plymouth and ran into what was presumed to be the Channel Fleet. Only when one ship opened fire was it realised that this was the invasion fleet. The resulting battle was heard at Plymouth:

> Soon after nine a heavy firing began just in sight from the Maker tower, which continued incessantly till near one o'clock, during which time expresses were sent off every way, under a supposition that the fleets were engaged; but an account was brought in by the master of a Cawsand smuggler, at four o'clock, that being at some distance under land, he saw the Ardent make towards the enemy's fleet ... Several frigates and three deckers chased her near an hour, when a very smart firing began from two frigates ... the fire became general from five sail which he could distinctly count, that had all opened upon the Ardent in very quick succession after the attack had been begun by the frigates. About 1 o'clock the firing ceased, when he supposed the Ardent had struck to the great superiority of the enemy.[12]

The *Ardent* was captured in sight of the naval base of Plymouth, making this the first successful engagement for the would-be invaders.[13] Everyone was waiting for the Channel Fleet to deal with the French and Spanish ships, and there was dismay when they remained unchallenged. John Carpenter was a steward of Sir Francis Henry Drake and wrote to him from near Tavistock, inland from Plymouth, about the turmoil:

We all consider ourselves deserted by Hardy's fleet, as we can
get no accounts with certainty where he now is, and all we with
certainty do know is that he knows the French and Spaniards
are braving Plymouth and the Cornwall coasts ... Our Empire
of the Sea is lost, it's not extravagant to conclude we must be
a lost people ... since hereafter whatever we hold must be by
the courtesy of France and Spain – a tenure till this fatal era
unknown to Britons.[14]

Drake, who was Eliott's brother-in-law, was then at Winchester,
and Carpenter related to him what was happening on the edge of
Dartmoor:

All business is at a stand in this county [Devon]. Everybody
attending to nothing but hiding, burying or removing what
little property they possess, to save themselves from want. 'Tis
really affecting to see, and to consider the consequences much
more so. Shoals of people, women and children, daily coming
through the town [Tavistock], looking like people bereft, and
not knowing whither to retire for safety, and lamenting their
friends left behind. As to myself, I have packed up my material
papers, etc. and shall remove them with Mrs. Carpenter [his
wife] and my daughter and father, as soon as I hear a landing is
effected. Myself and my boys will join the troops and stand or
fall with them.[15]

The panic spread across southern England and was especially felt at Portsmouth, which was an even greater target than
Plymouth. The Admiralty in London had by now been informed,
but was unsure of Hardy's location and whether or not he knew
about the enemy fleet. On the assumption that the French and
Spanish ships would sail eastwards with the prevailing winds,
naval ships were ordered to be stationed in the Channel off the
Kent coast, and Rear-Admiral Francis William Drake, commander-
in-chief at the Downs, was instructed to take a squadron across to
France to look for and destroy any transport ships that might be

part of an invasion force. Troops were also mobilised in southern England.[16]

One more day passed at Plymouth with the menacing presence of the invasion fleet off the coast, but then something strange happened. To their immense relief, the people of Plymouth woke up on the morning of 19 August to find it had disappeared. The Admiralty, though, was faced with two problems – not knowing where it had gone and not knowing the whereabouts of Hardy's Channel Fleet, comprising thirty-eight battleships, three 50-gun ships and seventeen smaller warships. The battleships included three 100-gun vessels (*Britannia*, *Victory* and *Royal George*), several 98-gun vessels, like the *London* and *Formidable*, and more than twenty 74-gun vessels, such as the *Invincible* and *Terrible*. Lieutenant Wheate estimated that the combined invasion fleet had sixty-three warships, of which more than forty were large battleships.[17]

Although Hardy was heavily outnumbered, his immediate problem was to get back into the English Channel. With contrary winds, it took another ten days before Land's End, at the tip of Cornwall, was even in sight, but suddenly the combined fleet was spotted. Sir Richard Bickerton, captain of the *Terrible*, related that they immediately prepared for battle:

> Sunday, 29th August, about four in the afternoon, a signal was made by the *Cumberland* for many ships in the S.E., the wind then being about E.S.E. Some ships soon afterwards let fly their topgallant sheets as a signal for a fleet. The Admiral in consequence thereof made a signal to call in his cruisers, and another for close order of sailing. About six o'clock the signal was made to tack; and soon after we had tacked, a signal for a line of battle ahead, which was cheerfully complied with, with a general cheer throughout the fleet, as we took them to be the enemy's fleet.[18]

At midnight the wind changed, forcing the Channel Fleet to alter its formation, but the next morning brought huge disappointment, because after all the tension of preparing for a major engagement there was no sign of the enemy ships. It was later realised that this was a convoy of French supply ships that was also looking for the combined fleet.

The next day, more ships were seen to the west. This time, they were positively identified as the invasion fleet, which had left Plymouth to look for the Channel Fleet. In the night both fleets had passed each other unnoticed, moving in opposite directions. Hardy's much faster ships continued sailing eastwards, and the French and Spanish ships were soon out of sight. At the beginning of the year, a programme to cover the bottoms of all British warships with copper sheets had begun, in order to protect the wooden hulls from 'shipworm' (actually a mollusc, *Teredo navalis*), whose holes could rapidly destroy the bottom of a ship. The copper also prevented weed from attaching to a ship's bottom, making vessels faster and more manoeuvrable. Francis Vernon on board the *Terrible* watched what happened after the invasion fleet was spotted:

We descried them from our mast heads early in the morning, and from their numbers resembled an approaching wood, consisting of near seventy sail of the line. Our fleet was scarcely more than half that number, and was fortunately between the enemy and our ports. Sir Charles clearing for action, and preparing for the worst, made a masterly disposition of his ships, and standing to the eastward, anchored off Plymouth, on the 1st of September.[19]

They remained off Plymouth for a few hours, long enough for Hardy to write a dispatch to the Admiralty, in which he explained that his plan was to lure the enemy further up the Channel, where a battle would be more favourable. His strategy was sound, considering that his fleet was outnumbered. Towards Portsmouth, the English Channel was not so wide, which would give an advantage to the British ships, and, being in constant use by the Royal Navy, it was rightly assumed that the French would not have detailed knowledge of these waters. After leaving Plymouth, Hardy continued as far as Spithead and anchored off Portsmouth on 3 September to take on supplies, offload sick seamen and hopefully find reinforcements. As for fighting the much-anticipated battle with the French and Spanish ships, nothing happened. The invasion fleet was not seen again, leading to rumours that, rather than fight the enemy, Hardy had run away. It was even alleged that seamen on board the *Royal George* felt such shame that they covered the eyes of the figurehead:

A boatswain's mate on board the Royal George stept over the ship's bows, and lashed a double hammock fast round the figure-head of the King. 'What are you doing there?' says a lieutenant on the forecastle. 'Only securing his peepers,' replies Jack. 'Peepers! What do you mean?' exclaims the officer. 'Why,' replied the man, 'we aren't ordered to break the old boy's heart, are we? I'm sure if the King once gets sight of this here day's work, and knows that we have run away like cowardly lubbers, it will be the death of him, poor soul.'[20]

The figurehead actually comprised two horses and their riders, with the monogram G.R., leading the seamen to believe they represented the king.

There was also concern that while the Channel Fleet was secure at Spithead, a huge enemy fleet with plans to invade the country was at liberty in the Channel. The king shared that concern and wrote to the Earl of Sandwich, who was First Lord of the Admiralty:

Our fine fleet being returned to Spithead for refreshments I do not object to, provided that is effected with the greatest expedition; but the times will not permit its waiting for every little convenience; therefore I trust on your not losing one moment in proceeding with the utmost dispatch to Portsmouth, and on your seeing that no time is lost in putting on board the several ships what may be absolutely necessary for enabling Sir Charles Hardy to go and meet the combined fleets of France and Spain now in the Channel.[21]

Sandwich took the hint and immediately left for Portsmouth, but the king kept up the pressure, writing to him again before he had even reached the port: 'We cannot be too expeditious, and show by actions not words that the putting the fleet in a state to pursue the enemy when thrashed, and to sweep up the Dons now before Gibraltar, make the present appearance of retreat not only wise but meritorious.'[22]

At Portsmouth, Sandwich tried to find out what was happening and urged Hardy to set sail as quickly as possible, but events were moving rapidly. Intelligence was providing a clearer picture, and even before Sandwich left Portsmouth, news of the state of the French and Spanish ships started to arrive. One report came from an Irish crew member of a Portuguese vessel that had encountered the invasion fleet. The Irishman was held on board a French ship, but was released after a few days: 'The informant says he was detained on board a 74-gun ship called the *Palmier*, and was told that they were sickly and in want of water and provisions and were going into Brest soon; that on a meat day, the allowance was only one ounce and a half of meat. The *Ardent* was with them, which ship they often showed him by way of mortification.'[23]

It was obvious that the invasion fleet was not as strong as feared. Because of the initial delays and hurried departure, their supplies were running low, and the French victualling vessels encountered by Hardy's fleet had failed to deliver their supplies, having been driven back to port by bad weather. More significantly, the invasion fleet was affected by disease, much more than the British, with countless seamen dying of various illnesses. Yet it was still at large somewhere in the Channel, and such a threat needed to be removed. A heavy defeat by Hardy would have destroyed the invasion plan and possibly lifted the siege of Gibraltar, but George III was now urging caution:

The Admiral will, I trust, in all his conduct be guided less by rumour than by what appears to him for the public good, and then I do not doubt he will give a good account of his opponents if he engages them. A victory over them will be a great advantage and glory to Great Britain; but I cannot desire to see him run *headlong* into a battle against a *superior force*, under *circumstances of disadvantage*, when we are upon the *defensive*, and when the season is so far *advanced* that the enemy's project, if not carried into execution in three weeks or a month, must be given up *without a battle*.[24]

As it was, the invasion fleet returned to the port of Brest in mid-September, beaten by disease, bad weather, shortage of supplies, lack of co-operation between the two allied fleets and poor planning. In the short term, the French and Spanish ships had lost so many men through disease that their fleets were crippled and would remain in port for months. The *Scots Magazine* described the true scale of the sickness, which had even taken the life of the son of Admiral d'Orvilliers:

On the 16th of September, twenty-five ships of the line, part French and part Spanish, and on the next day the remainder of the combined fleet, entered Brest roads ... An epidemic sickness is said to have raged in the fleet ... insomuch that they were obliged to disarm six sixty-four gun ships to man some of the others properly. 500 mattresses were burnt, being accounted contagious. The Count [Admiral] d'Orvilliers, being in a bad state of health, obtained leave to resign.[25]

Marie-Antoinette, Queen of France and wife of Louis XVI, commented to her mother: 'The public complains greatly that Monsieur d'Orvilliers, with forces far superior to those of the English, wasn't able to engage them in battle, nor prevent any of their merchant ships from returning to port. This will have cost a great deal of money to do nothing, and I still don't see any sign of peace being negotiated this year.' A month later, in mid-October, she said: 'Our fleet was not able to engage the English and has done nothing at all; it is a wasted campaign that has cost a lot of money. What is most distressing is that the sickness got into the ships and wreaked havoc.'[26]

In Britain, inertia and inaction had preserved the precious ships and seamen, but not the reputation of Admiral Hardy. It had also highlighted the weakness of the Royal Navy. The French and Spanish plans might have failed on this occasion, but the British people still lived in fear of invasion and would continue to do so until the end of the war. In the short term, though, the threat was removed. With the invasion plan shelved, the Spanish fleet returned to Cadiz from Brest at the end of the year, causing the *Annual Register* to comment: 'Thus ended the expectations of the enemy, and the apprehensions of Great Britain. Never had perhaps so great a naval force been assembled on the seas. Never any by which less was done, or, except by sickness, less suffered.'[27]

# CHAPTER FOUR

———— ·◆· ————

# FIREPOWER

An invasion of Britain was now out of the question. Instead, Spain's revised strategy was to concentrate on tightening the blockade of Gibraltar and get ready to attack. While the failed invasion had been a joint Spanish and French affair, the Spaniards were on their own when besieging Gibraltar. Such was the massive scale of reinforcement of their fortifications along the Lines that anxiety grew on Gibraltar, and many grumbled at the failure of Governor Eliott to take any action. The widespread feeling was that a bombardment by the Spaniards must surely be imminent, and the northern part of the town would be especially vulnerable. At the start of September 1779, Mrs Green was one of those voicing criticisms, especially about Admiral Duff: 'Most people now begin to think we ought to take some notice of our neighbours, as they continue to work on very briskly and are very busy at Fort Negro, Fort St Philip and Fort Barbara. Our Admiral and his small squadron remain perfectly quiet. Many town vessels go out – and are very active!'[1] Spilsbury simply noted: 'The Admiral continues to live on shore.'[2] Thirty-four-year-old John Spilsbury from Willington in Derbyshire, described as 'a brave and attentive officer, and a kind and humane man',[3] was a captain in the 12th Regiment and kept a journal throughout the siege, which is now curated by the Garrison Library. It is full of short and pithy remarks, often highly critical, such as these few words about Duff, who should have been on board his flagship, ready to react.

The size of the Spanish camp was increasing with the arrival of more and more troops, and working parties were constantly seen on the Lines. A mass of equipment was being brought in by sea and landed close to the Orange Grove, in the north-eastern part of the Bay, depicted as an idyll only a few years before by Francis Carter:

> Half way between Carteia [ruins of an ancient Roman town] and the Spanish lines, runs into the sea a little river, collected from different springs ... on its pleasant banks several Spaniards have established themselves, and planted gardens of orange-trees, sweet canes, pomegranates, and evergreens; the eternal bloom of the oranges, and the advantage of angling in a river full of fish, induced a gentleman of the garrison to erect a little hut of canes, under the shade of an enormous walnut, where the officers find beds, and the little requisites for passing an agreeable day in this amiable spot.[4]

It now looked very different from Captain Horsbrugh's viewpoint at Willis's battery:

> several covered carts went into Sta. Barbara [fort], and numbers of others uncovered passing to and from the landing place. The last convoy must have brought them a large supply, for the beach was crowded with all kinds of things, amongst which I could plainly see a number of guns lying on skids and a vast quantity of gun carriages. Two guns were mounted in front of the Guardhouse, a little to the west of Fort Negro to protect the bay at the Orange Grove and the landing place.[5]

Overlooking the bay, Fort Negro was situated at Point Mala, between Fort St Philip and the Orange Grove.

The civilians on Gibraltar were scared, expecting their homes and businesses to be destroyed any day, and so several applied for permission to erect wooden huts in the south, away from the Spanish artillery, where they began to move their possessions to safety. Mrs Green followed their example and shifted valuable furniture and various goods to her other home. 'I have also divided our stores and livestock between this house [in town] and the Mount,' she wrote, 'as it may be very likely I and the female part of our family will be under the necessity of being out there, in case the Enemy should fire upon the north part of the Garrison.'[6]

It felt as if the Spanish forces were being allowed to act unchecked, but Governor Eliott was a highly skilled military man, who was not inclined to act prematurely without careful analysis. He was watching and waiting. Like Mrs Green, his family had a long association with Gibraltar – decades earlier his uncle, Major-General Roger Elliott, had also held the post of governor.[7] Roger Elliott died in 1714, and three years later George Augustus Eliott was born at Stobs, just south of Hawick in the Scottish Borders, the youngest son of the large family of Sir Gilbert Eliott and his wife Eleanora. Educated at Leiden University in Holland, Eliott then attended a French military college and served in the Prussian army, before returning to England for further training at Woolwich. He received a commission as a field engineer and at the same time joined the 2nd Horse Grenadier Guards, probably through the assistance of another uncle who was its colonel. A distinguished military career followed, and in 1743 he was wounded at the Battle of Dettingen, in which George II led his troops into battle, the last time a British monarch did so. Eliott was again wounded two years later, at the Battle of Fontenoy, now in Belgium, which was the last occasion a French king (Louis XV) led an army into battle.[8]

One family member described Eliott as 'tall and good-looking, of a lively, genial disposition, and highly educated. He spoke and wrote French and German both fluently and correctly, and was a lover of books.'[9] In London in 1748, he married Anne Pollexfen Drake, the favourite sister of Sir Francis Henry Drake. She had two other brothers, and, no doubt in order to perpetuate the famous name of Sir Francis Drake in case any of them died, they all bore that name. Francis William and Francis Samuel were both in the Royal Navy, while another brother, Francis Duncombe, died in infancy. Anne also had a younger sister, Sophia.

Eliott subsequently became aide-de-camp to George II and left the Horse Guards after being selected to raise and train the 1st Regiment of Light Horse. His service in the Seven Years' War included fighting at Minden. Under George III, he was second-in-command in an expedition to Cuba, where the capture of Havana netted him substantial prize-money. In 1772, Eliott's beloved wife Anne died, and two years later he became commander-in-chief in Ireland, but asked to be recalled straightaway, unhappy at the petty interference.[10] Instead, at the age of fifty-eight in 1776, he was appointed governor of Gibraltar, little suspecting that three years later he would be in the thick of a siege.

Among the soldiers and officers of the garrison, feelings towards Eliott were divided. Mrs Green's views were ambivalent, no doubt through loyalty towards her husband, Colonel William Green, who tended to clash with him. On the other hand, he was rated highly by Mrs Catherine Upton, known as Kitty to her husband John, who was a lieutenant in the 72nd Regiment: 'Of all men living, General Eliott is the most likely to keep possession of Gibraltar. Though he is formed for great actions, he attends, with unwearied assiduity, to the minutiae of what relates to his important trust! He is, I think, take him, all in all, a most excellent character.' She summed him up in a few lines of verse:

Firm as this Rock is ELIOTT's steady soul,
Watchful he guards, and wisely guides the whole.
Alike he hates the Sycophant and Slave,
And gives his Favours only to the Brave.[11]

Horsbrugh, in a letter to his wife Peggy, wrote a first-hand account of the governor:

General Eliott continues to behave to me with great politeness, and I have the happiness to think no part of my behaviour has hitherto displeased him. He is a man of real worth, strict honor, steady and sincere in his friendship when he professes it, which he never does on a short acquaintance. In duty he expects a punctual and immediate compliance and constant attention to it. He is every morning on horseback by break of day, never misses the Parade, and from that time I generally ride with him till breakfast.[12]

One of the inhabitants was also full of admiration, rating him as 'a most able commander and excellent officer; he is ever vigilant and attentive to the great charge with which he is entrusted, the care of the important fortress; he rises at the dawn of day, and immediately rides round all the walls, takes notice of the several guards, and observes whether that due order is preserved throughout, so essential to the security of the place.'[13]

Since the end of August, the engineers had been hard at work on a new battery of five guns constructed at a height of some 900 feet. It was going to be called the Superior Battery, but was changed at Eliott's suggestion to Green's Lodge. On 11 September it was ready for use, which was the final piece of work that enabled Eliott to consider the garrison sufficiently prepared for their first attack against the Spaniards. According to Horsbrugh, he met with senior officers that same day: 'General Eliott (our Governor) called a Council of War, consisting of Lieutenant General Boyd (Lieutenant Governor), Major General La Motte (commander of the Hanoverian Brigade), Colonel Ross (Lieutenant Colonel of the 39th Regiment), Colonel Green (Chief Engineer), Colonel Godwin (Commander of Artillery), Admiral Duff (Commander of the squadron) and Sir Thomas Rich (captain in the navy).'[14] The purpose of this highly secret meeting was to plan an attack on the Spanish working parties and fortifications, and Eliott gave out his orders:

Captain [Vaughan] Lloyd with his Company, the Captain of Artillery with his picquet and the additionals of the 39th Regiment, to assemble on the artillery parade tomorrow morning at gun firing. The above detachment are to man the several batteries from Greens Lodge to Queen Charlottes inclusive, and are to begin to fire on the Enemy's works at half an hour after six o'clock, or as soon after as the batteries are ready. Captain Lloyd will point out the objects to be fired at and will make a signal for the whole to begin. He may make use of what mortars he [finds] most expedient for the service.[15]

Mrs Green had no idea what had been discussed, but noted in her diary that evening: 'the Colonel ordered his horses at gun fire the next morning, as indeed he does almost every morning'.[16] He was up very early on the 12th and rode up to the batteries at the north end of the Rock. Shortly afterwards, a terrific bombardment was unleashed.

Battles between armies on land used relatively light artillery that could be transported to a battlefield and was manoeuvrable during the action. Sieges were different. Strongholds were armed with larger, heavier cannons and mortars, and for any chance of success, the besiegers had to use similar artillery. Gibraltar was fortified with mortars, howitzers and long guns or cannons, all supplied from Britain. Mortars had short barrels with a large-diameter bore and were set on wooden frames or blocks called mortar beds. They lobbed ammunition in a high arc, enabling shells to fly over an obstacle such as a wall or rampart to the target behind. To achieve a high trajectory, mortar barrels were generally fixed at an angle of 45 degrees, while the range or distance over which they fired depended on the amount of gunpowder. The reinforced breech or closed end of the barrel was set into the bed, which absorbed the downwards thrust of the recoil.

A howitzer was a hybrid, with a large-diameter barrel that was longer than a mortar, but shorter than a cannon. Howitzers were used mainly for firing shells and were mounted on gun carriages. They were designed to fire ammunition upwards, but not so high as mortars, and they could also fire horizontally. Mortars and howitzers were identified by the diameter of the bore – 8-inch howitzers, 13-inch mortars, and so on.[17]

Although the term 'gun' covered all kinds of artillery, more often it referred to a cannon, while 'long gun' was specifically a cannon. Fired horizontally from wooden gun carriages, cannons

were identified by the weight of shot, so a 24-pounder fired cannonballs ('round shot' or 'shot') weighing 24 pounds. They had
much longer barrels and used a bigger charge of gunpowder than
mortars and howitzers, allowing a more accurate shot and a longer
range. The gunpowder was brought from England in barrels and
kegs of various sizes, usually of oak. Gunpowder was not a chemi-
cal compound, but a mixture of sulphur, saltpetre and charcoal,
which over time tended to separate and deteriorate, a process
accelerated by jolting during transportation. A more serious problem was dampness, which rendered it useless, though in what was
a hazardous operation it could be 'repaired' by being dried out and
mixed with good powder.

Gunpowder captured from the Spaniards was found to be
inferior to British gunpowder, possibly due to its method of
manufacture. Later scientific research would establish the ideal
proportions as 75 per cent saltpetre, 15 per cent charcoal and 10
per cent sulphur. Without saltpetre, the sulphur ignited easily and
set the charcoal alight, but if starved of oxygen (as in a gun barrel)
the burning charcoal fizzled out. When saltpetre was added, forming gunpowder, the heat from the initial burning broke down the
saltpetre, releasing oxygen, which generated more burning, more
heat and more oxygen, until all the sulphur and charcoal were
consumed or the saltpetre was exhausted. At the same time, a
cloud of smoke and gas rapidly formed, building up a tremendous
pressure that could fire a cannonball from the barrel of a gun.
The amount of gunpowder needed in any particular situation was
established by trial and error.

No artillery was consistently accurate because it was all smooth
bore, with the ammunition fitting loosely within the smooth
inner surface of the barrel. The direction of spin of a cannonball or shell was random, determined by which side of the bore
it touched when fired towards its target, so that it might hit the
target squarely, pass either side or land in front or beyond. Guns
of all types were made from cast iron or from an alloy of copper
and tin – what was then called 'brass'. Brass guns were easier to
cast and were less brittle, so they did not need such thick-walled

barrels as the heavier iron guns, though they had a tendency to warp or droop when overheated, making them unserviceable. When damaged, brass guns could be melted down and the metal reused, but useless iron guns were scrapped. Even so, iron guns were cheaper and more durable, though there was a danger of them exploding without warning if they became too hot.

All types of artillery were muzzle-loading, and the first step in firing was to place loose powder or a paper cartridge of powder down the mouth (muzzle) of the gun and ram it home. The artillerymen manufactured cartridges in workshops (laboratories) using specially made cartridge paper – the forerunner of the paper used by artists. The powder was followed by a wad of worn-out rope (called junk and therefore a 'junk wad'), though hay and straw could be used. The ammunition, such as a cannonball or shell, was loaded next and rammed home, along with another wad if it was likely to roll out before firing.

On the upper side of the breech of the gun, a small vent or touch-hole gave direct access to the gunpowder or cartridge. If a cartridge was used, a wire rod was inserted into the vent to break the paper and expose the gunpowder. The vent itself was then filled with gunpowder and ignited by a slow match of smouldering twisted cord, which set off the gunpowder within the gun barrel. The resulting explosion fired the ammunition, with the guns belching great clouds of white smoke and producing an acrid, throat-catching, sulphurous smell like a mixture of rotten eggs and wood smoke. The clothing of the gunners reeked with the stench, and the noisy, filthy work left them deaf and blackened from the pervasive soot and smuts.

The first bombardment of the Spanish Lines by Gibraltar's batteries on 12 September 1779, almost three months after the start of the siege, was a significant occasion. Early in the morning, after the Spaniards had paraded their men for work as usual at the Lines, orders were given for Green's Lodge battery and Queen Charlotte's battery (near the castle), as well as those at Willis's, to open fire. It was an event treated with due ceremony, and from this moment Samuel Ancell, a twenty-three-year-old soldier with the 58th Regiment, started to compile a daily journal. Born in Wapping, near London, he was described as 5 feet 8 inches tall and of fair complexion. He was an engraver, probably associated with the printing trade, and, unusually for a rank-and-file soldier, he was well educated. His journal was written as a series of letters to a brother, which may have been a literary device for publication.

Of this first bombardment, Ancell wrote: 'An officer's lady, whom curiosity had excited to our batteries, was encouraged to discharge the first gun, and having taken a lighted match, (with an intrepidity not peculiar to the sex), Gen. Eliott pronounced in a true heroic style, "Britons strike home", and immediately every battery and angle bellowed with rage, and foamed with destruction.'[18] The woman responsible was Jane Frances Skinner, just sixteen years old, who had recently married Lieutenant Thomas Skinner of the Royal Engineers. She was the eldest of six children, all born on Gibraltar to Sarah and Barry Power, and her father was a vintner. The first shot towards the Spanish Lines was therefore fired by a native Gibraltarian, and the choice of Mrs Skinner was no accident, because her husband was the grandson of Lieutenant-General William Skinner, who knew Gibraltar intimately and – at the age of seventy-nine – was Britain's Chief Engineer.[19]

Mrs Green told a slightly different story: 'The first shot was from the new battery called the Superior, above the North Lodgment, 900 feet high. It was fired by Captain Lloyd, Royal Artillery. We kept up a very heavy cannonading for an hour. Most of the Garrison got upon the Hill. I never heard such a noise in my life.'[20] Several batteries of guns probably opened fire simultaneously, including the ceremony with Mrs Skinner, but Mrs Green gave the honours to the battery high up on the Rock that had recently been renamed Green's Lodge after her husband.

For weeks, the Spaniards had toiled unmolested, and she now watched them as they retreated, panic-stricken: 'When the first shot was fired, they were relieving the guards at the Lines, and at the same time large parties were employed bringing down quantities of stores, as usual, in large waggons and carts, drawn by horses and mules. I saw several myself, whose drivers had left the poor horses &c standing, whilst they made off. We know that several mules and horses were killed.'[21] Horsbrugh also witnessed the events:

> The Spanish Guards had just marched into the Lines for the first time and had not all got to their posts when our batteries opened, which obliged them to take shelter under the nearest cover. The working parties abandoned their work in the greatest hurry, and the Guard of Cavalry broke from their pickets and went off on a full gallop. Our first and second round from the batteries fell rather short, but [after] a few more shots we got the proper distance, and we continued to fire at intervals through the day, particularly when any of their workmen were observed returning to their work.[22]

Ancell was amused by their reaction: 'At the first discharge our shot dropped short, so that their advanced guards had time to escape to their lines, and their precipitate retreat almost occasioned a general laugh, to view the Dons tumbling one over another, as they fled from the showers of shot.'[23] Because the remaining workmen were hidden by their covered way, Horsbrugh said the gunners tried a different tactic:

> It was therefore determined to try a few shells, one of which falling and bursting at the spot we wished, so effectually dispersed the workmen that none of them attempted returning for the remainder of the day. Many of our shells were extremely well directed, and the fire kept up so regularly that the Enemy never once ventured to appear in any number out of cover; an effectual stop was also put to their bringing forward more materials in the carts or wagons, for the drivers unyoked their mules and carried them off in great haste.[24]

When Ancell came off guard duty, he saw that the inhabitants were terrified: 'As I came up the street about two hours after, from Waterport (having been the preceding day and night on duty at

that post), I could not but remark the timidity and fearful apprehension pictured in the countenances of the inhabitants, as they
were held in expectation of as furious return from the enemy.
The Jews and Jewesses exhibited the most descriptive amazement, accompanied with significant shrugs, and eyes raised to
the skies.'[25] Nobody was injured that first day on Gibraltar, but
Horsbrugh tried to calculate the Spanish casualties: 'It was impossible for us to judge of their loss. We saw three Dragoon horses
laying dead with their furniture on, others wounded and unable to
move off, and it was generally believed we must have killed some
men, as our shot went into both the forts, and through the roofs
and walls of the guardhouses along the Lines, behind which they
had taken shelter.'[26]

The bombardment from the Rock became a daily occurrence,
a new phase in the siege, and quiet days would now be rare. Many
more inhabitants fled to safety in the south, leaving their houses
unprotected, and Horsbrugh said they 'began erecting wooden
sheds at the southward near Col. Green's country house' – a
shanty town was beginning to form on the edge of the extensive
grounds of The Mount. On 14 September, the General Orders
were: 'Eighty men for fatigue to parade at six o'clock tomorrow
morning to be employed by the Quarter Master General. N.B.
this party is for plowing up the streets from Waterport to Bethlam
Barracks.'[27] It was assumed that Spanish retaliation could happen
any day, and so Eliott wanted the stone surfacing of the streets
removed so as to prevent injuries from the ricochets of shells
and shot. The fastest method was to draw an agricultural plough
through the streets to rip up the cobblestones and setts, which
could be cleared to either side. As Spilsbury noted, 'The pave-
ments of the streets plowing up, the plow drawn by 80 men.' By
'pavement', he meant the street surface, not a sidewalk. The next
day, Captain Price wrote: 'Ploughing the pavement still continues – Irish Town looks as if it had undergone a siege already.' Mrs
Green mentioned that 'the streets in the Garrison were began
to be plowed up on Tuesday the 14th inst. They began in Irish
Town and plowed up the Main Street to the Grand Parade. This

day they are in our street [Engineer Lane] and have come within 100 yards of us.'[28] A little later, traverses or barriers were erected at intervals across Main Street and the parallel street, known as Irish Town, in order to give additional protection if they came under fire.[29]

The usual ammunition was cannonballs – solid spheres of cast iron of different weights and diameters for the different sizes of gun – but they were of limited use against groups of people, such as the Spanish working parties. Explosive shells, also referred to as bombs, were more effective. These were hollow iron balls, which the artillerymen filled with gunpowder and a fuse. The flash of the mortar when fired was enough to light a shell's fuse, and shells were designed to explode just after landing so as to cause fires and injuries to anyone nearby. On the 15th, Price recorded a lucky escape: 'two thirteen inch shells and an eight inch fired in a very good direction, a third thirteen inch shell burst soon after it left the mortar (owing to a flaw) and had like to have done mischief, a large part falling on the parapet of the Prince's Lines, and the smaller splinters among some officers, spectators, of whom I was one'.[30] The shells continued to be unsatisfactory, exploding before they reached their target or falling short. In Drinkwater's view, 'their [working] parties were at too considerable a distance (being near a mile) to be materially annoyed by our shot; and the works being surrounded with sand, the large shells sunk so deep, that the splinters seldom rose to the surface'.[31]

John Mercier, a captain of the 39th Regiment, thought that if smaller shells were fired from a 24-pounder cannon, and not from a mortar, they might reach their target, but experiments were needed to see if the length of the fuse could be calculated to control the timing of the explosion. A trial using shorter fuses proved very effective, as Captain Paterson of the artillery described: 'This afternoon some 5½ inch shells fixed to wooden bottoms were fired from a 24 pounder on Greens Lodge at a working party in the Enemy's Line. They answered very well with 8 lb powder and one degree elevation. The fuzes burnt all well.' Drinkwater agreed: 'These small shells ... were dispatched with such precision, and the fuses were calculated to such exactness, that the shell often burst over their heads, and wounded them before they had time to get under cover ... Less powder was used, and the enemy was more seriously molested.'[32]

Walter Gordon was a Scottish soldier from the 73rd Regiment who would arrive in Gibraltar a few months after these experiments, and he recorded how shells were filled:

> It is a large shell of cast iron, having a great vent to receive the fuzee [fuse], which is made of wood; if no defect is found in the globe, its cavity is filled with whole gun powder; a little space of liberty is left, that when a fuzee or wooden tube is driven thro' the opening, and fastened ... the powder may not be bruised. This tube is filled with a combustible matter, made of two ounces of nitre, one of sulphur, and three of gun powder dust, well rammed. This fuzee set on fire, burns slowly till it reaches the gun powder, which goes off at once, bursting the shell to pieces with incredible violence.[33]

Adjusting the length of the fuses and firing in a straight line from cannons (rather than in an arc from mortars) using Mercier's ideas ensured that shells exploded with devastating effect over the heads of the Spanish troops working out in the open or behind protective ramparts. Such techniques had never before been tried, and they were to revolutionise artillery warfare. Gordon added: 'Perhaps the bomb is the most hellish device, that has as yet been made for the destruction of mankind.'[34] Worse was to come. Henry Shrapnel was an officer in the Royal Artillery who was at Gibraltar after the siege, and he was able to see how shells had been used. He himself invented a more deadly explosive shell, and consequently the word 'shrapnel' instead of 'splinters' came into general use to describe lethal metal fragments from explosives.

With practice, the firing of shells from both mortars and cannons became more precise and less wasteful, though Paterson described some problems:

Our batteries have kept up a slow fire at the forts and working
parties in the lines since the 12th ... which must have retarded
the Enemy's works considerably. Most of our 13 inch mortar
beds broke or gave way near the trunion boxes after a few
rounds were fired from them with about seven or eight pounds
of powder. Many of the old shells broke in the mortar. The
beds were repaired and strengthened ... Continued to fire 5½
inch shells from the 24 pounders on Greens Lodge which were
observed to annoy the Enemy's working parties much.[35]

A week later, he added: 'Some 13 inch shells fell into Fort St
Phillips and did considerable damage to the buildings', while on
3 October Lieutenant Holloway noted: 'Last week the Garrison
fired about 150 shots and 300 of the 5½ inch shells from 24 pounders, besides 30 large shells.'[36] Three days afterwards, Thomas
Cranfield wrote a letter to his father in London: 'Upwards of
20,000 soldiers are now in camp before us, whom we hourly
expect to open upon us ... Every now and then we fire on them,
which they have hitherto refused to return. We expect, however,
that they will soon storm us; though, unless they starve us out,
it is impossible that they can take the garrison.'[37] Cranfield was
unusual among the rank-and-file soldiers because he could read
and write well. Originally from Southwark in London, he had
been a wild, careless youth who had absconded from an appren-
ticeship and enlisted in the 39th Regiment in 1777.

Another soldier was also observing the Spanish activity: 'They
are now employed in throwing up sand banks on the glacis [slop-
ing embankment] of the lines, to cover their men from our upper
batteries: they are also making a *boyau*, or covered way, from the
lines towards the camp, and have unroofed and demolished the
stone guard-houses within the lines, and pulled down most of
the sentry-boxes. From what we can observe, they are preparing
platforms at the lines, for their new mortars and cannon batteries.'
He then commented: 'It is astonishing they have not fired a shot
at us, notwithstanding our fire on them.'[38]

For the time being, the Spanish working parties continued

constructing further fortifications, while the garrison fired at them. The constant tension waiting for retaliation was more than some of the soldiers could bear, and one of the 58th was overheard saying that 'if the Spaniards came, damn him that would not join them'. Once Eliott found out, he declared that the soldier 'must be mad and ordered his head to be shaved, to be blistered, bled, and sent to the Provost [prison] on bread and water, wear a tight waistcoat, and to be prayed for in church'.[39] He could have had the man hanged for treason, but instead treated him as insane, prescribing what were the medical cures of the day. That same night, Horsbrugh related the desertion of another soldier from that regiment: 'Betwixt one and two o'clock in the morning, a soldier of the 58th Regiment on guard at Middle Hill was reported to be missing, and it being suspected he had not got off, but might still be skulking behind the Hill, a party was ordered round in a boat, who found him dead at the foot of the rock, his head clove almost in two, his body greatly mangled, and one of his legs broke.'[40] Mrs Green remarked: 'this makes 5 that have deserted since the investment, three Hanoverians, one of the 72nd and this of 58th'. On this occasion, the deserter was Private Eustace, who had served nine years in the regiment.[41]

The inhabitants, who were already uneasy at the prospect of a Spanish bombardment, became more concerned when familiar landmarks were removed on Eliott's orders: 'The Tower of the White Convent being a conspicuous mark for the Enemy, was ordered to be taken down, as were also some of the highest mirandas belonging to the inhabitants to prevent their making an improper use of them.'[42] Drinkwater explained that modern houses, constructed not long before the siege, generally had tiled roofs, 'but the flat terraced roofs remained in those erected by the Spaniards, and in some, the mirandas or towers; whence the inhabitants, without removing from home, had a beautiful and extensive prospect of the neighbouring coasts'.[43] The reason for removing the mirandas or towers seemed to be Eliott's attempt to prevent any untrustworthy inhabitants from sending signals, while other landmarks were demolished to stop them being used by the Spaniards for sighting artillery. The White Convent or White Cloister, formerly the Monasterio de Nuestra Señora de la Merced, was close to the Line Wall in Irish Town and had for many years been used as naval stores. It was also currently the headquarters of Admiral Duff. Another former monastery was the Convent, where Eliott was based, and the belfry belonging to that church (the King's Chapel) was also dismantled.

In early October, it was the turn of the bell tower of the Catholic – or Spanish – church of St Mary the Crowned, on the site of a former mosque, which Colonel James described two decades earlier:

> The Spanish church originally was a Moorish structure, though pulled down to build the present one, which is in the Gothic style; as a proof, the northern entrance is Gothic, and adjoining is the steeple and belfry; now, within this large gateway is a Moorish square (before you enter the church); the centre of the square is open, but round the sides of the area are Moorish pillars and arches ... Round the area are orange and lemon trees.[44]

Although appreciating the building, he could not help being critical:

> The church, were it kept in proper repair and good order, would make a very good appearance ... [and] would be light enough, did they not exclude the sun, by blinding their windows. However, to supply the place of this luminary, many lamps were burnt before the shrines on days of dedication and festivity. A great many amulets hang against the pillars and walls; silver legs, arms, pieces of cables, shirts, and such rubbish and trumpery, as offerings to saints.[45]

Part of the church had been requisitioned for naval stores by Admiral Duff in early September and was already partitioned off. Francisco Messa, a fifty-one-year-old Minorcan who had been in Gibraltar in charge of the Roman Catholics for the last six years, agreed to Duff's plans, 'as we were concerned that they would have taken over the church entirely, for more unbecoming purposes, as happened in the other siege [in 1727], when it was completely taken over as a hospital, as recounted by the older inhabitants, and I was further assured that it would only be for a short period of time'.[46] Since then, Father Messa had given permission for the upper part of the bell tower to be demolished, but had heard nothing more. He therefore hoped that it would not be carried out, as the clock and bells were such important elements of everyday life for the inhabitants:

on 6th October, my brother-in-law came to tell me that the order had already been given to dismantle the belfry and to demolish it as quickly as possible. On the morning when I went to the church, I found the engineers already there setting up the scaffolding for this undertaking, so that by the 7th ... the first and sad view that I had was of a soldier removing the first stone, which was the one at the very top. And everything was done so quickly that by the 13th of the month, that part of the tower containing the bells and clock ... had been dismantled.[47]

While the garrison was trying to make it difficult for the Spanish gunners when they chose to retaliate, they also made constant improvements to their own artillery and fortifications. 'The great command we had over the enemy's operations from Green's lodge,' Drinkwater commented, 'induced the engineers to mount still higher, and endeavour to erect a battery on the summit of the northern front. A place therefore was levelled, and a road for wheeled carriages begun at Middle-hill.'[48] After a few days, he said that 'The artillery were too impatient to have a gun mounted on the summit of the rock to wait till the new road was finished. They accordingly determined to drag a twenty four-pounder up the steep craggy face of the rock.'[49]

The higher the guns were mounted, the greater the advantage they had over the Spaniards, and Horsbrugh expressed his admiration: 'We began to prepare for carrying a twenty four pounder up to the Midshipman's look out on the summit of the Rock to the northward, and nearly 1400 feet in perpendicular height from the sea. Such an attempt would a few years ago have been thought impracticable, but our miners and workmen were by constant practice so much masters of their business that no difficulties now obstruct them.'[50] Paterson gave details about how they managed to haul this huge gun of about 2½ tons up to Rock Guard – almost the highest point of the Rock: 'The Artillery employed this morning in getting a 24 pounder up the Rock in a direct line to the top near the Rock Guard. A frame was laid down on which a slay [sleigh] with the gun was fastened upon it run on. Irons were fixed in the Rock at proper distances, and the whole drawn up by pulleys. It was taken up 120 feet the first 3 hours.'[51] Solid iron hauling rings fixed into the rock and through which ropes were passed are still visible in the Upper Rock, showing where guns were manhandled in this way.

It took 150 men four days, and on the 9th Paterson said: 'This evening our Artillery got the 24 pounder up to the top of the Rock, gave three cheers, and drunk the Governor's health in a quarter cask of wine he presented them with upon the occasion.'[52] Ancell found the achievement unbelievable: 'This day, a twenty-four pounder was dragged up the face of the Rock to Midshipman's look-out, or Rock-Gun; the labour and danger attending it is not to be conceived, as it was carried over points of rocks to a height of 1357 feet.'[53] One long-time resident recounted how the new battery was a blow to Spanish morale:

On the highest pinnacle of this mountain, which fronts the Spanish lines, is built a guard-house, called the Rock-Guard ... a battery was erected thereon, and called the Sky Battery. It was amazing to see with what spirit and resolution our British troops dragged the heavy pieces of cannon that are mounted on this battery up the precipice. The Spaniards, who at a distance saw our brave fellows at work, were astonished, and could hardly believe it possible men would attempt so laborious a task, and in the height of summer; they were, however, soon

convinced the work was compleatly effected. They perceived
an additional fort opened on them, and saw the fatal ball and
shell flying from the Sky Battery about their lines.[54]

In spite of all the incoming shells and cannonballs, the Spanish
working parties managed to keep up their hard work by night,
so that the threat facing the Rock grew ever more menacing.
By October, the cavalry and infantry forces before Gibraltar had
increased considerably in number, and Holloway reckoned that
the Spaniards had 16,000 men on land and about 6850 men on
board the various armed vessels in the Bay.[55] Unless there was a
full moon, it was impossible to discover exactly where work was
taking place, making it difficult to know in what direction to fire.
All that the garrison gunners could aim for was the general direction where flickering lights were visible or where noise could be
heard, both of which depended on weather conditions. 'Being on
Waterport Guard during the stillness of the night,' Price commented on one occasion, 'I could plainly hear the Spanish working
parties nailing their [gun] platforms.' He resented the attitude of
the opposing forces: 'The enemy continue to hold us in contempt
and as yet have never returned us either shot or shell,'[56] while
Ancell said: 'The enemy are quiet, but exceedingly watchful, and
labour much at their approaches; we cannot form any judgment of
what they are doing. We keep up a fire upon them.'[57]

The frustration of being literally in the dark led to the development of lightballs or fireballs, to illuminate enemy territory.
Initial experiments took place in early September, when Paterson
recorded one that travelled over 500 yards: 'Experiments were
made this evening with a light ball fired from an 8 inch howitzer
on South Bastion. One of them burnt 6 minutes.'[58] On the evening
of 19 October, Drinkwater described an experiment with a new
kind of lightball that took place in the presence of Eliott, 'the
invention of Lieut. [Abraham] Whitham, of the artillery. It was
made of lead, filled with composition, and weighed 14lb. 10 oz.
With 4 lb. of powder, at six degrees elevation, the ball was fired
out of a thirty two-pounder, upon the glacis of their lines. It burnt

well; and the experiment was to have been repeated, if a thick fog had not suddenly arisen.' Eliott had a reputation for sleeping very little, and he was soon back the next morning: 'the fog being dispersed, the Governor was at Willis's by half past four, to see a second trial, when the lightball answered to his satisfaction'.[59]

This was a new development, Price explained, enabling them to be fired much further: 'Some fireballs for a new plan – hooped with lead so as to make them weigh about 15 pounds ... Lt Whetham of the Artillery had the credit of the improvement, though not of the original invention. Four or five hundred yards used to be the usual distance to which these fire balls could be thrown, but by the addition of the lead they carried upwards of eighteen hundred yards, that being the distance of the nearest part to us of the Spanish Lines.'[60] Unfortunately, Drinkwater said, they failed to illuminate anything on this occasion: 'The enemy, during the night, had been uncommonly noisy; but when the lightballs were fired, no parties were discovered at work. At day-break, however, to our surprise, we observed 35 embrasures [for guns] opened in their lines, disposed of in three batteries.'[61] It looked as if Gibraltar was about to be bombarded.

# CHAPTER FIVE

———— •◆• ————

# SHORTAGES

At about five in the evening of 16 October 1779, one of the soldiers on duty at the Prince's Lines spotted a man dressed in a brown coat, laced hat and white stockings, traipsing through the market gardens near the inundation and heading towards the Spanish Lines. Governor Eliott immediately ordered Captain Horsbrugh to investigate. He was found to be a servant of Mr Davies, an agent-victualler of the garrison, and against all regulations he had been allowed to pass through the Landport barrier after pretending to search for his master's goat. Captain Price said that 'he imposed on the Captain of Landport by a cock and ball story, who allowed him to pass the barrier. For this, poor Sam Moore [captain] of our regiment got chocolate [a reprimand] from the Governor.'[1] This desertion was especially worrying, because in order to ensure a favourable reception it was believed that he might have taken information with him about the state of provisions in the garrison.

It was not long before Drinkwater complained that 'Provisions of every kind were now becoming very scarce and exorbitantly dear in the garrison ... Fish was equally high, and vegetables were with difficulty to be got for any money; but bread, the great essential for life and health, was the article most wanted.'[2] When two Walloon Guards succeeded in deserting from the Spanish Lines, they said it was believed that 'the Garrison was reduced to a fortnight's provisions'.[3] The regiments of Walloon Guards were originally recruited in the Netherlands, from an area now mainly within Belgium. By the time of the siege, recruits also came from places such as Switzerland, Italy and, especially, Ireland. Most of the deserters to Gibraltar were Walloons, and, being foreign troops, they did not have the same allegiances as those from Spain itself.

This information about the state of the garrison may well have been supplied by Mr Davies's servant, even though he and the other deserters into Spain were treated as spies and held shackled in prison. According to Price, the Walloon deserters also said that the newly invented shells had proved highly effective: 'they have had twelve men and a woman killed by our fire and about twice that number wounded, that the shells fired from cannon have annoyed them extremely and confused them at first by their novelty'.[4] Although the Spanish commander had intended firing on the garrison before now, it was decided to let starvation take its course and force Gibraltar to surrender.

The besieging troops were also hungry, and the Walloons pointed out that 'Bread is very scarce and dear in Camp, and water brought from a great distance.'[5] Spain was not blockaded and so was responsible for the provision of adequate supplies to the camp, but on Gibraltar the blockade by land and sea was badly affecting food stocks, even though Eliott had introduced various regulations from the outset. A fit man of frugal habits, he himself was a vegetarian who ate very little, drank only water and never slept more than four hours a night. In Europe in the late eighteenth century, vegetarianism was not common, though the mass of the population rarely ate meat because of its cost. Only in the early nineteenth century did the idea of abstaining from meat take hold, so he was an unusual figure. Around this time, he conducted a trial in order to see 'what quantity of rice would suffice a single person for twenty-four hours, and actually lived himself eight days on four ounces of rice per day'. Eliott, Drinkwater said, 'is remarkable for an abstemious mode of living, seldom tasting any thing but vegetables, simple puddings and water; and yet is very hale, and uses constant exercise'. While the shortages would never bother him unduly, Eliott was mindful of the dangers of reduced rations. Few others on Gibraltar willingly shared his habits, and as for his experiment, Drinkwater concluded, 'the small portion just mentioned would be far from sufficient for a working man kept continually employed, and in a climate where the heat necessarily demands very refreshing nourishment to support nature under fatigue'.[6]

As food stocks fell, prices rose, which shocked Spilsbury: 'Charged seven shillings sterling for dinner of salt beef and a little bit of fish and pudding.'[7] Because meat was a luxury for most people, those in the army or navy were fortunate to have meat as part of their rations. Soldiers serving abroad did not always have fresh produce, and that was certainly the case during the siege, when salt meat was instead shipped in wooden casks from England. Beef and pork were salted by cutting the meat into pieces and repeatedly rubbing them with dry salt and saltpetre, which preserved them by drawing off moisture and preventing bacteria. After a few days the meat pieces could be packed into wooden casks filled with brine. Salt meat was more palatable if soaked in water before cooking, but it still made the soldiers thirsty. If the meat portions were too large or if the brine leaked out, the contents would rot, which was a common complaint during the siege.[8] Ancell reflected that 'It is really vexing and mortifying to view the Spanish hills and heights, covered with cattle, while we can scarce procure a piece of salt beef, and that at a price', and Spilsbury grumbled: 'Rice sold at 21 dollars 6 reals per cwt., raised five times the usual price. Little fresh meat now. Geese at a guinea each, and ducks at 2 dollars, pork 5 reals per lb.'[9]

It was not just rising prices that affected the garrison, but the unfavourable fixed exchange rate for their pay, as Drinkwater explained:

The troops are paid in currency, which, let the exchange of the garrison be above or below *par*, never varies to the non-commissioned and privates. A serjeant receives weekly, as full garrison-pay, one dollar, six reals, equal to nine-pence sterling, *per diem*; a corporal, and drummer, one dollar, one real, and five quartils [quarts], in sterling about six-pence *per diem*; and a private, seven reals, or four-pence half-penny sterling, *per diem*. Officers receive their subsistence according to the currency: thirty-six pence *per* dollar is *par*.[10]

None of the soldiers thought their pay was enough to cope with the rising prices, but the problem for officers was that although they were paid at an exchange rate of 36 pence for a dollar, the actual exchange rate was often 39 pence and sometimes as much as 42 pence. Because their garrison pay was set in pounds, shillings and pence sterling, but paid in the local currency at an unfavourable rate, this amounted to a cut in pay. It was an issue that would continue to annoy them throughout the siege.

Exchange rates were a constant worry because various currencies were used, often at arbitrary exchange rates, and the local currency relied on Spanish coins. Visiting Gibraltar just before the siege, Richard Twiss said: 'All European coins are current here, but considerably under the value; a guinea [21 shillings] passes [at] no more than nineteen shillings and six pence; five Spanish reals are only three here.'[11] In the same way as British currency was based on the pound sterling, the Gibraltar currency was based on the Spanish dollar. Spilsbury jotted down the different values: '16 quarts is 1 real; 1 dollar is 8 reals; 1 cob is 12 reals [1½ dollars]; 1 pistol is 5 dollars 5 reals or 45 reals; 1 doubloon is 22½ dollars (or 22 dollars 4 reals) or 180 reals.'[12] Ancell explained the coinage in a letter to his brother: 'A rial is a piece of Spanish coin, Gibraltar currency, eight-pence value, equal to four-pence three farthings sterling. A quart is a Spanish half-penny, forty of which is given in change for an English shilling.' Small coins were in constant short supply, with quarts, reals (or rials) and cobs used in everyday transactions.[13]

Even those who had money found little to buy, and Ancell lamented how they were isolated and neglected: 'We have not received any supplies or intelligence … No prospect of relief:

We begin to think England has forgot that such people are in existence.'[14] The problem was not just a lack of a relief convoy from Britain, but that all supplies had to evade the Spanish blockade while sailing into the bay. Most provisions came across the Straits from Morocco (Barbary), as well as from the British-held Mediterranean island of Minorca, over six hundred miles away, or from Portugal's Atlantic port of Lisbon, a distance of nearly four hundred miles. There were no other allies closer to hand, but Gibraltar could not support itself. With steep, rocky hillsides, there was limited land fertile enough to be farmed, although the Genoese inhabitants did continue to cultivate their market gardens out on the isthmus.

Eliott ordered any supplies evading the blockade to be sold on the open market to the highest bidder – quite often to a merchant, who would resell at an even greater profit. Prices spiralled upwards, but any attempt to control prices would have deterred those captains of vessels who were willing to risk breaking the blockade. It was, after all, only the lure of quick profits that was the motivation to run the gauntlet of Spanish warships, but the feeling among the resentful population was that 'The Governor does not care how dear things are'.[15] For both soldiers and civilians, the lack of food and the rising prices were a source of antagonism and distress. Soldiers received some food rations, with extra rations given to officers, but additional provisions had to be purchased. Soldiers' wives who had permission to be with their husbands were entitled to half-rations and their children to quarter-rations.[16] The civilians had to pay for everything.

At great risk, vessels slipped unseen into Gibraltar by night or were concealed by the all-too-frequent fogs, while others eluded the Spanish guns by taking advantage of the awkward winds and currents. Not all were lucky. At the end of October, after a long trip from Minorca, the *Peace and Plenty* privateer, a Belfast vessel, had almost reached Gibraltar when several Spanish ships moved in to intercept, and Lieutenant Holloway described what happened: 'an English ship of 20 guns was engaged at the back of the Rock by a Spanish xebeque, a galley and several row-boats. The

guns at Europa Advance [battery] was fired and also the gun at
Middle Hill, which was found to be of great use in preventing the
ship from falling into the enemy's hands, besides protecting the
boats of our squadron which were sent round by the Admiral to
give assistance.' The privateer was trapped between the Spanish
ships and the coast and had no option but to run on to the eastern beach: 'notwithstanding all that could be done, the ship was
under the necessity of running ashore on the isthmus between the
Devil's Tower and Fort St Barbara, from which they fired on her,
killed the boatswain and wounded three men. Several of the crew
quitted the ship and came on shore near the Devil's Tower and
then along under the Rock into the Garrison. The Master with
the remainder of the crew were taken out of the ship and brought
in by our boats.'[17]

In response to the firing from Fort St Barbara, the garrison
retaliated: 'The enemy firing on the ship from Fort St Barbara
was the occasion of Willis's and all the upper batteries opening
upon the Fort which dismounted one of their guns and kept them
in pretty good subjection.'[18] There were still hopes of salvaging
something from the wreck, even if only firewood, so the batteries continued firing to keep the Spaniards at a distance, and guns
were hauled up even higher to protect the wreck, as Paterson
outlined: 'Two 24 pounders were moved to Farrington's Battery,
an officer and 30 men were sent up to reinforce the batteries, and
they kept up a pretty brisk fire upon fort St Barbara for most part
of the day, yet that fort fired many shot through the vessel. The
xebeqs came so near that it was thought two shot were fired into
them from Europa, two from Middle Hill, and one from Green's
Lodge.'[19]

The next day, an attempt was made at salvage. 'Some of the
crew of the stranded vessel attempted going on board her this
morning,' Price said, 'to get some livestock and other things out of
her, but the fire from the Spanish fort with round and grape shot
was so well directed and kept up that the poor fellows could not
accomplish their purpose and were obliged to desist. She has on
board hogs, poultry, sheep, several casks of beef and many barrels

of powder and letters for the Garrison.'[20] Grapeshot was a shower of smaller balls and miscellaneous projectiles, usually contained in a canvas bag and fired from a cannon over short distances. At about 8 o'clock at night, the vessel was set on fire, though nobody was certain who was to blame. Price was captain of the guard at Landport that night:

> between seven and eight the centry posted on Coverport Battery reported to me that a light ball had been thrown from Willis's on the eastern strand in a line with the privateer with intention of discovering whether the Enemy who had a xebeque all day at anchor off Fort Barbara had boarded her. Soon after I went to the centry's post, a carcass [an incendiary device] was thrown from our batteries at the ship. In two or three minutes I saw her on fire in three different parts. This had every appearance of being done by ourselves but the centry at the extremity of the Prince's Lines reported to his captain that he could perceive by the light of the fire ball burning on the Strand a boat putting off from the ship's side, a pretty convincing proof that this little exploit ought in strict justice to be ascribed to the Spaniards, though some in the Garrison are still of a contrary opinion. She was in a few moments compleatly on fire, and by some little sudden flashes, some loose powder seemed to be strewed over her deck, her guns and swivels went off as the fire reached them. I plainly saw several of the shot strike the water. Upon the whole, it was a splendid but awful spectacle ... in the morning she was burnt to the water's edge, but still continues burning.[21]

It was a bitter blow whenever vessels were captured or destroyed, and this one was a total loss. At the time, nobody seems to have noted the irony of the *Peace and Plenty*, the two things they desperately wanted, being completely destroyed when almost within reach.

Just as the *Peace and Plenty* was shipwrecked, an outbreak of smallpox was detected among the civilians. When the border was closed in June, the children sick with smallpox at San Roque were not allowed back into Gibraltar but had to stay in the area of the market gardens until they had recovered.[22] Eliott gave new orders to protect the troops:

> The smallpox having appeared in the Garrison, all the men of the different Corps who have not had that disorder to be removed to the southward this day at three o'clock. They are to remain there, and on no account be permitted to come to town. The Hanoverian Brigade [is] to occupy Wind Mill Hill, the other detachments will be quarantined by the regiments at the southward, the Grand Company of the 12 Regiment and Light Company of the 72 Regiment to come into town.[23]

Smallpox was not properly understood, and one theory, Mrs Green related, was that this outbreak was spread by the crew of the *Peace and Plenty*: 'It is not certain how this disorder got into the Garrison. Some think it was brought in by some privateers' men who were taken out [of] an English ship which run on shore near Fort Barbara, which ship was burnt.' The timing made this impossible, though smallpox may have been introduced by crews of previous merchant vessels. Three weeks later, Mrs Green described how it was brought under control:

> It began in an inhabitant's house, a poor Jew's. One child was nearly recovered before it was found out, and another taken ill. Every method is taken to prevent the disorder spreading, as it would have been a very bad thing at this time. The means were used as follows – an examination was made amongst the different regiments of those men who had not had the smallpox, and they were directly ordered out to the southward, and the same number sent in to do the duty; the Jew's family was removed to a house in Irish Town, a large airy place ... As other children were taken ill, they also were sent to that house; by which means it avoided spreading. There was 7 children in all that had it, but it never took amongst the troops.[24]

While a number of the Jews were wealthy, many Jewish families were poor, like the ones whose children had contracted smallpox, and they worked primarily as hawkers, porters and labourers. The Spanish historian Ayala held an unsympathetic view of Jewish people, as did many in Britain at this time:

> The Jews [of Gibraltar], for the most part, are shopkeepers and brokers, as much given to cheating and to lending money at exorbitant interest there as their brethren elsewhere. They have a synagogue, and openly practise the ceremonies of their religion, notwithstanding the conditions of the Treaty of Utrecht. They are chiefly managed by some principal one among them, whom they style King: he is in communication with the Governor, who through him regulates the imposts paid by them for his sole benefit.[25]

Under the terms of the 1713 Treaty of Utrecht, Jews were banned from living in the town of Gibraltar, and although many were running businesses and importing much-needed supplies, London had exerted pressure until they were removed. After a breakdown in relations with Spain, a treaty was agreed with Morocco in 1721 that gave Moors and Jews the right to settle and work in Gibraltar, and by the time of the Great Siege, Ayala reckoned that a thousand Jews were living there. The census two years earlier, in 1777, recorded 863 Jewish people, nearly three-quarters of whom were born on Gibraltar. The community had a synagogue in the town, with an entrance off Engineer Lane, not far from the official residence of the Chief Engineer, Colonel Green. It replaced a smaller synagogue nearby that was destroyed during a terrible storm in 1766.[26]

Although most of the Jews had come to Gibraltar from Morocco, primarily Tetuan, they were originally descended from those refugees who had been expelled from Spain – Sephardic Jews. As Ayala mentioned, the Jewish community regulated its own affairs, a measure that was introduced by Lieutenant-Governor Bland some three decades earlier in response to the unruly behaviour of some of the hawkers and labourers.[27] At the start of the siege, the leader of the Jewish community that Ayala called 'King' was Isaac Aboab, now sixty-seven years old, who had been born at Tetuan and was a considerable merchant and property owner in Gibraltar.

Despite the risks of the blockade, ships still tried to reach Gibraltar, and in mid-November, a fortnight after the *Peace and Plenty* was destroyed, it looked as if something was approaching from the Atlantic. 'This morning about 8 o'clock one of the row galleys in the gut made a signal to the Spanish admiral,' Paterson wrote, 'upon which he got under way with his whole squadron, consisting of one 74, one 50-gun ship, one frigate, 3 xebeqs and six or eight row galleys.'[28] With such a reaction from Admiral Barcelo, observers on the Rock assumed that a convoy was close – something everyone longed for, because of the dwindling supplies and soaring prices.

It was soon discovered that the entire Spanish squadron had been ordered out to pursue a lone cutter, the *Buck*. Captain Price watched what happened: 'This morning early the attention of the Garrison was greatly engrossed with attending to the manoeuvres of an English cutter which appeared to westward.'[29] Barcelo's ships positioned themselves right across the bay to intercept the vessel, and so the cutter tacked and made for the Barbary coast, luring the Spanish squadron towards Africa. The *Buck* suddenly changed course once more and headed directly for Gibraltar, while the strong westerly wind and the currents carried most of Barcelo's ships eastwards. Only the Spanish flagship managed to anchor in time and was now the only vessel upwind of the cutter. 'Our ships in the Bay loosened their topsails,' said Price,

> and every one was on tip toe for some great event. As the cutter approached Europa, the Spanish Admiral weighed and stood for her. She kept steady to her course, and as she passed Barcelo, he fired the greatest part of his lower deck guns at her. The cutter returned shot for shot in every good direction and between twelve and one o'clock came to an anchor off the New Mole, having ran the gantelope [gauntlet] through about one and

twenty vessels of various sizes and dimensions, without sustain-
ing any injury but a shot through the gunnel of her boat, which
went also through the jacket of a seaman who was sitting on it.[30]

The naval ships at Gibraltar had made no move to help, and
Spilsbury was unimpressed: 'Our Admiral unloosed topsails, but
did not unmoor.'[31]

The *Buck* cutter was a privateer from Folkestone in Kent,
which was a port renowned for building such vessels. Armed with
twenty-four 9-pounder guns, she was commanded by Captain
George Fagg. His seamanship was so remarkable that Drinkwater
felt obliged to write an explanation of why the *Buck* had not been
carried eastwards with the Spanish squadron:

> As it may appear very extraordinary to readers unacquainted
> with naval affairs that the privateer should not be equally
> affected by the current, it is proper they should be informed
> that a cutter, or any vessel rigged in the same manner, from the
> disposition of her sails can go several points nearer the wind
> than a square-sailed vessel [like warships]; which advantage, on
> this occasion, enabled Captain Fagg, by turning to windward,
> to stem in a great measure the current, whilst the Spaniards ...
> were carried away to the eastward.[32]

Those on Gibraltar who saw this drama unfold were amazed
at what Captain Fagg had done, even though the *Buck* was only
a little more heavily armed than the *Peace and Plenty*, which
had been wrecked. Ancell heard that before coming in sight of
Gibraltar, the *Buck* had been chased by three other cutters that
turned out to be English: 'They asked him where he was bound,
and answering to Gibraltar, they persuaded him to return, adding
it was impossible to get in safe. In a jocular strain he asked if there
was room for a coach and six to get in, which being answered in
the affirmative, he rolled his quid [chewed tobacco] two or three
times, and with an audible oath, swore he would get in if Belzebub
himself gave chase.'[33]

Paterson summed up everyone's feelings: 'It is difficult to judge whether the Captain deserves most praise for his maneuvering, for his courage, or for the modest manner of his relations of this fact, which the whole garrison were witnesses to. Upon his coming on shore he received every mark of distinction possible, in the most public manner from the Governor, and was received with open arms by the whole Garrison.'[34] On Gibraltar, everyone thought the *Buck* was the first of a convoy, and Drinkwater saw how the mood of jubilation soon changed:

The expectations of the troops and inhabitants, who were spec- tators of the action, had been raised to the highest pitch: few doubted that she was a King's vessel; and as no intelligence had been received from England for many weeks, their flattering fancies painted her the messenger of good news; probably the forerunner of a fleet to their relief. But what was their despon- dency and disappointment, when they were informed that she was a privateer, had been a considerable time at sea, and put in for provisions?[35]

The *Buck* had brought no supplies, though may have brought dispatches for Eliott. If so, they were delivered discreetly, which Ancell hinted at: 'What news he brings, is not made public, excepting that we are not to expect a fleet yet.' After such a spectacular manipulation of the Spanish squadron, Drinkwater admitted that they felt obliged to help Captain Fagg: 'What indeed could be refused to a man by whose manoeuvres the Port was once more open, and the bay and Straits again under the com- mand of a British Admiral?' As one soldier witnessed: 'All Barcelo's ships are *blackstrapped*, that is, they are dropped behind the hill [east of the Rock], and unable to recover their stations, so that we remain masters of the Bay till they can work up [westwards, once the wind changed].'[36]

In an era reliant on wind power, everyone was acutely aware of wind conditions, which were recorded in most of the diaries at the time. The winds and currents around the Strait of Gibraltar, a constricted shipping lane where the Atlantic Ocean connects with the Mediterranean Sea and where two continents almost meet, have always been troublesome. Any vessel sailing from the Atlantic into the Mediterranean had to pass the Moroccan port of Tangier at the south-western approach to the Straits. Next came Tarifa, at the southernmost tip of Spain (and Europe itself), a port exposed to the winds. The Bay of Gibraltar, some 15 miles north-east of Tarifa, was the first reasonably safe anchorage. Whoever dominated the Straits was therefore in a powerful position to control shipping and trade to and from the Mediterranean.

Because of the westerly wind and the skill of Captain Fagg, the Spanish squadron had been forced beyond Gibraltar into the Mediterranean. They had been blackstrapped, a word derived from the rough local Spanish wine known as blackstrap (there is also a Blackstrap Cove on the eastern side of Gibraltar). For ships sailing westwards from the Mediterranean towards the Atlantic, conditions were especially difficult, and they could find themselves going backwards, which was why the Spanish squadron now had to wait for an easterly wind, as Drinkwater explained: 'The rapidity of the superior current renders the passage from the Mediterranean to the westward very precarious and uncertain, as ships never can stem the stream without a brisk Levanter, or easterly wind. Vessels, therefore, are often detained weeks, and sometimes months, waiting for a favourable breeze.'[37]

As long as there was a westerly, the Spanish warships were out of harm's way, but there was no way of judging how long the garrison's luck would last. Rapid action was therefore needed to take advantage of their unexpected situation. A few vessels did manage to slip in with supplies, but Gibraltar's naval squadron failed to grasp the opportunity, and Mrs Green reflected the feelings of many in her diary: 'From this time, the enemy's fleet was dispersed and left us sole masters of the Bay; it was therefore expected that we should have availed ourselves of it. However it did not turn out so! as our men of war made no attempt to move.

All this seeming neglect hurt every individual in the Garrison; and several very severe papers were put up on the different parades reflecting upon the Admiral's conduct.'[38]

There was a tendency for different elements of the garrison to be critical of each other, with derogatory remarks appearing in journals, such as that of Spilsbury who was especially quick to find fault with the artillery. Discontent with the navy became widespread, but Mrs Green said that Admiral Duff 'carried it with an air of indifference'.[39] Even so, suspicions were aroused over his constant lack of action. When two Spanish frigates arrived from the west and anchored off Algeciras only twenty-four hours after the *Buck*, this was a real chance for the squadron to act. Spilsbury was scathing: 'It seems a council of war was held among the Navy, and it was agreed to go over to Algazeras, and attack two Spanish frigates that came in last night, and ride by themselves. But nothing was done, but [it is] alleged that the Admiral is bribed.'[40] The westerly wind effectively put the Spanish ships beyond reach for several days, but finally the wind changed to the east and they returned. The opportunity to make use of the accidental lifting of the blockade by the *Buck* was lost.

Soon after, Duff was again bitterly criticised. He had been informed by some of the merchants that they were expecting a vessel with supplies, but he failed to act on this information, as Paterson recorded: 'A Swedish snow [large, two-masted merchant vessel] appeared about 9 o'clock [on 20 November] from the westward, was boarded by the row gallies and carried into Algaziras. By her signals it appeared that she was consigned to Mr. Spinosa with provisions for the Garrison.' Later on, it was learned that the supplies had included 350 tons of coal, which was a huge loss.[41] It was not just hunger that sapped everyone's morale. With coal and wood scarce, they were continually cold and wet. Coal used to be brought to Gibraltar in massive quantities by colliers from the Newcastle area, as Colonel James mentioned two decades earlier: 'Fires in winter are absolutely necessary, nor can you do well without them; and the fuel is coal from Great Britain, which you get as cheap as in the Pool at London.'[42] The lack of fuel now added to their misery, which Mrs Upton described: 'Our cloaths were washed in cold water, and put on without ironing; but when the rainy season came on, I suffered more from the cold than I ever did in the severest winter in England: for what is the inconvenience of a cold day by the chearing warmth of a good fire-side? – You can form no idea of the periodical rains in Gibraltar!'[43]

Mrs Upton's life in England had been very different. Before her marriage, she was Catherine Creswell, brought up in Nottingham, where her father Samuel was a bookseller, printer and political activist, with his business located in the market place.[44] One of her brothers, Edward Creswell, would become vicar of nearby Lenton and Radford. Unusually for a girl at that time, she was well educated and undertook one of the few respectable jobs available to young women – teaching children. It is possible that her early employment was as a governess in London, from where she penned a poem to her father, revealing how much she missed Nottingham and how desperate she was to write: 'My love for scribbling still torments me here'.[45] Back in Nottingham, she ran a boarding school at Bramcote, though by 1771 she had moved to the growing town of Manchester and placed an advertisement for her new school in the local newspaper:

Miss CRESWELL, (Late a Partner at BRAMCOTE Boarding-School, near NOTTINGHAM) Takes this Method of acquainting her Friends and the Publick, THAT she has taken a genteel and commodious House of Mr. *Budworth*, near St. *John*'s Church, in Manchester, where she proposes Boarding, and teaching young Ladies English Grammar, and various Kinds of Needle-Work, at fifteen Guineas a Year, and two Guineas Entrance ... She will open her School on the 10th of April next, and may be spoke with, or wrote to, at Mr. *Creswell*'s, in *Hanging-ditch, Manchester.*[46]

The school was not to last because two years later, in May 1773, she married John Upton, known to her as Jack, who was a

chapman or bookseller in Manchester, though in 1778 he joined
the 72nd Regiment, initially as an ensign but soon promoted to
lieutenant. Mrs Upton accompanied her husband to Gibraltar,
and by then she had one son, Jack, and her daughter Charlotte
was born not long after the siege started, probably in late 1779.
Her entire life became focused on caring for her children and her
husband in the midst of the siege.

In late November 1779, Eliott gave out new orders: 'No more
fuel is to be issued to officers or soldiers than what can be allowed
to dress [cook] their provisions.'[47] Coal was so scarce, Drinkwater
said, that they were issued with wood from ships, 'bought by
Government, and broken up for that purpose, but which had so
strongly imbibed the salt water, that it was with the utmost difficulty we could make it take fire'. Shortly afterwards, 'Mr Holliday,
the principal baker in this garrison, refused to bake, owing to
the want of wood. He had at the time 51 sacks of flour left. The
Governor took them all away except two, which he allowed him
to keep for his family.' This was fifty-eight-year-old William
Halliday, a resident of Gibraltar for nearly four decades, who lived
with his Gibraltarian wife Phoebe and their two children.[48]

Some families found it impossible to cope. 'It is really griev-
ous to see the fighting of the people for a morsel of bread,' Ancell
wrote sympathetically, 'at a price not to be credited by those who
never knew hardship or their country's service. Men wrestling,
women intreating, and children crying, a jargon of all languages
piteously pouring forth their complaints. You would think sensibility would shed a tear; but yet when we are in equal distress
ourselves, our feelings for others rather subside. Compassion is
very extensive, but self-preservation shuts out all condolement.'[49]

At the start of December, two more Walloon Guards deserted
in the night, and Ancell heard from them that the troops in
the Spanish camp were still suffering, though ever hopeful of
Gibraltar's capitulation:

> they report that the enemy are not to fire, while they can keep
> the place blockaded, as General Alvarez [who had replaced

Mendoza] is confident that famine will oblige us to surrender. We are certainly greatly distressed for want of fresh provisions and vegetables. Salt meat is scarce to be purchased ... Yesterday a baker was obliged to shut up, not having flour sufficient for his family for one month. Appearances are rather dreadful. God grant that a fleet may soon arrive, or the consequences are to be feared.[50]

In spite of the shortages, Captain Price was more amused than annoyed when the Spanish troops began to raid the market gardens: 'Some Spaniards got into the gardens outside Landport and rooted up some cabbages, etc. The lanthorns they brought with them discovered them, and the grape shot from the extremity of Prince's Lines scoured the gardens so effectually that the lights soon set a scampering towards the [Spanish] Lines. Our loss in the night expedition by the most authentic accounts to eight cabbages and a pennyworth of parsley!'[51] Ancell heard another deserter say that 'they are much distressed in camp for fresh water, and that a great many die of the flux, occasioned by drinking of the salt springs'.[52]

Amongst all this privation, 4 December turned out to be somewhat surreal. At first light, Horsbrugh was enchanted by the beauty of the scene before him: 'Just as I got to the look out this morning, a sudden fog overspread all the lower ground. When the sun got above, it looked like a frozen sea covered with snow, the tops of the mountains towering a considerable height above its surface on which the sun shone, appeared like so many islands and afforded a most picturesque scene.' The curious day continued when a would-be deserter was returned to Gibraltar:

An officer came out from the Enemy's Lines attended by a trumpeter sounding a parley, and a soldier leading a mule, and the Town Major [Burke] being sent out to know the purport of his message was informed that the Spanish General, Don Alvarez, sent his compliments to our Governor and returned a mule which two days before had strayed to the Lines. This being notified to the Governor, he desired his compliments might be presented to the Spanish General with thanks.[53]

Price added that 'the officer who brought the message, Colonel Cadalso, his aid-de-camp and Lieutenant-General to the Regiment of Bourbon, [is] known to myself and many other officers of the Garrison' – a reminder that several officers on each side were well acquainted with each other.[54]

In the hardship and tedium of everyday life under siege, each incident was a potential diversion. Anything that happened within sight of the Rock passed for news, especially if it afforded the slightest amount of interest, and deserters to and from the Rock always provided some sort of story, though all too often a tragic one. Any deserters seen running across no man's land towards the Spanish Lines from Gibraltar were fired at by the garrison soldiers on guard duty, and if they were not brought down by lead balls from muskets, then the batteries would fire explosive shells and cannonballs to try to stop them. The Spaniards might send out horsemen to pick up these deserters, but they would try to ride down their own deserters or slash them with swords. Any caught alive before they reached safety were tried, sentenced and executed. Because of the information they could give to the enemy, leniency was rare. Deserters were regarded as traitors and treated as spies. Those from the Spanish camp mainly tried to head further inland, but a minority tried to reach Gibraltar. Not all were successful, as Price himself saw in mid-December:

This morning between 8 and 9 o'clock one of the Walloon Guards attempted deserting to us off his post at the Spanish Lines. The centries fired two shots at him, one of which wounded him, for I saw him lying on the slope of the glacis in front of the 7 gun battery. Our batteries on the heights fired smartly to protect him, but in vain. Two Spanish Dragoons rushed out at the barrier of the Lines, alighted off their horses, and after wounding the bleeding wretch, put him into one of the nearest embrasures and galloped off at full speed.[55]

They then prepared for his execution, which Paterson witnessed:

At 4 o'clock this evening they were employed erecting a gallows on the top of the sand hills about halfway between their camp and Lines, to hang the deserter taken. This morning, a great number of people, assembled to see the execution, were fired upon by our batteries and several of them killed and wounded. They desisted from their enterprise and removed the gallows during the night near to their fascine park, where the deserter was hanged this morning [15th] in great form, the pickets of the army and Walloon Guards attended the execution.[56]

Drinkwater said that 'the body, according to custom, hung till sun-set', but Price was very much a gentleman where women were concerned and was more disconcerted by a rumour that ran through the garrison: 'Strange as it is to relate, a Lady was seen at this melancholy spectacle who, by the number of her attendants, seemed to be the Spanish General's wife. As I have this merely from hearsay, I am willing for the honor of the female gentleness and sensibility to reject it as an absolute fiction coined by some disappointed old bachelor inveterate against the sex.'[57]

Rice Price, himself a bachelor, came from Wales (Rice is a version of the Welsh name Rhys or Rees). He would eventually return there – to the Williamsfield estate at Myddfai, Llandovery – after leaving the army and marrying Ann Stewart. He had joined the 56th Regiment as an ensign at the age of thirteen, and at the start of the siege he was thirty-three years old. The 56th Regiment had been in Gibraltar since 1770, and so Price knew the place well, and he had risen to the rank of captain by the time the siege started. He was described as having 'a mind naturally strong, and a memory unusually retentive', to which 'he added all the information to be acquired from extensive reading'. He was particularly fond of history and poetry (like Colonel José de Cadalso) and was appreciated for his sense of humour.[58]

Just after Christmas, during the night of 26 December 1779, a violent thunderstorm with strong westerly winds and torrential rain drove into the sea about 5 tons of timber and brushwood that was stacked along the banks of the Palmones and Guadaranque rivers, ready for use by the Spanish forces in their camp. Swept across to Gibraltar, it was rapidly salvaged during the morning of the 27th, to the delight of many people, including Horsbrugh:

A great quantity of brushwood, some pieces of timbers and stumps of trees, intermixed with canes and landweeds, which had been washed down the rivers by the late floods, were brought by the wind and tide close to the foot of our wall. Fourteen boatloads were taken up before it drove on shore, and the poor people being then permitted to go along under the Line Wall, they collected and brought a very considerable quantity of it, which proved of infinite service to the poorer inhabitants who had no fuel to dress their victuals.[59]

At about noon that same day, some of the Genoese fishermen were dragging their nets on the western beach, a little closer to Spain than normal, when without warning they were fired on by guns at Fort St Philip. Spilsbury was perhaps more accurate in saying that they were fishing for firewood. They rapidly retreated, leaving behind their nets, though one of the fishermen, Bartholome Guillasa, picked up one of the cannonballs that had fallen in the nearby market gardens and took it to Father Messa, who told him it was a 26-pounder.[60] Nearly three weeks earlier, the same fort had fired at two fishing boats, and so this new firing could have been another warning, but Horsbrugh believed that the final shot was actually targeted at the garrison's defences:

the fourth [shot] struck the retaining wall as you enter into Alls Well, broke down part of that wall and stuck. This last shot being considerably out of the line of the others, and having a much greater elevation, we therefore conjectured the first three were fired to take off our attention, and that the fourth was intended to try the range or what effect it might have against our works, or perhaps it was wantonly fired at a number of our officers and soldiers who were looking out from thence, but whatever may have been their reason for it, we return the compliment with several shot and shells at that fort.[61]

Up to now, the Spanish forces had fired only at shipping. This was therefore their very first shot directed at the garrison, and so Spilsbury commented: 'Many bets lost, as it was thought they would not fire at the place.'[62] Some feared that the Spaniards were about to begin the new year, 1780, with a bombardment.

On the same day as these first hostile shots at the Rock, three more deserters successfully made their escape from the Spanish Lines. One was a Dragoon, from whom Price heard that 'there are strict orders from Court [Madrid] to carry on the blockade with all possible alertness. We are thought to be near starving and our surrendering in a month or two at most looked upon as inevitable.' However, the blockading ships had failed to notice a packet boat come in with supplies earlier that evening, belonging to the Jewish merchant Abraham Israel. The boat had gone unnoticed to Tangier a fortnight previously, carrying dispatches and letters, and at the time 'their safe arrival was notified to the Garrison by their making two fires at the hours agreed upon Ape's Hill'. The vessel was now back from Barbary, loaded 'with forty goats, some poultry, onions and oranges'.[63] Without any convoy from England, Gibraltar was increasingly reliant on supplies brought by small vessels from Tangier and Tetuan that managed to evade the blockade in the dead of night. The Court at Madrid would not have been happy.

Despite a few distressed voices, Mrs Green reckoned that on Gibraltar 'The troops are in good health and spirits, and have been so during the whole blockade.' The mood was muted, though, and on the first day of the new year, 1780, she said with sadness: 'We had only 8 friends at dinner by way of keeping up an old custom; the times were too bad to allow any family to entertain; not only that but I was greatly indisposed and totally out of spirits ...

Several persons called as usual this forenoon; but not near so many as on former occasions, indeed most people now began to look rather unhappy at our uncomfortable situation.'[64] One soldier summed up the prevailing mood: 'A most melancholy prospect for the inhabitants, and women and children in the army! The troops may hold out for some months longer, but, if Providence does not relieve us soon, I tremble for the approaching conflict!'[65]

# CHAPTER SIX

———— ·◆· ————

# MOONLIGHT BATTLE

Crimes committed by the rank-and-file soldiers in the garrison were generally dealt with by corporal punishment. In the years since Eliott became governor, nobody had been executed, but many robberies had occurred of late, so that when Patrick Farrell of the 58th Regiment was tried and found guilty at a General Court Martial for theft from a winehouse early in the new year, he was sentenced to be hanged. The day before his execution was a Sunday, and Mrs Green was perplexed by his behaviour: 'The man of 58th would not go to Church; or even allow our clergyman to go to him!'[1] The following day, 10 January 1780, he was hanged, watched by his regiment, along with pickets from all the other regiments. Mrs Green commented: 'The man went out at South Port at 11 o'clock, the usual ceremonies being observed. He appeared perfectly stupid, stayed but a little time at the place of execution and had refused to have any clergyman till at the hour of his suffering. He did allow of the attendance of our clergyman, owned he had often deserved such a fate, said he was bred a Quaker. An Irish Man.'[2] Farrell was from Richhill in Armagh and had enlisted with the regiment at Cork almost ten years before. Once a farm worker, he was described as a man of dark complexion, dark hair, grey eyes and an extraordinary height – 6 feet 6¼ inches, about a foot taller than most of his comrades.[3]

The day following the execution, four shots fired from Fort St Philip were aimed at a funeral for a soldier of the 72nd Regiment that was taking place at the burial ground by the Governor's Meadow, beyond the Rock's northern defences. Two fell in the market gardens, one in the Governor's Meadow and another in the inundation. 'There was a funeral party going out at this time,' Mrs Green related, 'and as the burying ground is very near to where the shot fell, it greatly alarmed them. They only stayed to put the corpse hastily into the ground, and the clergyman came back as fast as his horse could bring him!' Captain Price complained that 'their gunnery was below contempt'.[4]

Even though the working parties were being constantly targeted by the garrison, nobody expected the Spanish guns to be active, because conditions in their camp and siegeworks had become terrible, due to flooding and sandstorms. Horsbrugh could see a 'great quantity of standing water in and about the Enemy's works, which they were endeavouring to carry off by means of drains, and the boyau and communications along the Lines appeared to have suffered a good deal from the weather'.[5] Paterson also observed that the 'high winds which we have had for this week past has drifted a great deal of sand into the enemy's boyeaux or trench communication. In some places it is filled with water from the rain, as are their works in general in the lines, which lay so low that they cannot drain them.'[6] Added to the camp's woes, several of their large wooden huts that they were roofing with brushwood to replace their tents had recently caught fire late at night, fanned by the strong winds. Price had watched as they 'burnt furiously for a considerable time. The drums beat to arms and the alarm was general. The blaze was so very bright that we could see for some miles around.'[7] Two more Walloon deserters reported that 'the camp is in a most wretched condition – bread scarce, water infamous, the troops sickly and heartily sick of the service'. They also claimed that a great deal of propaganda was being spread about the state of the garrison, but that if the truth was known, about six hundred men would desert.[8]

On 12 January, shots from Fort St Barbara hit a garrison working party using mule carts to collect stone quarried from near the Devil's Tower, an old watchtower close to the eastern side of the North Front. Firing also took place again from Fort St Philip towards the Landport area, and one shot hit a sentry box. Mrs Green thought 'it was supposed to be intended for the Flag Staff, as there was a great many of our artillery officers there. They also hurt a mule who was in a working cart. The Colonel [Green] was looking over the Ramp at Landport when this happened, and one of the twenty-four pounders fell within 3 feet of him!'[9]

Another shot went into the town. According to Father Messa, it 'passed over the walls of Land Port and hit the roof of Antonio Quartin, which happened to be unoccupied, and only made two holes in the roof and fell in the street near the house of the carpenter, Mr. Boid.'[10] Quartin's house was in Governor's Street, a back lane leading into the French Parade (now Governor's Parade), and it was empty because he had gone to Spain with his wife at the start of the siege, taking with them their children. Although he had lived all his life on Gibraltar and was the clerk of the coal yard, his wife Frances was originally from Spain.[11] Price said that this shot 'went through the roof of Mr Quartine's house and lodged in the opposite wall of the Artillery Hospital. It passed so close to Mrs. Hamilton who was crossing the street as to raise a slight contusion on the calf of her leg. This is very unlike the Spanish gallantry to injure the sacred persons of the ladies. It weighed seven and twenty pounds [and] some ounces.'[12] Everyone was surprised and disturbed, because they never expected a shot to reach so far, and this first British casualty was a civilian woman, not a soldier. Drinkwater thought 'it was singular that a female should be the first person wounded in this remarkable siege'.[13] Mrs Hamilton's husband was a merchant, and she found herself the centre of attention, which exasperated the stalwart Mrs Green:

A woman who keeps a milliner's shop was standing on the opposite side of the street and was thrown down by something, striking her leg. She insisted upon it that it was the ball but that could not possibly be the case, as it was only some splinters of the roof or else some of the shell work out of the front of the house, as the least stroke of the ball would undoubtedly have broke her leg. It hurt no-one else, and she was more alarmed than any real hurt. However, it alarmed everybody.[14]

Family tradition was passed down in the Skinner family that Mrs Jane Skinner, who fired the first shot at the Spaniards four months previously, was also the first person to be injured by incoming shot. It supposedly happened not long after the birth of her first child, William Thomas Skinner, and his son wrote decades later that his father William 'was born at Gibraltar in 1780, during the siege, my grandmother being the first to be wounded, by a shell bursting over the [Moorish] castle, while she was nursing her son'. If this did occur, she was not the first civilian to be wounded, because William – the first of eight children – was not born until July 1780, some six months after this attack.[15]

Because the garrison's main burial ground on the isthmus was too dangerous to use, Eliott gave immediate orders for funerals there to cease. All soldiers and other inhabitants were ordered to bury their dead on part of the red sands in the south, behind the Prince of Wales lines. Elsewhere on Gibraltar, officers were buried at Southport, the Jews had their own burial ground in the south, while the King's Chapel was reserved for noteworthy Protestant members of the garrison, and, as Colonel James described a few years earlier, 'All the Roman Catholics are buried in the Spanish church; they put them in a deep pit, throwing a quantity of lime upon the corpse, to consume the body the sooner.'[16]

In the evening of this eventful day, the soldiers were told that because of shortages their weekly allowance of provisions had to be cut. 'Disagreeable as this intelligence was,' Drinkwater reported, 'and particularly when we consider the distress which many experienced even with the full allowance, the men received it without the smallest appearance of discontent.'[17] Ancell, though, was worried:

Our situation every day appears more alarming, there being a scarcity of almost everything in the garrison – fire-wood a cob per hundred, flour five rials per pound, no fresh meat except an old cow, or worn-out ox, (only one perhaps killed in a month) which is sold at four and a half and five rials per pound, fowls twenty to twenty four rials each, a goose ten dollars, a turkey twenty dollars, eggs a cob the dozen, and every other necessary in proportion.[18]

Now that the fishermen were being targeted by the Spaniards, the besieged population could no longer benefit from the plentiful supplies of fish and other seafood, and Mrs Upton was critical of the fishermen: 'Though Gibraltar is surrounded by the sea, we were no better supplied with fish than with the other articles of life. The fishermen were Genoese, and they chose to catch very few, that they might have a pretence for enhancing the price:– a quantity that would dine but two persons, cost four shillings.' Drinkwater agreed: 'our fishermen were foreigners, and being under no regulation, they exacted, by degrees, most extravagant sums for what some months before we should have looked upon with disgust.'[19]

Soon after the rations were cut, on 15 January, smallpox made an unwelcome return, though as the previous outbreak had occurred only a few weeks earlier, it probably never left. This new outbreak threw Mrs Green into panic: 'Doctor Baynes called in the forenoon and greatly alarmed me by telling us of the smallpox being again broke out! The child was a son of Captain Evelegh's of the Corps of Engineers; this is a fine boy, about six years old. He did not seem very well when we supped there on last Tuesday evening [the 11th]. They have 2 younger girls to have this disorder. It hurt me to hear of this, as it is not a thing to be wished ... when we can only manage people in health.'[20] John Evelegh, who was captain-lieutenant of the Engineers, was born at Exeter in Devon in 1740. He had been in Gibraltar since 1771 with his wife Ann. By now, they had eight children, including the oldest son, also called John, who was fourteen years old and became an ensign in the 72nd Regiment the following year. Information about three of the children is scanty, and they may have died very young. The six-year-old boy who contracted smallpox was Henry, and the two younger girls mentioned by Mrs Green were Mary Ann, aged three, and Eliott Ann, aged one, who had been named after Governor Eliott.[21]

Since 1772 Evelegh had been one of the engineers in charge of the new 'Soldier-Artificer Company', which had been formed by William Green as a body of skilled military workmen to replace the unsatisfactory system of using civilian labourers brought from England. Many soldiers in the various regiments had their own trade, and some had enlisted because their industries were ailing, such as the textile workers in the Manchester area who joined the 72nd. Many had been labourers and agricultural workers like Patrick Farrell of the 58th, while others in his regiment – who came from all over the British Isles – included tailors, bricklayers, shoemakers, barbers, masons and butchers.[22] Those with useful trades at times transferred to the Soldier-Artificers.

Mrs Green thought that Evelegh's son Henry had caught smallpox by mixing with civilian children: 'We were in hopes that by the great care that was taken in November last ... that it was all over; however it could not be so. Undoubtedly this little boy had taken it by having been at play with the Spanish and Jew children after they had returned home.'[23] Smallpox was very common – a frightening and highly contagious viral disease that affected all classes. Epidemics were devastating enough for those in normal health, causing the deaths of up to a tenth of any population, let alone a community under the stress and privations of a siege. It started off like influenza, with aching, vomiting and a rash that developed into blisters that could cause permanent scarring and blindness. Over half of those who contracted the disease tended to die, but the mortality rate for children was significantly higher. From the mid-eighteenth century in Europe, it was a major killer.

It was Surgeon Major Arthur Baynes who had brought Mrs Green the unwelcome news about smallpox. Now fifty-nine years old, he had been in charge of medicine for the army on Gibraltar for many years, while his younger brother Alexander was based at the naval hospital with the rank of surgeon's mate.[24] There was no single medical service, but the civilians were subject to military law and so had to comply with orders such as isolation during a smallpox epidemic. Before anaesthetics and the ability to control infection, hospitals were dangerous places, where much disease could be spread, and they were used largely as a place of last resort. A civilian hospital of San Juan de Dios (St John of God) had been established at Gibraltar in 1591, but was taken over as a military hospital under British rule. By the time of the siege, the site had been converted to use as army barracks. It was not until 1815 that a hospital for the civilian poor would be opened, 'divided into three branches, for patients of the Catholic, Protestant, and Hebrew persuasions' – mirroring Gibraltar's tripartite society. Sick and wounded civilians were more likely to rely for help on religious charities, age-old remedies, folklore and even pilgrimage in the hope of a cure. In the 1777 census, no civilian surgeons or physicians are listed, only one midwife and two apothecaries.[25]

Soldiers were looked after by the surgeons and surgeons' mates of their respective regiments, who established their own hospitals. Provision for the navy was more developed, with a substantial, purpose-built hospital over a mile south of the town.[26] The two-storey quadrangular building had been constructed some three decades earlier and was not solely for the use of the small squadron at Gibraltar, but for seamen from any Royal Navy vessel that called at the naval base. Colonel James described its appearance before the siege:

> The sailors hospital is a noble, capacious, well adapted pile of building; it is square of masonry and tiled, with an area in the center, and piazzas round it, by which the men may either enjoy the sun or shade, and are kept properly, without confinement: there are apartments for a thousand sick, with all conveniences: it is erected to the southward of the new mole, upon a plain, and walled round, in a free, salutary, airy height, greatly to the advantage of the distressed seamen; for the cool breezes off the sea render it a happy residence in summer, and its situation and compactness make it comfortable in winter.[27]

Baynes also informed Mrs Green that Eliott would not allow inoculation. Introduced to Britain in 1721, inoculation (or variolation) had proved highly effective in giving people immunity with a mild dose of the disease, which was achieved by cutting a person's arm and introducing pus from someone already ill with smallpox. Unfortunately, nearly 2 per cent of those inoculated died, while others could become unwell. They were also infectious until they recovered from the effects. The safer form of inoculation using cowpox ('vaccination') was not yet available, and so deciding whether or not to inoculate was a difficult decision for Eliott to take.

After hearing about the outbreak of smallpox in the morning of 15 January, better news arrived of a British fleet on its way to relieve Gibraltar: 'This afternoon, an English brig appeared in the offing,' said Ancell. 'She was chased by a xebec and several gallies, but fortunately got safe into New Mole. She brings the joyful and happy intelligence of a fleet being within twenty-four hours sail of the garrison.'[28] Not only that, but a decisive battle had been won against the Spaniards.

Until the combined French and Spanish fleet gave up their intended invasion of Britain four months earlier, the British had been unable to augment their forces in America or the Mediterranean. Although the French and Spanish ships had retreated to Brest, little was known about what they were doing. Once the danger of invasion had passed, the most pressing priorities were to reinforce the West Indies and take supplies to Gibraltar and Minorca. Despite Admiral Hardy's widely criticised handling of the invasion threat, he was still in command of the Channel Fleet, but instead of involving him in these new operations it was decided to place someone else in charge.

Admiral Sir George Brydges Rodney was eventually selected to escort a massive convoy of merchant ships, victuallers and transports to Gibraltar and Minorca, before heading off to the Leeward Islands in the Caribbean where he had been appointed commander-in-chief. Born in 1718, Rodney had joined the Royal Navy at the age of fourteen and was a highly successful naval officer. He became so famous that by the end of the eighteenth century his surname 'Rodney' would be popular as a boy's Christian name. He had also served as governor of Newfoundland and was at various times a Member of Parliament for Saltash, Penryn, Northampton and Okehampton. The money he spent on political campaigns during elections and the huge sums he lost through gambling had forced him to flee to France to avoid his creditors, and although he was back in England and solvent again he remained desperate for money.[29]

Two rear-admirals, Robert Digby and Sir John Lockhart Ross, were put under Rodney's command. Digby had previously served under Hardy and brought with him a detachment of ships from the Channel Fleet to boost the strength of the convoy's escort. It was Digby's role to return to Britain with the empty merchant ships after delivering their supplies and reinforcements to Gibraltar and Minorca. The warships escorting the convoy included Rodney's own flagship, the *Sandwich*, and large warships from the Channel Fleet such as the *Prince George*, which was Digby's flagship, the *Royal George* and the *Terrible*. One midshipman on the *Prince George* was the third son of George III – the fourteen-year-old Prince William, who was destined to become king when his elder brother died in 1830.

From late October at Portsmouth and Plymouth, preparations had begun on board the warships, while the store vessels were loaded with supplies and troops were embarked in the transports. By 10 December, the two parts of the convoy in both ports were ready to sail, and the Admiralty in London was agitated. Two days earlier Lord Sandwich wrote to Rodney at Portsmouth: 'For God's sake go to sea without delay, you cannot conceive of what importance it is to yourself, to me, and to the public that you should not lose this fair wind. If you do, I shall not only hear of it in Parliament, but in places to which I pay more attention.'[30] Unfortunately, stormy weather prevailed at Portsmouth, and another fortnight passed without any change. It then improved sufficiently for the ships to sail, and on Christmas Eve, after the fleet had struggled from Portsmouth to Plymouth in adverse conditions, Rodney wrote to his wife Henrietta in London from Cawsand Bay: 'I am this moment arrived here, after beating down the Channel against the wind, which proved bad the moment I got on the back of the Isle of Wight. I dare say every person at Portsmouth expected my return.' At Plymouth, he told Henrietta, the wind was still against them: 'Nothing but the extreme badness of the weather could have induced me to anchor here ... While the weather continues to blow at south-west, I must remain here, as there is little likelihood of my getting down the Channel at this season with a foul wind.'[31]

Being Christmas Eve, his family was inevitably in his thoughts, and Rodney ended the letter: 'Our dear girls' pictures are hung up in my cabin. I own it is a very great relief to me when I look at them. At the same time I abuse the painter most heartily. The dog shall never draw mine, he has done so much injustice to them. Give my dearest love to them, and the other little ones. Adieu.'[32] It would be many months before he saw his wife and children again, and in an era before photography, artists' portraits were the only images of loved ones that could be carried as mementoes.

Waiting for Rodney's fleet at Plymouth was the second battalion of the 73rd Highland Regiment. In late November, after the invasion threat had receded, these men had been moved from their camp near Maker church back to barracks at Plymouth. They knew they were going abroad, but their destination remained secret. These Scottish soldiers looked and sounded completely different from the other troops at Gibraltar, since many of them wore a plaid as part of their uniform. This single-piece garment of woollen cloth wrapped around the body to form a skirt that reached to just above the knee and a covering over one shoulder like a large folded shawl. It was the forerunner of the kilt and was woven in a tartan pattern conforming to regulations, apparently a combination of green, blue and black similar to the modern Black Watch tartan.

As well as a plaid, these Highland troops wore a red jacket which was shorter than that worn by other soldiers, as well as a bonnet with a plume, stockings that left the knees bare and shoes.

It was not just their appearance that set them apart, because they spoke mainly Gaelic, and many could not speak English. They were also accompanied by regimental pipers with their bagpipes. John Macdonald was a piper who could speak English, and he recorded that the soldiers were put aboard transport ships long before Rodney's fleet arrived: 'On the 8th December 1779, we marched from Dock Barracks, and that same day embarked on board the transports that lay then in Catwater [where the River Plym runs into Plymouth Sound] waiting for such troops as were going aboard. It was my chance to go on board the "Dispatch" transport, Captain Munro, who behaved very well to the men in general.'[33] The troops, Macdonald said, were kept at sea in the transports off Plymouth for nearly three weeks:

> We were detained there at anchor waiting for a convoy till the 27th December, and then sailed from Plymouth Sound under convoy of six sail of the line and two frigates, and joined the grand fleet under the command of Admiral Sir George Bridges Rodney off the Ram-head that same evening. The fleet was really a very pretty sight, consisting of about twenty-four sail of the line, nine frigates, with a considerable number of armed ships, store ships, and a great many merchantmen, to the amount of one hundred and fifty.[34]

Part of the convoy was intended for the West Indies and Minorca, but the fleet was delayed again by awful weather. On board the *Terrible* was Francis Vernon, a fourteen-year-old midshipman like Prince William. He was not impressed by this part of Devon: 'Plymouth is one of the most considerable sea port towns in the kingdom. It is situated in the west of England in Devonshire, and surrounded with a mountainous country, that so frequently attracts the rain, as occasions it being called, "Le Pot de chambre du Diable" [the Devil's piss pot].'[35] On 29 December the fleet finally left Plymouth.

Nine days later, about 350 miles west of Cape Finisterre, the merchant ships for the West Indies broke away with a small

naval escort, leaving a considerable naval force to continue with
the convoy towards Gibraltar. Less than twenty-four hours later,
enemy ships were spotted: 'About four o'clock in the morning [8
January 1780],' Macdonald said, 'we discovered a large fleet bearing down upon us mistaking us for a convoy of their own, but
finding their mistake they tacked about immediately. Our admiral
hoisted a signal for a general chase, and ordered the transports to
lie to with one ship of the line and two frigates.' While the warships chased the enemy convoy, Macdonald was left behind in
one of the transports, but the next day he learned what had taken
place: 'we had the happiness of being informed of the capture of
the enemy's whole fleet, consisting of one sixty-four gun ship, five
frigates, and twenty-three sail of merchantmen, called the Carraca
fleet, all belonging to Spain, not one of them being able to escape
the vigilance of our brave British tars'.[36]

Rodney immediately wrote a report to inform the Admiralty
how he had captured an entire Spanish convoy belonging to the
Royal Company of Caracas (which traded with South America)
that had set sail a week before from San Sebastian on the north
coast of Spain. He had also captured its naval escort of seven
warships after they offered only a token resistance. 'Part of
the convoy was loaded with naval stores and provisions for the
Spanish ships of war at Cadiz,' he said, 'the rest with bale goods
[merchandise in bales, such as textiles] belonging to the Royal
Company. Those loaded with naval stores and bale goods, I shall
immediately despatch for England under convoy of his Majesty's
ships the America and Pearl. Those loaded with provisions I shall
carry to Gibraltar.'[37] This unexpected capture ensured prize-
money for Rodney and his men, while Gibraltar benefited from
the extra supplies, but a battleship was needed to escort the
captured ships to England. To fill the gap, he commandeered the
Spanish *Guipuscoana* into his fleet: 'I have commissioned, offi-
cered, and manned the Spanish ship-of-war, of the same rate, and
named her the Prince William, in respect to his Royal Highness,
in whose presence she had the honour to be taken. She has been
launched only six months, is in every respect completely fitted

for war, and much larger than the Bienfaisant, Captain McBride, to whom she struck.'[38]

The unfortunate Spanish crews were also taken to England as prisoners-of-war, ending up in a prison at Winchester. In the cramped conditions, many of them caught typhus, also known as gaol fever, which was carried by lice. Although the exact cause of the spread of the disease was unknown, one of the doctors treating them, James Carmichael Smyth, rightly suspected the clothes and bedding that the seamen had insisted on bringing, 'so much afraid of the cold, and particularly the dampness of our climate'. Smyth also believed that their mental state was a contributory factor: 'Many of the prisoners belonged to the Caracca company, and had private adventures [goods to trade] on board. These men, when captured, having lost their all, were particularly low spirited, and consequently were more liable to suffer from the distemper. It was remarked that they were the first who were seized with it, and most of them died.'[39] The epidemic at Winchester was not brought under control until the lice-infested clothes and bedding were burnt and a higher standard of hygiene maintained. At its peak, the prison housed more than 1500 Spanish sailors, and over the next few months hundreds of them contracted typhus. Many recovered, but 265 men died.[40]

The day after capturing the Caracas convoy, the men of the 73rd were distributed among the warships to replace the seamen and marines who had taken over the captured Spanish vessels. Some days afterwards, reports reached Rodney that an enemy fleet was ahead: 'Having received repeated intelligence of a Spanish squadron, said to consist of fourteen sail of the line, cruizing off Cape St. Vincent, I gave notice to all the captains upon my approaching the said Cape to prepare for battle, and having passed it on the 16th [January] in the morning with the whole convoy, at one p.m., the Cape then bearing N. four leagues, the Bedford made the signal for seeing a fleet.'[41] Macdonald was now watching events from a warship: 'About twelve o'clock they were observed, and at four in the afternoon the two headmost ships, viz., the "Edgar" and the "Bedford", engaged them and resisted their fire for a considerable time until some more of our ships came to their assistance, and then the engagement became general.[42]

Rodney's convoy had encountered a squadron of warships commanded by Admiral Don Juan de Langara. Realising he was outnumbered, Langara attempted to flee to Cadiz, which Vernon in the *Terrible* witnessed: 'Our fleet forming line of battle a-breast, gave chase. For some time the Spanish fleet, consisting of thirteen ships of the line, lay to ... for having sailed from Cadiz to intercept the ships destined to relieve Gibraltar, had supposed our force to be inferior, but being convinced of their mistake, attempted flight to escape back to their port.'[43] Rodney gave the order to pursue the ships. 'Sir George considering that a chase before the wind is in general a tedious one, and that night approached,' Vernon said, 'made the signal to continue chase without observing the line of battle. The emulation shewn by each captain, in crowding sail to reach their antagonists, proved they had not forgotten their warfare.' Vernon's ship was out in front, but then suffered a setback: 'The Terrible was sheathed in copper, and sailing well, gave hopes of being one of the first in action, when in hoisting the main-top sail, the yard sprung, and by the delay occasioned in getting up another, [and] with bending [tying on] the sail, several of our ships were sooner engaged, and a line of battle ship blowing up, assured us the work was begun.'[44]

With the delay in replacing the damaged maintop yard, other British ships surged ahead, and the first broadside was fired from the *Edgar* into the stern of the *Santo Domingo*, the trailing Spanish ship. It was a race between the Spanish vessels fleeing for safety and the British trying to catch them, with the added danger of the wind blowing both fleets towards the rocky coast. The next broadside was from the *Marlborough*, followed by one from the *Ajax*, and shortly afterwards the *Santo Domingo* erupted in a sheet of flames and disintegrated.[45] In the mid-January afternoon, the sun was already low in an overcast sky and the weather was hazy, with occasional squalls and a heavy swell. The explosion was made even more dramatic by the gathering gloom.

As the light continued to fade, the *Bedford* subsequently clashed with the *Princesa*, which surrendered after an hour. The *Defence* then caught up with Langara's flagship, the *Fenix* (or *Phoenix*), and began a lengthy struggle. The *Montagu* was next to fire two broadsides into the *Fenix*, and after the *Prince George* and *Bienfaisant* joined in, the badly damaged Spanish flagship surrendered. The *Montagu* then caught up with the *Diligente*, which surrendered after a broadside brought down the mainmast. By now, the *Terrible* had reached the scene of the battle, capturing the *San Julian*, as Vernon described:

> At the edge of night, having singled out a Spanish 70 [-gun warship], we engaged, and remained by her till she struck, after an action of an hour and forty minutes. The sea running high, endangered our ships, in opening their lower deck ports, and prevented any further communication with the prize, than sending an officer and a small party of seamen to take charge, receiving in return, the Marquis of Medina, her captain. She was called El San Julian, and now lay almost a wreck, the fore-mast and main-top-mast being shot away, and her decks covered with the killed and wounded.[46]

He reflected on his role of bringing gunpowder cartridges to the guns: 'My station in the fight was what is commonly called a powder-monkey, supplying two of the quarter deck guns with powder from the magazine. For the younger midshipmen, not having the experience necessary for a greater charge, are hereby made useful, and also accustomed to the smell of gunpowder.'[47]

The *San Eugenio* also surrendered, helpless after the *Cumberland* shot away all her masts, and at around two in the morning the *Monarca* was finally captured, bringing an end to the battle. In twelve hours of fighting, only four battleships and two frigates managed to escape from the Spanish squadron of thirteen ships. The battle had continued in darkness into the early hours of the 17th. Because it was rare for such actions to take place at night, it became known as the 'Moonlight Battle'. The moon had risen just after noon and did not set until past midnight, but it was eight days before a full moon. With so much cloud cover, conditions would have been very dark, though years later the battle was imagined to have been fought by moonlight.

Having chased the Spaniards with a strong following wind, the British fleet and their prizes found themselves perilously close to the coast. With a heavy sea and on-shore wind pushing them towards the rocks, and with the deep winter darkness, the crews struggled to keep their vessels off shore until daylight. Rodney reported the circumstances to the Admiralty:

> The weather during the night was at times very tempestuous, with a great sea, which rendered it difficult to take possession of and shift the prisoners of those ships that had surrendered to his Majesty's arms. It continued very bad weather the next day, when the Royal George, Prince George, Sandwich, and several other ships, were in great danger, under the necessity of making sail to avoid the shoals of St. Lucar [north-west of Cadiz], nor did they get into deep water till the next morning.[48]

In the struggle to avoid being wrecked, the ships had drifted along the coastline, and some, like the *Terrible*, were out of sight of the main fleet, as Vernon observed: 'This engagement during the night had dispersed our fleet, and at day break we found no ships in company but the prize, and the Monarch 74 ... it blew strong, with a heavy sea from the westward, and the crippled situation of the San Julian prevented our carrying sail [and bringing the *San Julian* away from danger].' The next day, they were perilously close to Cadiz:

> On the 18th, early in the morning, having drifted near Cadiz, we plainly perceived it under our lee, with a Spanish squadron at anchor in the harbour. Two strange line-of-battle ships were also in sight, under sail. When making the private signal, and it not being answered, [we] supposed they were enemies, and might have engaged them, yet if crippled so near an enemy's

port, there was little probability to escape being taken. It was therefore resolved to abandon the prize [the *San Julian*], which, (as we were afterwards informed) was lost at the entrance of Cadiz. Crowding a press of sail, in the evening the Terrible joined Sir Rodney and fleet, at the entrance of the Streights of Gibraltar.[49]

The *San Eugenio* also proved impossible to save and was wrecked on shore, leaving the British with only four captured ships, but the soldier Walter Gordon of the 73rd Regiment, who witnessed the fighting, was full of praise for the Royal Navy: 'I cannot do proper justice to the bravery of Admiral Rodney's fleet ... the eagerness for battle shewn by the tars is almost incredible, the ideas of danger or death seem never to enter the hearts of British seamen. Every one exerts himself as if the whole business depended upon his single arm, and the only fear they betray is lest the enemy should escape.'[50]

One Spanish ship had blown up and six were captured, though two of them were wrecked. This meant that Langara had lost over half his squadron, while Rodney had successfully brought his warships and convoy as far as the Strait of Gibraltar. He now sent word into Tangier: 'having joined the convoy, and made Cape Spartel, I despatched two frigates to Tangier to acquaint his Majesty's consul [Charles Logie] with our success, that Great Britain was again mistress of the Straits, and desiring him to hasten a supply of fresh provisions for the garrison. At sunset we entered the gut.'[51]

# CHAPTER SEVEN

———— •◆• ————

# RODNEY'S RELIEF

Soldiers and civilians alike had despaired of ever seeing a relief convoy until the welcome news about Rodney's fleet was brought by the brig on 15 January 1780. Suddenly, the mood changed to excitement, and Ancell remarked that 'It is almost beyond the power of words to describe the general joy which pervaded the soldiery as well as the inhabitants upon this gladdening intelligence. Even avarice and extortion seem to pause from their iniquities, and to participate [in] the pleasure inspired by our hopes.'[1] The very next day, however, Mrs Green voiced everyone's changing spirits:

We grow very uneasy about the fleet. Those 3 officers of artillery [from the brig] are very young men, and they do not exactly agree in their accounts, and for the most part, they all say they do not know whether all or part of the convoy is for this place, or even who they all are. All this makes us full of hopes and fears . . . We are in hourly expectation of the Convoy, but nothing appeared till about 7 in the evening, at which time we heard some signals [guns] from our Admiral to a vessel who was coming into the Bay, who was going up too high. She was ordered into the New Mole, and proved to be a ship belonging to Merchant Anderson, loaded with flour, and had left the Grand Fleet 5 days ago. She brings a confused account, of an engagement. We all long for morning to know more.[2]

Uncertainty remained for another day, and the tension was intolerable: 'Find myself remarkably ill, and my anxiety very great,' wrote Mrs Green. 'The troops were this day put upon a shorter allowance as to beef and pork ... We are all uneasy. No further news, or sight of ships, all day. Let anyone judge of our anxiety – but that is not possible, except by those who have experienced the like situation as we are now in.' Everyone imagined that the convoy and fleet had been defeated in battle and captured. It was not until the next morning that Mrs Green's mood improved significantly when two of the captured Caracas ships appeared:

About 10 o'clock a joyful sight presented! A prize brought in, taken by some of our expected convoy, a very large ship loaded with oil, tobacco, soap, and bale goods. At noon a much larger and more valuable one came in, a prize to one of our men of war. She was brought in by a Lieutenant of the man of war who had taken her, is loaded with brandy and masts. Now we are certain of the good news. There has been an engagement indeed! The particulars are not well known as yet – any hour we now expect the ships.[3]

By the end of the day, the convoy and its naval escort were getting closer, and Mrs Green observed the reaction of one Royal Navy frigate captain, who expected on his arrival to be greeted by Admiral Duff: 'Several large ships in sight, and in the close of the day, an English frigate came in, which proved to be the Apollo frigate, Captain Pownoll. He was greatly surprised when going on board the Panther, to find that Admiral Duff was not on board. But he was informed that the Admiral was a *Quiet Man*!'[4] Captain Philemon Pownoll not only brought news about the battles and ships captured, but confirmed that a convoy was heading their way with provisions. He himself was a highly successful and wealthy officer from Plymouth, who would be greatly mourned when he was killed only five months later in an action against a French privateer.[5] Drinkwater learned the story behind the success of Rodney's convoy:

We now found that the plan for relieving Gibraltar had been conducted at home with such secrecy and prudence that the Enemy never suspected that Sir George meant to convoy the transports to the Straits with so strong a fleet. By their intelligence from Brest, they understood he was to separate in a certain latitude, and proceed with the main body of the men of war to the West-Indies. Thus deceived, they concluded that the transports with their convoy would fall an easy prey to their squadron.[6]

Instead, the Spanish Caracas convoy and Langara's squadron had turned out to be easy prey for Rodney.

With the bad weather and difficulties of the winds and strong currents, the bulk of the convoy overshot the Bay of Gibraltar into the Mediterranean, which meant it took some time to come back. Initially, it was mostly warships that managed to sail into port, including the captured Spanish flagship *Fenix* with the injured Admiral Langara on board. During the battle, the *Fenix* had surrendered to HMS *Bienfaisant*, but because some of Captain Macbride's crew had smallpox, it was agreed with Langara that the *Fenix* should sail to Gibraltar without a full prize crew in charge. The Spaniards kept their word and did not attempt to flee, which would have been highly dishonourable.[7] In the afternoon of Langara's arrival, Horsbrugh, who spoke Spanish well, was sent by Eliott 'to enquire after the Spanish Admiral's health and to invite him and his officers on shore'.[8] This might be war, but there was a code of honour to observe between officers and gentlemen.

Mrs Green heard about the admiral: 'Don Juan Langara was brought on shore and taken in a sedan chair to a house prepared for his and his officers' reception. He was allowed to bring all his attendants and baggage on shore. He is not dangerously wounded.'[9] Paterson downplayed Langara's injuries even more: 'the Spanish Admiral (who was slightly wounded in three places) was brought on shore with some of his officers and lodged at Mr Dallins.'[10] The house, in Bombhouse Lane, belonged to Edward Dallin, who worked in the navy victualling office. Once he was safely there, Captain Price seized the opportunity of a tour round the damaged flagship: 'I went on board the Phoenix, the captured prize. She has been much shattered in the action ... her mizen mast shot by the board, her main mast wounded, sails and rigging much damaged and several shot through her hulls. She is a fine modelled vessel.'[11]

Thousands more prisoners-of-war captured at the Moonlight Battle were also brought on shore. Being expensive and inconvenient to look after, it was customary for warring factions to exchange them. A batch of prisoners such as seamen and soldiers was usually exchanged for the same number from the opposing side, but officers were primarily from the upper strata of society and were therefore regarded as gentlemen who could be trusted, whatever their nationality. They would be released after giving their word of honour – their parole – not to resume fighting until a similar officer was exchanged. In the siege so far, the conflict had consisted largely of long-range artillery fire rather than close combat, with few prisoners captured. The sheer number brought in by Rodney's fleet proved overwhelming. While Langara was housed in the town, in recognition of his status, most other prisoners were taken to the naval hospital.[12] The sick and wounded were returned by boat to Spain if they could be moved, while the badly injured men were treated at the hospital, and negotiations began with the Spanish authorities to exchange the remaining prisoners. It was important to get rid of them quickly, because they had to be guarded and fed.

With the arrival of the convoy, the initial exultation was replaced by fears that Spain would start a relentless bombardment of the defences and town. 'The 20th being the anniversary of the King of Spain's birthday,' Drinkwater explained,

Admiral Barcelo's ships were decorated according to custom. When the colours were struck in the evening, the flag-ship, with her consort of 50 guns, was hauled close in land, and the next day a large party began to erect a battery on the shore for their protection, being apprehensive, probably, of an attack from

the British fleet. The night of the 21st, the Enemy unmasked
the other batteries in the lines, which again caused a general
disturbance amongst the inhabitants. Everything seemed now
prepared to fire upon the town.[13]

When the gun batteries on the Spanish Lines started firing at
midnight, Mrs Green feared the worst, but the firing was limited
to four British warships that the tide had pushed towards them:

> We naturally concluded it was now their intention to begin, and
> I declare I did expect to see the shells in the town any moment;
> it was now that I really was alarmed ... it alarmed the enemy
> more than us, as no doubt they expected it was an attempt to
> set fire to their camp. They fired an amazing number of balls
> and one shell. It wounded and hurt the rigging of the Terrible
> man-of-war and hurt a few sailors, also one Spanish sailor who
> was on board the Terrible ... It was a very fine moonlight night.
> The appearance of the enemy's firing was a grand, though
> alarming sight, and I own I suspected it was their full intention
> to throw some shells into the town. Thank God they did not,
> and we all went quietly into our beds at 3 o'clock.[14]

Little damage was done to the ships, but some Spanish prisoners-
of-war still on board the *Terrible* were killed and wounded.

As more ships arrived, one soldier was amazed: 'Our bay, from
lying empty for so many months past, is now become a wood',
and Ancell said that the vessels coming in 'are so thick I cannot
number them with any precision'. Horsbrugh calculated that
Rodney's naval escort alone had twenty-two warships with more
than thirteen thousand men.[15] Much effort was focused on dealing with the provisions that the convoy had brought, but the sheer
quantity presented its own problems. New cranes for unloading
vessels were erected on the Line Wall between the south end of
the town and the New Mole beyond, but with such a shortage of
storage space they ended up covering stores with canvas sails as
they were landed in order to protect them from the heavy rain.

A great deal was then temporarily housed in the Protestant and Catholic churches, as well as the synagogue. To speed up the process, Eliott decreed that 'As many men as can be employed are ordered daily for unloading, transporting, and stowing stores and provisions.'[16] Captain Paterson described the problem: 'Every effort has been used to unload the transports and get them and the men of war fit for sea, but they have been much retarded for want of proper craft and wharfs for that purpose. A punt with six 26 pounders from one of the prizes sunk alongside of the ship ... The guns, shot and punt were totally lost.'[17]

Rodney decided to let the garrison have many of the supplies from the captured Spanish ships, and when writing to the Admiralty he emphasised the convoy's importance: 'The Spanish Admiral [Barcelo] and their whole army have the mortification to see the garrison receive that reinforcement that was meant for them which adds two years' provisions to the garrison, and has deprived them of every hope to take it through famine.'[18] Eliott was full of praise about Rodney's achievements when writing to Trayton Fuller, his son-in-law in England: 'You'll see a glorious gazette of the success of our fleet. Five Spanish ships of the line now at anchor in the Bay, and a Rear Admiral prisoner in the town, [and] three or four thousand other prisoners. We have an ample supply of everything and universal joy runs thro' the whole.'[19]

Drinkwater was not quite so jubilant, as he regretted that no ships carrying coal had sailed with Rodney's fleet, so they were still desperately short of fuel, and while the relief was welcome, it was inadequate: 'Though it was generally imagined in England that the Garrison had been amply provided with every article and necessary of life, when Sir George Rodney arrived with the transports and relief from England, our wants, in reality, were far from being supplied. In the articles of ammunition and salt provisions, the Garrison had probably as much as they could dispense with; but of fresh provisions, wine, spirits, sugar, &c. we began to find a great scarcity.'[20] Mrs Upton was also disappointed and complained that the provisions consisted largely of salt meat.[21] Charles Logie at Tangier had been asked by Rodney to prepare a huge shipment of live cattle and fresh provisions, but the arrangements became completely confused, because the vessels from the fleet that were sent to pick up the supplies had virtually no cargo space, being full of equipment for the next stage of their journey to the West Indies. Because the winds became variable and then changed to the east, it proved impossible to send other vessels to Tangier, as they would have been unable to return to Gibraltar fully laden.

Despite these setbacks, most of the population felt triumphant that the convoy had reached them and that Rodney had been victorious, but Mrs Green was then shocked to hear that the smallpox infection was spreading, with one inhabitant falling ill, as well as Captain Evelegh's three youngest children: 'he is obliged to leave his house for the time, not being able to stray from his respective duties at such a busy period as this. No one is allowed to go to see Mrs Evelegh except the Doctor. This seems nearly unnecessary, as no doubt it will now spread. No inoculation allowed of as yet but says he [Eliott] will, as soon as it gets amongst the troops.'[22]

Hardly anyone else was perturbed by the smallpox outbreak, and even Mrs Green rallied when she started receiving supplies from the ships: '2 English sheep from our old friend Admiral Digby ... This day we get a box of things from on board one of the ordnance ships which had been on board six months, consisting of family matters for myself and child. Also we receive 3 sheep and a cask of butter from Mr Veale at Portsmouth ... Get some oranges as a present from Captain Pownoll who has been over to Barbary.' Two days later she managed to 'get 4 sheep from on board the Nottingham'. Officers with friends in Britain and contacts in the warships did rather well. A post-chaise had even been brought for the Greens, but there were disappointments. 'We had 2 hampers of sugar brought on shore this day,' wrote Mrs Green, 'which was on board the Nottingham. We understand they were for us, being on the bill of lading, though the directions were off. They are totally destroyed, and not one pound will ever be used in the house. They are wet and have also been destroyed by all sorts of vermin.'[23]

Although the attempt to bring fresh food and live animals from Morocco had failed, the very presence of Royal Navy warships meant that smaller vessels were taking the opportunity to bring in produce, as Ancell saw: 'This morning arrived from Tangier, a small boat with lemons and oranges, a most useful article, as they are very salutary in the cure of the scurvy.' The next day 'arrived a boat from Tangier, with a few dozen fowls. Also a settee with bullocks and other refreshments from Tetuan. One of our frigates cruizing in the offing captured a settee bound for the [Spanish] camp.'[24] Because the Royal Navy was preventing supplies reaching the Spanish territory of Ceuta and the camp beyond Gibraltar, conditions became even more miserable for the thousands of besieging troops. Drinkwater said that three deserters 'gave dismal accounts of the Enemy's sufferings in camp, where universal discontent prevailed on account of the great scarcity and dearness of provisions', while Horsbrugh heard that 'the allowance of bread for the soldiers in camp is reduced to a small pittance and irregularly served, are greatly distressed for every other species of provision, and that the Spanish Regiments were very sickly'.[25]

Those living on Gibraltar had suffered for months under the blockade, so they understood why some soldiers chose to desert into Spain, but Drinkwater was perplexed by the motives of those who deserted from the Spanish camp to Gibraltar: 'the neighbourhood of their camp, from our own knowledge of the country, was not capable of subsisting so large an army; consequently they were obliged to be supplied with provisions &c. from places at a distance; and these resources, since Admiral Rodney's arrival, had been cut off.' Even so, escaping to Gibraltar was hardly a solution: 'What could these unhappy men expect in a confined and blockaded garrison, and even at a time when they could not fail to be acquainted with the distress and difficulties under which we laboured?'[26]

When Rear-Admiral Sir Samuel Hood at Portsmouth heard the news of Rodney's victory, he expressed his delight in a letter to a friend:

What a glorious business! I dare say the Spaniards will secede
from France altogether very soon. I am persuaded they will
never make a junction with the French fleet again. The arrival
of Sir George Rodney was very providential, as the garrison
had but a few days' provisions left. 30,000 troops encamped at
St Roche [San Roque] immediately made off, with great pre-
cipitation, upon the appearance of our fleet. This is the account
brought here this day by the lieutenant of ... the *Hyaena*
frigate.[27]

The report of a mass desertion of Spanish troops was incorrect,
but Rodney himself was struck by the attitude of the Spaniards
towards the French, who were supposedly their allies:

I find ... their resentment against France is inexpressible,
and the treatment they meet with [in Gibraltar] is such as
astonished them. In all their letters to their friends, which
we suffer to pass [after reading them], they express a just
sense of humanity they are treated with; and the Admiral
[Langara] this morning assured me, if they were permitted
to return home upon their parole of honour, they would never
serve against Great Britain, but be happy to join her against
France.[28]

Ironically, while deserters were coming into Gibraltar, some
prisoners-of-war were being returned to Spain, as Rodney
informed the Admiralty:

The Spaniards are extremely thankful for the humanity shown
the prisoners; I have sent them all the wounded and sick, taking
receipts for them. The Spanish Admiral [Langara], who is prisoner, has requested me to make an exchange of prisoners. I
told him I was ready to do so, man for man; but that it must be
done soon, or else all the prisoners would be sent to England. I
said this to hasten the exchange, and assured them that no one
prisoner would remain at Gibraltar.[29]

While recovering from his minor battle injuries, the high-profile prisoner Langara received a stream of visitors and also visited some of the British ships, such as the *Prince George*, Rear-Admiral Digby's flagship:

> The Spanish Admiral, Don Juan Langara, one morning visited Admiral Digby, to whose charge the Prince [William] was intrusted, and Don Langara was of course introduced to his Royal Highness. During the conference between the Admirals, Prince William retired, and when it was intimated that Don Juan wished to return [on shore], His Royal Highness appeared in his character of midshipman, and respectfully informed the Admiral that the boat was ready. The Spaniard, astonished to see the son of a monarch acting as a warrant-officer, could not help exclaiming, 'Well does Great Britain merit the empire of the sea, when the humblest stations in her Navy are supported by Princes of the Blood'.[30]

The prince was of German descent with strong links to Hanover in Germany. When Queen Anne had died in 1714, her successor was George I, the ruler of the principality of Hanover, who spoke no English. His great-grandson George III continued as ruler of Hanover, from where loyal German troops were hired to serve alongside the British forces in places like Gibraltar and Minorca. Three battalions of Hanoverian troops served on Gibraltar during the siege, and they felt a particular affection for the prince as a representative of their own royal family. One of their officers proudly declared: 'Our Prince William is a most favourite man. I have not yet seen him in anything other than his blue sailor's jacket, long trousers and leather hat; everything about him is charming; every morning, before he comes to breakfast, he has firstly to climb to the top of the [ship's] rigging, at the express command of the King.'[31]

On the prince's first day ashore, Horsbrugh recorded that the royal midshipman 'landed in the forenoon, without any other ceremony than the compliments of rested arms, a salute and march from the ordinary guards. After waiting upon the Governor, he went up the Hill to the Governor's Lookout and Willis's to get a view of the Enemy's camp and works, and returned on board to dinner.' New orders were issued: 'For the future no compliments be paid to His Royal Highness the Prince, unless he has his Star and Ribbon on; but if he is in company of an Admiral or General Officer, they are in that case to pay the proper compliment due to such Admiral or General.'[32] The next morning, attended by senior officers, the prince walked down the Main Street towards Landport, stopping on the way at the Spanish church. When Father Messa heard, he hurried there, 'and offered to show them the treasures of the church, but they replied that they had already seen the images. And so they departed and I accompanied them down the Main Street and along the walls of the Land Port and even near to the Lieutenant Governor's house'.[33] When Messa realised they were about to dine, he left – there was no invitation for somebody like him to join the illustrious party.

Rodney did what he could to help the garrison, and on 28 January Horsbrugh delivered to his flagship a specific request from Eliott: 'Being ordered by the Governor to go on board the Sandwich with a letter to Sir George Rodney, I was obliged to take a common fishing boat and with some difficulty reached the ship.' It was a short message, requesting wine or strong liquors, coal, gunpowder, 24-pounder guns and shot – if they could be spared from the King's ships or the Spanish prizes.[34] After consulting with Rodney and his subordinate admirals, Eliott also decided to retain the 73rd Highland Regiment to reinforce Gibraltar, rather than let the troops continue to Minorca to strengthen that garrison. The piper John Macdonald described how they came ashore: 'On the 29th January 1780 the 73rd Regiment landed at New Mole and were marched to Irishtown, a part of the town of Gibraltar so-called. The inhabitants for the most part having never seen a Highland regiment were very much surprised at our dress, and more so at the bagpipes.'[35]

While the townspeople were surprised at the strange appearance of the Highlanders, the Scottish soldiers were shocked at the desperate state of Gibraltar. Walter Gordon, one of the Highland soldiers, considered that Rodney's fleet had come at a critical moment: 'Upon our arrival at Gibraltar, we found the garrison reduced to great distress for want of provisions; their situation may be conceived, from attending to the prices of the necessaries of life at the time of our arrival, and the weekly allowance of each soldier.' After noting down the cost of many goods and the weekly rations, he wrote: 'Add to this scanty allowance their almost continual watching and hard duty, and men can scarcely be imagined in a more distressed situation; the supply we brought in greatly relieved the garrison for some time.'[36] John Macdonald began to assist in their hospital in the town: 'Soon after our arrival at Gibraltar Colonel Mackenzie thought proper to send me to the hospital to take care of the sick, under the direction of Mr Andrew Cairncross, head surgeon of the regiment, an able surgeon and a humane gentleman.'[37] With the 73rd disembarked, Rodney now dispatched the remaining convoy for Minorca, which was escorted by three battleships and a frigate.

While Rodney's fleet remained, Gibraltar enjoyed a time of peace. Even the ordinary soldiers could hear news of home from the newly arrived reinforcements, and the officers had a host of new faces and old friends from the fleet to socialise with. After the tedium and isolation of many months of siege, the arrival of so many people had a huge impact, and they included some officers who had come from England to join their regiments, such as Colonels Picton and Mawhood. Because Colonel Green had been unwell for many days, it was highly disappointing for Mrs Green to be forced to cancel many of their social engagements, but by early February he was greatly recovered. Being the wife of a high-ranking officer, she was in a position to entertain the royal midshipman at The Mount. Her husband had acquired the land in 1775, cleared it and built the house, since when he had devoted much effort and expense on landscaping and planting the estate, which extended to around six acres.[38] 'The Prince &c came after they had taken a walk to the cave. I had proper refreshment for them,' she wrote. 'He was much delighted with the gardens and walks; it was favorable, so pleasant a day; more so as it was the only fine one since the Fleet arrived. I was as much pleased with him. He is a very fine youth and must be liked in any situation. His questions were proper; they all wore the face of being the result of a proper curiosity.'[39]

For Mrs Green, Prince William was on his best behaviour, but at night he headed to the taverns with friends from his ship. Increased night-time patrols were taking place, who were instructed 'to take up all idle people, inhabitants without lights, or soldiers they find on the streets, excepting officers' servants who may be necessarily employed on their masters' business; to search all wine houses where they hear any noise or disturbances or soldiers in them, and carry the master of the house, and such persons as they find there, prisoners to the Main Guard'.[40] When Prince William's party was involved in a drunken brawl with some soldiers, it was quickly broken up and they were arrested. The news that 'a son of the King of England was in custody' flew round the garrison, and Admiral Digby had to arrange his release. After that, he was allowed on shore only if accompanied by a superior officer.[41]

Everyone was making the most of the last few days before the fleet sailed, and Mrs Green was fully occupied writing letters and entertaining. She was devoted to her absent family and constantly tried to keep in touch:

I am as busy as I can spare time, in transcribing a small journal for my son, but am frequently broke in upon by the number of visitors that are constantly calling. Not only that, but the daily necessity I have in attending to all sorts of family business makes it almost impossible to go on in the writing way. I shall at last get into a total disregard to method, style or sense, I fear, for as I wish to write to the very moment, so it can never be the effect of a studied writer.[42]

A few days later, she added: 'Busy writing for the fleet, as it is expected it will soon leave us. We have a very large party at dinner this day, Sir J. Ross and many of our Navy acquaintances;

and also of the Highland Regiment . . . A very large party at night.'
She was also hoping to have a tour of the famous battleship, the
*Royal George*, but feared there was no time left:

> Sir J. Ross has pressed me exceedingly, to go on board the *Royal
> George* and to take a rough dinner with him on Wednesday, also
> to take my own Party, all which I have promised to do, though
> at the same time, think it will not be possible; as it is very likely
> the wind may be easterly; in which case I understand it is likely
> that division may have orders for sailing. I should very well like
> to see so fine a ship, particularly as Sir John is so pleasing and
> so cheerful an old man.[43]

Her prediction was unfortunately correct, because the very next
day saw the gradual departure of the fleet, and everyone became
frantic to complete their tasks. On the day that she was to have
gone on board the *Royal George*, Sir John Ross sent his apologies
and sailed that afternoon. Prince William was her next visitor: 'the
Prince took leave of me and was again at the Mount . . . my letters
going by different hands'.[44]

Later that afternoon, Admiral Langara was also allowed to
leave. One of Rodney's final tasks had been to sort out the
exchange of prisoners with Spain. In a letter from Sir John
Hort, the British consul at Lisbon, he had been warned that the
Spaniards were being slow in honouring their part in prisoner-of-
war exchanges, and so he had taken a firm line in negotiations.[45]
Eventually an exchange was arranged, totalling over a thousand
prisoners, including Langara who so impressed Mrs Green that
some of her earlier fondness for the people of Spain was restored:
'This day the Spanish Admiral went away, great civility shown
him. He went in a carriage of our Governor, was drove quite close
to the Spanish Lines. The Town Major attended him and a drum
as usual. Langara went away fully convinced that he had met with
the utmost politeness he ever could have wished for and much
more than he could have expected. He seemed a good sort of
man; was very highly displeased with the French.'[46]

Horsbrugh was amused to hear that Langara's defeat was being treated like a victory: 'Just before their departure the Admiral received the accounts from Madrid that the King of Spain had promoted him to the rank of Lieutenant General and given all the other officers down to the midshipmen an additional step as reward for their behaviour in the action with our fleet.'[47] Other prisoners were not so lucky. Five hundred were left on Gibraltar, so that they could be exchanged for British prisoners once the Spaniards stopped dragging their feet, while the remainder were to be transported to England.

The warships that had escorted the convoy to Minorca now returned, and the remaining fleet left in mid-February after being at Gibraltar for nearly a month. Rear-Admiral Digby's ships were carrying not just Spanish prisoners, but also all the invalids from the garrison who were unfit for service, as well as military wives and children who had been ordered by Eliott to leave, because they did not have in store a sufficient quantity of flour or biscuits for a year, which he specified as 250 pounds of flour or 360 pounds of biscuit per person. They were joined by other families who, although not ordered out, could not bear the siege conditions any longer. Two days later, Digby's squadron parted company from Rodney's fleet and continued to England, encountering a French convoy on the way and capturing three merchant ships and the 64-gun battleship *Le Prothée*, which was found to be carrying around £60,000 in coins.

On board the *Royal George*, Vice-Admiral Robert Duff was also travelling home. A few days earlier he had sent a letter to Rodney, informing him that he felt the small force at Gibraltar was incompatible with his status as vice-admiral and requested a new appointment elsewhere, especially as his health was impaired. Rodney expressed sympathy, but declared it was not within his power because he had secret orders. Duff regretted this fact and advised Rodney that he therefore felt obliged to return to England on the grounds of ill health.[48] Some two decades earlier, in the West Indies, he had refused to serve as Rodney's flag-captain, claiming he was too senior for the post, even though it was a prestigious role. He lived by the rules of status, not service, and had proved ineffective and unpopular in Gibraltar. At the age of fifty-nine, his voyage home marked the end of his naval career. He was an afterthought in Mrs Green's diary: 'I have omitted to mention that Admiral Duff went on board the Royal George on Saturday last with an intention not to come on shore any more. He goes home as a passenger to England with Sir J. Ross. There was no ceremony used at his going. He called upon a few persons only. We were of the number. He seemed a good deal discomposed and disconcerted.'[49] His final years would be marred by ill health, and he died seven years later.

As soon as he left Gibraltar, Rodney wrote to his wife, vividly describing his feelings: 'I am now at sea, and on my way to the West Indies. Thank Heaven I have got from Gibraltar, I hope never to see it again, for I have not had one day's health since I went there. A violent cold has hung by me, and I still have it, though not so bad as when I was there. The weather is now remarkably fine, and as warm as the middle of summer in England.'[50] Rodney sailed to the West Indies to join the action against the combined French and Spanish fleet there. Before his convoy, the Royal Navy had been mostly on the defensive, but the expedition to Gibraltar was Britain's first major naval victory in the American War of Independence. Gibraltar and Minorca had been resupplied just in time, enemy warships and supply ships had been destroyed or captured, and several thousand prisoners taken. There were relatively few British losses, and the prize-ships and cargoes were valued at over a million pounds.

Not everyone left with the fleet, because after gunfire on the last day of sailing, a search was made for seamen who had absconded, and forty were found who were handed over to the new commodore, John Elliot.[51] Rodney had left Captain Elliot's 74-gun battleship HMS *Edgar* at Gibraltar to bolster the Mediterranean Fleet of one 64-gun battleship, two frigates, an armed brig and an armed sloop. While Rodney's fleet was at Gibraltar, the Spanish troops had done very little and Admiral Barcelo had withdrawn his own blockading vessels to the safety of

Algeciras and Ceuta, but they now re-emerged into the Straits and the Bay of Gibraltar. Arranged against the Royal Navy warships was a Spanish force of over forty vessels of varying sizes, with a total of 320 guns and 5000 men. The balance of naval power tipped firmly in favour of Spain once again, and the blockade was back in place, with the renewed intention of starving Gibraltar into submission and continuing to prepare for a final assault.

# CHAPTER EIGHT

·◆·

# SMALLPOX

By the end of February 1780, numerous children had contracted smallpox and several fatalities had already occurred, which would continue over the following weeks. Normally possessing a robust attitude to life, Mrs Green became very depressed with all the suffering and grief felt by their parents, a mood exacerbated by her own periodic bouts of illness. She confided in her diary in mid-March:

Find myself exceedingly indisposed, could not get up to breakfast. The hurry and daily hopes and expectations which now prevailed, particularly in weak minds, began to affect me, and I grew exceedingly ill. My head and eyes very bad, hardly indeed am able to write this, and fear I am going to be very ill. It was the same with me some weeks ago, but as I only write for the amusement of myself and if ever it so happen for my own family's information in a few points, so I am the less anxious about the style or manner.[1]

Mrs Green's diaries were full of comments about her health, with minor and acute symptoms interspersed with periods of being completely well. Even before the siege had started, when the way of life was pleasant, she was constantly afflicted by episodes of ill health and had been very sick for much of June 1779. In July she had been 'taken with a cold shivering like an ague', and two months later she had great pain in one foot, while in October she wrote: 'At this time I was taken exceedingly ill and continued so till the end of the year.' For many weeks, her diary was patchy, but at the start of January 1780 she wrote: 'Find myself not quite so lame or ill as I was yesterday', though she recorded two weeks later: 'I was taken ill again, in the course of the evening, a cold shivering and a pain in my left arm.' The very next day, she heard about the new outbreak of smallpox from Dr Baynes, when she herself was 'exceedingly ill, pains all over'.[2]

By Easter Day, which was early that year, on 26 March, Mrs Green's health was still unpredictable: 'I walked out before dinner with the child [her daughter Charlotte], find myself very indifferent whilst out and come home very low.'[3] Looking at all the symptoms that she describes over the following months, various conditions (such as heart disease) can be discounted. One likely cause was relapsing fever, a tick-borne infection that is treatable today with antibiotics. Known then as remitting fever, it was endemic in north Africa and Spain and was characterised by periods of feeling unwell and short periods of feeling fine, while the leg pain she suffered could well have resulted from septicaemia.[4] She tried all sorts of remedies that may have made her worse, such as dosing herself with an assortment of potions, and in spite of being in the care of Dr Baynes she had no idea of the reason for her problems and neither did he, which caused her acute anxiety and depression.

In between the recurrent attacks, Mrs Green recorded the events around her. Reviews of the different regiments tended to take place in March each year, and she was particularly intrigued by a strange incident a few days after Easter during a routine review of the 39th:

to the astonishment and wonder of many people, Colonel Ross attended at the 39th review and went through that business. It was not known to any of the officers that he would be there, but just before the regiment went on, he sent to Colonel Kellet and informed him [that] he had let the Governor know he intended to fall in with the regiment. In the same time, General Boyd went on to the Parade, but never joined the regiment, only as a spectator as on other days. The whole went on pretty well, better indeed than it could be expected, as it was very reasonable to think the men were taken at a disadvantage by the changing [of] the commanding officer that very morning.[5]

Lieutenant-Governor Boyd was colonel of the 39th, and according to Mrs Green, he normally watched his regiment at reviews, though played no active role so as not to undermine the authority of the commanding officer. This was normally Major William Kellett, as Lieutenant-Colonel Ross had not participated for some time. Several weeks earlier, she had mentioned Ross being very ill for several months, though in early February, while Rodney's fleet was present, she had noted a change in him: 'Colonel Ross quite in spirits now his friend [Admiral Lockhart Ross] is here. We all wish, for his own sake, he could go home with the Admiral.'[6] Boyd and Ross were not the only examples of a full colonel of a regiment being in the same place as the lieutenant-colonel, because Colonel Charles Mawhood of the 72nd Regiment and Colonel William Picton of the 12th had both come to Gibraltar with Rodney's convoy to join their respective regiments, but in the case of Boyd and Ross it had turned into a feud.[7]

After the review, Mrs Green said that all the officers dined together at the Convent, including Boyd, who was present as the deputy governor 'in his general's uniform with his aid de camps, not making himself Colonel of the 39th the whole day. He or Colonel Ross did not speak to each other.'[8] Their quarrel dated back a considerable time, supposedly over an officer in their regiment, though at a court-martial several years later, it was stated that Boyd 'being on the spot with his regiment at Gibraltar, took the business of orders and regulations upon himself, without attending to the etiquette observed. Lieutenant Colonel Ross first spoke to the Colonel upon this unusual interference, and afterwards remonstrated against what he considered as a reflection upon his military character.'[9] Because he had arrived in Gibraltar years after Boyd, Ross felt at a disadvantage and a rift developed, not helped by their class difference. Boyd had been brought up on Minorca and became the civilian storekeeper of ordnance there, a role that his father had previously held. He distinguished himself in the attempt to take dispatches to Admiral Byng's fleet when the island was besieged in 1756 and for that gallantry was rewarded with a commission in the army, but most army officers were sons of the upper echelons of society, like Charles Ross. The evening after the review of the 39th, Ross went to the Greens' house, where Mrs Green 'as usual heard all the story'.[10] She afterwards lamented that both Boyd and Ross were valuable officers, and yet their feud was intensifying.

While Ross may have been under severe mental strain, making him sensitive about his status, other troops were in poor physical health, as were numerous Spanish prisoners-of-war still being held at the naval hospital. 'One man was ordered from each regiment ... to carry water for the Spanish prisoners in the Hospital,' Horsbrugh noted. 'They were to deliver the water at the kitchens and doors, but on no account to enter the wards.'[11] All water on Gibraltar needed to be fetched from wells, cisterns and fountains, and this may have been an attempt at disease control or to prevent fraternisation with the enemy. Within a week the captives were well enough to be sent back to Spain, 286 men in all, in response to Spain returning almost four hundred British prisoners-of-war as their side of the exchange deal. Just twelve Spaniards were left who were too sick to move.

Like the prisoners-of-war from the Moonlight Battle, the soldiers of the 73rd Highland Regiment had also come to Gibraltar with Rodney's convoy. The Great Siege was taking place on the southernmost edge of Europe, within sight of Africa, yet the thousands of men on both sides were drawn from right across Europe. Many of the 73rd had never before travelled beyond Scotland, but Gibraltar was to be the final resting place for some, as many now fell ill with typhus. John Macdonald was still helping in the regiment's hospital in the town: 'The change of climate and like-wise of diet had such an effect upon our men that a great many of them fell sick of the flux, of which numbers died. From the beginning of the month of March to the end of June, we never had fewer than one hundred or a hundred and twenty or thirty men sick in the regimental hospital.'[12] In late April Mrs Green recorded: '7 men died of the Highland Regiment between last night and this evening, of a flux and fever. They had lost near 100 before!' Four days later, she wrote: 'Great complaints now making about salt fish.' Many attributed this 'putrid fever' epidemic to the salt fish, and it would likewise be blamed for scurvy, which was starting to afflict people. Eliott had purchased cargoes of salt cod from two Newfoundland fishery vessels, with Mrs Green remark-ing at the end of February: 'the troops had for the first time salt fish delivered them, instead of meat, and some rice and peas; not any butter, which occasioned great discontent; as it seems hard to oblige them to take the fish in place of meat and not to give them a little butter with it.'[13]

A month later, things were no better: 'The troops ... think it hard to be obliged to eat so much salt fish when it is well known there is an amazing quantity of beef and pork in store! Salt fish without the proper sauces is but poor diet, and particularly in the hot season coming on.' Drinkwater simply commented: 'The salt cod being indifferent in its kind, and the soldiers not having proper vegetables to dress with it, proved very pernicious.' This supply of salt cod lasted several months, and when a Swedish ship came too close and was forced to come in, it was cruel to find that the entire cargo was salt, and not fresh provisions. Small boats from Morocco did now and again evade the blockade with supplies of meat, fruit and vegetables, but it was sold on the open market at very high prices. One small boat from Tetuan arrived with twelve dozen fowl, including several cocks that the crew had to kill for fear that their crowing would alert the Spanish cruisers.[14]

Mrs Green now heard that the 73rd was also the first regiment to be affected by smallpox: 'Doctor Baynes informs me that the smallpox is broke out upon a man of the Highland Regiment on Friday last. NB This is the first soldier that has got that disorder. At the same time there is now a number of children ill with it.' She added: 'It is supposed the Governor will allow of innocula- tion, as he has said he would not have any objection to it when once it got among the troops.' The tedium and hardships of the siege oppressed everybody, but the dread of smallpox, real and imagined, was proving too much to bear, and so Mrs Green was in a state of panic when her daughter developed a fever: 'Charlotte was greatly indisposed all night, quite burning with heat. I gave her one of the small pills, and she grew very ill afterwards. Doctor Baynes is of the opinion she is breeding the smallpox. The child has not been quite well these last ten days.' Her ailment turned out not to be smallpox, and Charlotte rapidly recovered, but a week later Mrs Green lamented: 'Smallpox raging very bad, chil- dren dying every day', and a few days afterwards: 'The smallpox is now getting into all the regiments. A man of the soldier artificers exceedingly bad with it. No innoculation yet!'[15]

She herself continued to suffer from multiple ailments, with violent headaches, a pain in her left knee and then her right leg. In some despair, she wrote: 'am worse this day than yesterday, and at night beyond all possibility of bearing it with any degree of patience', followed by 'the worst night I have ever experienced in my life'. In mid-April she took to her bed for several days. Although Eliott had promised to allow inoculation once the dis- ease spread to the soldiers, he changed his mind, and at the end of April Mrs Green vented her anger: 'it is not very easy to tell, how exceedingly uncomfortable all ranks of people now are. This circumstance of the General's refusing to allow of innoculation has hurt all degrees of people. Several men are quite miserable at not being allowed to innoculate ... and it is the more to be won- dered at as the Governor did actually say he would not have any objections if it once got amongst the troops, which it has now, and likewise has been already fatal.'[16] Mrs Green was evidently trusted not to spread gossip, because Dr Baynes and others often confided in her, and he now told her of his failure to persuade Eliott:

Doctor Baynes ... asked the Governor this question, if the smallpox happened in any family where there were more than one child, would it not be a better way to innoculate the other children as it is not to be questioned but they would get it, and it would be the means of its being sooner over. He answered 'No, by no means! He could not answer it to his conscience!' What the Governor's meaning is, I know not. I think he should make a point of getting this cruel disorder over as soon as possible well knowing the violent [hot] season coming on and also to comfort so many anxious people.[17]

There was too much to worry about, from smallpox to typhus, lack of food and the intentions of the opposing forces, and for Mrs Green the uncertainty over Spain's plans was unbearable: 'Would to God, they either would leave us, or show themselves in earnest.'[18] Since the departure of Rodney's fleet, the Spanish squadron was at large once more in the bay, but work in their camp had slowed down and several regiments departed, to be redeployed in the West Indies, while new ones gradually took their place. 'The enemy at this time was not particularly active,' Drinkwater commented. 'Some new arrangements were made in their artillery-park; and in their camp they were busy collecting brush-wood for fascines, which caused various conjectures in the Garrison concerning their future operations.'[19]

In early May, the camp became much busier, with carts bringing in artillery, shot and shells, and the troops undertook exercises each day, so it appeared as if they were planning an attack. The nervous inhabitants of the garrison began to erect more wooden sheds south of the Greens' Mount Pleasant estate, away from the dangers of shot and shells. On 6 May, the entire Spanish army in the camp rehearsed an assault of Gibraltar, which Ancell described to his brother in England:

This afternoon the Spanish army were arranged in two divisions, and about four o'clock began a sham fight, similar to an attack upon the garrison. One division took post on the rising ground under the Queen's Chair (supposed to be the British) while the other division, in the valley on the common, endeavoured to dislodge them, and take possession of their intrenchments. The fire was well supported on both sides for three hours, when the British forces were entirely routed ... I assure you that the fight afforded great entertainment, and the army displayed some merit in their performance. They have been practising several days. It is evident they mean to familiarize their troops to the nature of an attack, so that they may be more expert when they make a regular assault.[20]

Horsbrugh wrote down a detailed description of the sham fight, which he judged to be tolerably performed, and 'the only fault seemed to be a great number of small detached parties from both sides placed too much in the line of fire to be of an essential service. The whole however viewed from our heights had a very fine effect, was extremely picturesque, and afforded us a few hours agreeable amusement.'[21]

On the following night, four deserters tried to escape to Gibraltar, but two were taken and one was shot. Horsbrugh had earlier heard that 'there was a general murmuring throughout the country against the present war, and that great numbers (particularly the Catalonians) had lately deserted both from the fleet and army through discontent'.[22] On this occasion, one Walloon deserter made it and brought intelligence that Madrid had given General Alvarez permission to start a bombardment whenever he thought fit. The next day, two men were executed in the camp, who were presumed to be the unsuccessful deserters,[23] but that did not deter a native Spanish deserter two days later. All previous ones had been from Spain's foreign forces, and so Drinkwater wrote:

Another deserter, belonging to the regiment of Estremadura, came in on the 11th [May 1780], and was remarkable for being the first native of Spain who deserted. The Spanish army are all raised upon a local establishment. Each district is required to

The capsizing of the *Royal George* at Spithead on 29 August 1782

Typical Mediterranean vessels – a tartan (top left), settee (bottom left) and xebec (above)

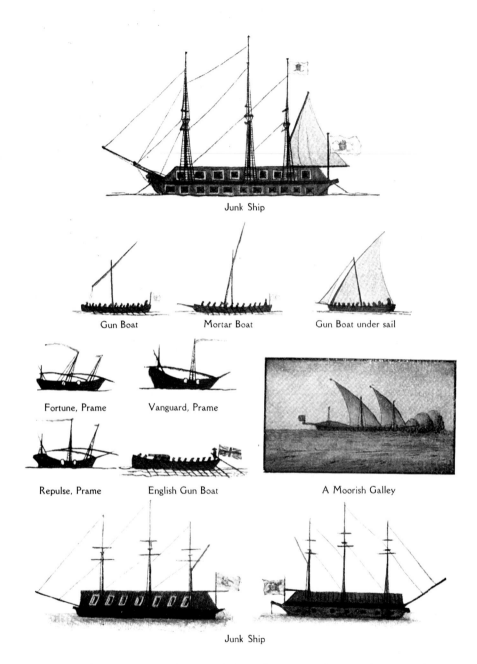

Junk Ship

Gun Boat

Mortar Boat

Gun Boat under sail

Fortune, Prame

Vanguard, Prame

Repulse, Prame

English Gun Boat

A Moorish Galley

Junk Ship

The *Pastora* floating battery ('junk ship') (top); Spanish gunboats and a mortar boat; Royal Navy prames and a gunboat; a Moorish galley; and a smaller floating battery (bottom, two views)

George Augustus Eliott,
Governor of Gibraltar

Captain John Drinkwater, depicted with
writing materials and plans and holding his
published book on the siege

Admiral Sir George Brydges Rodney
(above) and Admiral Lord Richard
Howe (right)

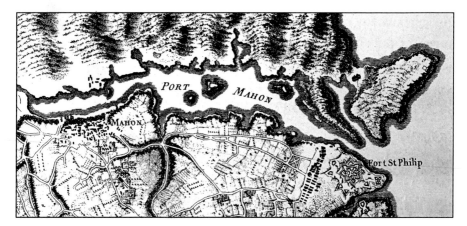

Port Mahon and Fort St Philip, Minorca

Comte de Crillon

The British surrendering to the
combined French and Spanish
forces at Fort St Philip, Minorca

The quadrangular naval hospital, surrounded by a wall, with Parson's Lodge battery behind

Koehler's depressing gun carriage (left) and (right) gun carriage elevated at 45 degrees, developed by Lieutenant-Colonel Williams of the Royal Artillery

Tunnel cut through rock between the King's and Queen's Lines

An encampment of huts, probably part of Hardy's Town, looking across the Straits to Africa

A house below the Moorish Castle, before and after the initial Spanish bombardment in April 1781

*Opposite:* Eliott (on horseback) on the defences, pointing to Captain Curtis stood in a gunboat (bottom left) rescuing survivors from the floating batteries. On Eliott's right is Lieutenant-Governor Boyd, with Major-General La Motte between them. On Eliott's left is William Green, then Lieutenant-Colonel Dachenhausen and Colonel William Picton. Captain John Drinkwater is shown top right, and in front of him is the engineer Charles Holloway. At the bottom right is Captain Colin Lindsay of the 73rd Highlanders. From a painting by J. S. Copley

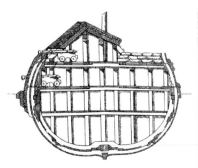

*Above:* Cross-section through a floating battery

*Right:* Captain Roger Curtis and his gunboat crew rescuing French and Spaniards from the floating batteries in the early hours of 14 September 1782

Massive explosion of a floating battery

furnish a certain proportion of troops; and the men are enrolled for, I believe, about seven years service, after which time they are permitted to return to their respective provinces. And as the Spaniards are all strongly attached to their native spot, desertion is consequently less common with them than with any other troops. Most of the men, therefore, who deserted to us came from those regiments in their service which are composed of foreigners.[24]

The Estremadura Regiment had arrived in the camp at the end of March, and, according to Ancell, the deserter 'says that the duty in the Spanish camp is incessant and fatiguing, and that cannon and mortars are mounted for the purpose of opening a fire upon us immediately'.[25] Intelligence from merchant boats also suggested that a bombardment would begin at the start of May and that many Spanish and French troops were marching towards the camp.

Deserters might not have been so keen on coming to Gibraltar if they had realised smallpox was still raging, and at this point Mrs Green's daughter Charlotte fell ill again: 'Our little daughter seems heavy and dull today ... It is dreadful to hear the number of children that are dying. Our Charlotte not able to hold up her head. We are exceedingly anxious, indeed I am quite miserable from fears.' The next day, her anguish continued: 'Abundance of children dies with the smallpox. Charlotte very bad and sleepy all day. This is the 2nd day when she has been so ill. On each side of our house and directly opposite three very fine children have died since yesterday after being 9 days bad ... Doctor Baynes seems to think our child will get it now, indeed it seems an absolute certainty as it is in every house in our street, and in the opposite door.' Within twenty-four hours, her daughter was desperately ill: 'Charlotte had an exceeding bad night and is quite delirious to day. Dr Baynes has no doubt of it being the smallpox.' In the evening Mrs Green recorded the appearance of the distinctive pus-filled blisters: 'We observed some spots coming out, and she grew more cool and composed. She is kept in the air, and drinks cold drink, chiefly toast and water.'[26]

After a few days, on Thursday 11 May, she wrote with relief about Charlotte: 'Going on well, but very sore, and bad nights. Still everything appears well. She was very patient, though in a good deal of throbbing pain.' It was more than a week before she had time to set down her child's gradual recovery:

Her nights very restless, notwithstanding her taking opiates. On Monday they were at the height and highly inflamed ... All the next week continued doing right and had hardly any second fever which is common upon the turn ... she was put into a bath of warm water and herbs ... She has had about 300 [blisters] all over her body and of the finest kind. During the fortnight she has been ill, more than 50 English children have died and several soldiers besides inhabitants. The whole air is infected and very dangerous. A very dangerous fever [typhus] is also in the garrison. Every means has been tried to obtain the Governors leave to innoculate. His refusals make everybody unhappy. Not any fresh provision comes near us now; so that we are badly off indeed.[27]

Just as Charlotte was improving, her maid Elizabeth Dixon became ill. Because it was a Sunday, Elizabeth had some hours of leisure, and Mrs Green wrote: 'Betty Dixon first complained of a headache but not so bad as to prevent her walking out with some of our servants in afternoon to New Mole. Seemed greatly indisposed when going to bed. NB She sleep in a room close to my bed chamber and I found she was ill all night and frequently sick, attended with a griping.' The following morning brought worse news: 'Doctor Baynes pronounces the maid's complaint to be the smallpox. Great uneasiness on that occasion. Thinking she had had it long before, therefore she was no ways prepared and is a remarkable, strong, hearty person, 25 years old, full of health and fat ... a very tall large-made woman.' The fact that she had suc-cumbed to smallpox with such a robust constitution worried Mrs

Green greatly: 'This adds to our uneasiness and the more so, as she is solely friendless in the world. Doctor Baynes is as attentive to her as he was to our own child. We put her into a most charming airy apartment.' Two days later, Mrs Green was very agitated: 'We are greatly distressed in our family. The young woman very bad. I am particularly hurt at it as she now wishes she had been innoculated.'[28] She later wrote:

> any one who knew her, were of the opinion she must have had this disorder when she was an infant. A brother and sister of hers had died of it. It was therefore most likely she had it, though it was supposed very slightly, but as the parents both died before she had knowledge of them, it remained an uncertain matter. She had lived in two families where 3 or 4 children had also died. From all the above circumstances, she never allowed herself to harbour a doubt, nor had the young woman any idea of fears, on the contrary, was the first to go to any house where she heard of the smallpox.[29]

Over the next week, Elizabeth became much worse, and her employer could not contain her anger: 'Our servant maid is past all possibility of recovery. Every means is tried but we find it will not do. Men, women, and children dying every day and the utmost distress now appears in everybody. The air is full of this cruel infection. It is to be wished that the innoculation had been allowed. That would have stopped this weeks ago.'[30] Ancell said much the same: 'Our garrison are beginning to be very sickly – the smallpox rages with great violence, and carries off 18 or 20 per week, but mostly children.'[31] Apart from Mrs Green, his comment is a rarity within the military garrison. Especially for those without children, the smallpox epidemic was not sufficiently newsworthy to be mentioned, because it fell heaviest on the civilians and the families of the rank-and-file soldiers.

Elizabeth was being cared for by Mrs Green's own maid by day and a nurse at night, with the housekeeper assisting. She became totally helpless, and on 31 May Dr Baynes was extremely uneasy and similarly helpless. Being the army doctor, he was not obliged to treat the servants, but was doing all he could, and Mrs Green was grateful for his compassion: 'Baynes hardly ever leaves the house and, I sincerely believe, tries anything that art or study can do.' In desperation he 'applied garlic upon the soles of her feet', which was in the form of a poultice. Mrs Green thought it helped her to sleep, and because her feet did not swell or blister, other poultices were also tried 'in hopes to draw down the swelling and disorder'. Nothing worked, and Mrs Green was in despair. Elizabeth lasted three more days: 'At 20 minutes before 3 all was over with our maid servant, upon the 15th day from her being taken ill. It is a most unwelcome circumstance and has greatly affected the Colonel [William Green]; I am not able to tell what I experience.'[32] Two days later, Colonel Green dismissed his servant James, because the man's children had smallpox.

Around the time Elizabeth Dixon first fell ill, the garrison heard bad news about the *Buck* that had so valiantly beaten the blockade. The vessel had stayed at Gibraltar for a month before heading into the Mediterranean for Minorca, but, Drinkwater said, 'she unfortunately fell in with a French frigate, which, after a few broadsides, captured the Buck; but before she could be got into port, she sunk, from the damage received in the action'. Captain Fagg and the crew survived, but some years later, in 1794, Fagg was commanding another privateer named the *Buck*, which was tragically lost with all hands off the east coast of England.[33]

Rather than attack the garrison, as deserters thought would happen, the Spanish army undertook yet another sham fight at the end of May, which Horsbrugh watched: 'In the afternoon the whole of the Enemy's army was put under arms and marched from camp in two columns, one to the north, the other to the west, formed and afterwards performed the following manoeuvres.' He then described how one half of the infantry and cavalry lined up along the shore as if to protect a convoy, which they acted out with covered waggons and loaded horses, while the rest of the army attempted to intercept the convoy, with gun fire and small-arms fire. The weather in the afternoon was so murky that Horsbrugh could barely make out what was happening. 'We imagined,' he commented, 'this general Field Day to have been in honour of San Fernando Rey de Espana, which is one of the great Gala days at Court.'[34]

Nearly twelve months had passed since Spain's declaration of war on Britain and the start of the siege of Gibraltar. The joint Spanish and French invasion of Britain had failed, and although the Spaniards continued to build up a formidable military zone all round the bay, they were increasingly anxious to force a surrender of Gibraltar through starvation. Hungry themselves, the Spanish soldiers kept raiding the garrison's market gardens, just outside the defences. If they were heard, the guards fired in their direction, and in the early hours of 4 June Horsbrugh said that 'Bayside Guard having heard a rustling noise resembling the approach of persons through the nearish garden, they turned out and fired several shots that way.' On this occasion, they were mistaken about Spanish soldiers pilfering vegetables, because 'In the morning one of our mules which had strayed towards the Enemy's Lines was found dead.'[35]

The Royal Navy warships stationed at Gibraltar occasionally helped those few small vessels that were still prepared to risk breaking the blockade to supply the garrison with fresh food, albeit at exorbitant prices. To complete the blockade, Spain needed to destroy those warships, and Admiral Barcelo decided to set them on fire. His task was made easier, because the Admiralty had disagreed with Rodney's decision to leave Captain John Elliot and his 74-gun battleship *Edgar* at Gibraltar. Having been recalled to England to join the Channel Fleet, the *Edgar* had sailed towards the end of April, which was a severe blow because the Mediterranean Fleet was left with only five warships – the *Panther* (a battleship of 60 guns), the *Enterprise* (a frigate of 28 guns), the *Porcupine* (a frigate of 28 guns), the *Gibraltar* (an armed brig with 10 guns) and the *Fortune* (an armed sloop with 10 guns).

Spanish workers were converting nine old vessels into fireships by packing them with tar, gunpowder, other flammable material and fuses. The idea was to sail them across the bay with a skeleton crew, set the fuses alight, ram the British warships and use grappling hooks to entangle them. The Spanish crews would escape in small boats, while the Royal Navy squadron was consumed by fire, but in case any vessels cut their cables and attempted to sail to safety, Admiral Barcelo's warships would be waiting. It was hoped that fires would spread to all the other vessels in the New Mole and the nearby naval stores, and when flames reached the gunpowder stores in the warships, they would blow up and cause catastrophic damage on Gibraltar.

Late at night on 6 June, the fireships set sail from Algeciras, with the help of a westerly wind. Because it was so dark, they managed to cross the bay undetected. It was well past midnight when an alert guard on board a boat from the *Enterprise* frigate made out a vessel close to the New Mole, which, when challenged, claimed to be a beef boat from Barbary. Suspicions were raised, and the guard went back on board the *Enterprise* and immediately fired a shot to raise the alarm. According to Ancell, 'the enemy finding they were discovered, took to their boats, and set them [the fireships] on fire, one after another ... The wind now dropped, and a dead calm ensued; the garrison and shipping kept a brisk fire on the boats as they retreated, from which they must have suffered considerably.'[36]

Eliott gave orders for the drums to beat to arms, and the soldiers hurried to their stations, leaving everyone else panic-stricken, while the artillery was ordered to try to sink the fireships. Nobody on Gibraltar had seen anything like it, and they waited with dread for the Spanish land batteries to open fire as well. 'The terrified inhabitants,' Ancell related, 'together with the women and children, were wringing their hands, weeping with the most bitter and inexpressible anguish, expecting every minute a bombardment from the land-side. Such a scene would pierce the most insensible heart, to hear their piteous lamentations ... the Rock appeared as bright as if Aurora had just risen, to bless the creation with her enlivening rays.'[37] Even Mrs Green admitted her own terror:

> It was a most grand though alarming sight as they burnt with great violence. It seemed to me just so many moving mountains of fire. Every regiment was at their alarm post ... to hear the drums beating, the noise of the guns, guns from the garrison, all our ships, together with the bursting open of the port holes in the fire ships, was beyond the power of my pen to express ... I little expected such a shock but I believe I am not born to partake any very common fate; otherwise I must have long ceased to exist, considering all I have experienced. My heart now seems totally full of concern and vexation; my bad state of health has rendered me miserable ... I was actually stupid with fright.[38]

The fireships kept approaching, burning fiercely, and Royal Navy crews risked their lives by towing them out of the way. Ancell documented their efforts:

> Our seamen in an undaunted and gallant manner, rowed alongside of the flaming devourers, and having grappled to their burning sides, they towed them quietly to the back of the New Mole, among the clefts of the rock, where they burnt to the water's edge ... Three of the fire-ships drove to the eastward; two dropped very near the Panther in Rosia Bay; and the others to Europa and Little Bay. They burnt with surprizing fierceness for three hours. The masts of some stood to the very last, and appeared as under sail. The largest was a 40 gun ship, and burnt till this afternoon.[39]

Father Messa said that the largest fireship almost made it to the entrance of the New Mole:

> the English launches managed to steer it towards the walls in front of the Naval Hospital. This vessel was so large that it

alone could have set alight the whole mole, as it was made up of so much combustible material that, despite the amount of sea water poured on it by the sailors, it continued giving off smoke for more than 40 hours. On this occasion, the English sailors carried out their duties so well that seven of them suffered burns to their hands and backs and had to be taken to the hospital. It is said that the naval commander [Captain Leslie] has rewarded them with the equivalent value of burnt ships, that is, with whatever could be salvaged.[40]

The wrecked hulls of the fireships were now recovered and sold as firewood.

When the next batch of prisoners-of-war was returned by Spain to Gibraltar, they included the crew of a boat that had been bringing supplies from Morocco. Horsbrugh said that among them was a very intelligent man who was proficient in both Spanish and Catalan and who had overheard much information while held prisoner. The original plan, he told Horsbrugh, was for the batteries along the Spanish Lines to join in the fireship attack once they received the agreed signals. Because the mission had already been aborted twice, it was thought that the garrison must have realised what was planned, and so it was decided to seek further instructions from King Carlos, but 'Admiral Barcelo objected, said he would make another attempt and take the consequences upon himself, which was at last agreed to, and the attempt accordingly made on the morning of the 7th June ... But when he found the fireships had miscarried he was outrageous [outraged] beyond measure, and for many hours would not suffer anyone to speak with him.'[41] A deserter from the Walloon guards confirmed the story, saying that on the night of the attack he was himself on duty as a gunner, ready to fire at the garrison: 'From him we learned that the matches were lighted and everything in readiness to bombard us the night they sent in the fireships, which would have been put in execution had they succeeded in burning our shipping in and about the New Mole.'[42]

Captain Price thought the scheme could easily have worked:

'The enterprise, however defective in point of execution, was by no means ill planned. The wind was not perfectly favorable and the Enemy appeared to want that kind of daring intrepidity required in the conduct of similar exploits. The vessels in succession were fired [set on fire] at too great a distance from their objects and left too much to the guidance of chance to succeed.'[43] The garrison had had a lucky escape, but word was that further fireships were being prepared.

# CHAPTER NINE

———·◆·———

# GUNBOATS

After beating off the fireship attack in early June 1780, the garrison may have hoped for a quieter summer, but Admiral Barcelo was already plotting his next move – night-time gunboat attacks. The first strike was in the early hours of 27 June, though Ancell said it was not possible to determine what kind of vessel was attacking them: 'It is conjectured they were gun-boats or floating-batteries, for it being very dark, it was impossible to perceive their form.' Horsbrugh was able to observe them more closely as they approached Rosia Bay, where the 60-gun *Panther* was moored:

> A little before two o'clock in the morning, it being then quite calm, the Enemy made an attempt against the Panther man of war with four gun boats, who as soon as they were discovered by our guard boats, began to fire which gave us the alarm on shore. The whole of their fire being directed against the Panther, she returned it very briskly, but the morning being dark, the objects small, and lying low in the water, we had nothing to direct us in pointing our guns but the flashes of theirs, which against boats who were using oars, and could quickly change their situation, was extremely uncertain.[1]

In Ancell's opinion, this new venture would harden the resolve of the garrison:

Several shot (26lb. weight) came on shore at South-barracks, but happily did no damage. The shipping and garrison kept up a brisk fire, the picquets of the several regiments were under arms, and the women and children roused on hearing a general discharge of cannon. It is not improbable that this is a stratagem of Admiral Barcelo's, to harrass and fatigue us with repeated firings and alarms from the Bay, and then give the decisive stroke; but they have Britons to encounter. The more we feel our Enemy, the more ardent are our desires to engage them.[2]

One of the women he referred to was Mrs Green. At the time, she was suffering greatly from stress and had left her townhouse three days earlier to go to The Mount, 'with an intention to remain ... come up in very great dejection of spirits – fear I shall soon feel the fatal effects of it'. Instead of some calm recuperation in its beautiful location, she was woken on her third night by the noise of the attack: 'I got up, and my windows at the Mount afforded me the means to see much more of this attack than I expected or desired.' When it was all over, she said everybody remained nervous: 'From this time, and for many nights after, we were constantly alarmed by shot firing, sometimes by the frigate mistaking the watch boats, sometimes from the enemy at Algezira.'[3]

Horsbrugh, and doubtless the rest of the military command on Gibraltar, could immediately see the advantages these gunboats gave to the Spaniards. They were small boats fitted with simple sails and banks of oars, each of which carried a 26-pounder cannon in the bow. Even in daytime, they were difficult to hit, but it was their manoeuvrability that made them so dangerous, being able to approach larger warships from directions where it was difficult to fire back, and they could escape by rowing into the wind, where sailing ships could not follow. Worst of all, they could fire on the southern parts of Gibraltar that were previously considered safe, being beyond the reach of the Spanish land batteries.

The intention of the gunboats on this occasion was to destroy the *Panther*, which had been Admiral Duff's flagship. Five days later, the *Panther* left quietly for England during the night. The

Spaniards did not believe it possible that such a large warship could slip past them unnoticed, and Mrs Green said that at about noon,

> a row galley came over from Algezira ... to look if the Panther was in the Mole, or if actually gone. It was universally believed that Admiral Barcelo was on board in disguise. They came by much too near and in a very insulting manner, paraded about. It was plain to be seen that a person in a fisherman dress was the whole time looking through a spy glass, as many of our officers were doing the same. He seemed to be making particular observations, sometimes standing up. This person was either Barcelo or some officer of trust. Our frigate and another vessel fired at the galley. She kept her colours up the whole time and when she had sufficiently amused herself, went off.[4]

The garrison had learned about the gunboats a week earlier from the crew of a vessel from Minorca, who said they were being constructed at Majorca and towed to Algeciras. Everybody expected more attacks, but Barcelo next deployed them to tighten the blockade. Their presence meant that boats with fresh food supplies had even more trouble breaking the blockade. Before the siege, a constant supply of livestock came in by sea from Morocco and elsewhere, along with other fresh produce. Households could then buy whatever food they needed on a daily basis, because perishable produce turned bad rapidly in Gibraltar's hot and humid environment. Writing just before the siege, the former resident Francis Carter said that although the climate was healthy, 'eight months in the year are disfigured with the levanters [easterlies] that blow in whirlwinds round the hill, obscure the sky with mists and clouds, and render the atmosphere heavy and insupportable; they cause such a dampness, that all the furniture mildews and rots, steel and iron utensils rust ... and no provisions will keep a day'.[5] These easterly winds could create unbearable conditions and spark violent storms, though the heavy rainfall did ensure a reasonable water supply, considering the absence of streams and rivers on Gibraltar.

Although wildlife was relatively abundant on the Rock, little mention is made of anyone trapping or shooting birds or other creatures for food. Drinkwater did say that game birds and wild rabbits were caught, but that 'garrison-orders ... forbid officers to shoot on the western side of the rock; but parties often go in boats around Europa point, to kill wild pigeons, which are numerous in the caves'. Some wildlife was less welcome: 'Moschetoes are exceedingly troublesome towards the close of summer; and locusts are sometimes found. The scorpion, centipedes, and other venomous reptiles, abound amongst the rocks and old buildings; and the harmless green lizard, and snake, are frequently caught by the soldiers, who, after drawing their teeth, treat them with every mark of fondness.'[6]

Carter described one unexpected species: 'On casting an eye up this barren hill, one would not imagine any living creature could exist upon it; yet it is inhabited by a numerous species, that occupy the tops of the highest rocks, and who may be said to be the true lords of the hill, whence neither Moors, Spaniards, nor English, have ever been able to dispossess them, I mean the monkies.' They could be a real nuisance, he explained: 'so little are they afraid of man, that often they declare war, and act in a hostile manner; not long ago, they had got a trick of throwing such a number of stones on our miners at work under the head of the rock, that they frequently obliged them to leave off and retire without their reach.'[7]

Starving people will eat virtually anything, but monkeys were perhaps too abhorrent, and in any case only soldiers on duty were allowed on the Upper Rock where they congregated. Monkeys were more likely to be a source of sport, which the Anglo-Dutch travel writer Richard Twiss observed on a visit just six years before the siege started: 'Many apes and monkies inhabit its caverns and precipices,' he said 'and are frequently shot.'[8] According to Drinkwater, they were certainly present during the siege: 'The hill is remarkable for the number of apes about its summit, which are said not to be found in any other part of Spain. They breed in inaccessible places, and frequently appear in large droves, with their young on their backs, on the western face of the hill. It is imagined they were originally brought from Barbary by the Moors, as a similar species inhabit Mons Abyla.'[9] These Barbary macaques have no tails and are often called apes, but are in fact the only free-ranging monkeys in Europe.

Morocco was Gibraltar's most valuable source of fresh supplies, and so it was extremely unsettling to hear that the emperor, Mahomed I, was being enticed into favouring Spain, his former enemy. On 11 July, information came by boat from Tangier that two garrison boats had been chased on shore there by the Spaniards and that the emperor 'winks at the hostilities committed by them and even countenances their depredations, by permitting the Spanish boats to seize our vessels coming into Tangier; several have been taken under the walls of the place'.[10]

A few days afterwards at Gibraltar, another night-time gunboat assault took place, which Ancell described: 'Between one and two o'clock this morning, the Spanish gun-boats began an attack upon our shipping. The fire was returned by us, but it is imagined without any effect, they being imperceptible to the eye, the flash of their guns being the only object we had to direct us.' Forty-eight hours later the gunboats were back: 'About two this morning, little wind, the enemy's gun-boats again attacked the shipping and garrison, without doing any particular damage, except rousing the wearied soldiery and timid inhabitants from their nightly slumbers.' Some hours later, a soldier deserted from the north front of the Rock, where he was working. After managing to climb down a ladder, he was seen running across the isthmus sands, and the fear was that 'there is not the least doubt but he will inform the enemy how far their shot reaches'.[11]

By now, the smallpox epidemic was almost over, after claiming many more victims in June and July, especially children. 'One only comfort', Mrs Green noted, 'is that the smallpox seems to be dying away. Indeed it was dreadful to hear the daily losses. More than 500 have died. The smallest number has been of soldiers, as there has not been more than 50 died, but their poor families are greatly thinned, and their grief is great at not having been allowed to innoculate. It might have saved the lives of scores, therefore it is a very great distress to think of this misfortune.'[12] In terms of saving Gibraltar and in saving more lives, Eliott's decision not to allow inoculation was sound, even though it caused immense sorrow.

If possible, their troubles worsened when, on 12 August, the *Dolphin* from Lisbon was taken, and there was more criticism of the navy's inactivity. One soldier wrote:

Early this morning, a brig from the westward was attacked, at the entrance of the Bay, by several Spanish cruisers. She fought them all, and made a running fight of it, till she got within long-gun-shot of Europa, when it fell a dead calm, and was boarded and towed off by the gun-boats and gallies. We know the vessel to be the Dolphin brig, Captain Grant, from Lisbon, with supplies for the garrison, belonging to the [merchant] house of Messrs. Moubray and McKellar. The loss of the vessel has chagrined us much, especially as it is the general opinion, she was lost for want of due assistance.[13]

Both merchants were from Scotland. Henry Moubray had lived on Gibraltar since 1762 and Donald Mackellar came three years later. Mrs Green was furious:

she was directly known to be a brig belonging to Merchant Mackellar, called the Dolphin. He has long expected her, is loaded with oils, sugars, etc. The same vessel had been a long time in Tangier harbour, has been fortunate enough to get in here with supplies. She now sailed in with a fine wind at the day break. Unluckily, it failed at half past 4. She made for Europa, their batteries fired and from Bonna Vista [Buena Vista], but not one shot hit the galleys. We fired our shot from the New Mole Head to encourage her. She came at last very near our guns and we flattered ourselves she was out of danger, as the small galleys seemed shy of our batteries.[14]

It was not to be, because two large row galleys from Ceuta suddenly appeared:

> This encouraged the others, so that to the universal concern
> of the whole garrison, they boarded her. She would not strike!
> I saw the whole manoeuvres from the instant she first came
> round, saw all her sails shot away, the grape shot flying all over
> her rigging. The last shot carried away her lower sails and
> yards, then it was easy to board her, and I plainly saw the first
> Spaniard get on board. It is impossible to express the discon-
> tent of the garrison on this occasion. The Enterprize was in
> the Mole, but everybody expected all the boats would have
> been armed and sent out, which if they had when the first
> signals were made from the point, it is beyond all doubt we
> should have got her safe in. It certainly is the most unpleas-
> ant circumstance that has happened to us and has occasioned
> many severe things to be said against our <u>Navy Folks</u>. No
> wonder.[15]

The badly damaged *Dolphin* was towed to Algeciras, and only
three days later the prisoners-of-war were returned, including
Cumberland Adams, also originally from Scotland, who was Mr
Mackellar's clerk and had been wounded in the wrist by grapeshot. 'Admiral Barcelo was exceedingly kind to them,' Mrs Green
noted, 'and at the same time expressed his wonder that our boats
had not been sent out. He made the captain a present of 70 cobbs
and told him, he was under the necessity of putting down in his
journal of what prizes was taken by them, [and] that this brig was
taken within gun shot of this garrison.' Among the passengers
were an officer of the 56th, the merchant Mr Hamilton, who was
the husband of the first woman to be injured, and Mrs Gray, her
sister-in-law, who Mrs Green described as 'a smart looking person
who says that Admiral Barcelo was exceedingly polite and kind
to her'. Mrs Gray also told her that there were letters on board for
the garrison, but they were kept, which added to the widespread
anguish.[16]

At the end of August, it was clear that the emperor of Morocco had been persuaded to lease Spain his ports, including Tangier, making Mrs Green very agitated: 'This morning a small boat with 5 men came over from Barbary, last from Tangier. They had no possibility of bringing any supplies, only a packet from our consul Mr Logie to the Governor, containing very unwelcome news, which is, that all communication between us and Barbary is stopped and in consequence, we cannot expect any supplies.'[17] Logie had written his letter over ten days before, warning Eliott that many vessels were being held at Tangier:

if the Emperor had sold his ports and the sea coast of his territories to our enemy, he ought first to have declared his intention, or ordered the British subjects to quit his dominions. The crews of all the boats taken, I am at the expense of subsisting and in a very short time the remaining crews of all the garrison boats and vessels will be destitute of money or credit to subsist with, which will oblige many to enter into the Enemy's service to prevent starving. The Enemy take all the Portuguese boats and vessels that attempt coming on this coast, so that excepting from Spain, no vessels are permitted to enter this port.[18]

He added: 'The Emperor gives no answers to the letters of complaints I write to him.'[19]

British ships could no longer even use the Moroccan ports for shelter, as Drinkwater explained:

a small boat arrived from Barbary, with information that the Moors permitted the Spaniards to capture every English vessel which took refuge under the protection of their guns; that the Spaniards would not allow any boats to leave the Bay of Tangier, and only waited for orders from Admiral Barcelo to burn and destroy what remained. This intelligence very sensibly affected us. To be cut off from what we had always considered our domestic market, was a stroke we little expected.[20]

The closest places that were now able to supply Gibraltar with fresh produce were Portuguese ports and the island of Minorca, and one soldier commented: 'The enemy now keep us blockaded closer than ever; there are not less than eight or ten armed vessels constantly under Cabrita Point, two or three at Tariffa, six or eight at and about Tangier, three or four at Tetuan, some at Ceuta, and, I believe, several off the Gut's Mouth; so that it is almost impossible for any vessels to escape ... When a sail appears standing for the Streights, signals are made at the watch-towers along the coast.'[21] These watchtowers or signal towers were originally constructed to give warnings when pirates from Barbary were spotted, and they still proved invaluable to the Spaniards.

With a bombardment seeming ever closer, William Green had a 'bombproof' with immensely thick stone walls built in the garden of his townhouse to protect his family from cannonballs and shells. Mrs Green described the structure when it was complete:

> The Colonel had a bomb proof begun in our house in town by digging under the garden and making an opening in the front courtyard, opposite the eating parlour. It will consist of three apartments, and it runs deep in, and in the further part, near to the coach house in the street, is an apartment with a window large enough for a man to get through, which may be very useful, in case of any quantity of rubbish should ever chance to fall into the front court. The top of this cave is covered over with hardened clay and done as is usual with bomb proofs. If it is never wanted as such, it will make most excellent cellars.[22]

The garrison defences were also improved, which pleased Ancell: 'Our Governor has made great additions to our fortifications; several new batteries have been erected upon the hill, and others planned out. Should the enemy not open [fire] till these are completed, we shall sing to the Dons, the old song of Defiance, and laugh at their approaches.'[23] While the defences and guns on the Rock were being upgraded, the Spaniards were systematically developing their own fortifications, and not everyone shared

Ancell's determination and resilience. In the extreme summer heat that August, many were finding it difficult to cope, and tempers of the soldiers became extremely frayed. The officers had more opportunity than the men to maintain some semblance of a normal life, and in mid-August Charles Mawhood, colonel of the 72nd Regiment, dined with Captain Phipps of the Royal Engineers, followed the next day by a dinner hosted by Colonel Picton and another at Major Fancourt's the day after that. Mrs Green also reported on a remarkable dinner that was hosted in part by Charles Ross, lieutenant-colonel of the 39th, 'he sending an English sheep to the Master of the Assembly House. 21 gentlemen. Very riotous.'[24]

The following day, the Greens also had a few gentlemen to dinner and a 'pretty large party in evening'.[25] The main meal of the day was dinner, which was eaten in the early afternoon, and years later Colonel Landmann wrote that 'three o'clock was the ordinary time for this meal; but on occasions of hard service it was postponed till four'.[26] Colonel Mawhood was not among the guests of the Greens, as he had been suddenly afflicted 'with a complaint in his bowels' and appeared dangerously ill. He was fifty years old and had been in Gibraltar for only a few months, having arrived with Rodney's convoy in January, two years after being appointed colonel of the newly raised 72nd Regiment, the Royal Manchester Volunteers. His lengthy military career had included service in America during the War of Independence, during which time he had been defeated by Washington's army at the Battle of Princeton in what was nevertheless called 'one of the most gallant exploits of the war'.[27]

On 23 August, it was reported that Mawhood was not expected to live. This was by far the hottest day, for which fires around the bay were blamed. 'Immense fires in Spain and Barbary occasioned by their burning the old grass,' Horsbrugh said, 'which affected the air so much that the thermometer rose to 93, and the evening was insupportably hot.' Spilsbury agreed: 'For these three days past great fogs in the mornings, and very hot afternoons; last night Apes Hill [Barbary] was on fire, and made this place so hot it was hardly bearable. The thermometer 92°.'[28] During these intolerable conditions, Mawhood clung on for several days, and on the 28th Mrs Green heard that, in a disturbed state of mind, he had twice tried to commit suicide:

This evening Doctor Baynes called and acquainted us of the very bad way Colonel Mawhood was in, and telling us it was not possible for him to hold out many hours. He had made two alarming attempts, proceeding it is supposed from delirium – one, of some nails; one of a bathing tub – everybody is concerned, as he was a man much esteemed in the world and quite a gentleman. He has not been well from the first of his coming to the Garrison in January.[29]

Luckily his suicide attempts failed, as he would have been denied a Christian burial. The very next day he died, and at night an autopsy was performed. Mrs Green learned the results: 'A mortification in his bowels had taken place, and likewise a stone as large as a pistol ball was found in his gall bladder. It was no wonder he had been long ill and oppressed. As the doctors agree, he could not have been in any health or spirits for a long time past.'[30] The gallstone was unlikely to have been the cause of his sudden deterioration, as it was probably too large (about half an inch) to enter the narrow duct from the gall-bladder to the bowel. Being unwell for several months was likely to have been due to twisting of the gut leading to the death of the tissues as the circulation was cut off, something that today can be dealt with by surgery. The toxic effect of the dead gut and loss of absorption of fluids and nutrients would have caused Mawhood to die.[31] His death is an extreme example of the range of medical problems they all might have suffered, with little prospect of treatment.

The next evening, Colonel Mawhood was laid to rest in the burial ground for officers, just outside the walls at Southport, where stones were placed on top of the graves to prevent them being washed away by violent winter rains.[32] Considering the siege conditions, there was surprisingly elaborate formality, but rather less ceremony than Mrs Green expected, especially as she felt that, for somebody of his status, he should have been buried inside the King's Chapel:

> The whole 72nd Regiment with their colours and arms as usual on such occasions. They formed a lane from the Colonel's house to let the corpse pass through. The Governor was chief mourner, his four aid de camps walking before him, and the Adjutant General and Quarter Master General on each side of the Governor. Every officer off duty in the garrison. Lt Gen de la Motte walked at the head of the brigade of Hanoverians. Pall bearers – Colonel Green, Colonel Picton, Colonel Godwin, Lt Col Cochrane, Lt Col Trigge, Lt Col Mackenzie, Lt Col Craig, Lt Col Kellet. All with crapes round their arms, and all the 72nd with crapes, which they wore about a fortnight afterwards … Capt Lesley [Leslie] of the *Enterprise* frigate paid a very handsome compliment to Colonel Mawhood's corpse, as he had minute guns fired from the time the body moved to its being buried, and all the King's vessels had their colours half-staff.[33]

Three weeks later, Mawhood's belongings were sold, which was a customary way of raising money for any widow and children. It took two days to complete the sale, and Mrs Green was amazed at the price everything fetched. 'It is astonishing how the books and any article sold,' she added, 'merely it would appear as if it was because they had been Colonel Mawhoods! NB The Governor and General Boyd had been allowed to take their first choice of books. The Governor also thought fit to take all the maps. They were good ones.'[34]

The day before Mawhood died, two young officers had attempted to settle a quarrel with a duel, out on the isthmus: 'Mr Stephens of 39th and Mr Johnson of 56th,' Mrs Green wrote, 'went out to the windmills in order to settle an idle business, merely the effects of their being young men. They were parted, and the affair is to be settled by commanding officers.' It was not settled, because the next day, 'The same two young gentlemen that went out yesterday went out again this morning, attended by seconds. Mr Stephens' pistol shot away three of Mr Johnson's waistcoat buttons and part of his shirt but did not hurt him.'[35] Another quarrel was to have far-reaching consequences. In the last few days when Mawhood clung to life, Lieutenant-Colonel Ross seemed set on destroying his own career. Barely forty-eight hours after hosting his magnificent dinner, he turned up to the 39th Regiment on the Grand Parade in a frenzied state, perhaps triggered by the violently hot weather. Mrs Green heard what happened:

> The Lt Col, Colonel Ross, went there under a visible agitation, and after the Regiment was drawn up, he asked if General Boyd as commanding officer of the 39th was upon the Parade. He was told not. He then ordered the articles to be read, after which to the surprize of everybody, addressed the officers and soldiers, talking first of the true meaning of those articles and afterwards attacking the Colonel of the 39th, calling him Bob Boyd, and the Regiment the Storekeepers Regiment, and said a vast deal tending to hurt General Boyd in the eyes of the men; and he also ordered the Adjutant [Horsbrugh] to tell the General all he had been saying! but as he declined it, one of the General's aid de camps did. It is supposed this will occasion much confusion.[36]

To denigrate a senior officer in front of the men was extraordinary, seditious behaviour, and Ross was placed under arrest by the very man he had insulted, Robert Boyd. A court-martial began on 29 August in front of Colonel Green as president and several other senior officers, and Mrs Green related what she had learned about the charge: 'It was that Colonel Ross had spoken disrespectfully of General Boyd at the head of the Regiment and had shewn an intention to hurt the general in the eyes of the officers and soldiers of the regiment, as his discourse tended to that purpose. I may not be exact as to the words, but the above is the substance. NB It was by everybody thought a very mild charge, all things considered.'[37]

Ross pleaded not guilty, and on the third day of the trial, she said, he tried to justify his behaviour:

> he did not mean to depreciate General Boyd 'but only to put him to his true standard, just as we do to good or base metal ...' The above and many other such like speeches he made. He very freely and openly confessed that he had said all and everything which had been mentioned by all General Boyd's evidences, such as having called the General 'Bob Boyd', for he knew the General was a man of humour and liked to be free with his superiors. Nor could he conceive any harm in calling the 39th the Storekeepers Regiment, as everybody knew General Boyd had been a storekeeper.[38]

Ross was found guilty and sentenced to a suspension of twelve months from rank and pay and banned from serving in the 39th Regiment. For a common soldier, the punishment would most likely have been a severe flogging, but officers were treated differently. The members of the court-martial were not happy when Eliott interfered and reduced the sentence to a suspension of three months. Ross remained steadfastly aggrieved and even considered the reduced punishment to be severe. 'So I hear do others in the Garrison,' added Mrs Green, 'but in general it is all those of a certain set who are partial to their country man.'[39] She was referring to the large number of officers who, like Ross, came from Scotland. Although her husband's mother was Scottish, his own birthplace was London, while she came from Portsmouth.

During the very hot summer of 1780, more rank-and-file soldiers made attempts to desert to the Spanish side, a few successfully, though others were caught, tried and punished, as on 8 September when 'A man of 39th received 300 lashes upon the Grand Parade this morning for attempting to desert. In the course of last night, 2 men of 56th deserted.' What the deserters failed to realise was that the Spanish camp was in a poor state, badly affected by illness and hunger, because it was proving so difficult to bring in provisions for the thousands of troops there, already more than twice the number on Gibraltar. The most recent deserters from Spain had said that 'They were very sickly in Camp, and all the hospitals at St Roque, Algaziras and all the adjacent villages full. Their bread bad and other provisions scarce, most of the wells being dried up. The cavalry much out of order, many of the horses dead.'[40]

The cattle roaming the Spanish hillsides at the start of the siege had long since disappeared, and Ancell lamented: 'O! how should we triumph to sweep their camp and coast of men and cruizers, that have so long prevented our receiving refreshing and agreeable supplies: We long to visit the Common, at the foot of St. Roque, to clear the ground of marquees, tents, huts and sheds, and to let nothing remain but the herbage for the cattle.'[41]

# CHAPTER TEN

—— ·◆· ——

# SCURVY

In September 1780 it looked as if Spain was close to starving Gibraltar into submission, because scurvy began to have a terrible effect. 'The blockade was,' Drinkwater said,

> if possible, more strict and vigilant than before. Chains of small cruisers were stationed across the Straits; at the entrance of the Bay; and on every side of the rock; and the late disagreeable intelligence from Tangier seemed now confirmed, by our having never heard from that quarter during the month. What little assistance we therefore received, came from Minorca, but the supplies from that place were so trifling, and sold at such enormous prices, that few were able to purchase them. We had not been favoured with a cargo of cattle for a long period, and the scurvy began to gain considerable ascendency over the efforts of our surgeons.[1]

The reasons for scurvy were not fully understood, nor the cure, and some believed that fresh meat was a solution. Newspapers frequently carried advertisements offering potions that claimed to cure all manner of ailments, including scurvy. In the same week that Drinkwater was expressing his concerns, a typical advertisement appeared in the *Stamford Mercury*:

DR. ANDERSON'S only genuine SCOTS PILLS are prepared by the sole Proprietor, JAMES INGLISH, at the Unicorn, No. 165, opposite the New Church in the Strand, London. More than 150 Years Experience has proved this Medicine to be extremely useful in Disorders of the Stomach and Bowels, particularly in Bilious and Dropsical Complaints, Indigestion, after hard Drinking, Surfeits, Want of Appetite or Sleep, Rheumatism, Gravel, and all Obstructions. Worms cannot breed in the Bodies of those who frequently take this Medicine. One or two Pills taken twice a Week, or oftener, will prevent the Scurvy. It will keep its Virtues many Years, and in all Climates; is therefore the best Medicine for Seafaring People.[2]

Scurvy was a non-infectious dietary disease caused by a deficiency of vitamin C. Just as deadly as smallpox, it was very much a disease of sailors confined on board ship, who had scant access to fresh fruit and vegetables – just like being on Gibraltar during the siege. Those succumbing to scurvy gradually experienced a lack of energy. The small blood vessels would weaken, causing haemorrhages in any part of the body. Bleeding often began around the hair follicles (particularly on arms and legs) and then the gums, followed by loose teeth, foul breath, constant pain in joints and muscles and the opening up of old wounds. Anyone with injuries, such as bruises and fractured bones, failed to recover. On the skin, haemorrhages caused purple patches to develop that eventually turned black, and patients became utterly weak and eventually died.

Drinkwater said that the condition of the soldiers was grim: 'The scurvy had made dreadful ravages in our hospitals, and more were daily confined. Many, however, unwilling to yield to the first attacks, persevered in their duty to its more advanced stages. It was therefore not uncommon at this period, to see men, who some months before were hale and equal to any fatigue, supporting themselves to their posts upon crutches, and even with that assistance scarcely able to move along.'[3] Andrew Cairncross, the surgeon of the 73rd Regiment, whose men had earlier been ravaged by typhus and smallpox, saw the scale of the problem:

The scurvy which attacked the Garrison of Gibraltar differed in no respect from that disease usually contracted by sailors in long voyages; and of which the immediate cause seemed to be the subsisting for a length of time upon salted provisions only, without a sufficient quantity of vegetables, or other acescent foods. The circumstance related in the voyage of that celebrated circum-navigator, the late Lord Anson, of consolidated fractures disuniting, and the callosity of the bone being perfectly dissolved, occurred frequently in our hospitals; and old sores and wounds opened anew from the nature of the disorder. Various antiscorbutics were used without success, such as acid of vitriol, sour crout, extract of malt, essence of spruce, &c ... Women and children were equally affected, nor were the officers exempted from this alarming distemper. It became almost general at the commencement of the winter season, owing to the cold and moisture.[4]

Mrs Upton was especially fearful for her baby daughter, who was born at the start of the siege: 'I was in continual dread of the scurvy; and my beloved Charlotte, who I have suckled for fifteen months past, will, I am much afraid, feel the effects of my unwholesome diet as long as she lives. Yet, what could I do? My husband's pay, though a lieutenant, would not purchase milk for my children! The "silken sons of ease" in England know not what the army have endured in Gibraltar!'[5] Several soldiers' wives made the difficult decision to return to England with their children, setting sail on board two transport ships in the darkness of the early hours of 26 September. Gun fire was heard, and a few days later the same vessels were seen being taken into Algeziras, after having been captured. One of the women was Mrs Elizabeth Gledstanes, wife of Colonel Gledstanes of the 72nd Regiment, who had himself gone home in June because of illness. The next day, her friend Mrs Green wrote:

We are now certain that it is the vessel with Mrs Gledstanes on board and another [vessel] ... Mrs Gledstanes, her 5 children &c was plainly seen through our glasses this morning, as the

Enemy was removing her from the ships. Everybody is greatly concerned for her. She took a letter from our Governor desiring if she should be taken, the Spaniards would forward her and family to Faro or to Lisbon, informing them that she was a field officer's wife who was gone to England on account of bad health. We all hope such a letter will lead Barcelo to shew proper attention to her and send her to Cadiz rather than back into this wretched garrison.[6]

The Gledstanes had married in about 1768, and Mrs Gledstanes had so far given birth to eight children – a daughter in Dublin in 1769, and the rest in Gibraltar from 1771, though the first three tragically died.[7] She was now returning home with Eliza aged eleven, Susanna aged five, George aged four, Charlotte aged two and one-year-old Ann. Mrs Green learned that two other transport vessels were taken the following night, with several officers on board, 'such as have of late sold out of the regiments in this garrison, in particular Mr Gregory of the 58th and Mr Cook of the 56th'.[8]

The capture of these transport vessels was a small incident compared to the huge capture of vessels that had occurred in early August, though Mrs Green only heard definite news at the end of September: 'A deserter came in this morning ... He brings a confirmation of the enemy having taken our West India convoy and that there are 59 [actually 55] vessels now in Cadiz. The men of war that was [escorting] the convoy are got away, we hear.'[9] French and Spanish warships from Cadiz under the command of Admiral Cordoba had intercepted a huge convoy sailing from England to the West Indies and America. Fifty-five out of sixty-three vessels were captured, with their cargoes and thousands of crew, though the five escorting warships commanded by Captain John Moutray escaped. For Britain, it was the greatest disaster of the American War of Independence so far.

The women, children and invalids from the captured transports that had sailed from Gibraltar were quickly returned to the garrison, but the seamen were kept, and Mrs Green was relieved to learn that 'Admiral Barcelo is exceedingly polite to Mrs Gledstanes'. She and her family were allowed to stay at Algeciras until an answer came from Madrid and were eventually permitted to go to Cadiz. One soldier commented on the seamen being kept: 'I do not think they act conformable to the spirit of their agreement with Admiral Rodney. By the last settlement, St. Roque [the headquarters] remained debtor to Gibraltar three hundred prisoners.' Ancell was perplexed: 'What the Spaniards mean by this is not known. If they mean to starve us into a surrender, they should send every man they take prisoner. For the more we have to maintain, the sooner will our provisions be consumed.'[10]

Incredibly, salt fish was still being distributed to soldiers, with the garrison orders for 8 October 1780 stating: 'The men to receive to-morrow, two pound of salt fish, one ditto of pork, and half a pound of beef', but Ancell thought that much of it was rotten, particularly the salt fish, while 'the wheat delivered to the troops is of no service, as the inside is destroyed by insects, and only the integument remaining'. Two weeks later, to the great relief of the garrison, the supply of salt fish finally ran out.[11]

Even so, Mrs Upton was surprised that the men were willing to accept the rations: 'Each man's allowance of meat was reduced to a pound and a half a week, and such meat! – the dogs in England would have turned from it in disgust! But it was not *all* in that *putrid* condition, for some of the pork was very good.' Mrs Green agreed: 'The beef is exceedingly bad, quite stinking. It seems to hurt everybody. The troops are far from well; and to a certainty are very weak and greatly fallen off in their strength and likewise in their spirits.' If the meat was cooked properly, they could have avoided being sick, but she was concerned that fuel was in short supply. 'The great want now seems firing [fuel]. There is plenty of flour thank God, but the wood is so scarce that the bakers are not allowed enough to bake as much as formerly. The poor women and children are round the bakers' doors every morning, in vain, waiting with their money. It is hard upon those people.'[12]

From late September, Mrs Green had also felt unwell once

more: 'Find I am growing much indisposed and am fearful it will
increase. Quite lame.' Two weeks later, she wrote: 'In the course
of last night I was taken violently ill, with a dreadful pain in my
leg, attended with a fever. Continued in bed all day', while the
next day she felt 'Worse than before, grew so bad that Dr Baynes
was obliged to bleed me on Saturday evening. Not able to be
taken out of bed.' Her condition deteriorated, and a few days
later, on 10 October, she was particularly low: 'My spirits exceedingly bad and not to be wondered. Disappointed in many things,
particularly Dr Baynes. NB I am totally left to myself now.'[13] She
was very loyal to her husband and yet gives the impression from
comments like these of being extremely unhappy.

Every small cargo that arrived was good news, and the day after,
the 11th, one cargo provided an almost miraculous remedy for
scurvy. While boats from Gibraltar were waiting in the thick fog
to escort two merchant vessels from Minorca into the bay, a large
Dutch convoy was seen approaching from the Mediterranean. One
Danish vessel, the *Vrow Helena*, sailed too close to the Rock and
was captured. Denmark was a member of the League of Armed
Neutrality, an alliance that had been formed with Russia and
Sweden to protect their neutral shipping during the American
War of Independence, particularly because Britain was trying to
prevent supplies from the Baltic reaching the rebels in America.
Dutch ships were the main carriers of this trade, and, two months
after the *Vrow Helena* was taken, in December, Britain declared
war on the Netherlands just before they too joined the Armed
Neutrality, so that their shipping could now be legally captured.
This left Portugal as Britain's only ally in Europe, so that Gibraltar
was very isolated.

Eliott purchased the cargo of the *Vrow Helena*, because it was
so valuable – oranges and lemons, as well as figs and raisins.
He then offered to sell it to various sections of the garrison, to
which Captain Patrick Leslie responded that he 'would be glad
to receive from the Danish fleet, for the use of the Naval department, including the Hospital, one hundred barrels of raisins, and
fifty chests of lemons and oranges, for which any settlement shall

be made, as you shall think proper to direct, for the amount of the same'.[14] High doses of vitamin C, especially from lemons, can stop the bleeding caused by scurvy within a day or two, and so, just when it looked as if the garrison would capitulate, this stroke of luck meant that the desperately sick rapidly recovered. Drinkwater was amazed: 'The salutary effects were almost instantaneous: in a few days, men who had been considered as irrecoverable, left their beds to congratulate their comrades on the prospect of once more becoming useful to their country.'[15]

Some lemon juice was preserved by mixing it with several gallons of brandy, but Surgeon Cairncross found that, as a medicine, it was not so effective. In his opinion, fresh lemons and oranges were much better in dealing with scurvy 'or when they could not be procured, the preserved juice in such quantities, from one, to four ounces *per diem*, as the patient could bear. Whilst the lemons were sound, from one to three were administered each day as circumstances directed. The juice given to those in the most malignant state, was sometimes diluted with sugar, wine or spirits; but the convalescents took it without dilution.'[16]

The month of October 1780 also brought a dramatic change in the operations of the besieging forces. For the first time, they began to extend their siegeworks forward into the isthmus. Over the past year, they had extensively remodelled and strengthened the forts and batteries along the Lines, as well as new positions all round the bay as far as Algeciras and Cabrita Point, protecting the rivers, landing stages and the camps. They had built artillery parks, magazines and camps, brought in vast amounts of artillery and ammunition, constructed bridges of boats over the Palmones and Guadaranque rivers and expended vast amounts of material and manpower into creating numerous trenches linking strategic points that acted as defensive positions and covered lines of communication. And yet virtually nothing had been done with all the menacing armament, making the garrison rather complacent about their preparations. As Drinkwater said, 'The Enemy's operations on the land side had been for many months so unimportant, as scarcely to merit our attention.'[17]

Now new plans were afoot, beginning in the early hours of 1 October, when the Spaniards set fire to the huts in the market gardens, as well as the wheel used to raise water from one of the wells. They also tried burning the wooden palisades of the barriers at Bayside and Lower Forbes by fixing strange combustible devices to the gates and fencing. The guards, Ancell explained, 'did not observe them, owing to the darkness of the night, and the roaring of the sea and wind', and Spilsbury said that it did not help that they were able to advance 'under cover of heaps of dung, rubbish, &c., that have been let to remain outside those outposts'.[18] The same darkness and noise concealed the activity of the Spanish working parties, and at daybreak it was a shock to discover that all their batteries on the Lines were manned and the guns were elevated, ready to fire. Overnight they had also constructed a substantial breastwork, or epaulement, forming a long mound about 700 yards in advance of their Lines, which Drinkwater described as 'about 30 yards in extent, of a simple construction, composed of chandeliers [wooden frames], fascines, and a few sand-bags ... erected near the windmill or tower on the neutral ground, distant about 1100 yards from our grand battery'.[19]

The next day, the Comte d'Estaing, a French general and admiral, was shown around the refurbished Lines by the Spanish general Don Alvarez, and, according to Drinkwater, 'They remained three quarters of an hour at Fort St. Barbara, viewing the rock with glasses.'[20] One deserter reported that several French regiments were expected to reinforce the Spanish army in the spring, 'though they flattered themselves at St. Roque that the garrison would be in their hands much sooner'. A few days later, Captain Burke, the town major, went out under a flag of truce into the neutral zone, heading towards the old tower which was the normal place for parleys, but the Spanish guards tried to stop him. In the end, they relented, and an officer came to receive his letter, 'but looked very sullen, not pleased with having their works examined'.[21] Burke reconnoitred as much as possible, but General Alvarez sent Eliott a message that in future all communication was to take place at sea. The neutral zone was no longer neutral, but an active war zone.

Over the next few months, between the Lines and Gibraltar, the Spanish work on the sand dunes of the isthmus was unrelenting, particularly at night and irrespective of the weather. Trenches were pushed across the neutral ground and gun batteries built, most notably a huge battery right by the old Mill Tower, which the garrison initially referred to as the Mill Battery or sometimes the Tower Battery, before finding out that the Spaniards had named it St Carlos battery.

From their new St Carlos fortifications, the Spanish soldiers kept firing on the Genoese gardeners, making it difficult for them to work in the market gardens. Until now, they had managed to keep up some cultivation. At the same time, the Spaniards kept raiding the gardens for cabbages and other greens, and Ancell complained that 'they have plundered the gardens every night of late, but now, in the most audacious manner, they come forward in the day time to gather vegetables'.[22] On one occasion, Horsbrugh saw that '25 men came out from the Mill Battery into the gardens and began to pull up and carry away the cabbages till dispersed by some grape [shot]', and soon after 'about a dozen men ... came forward to the middle garden and very coolly took away what greens they thought proper, and did not seem in the least intimidated at the fire of our marksmen from the Lines or the shells thrown at them from above'.[23] The Spanish troops were obviously too hungry to care about the risk.

Eliott eventually allowed the gardeners to use part of the Governor's Meadow, just beyond the inundation and much closer to the safety of the barriers at Landport. More effort was also made to create gardens on the Rock. 'Our barren rock yields but little,' Ancell said, 'but ... many have begun to convert the solid parts of the rock into kitchen gardens, which some have effected by raising walls one height above another, and filling the enclosed with earth. It will appear a scene of enchantment to Admiral Barcelo, when he beholds the face of the dry and barren Rock in a state of vegetation.' Drinkwater agreed, saying that their attempts at cultivating the Rock were 'crowned with tolerable success, especially during the winter months, at which time the produce was increased to be *almost* equal to the consumption. The supplies from the [market] gardens had indeed begun to fail for some time before; and we soon had little reason to regret their loss.'[24] Drinkwater may have been too optimistic, because by early November most regiments were again suffering from scurvy.

For well over a year the garrison had bombarded the Spanish Lines, attempting to stop their working parties from improving the fortifications. Now that the advance siegeworks were coming closer, they began a determined bombardment every single night, when most of the working parties operated. At times, damage to the fortifications could be seen the next day, though the number of casualties was uncertain, as they were generally removed before daybreak. Some men were definitely hit, Mrs Green explained: 'We know that some of our shot and shells have taken effect, as our people upon the high batteries frequently hear the groans of the enemy and likewise we have seen them, this very morning [2 November] carry away several wounded men upon hand barrows.' Her townhouse was near one of the gun batteries, and she found the constant firing intolerable: 'It now is become exceedingly uncomfortable, for as soon as it is dark, the enemy begins to work, and of course we begin to fire. Our house is just in the line of fire, and we are shook by every shot, particularly from the *Montague* [battery]. It absolutely shakes my bed with violence. I believe I may add with truth that there are hundreds [who] keep awake beside those on duty, and this is the case every night.'[25]

There was still no retaliatory fire from the Spaniards, apart from the hostile attacks of the gunboats. On many occasions, especially at night, the gunboats fired at the fishing boats, preventing them from going right out into the bay. This was especially hard on the inhabitants who depended on their catches, not being eligible for rations of salt provisions like the troops. The gunboats were particularly active in maintaining the blockade, and they also attempted to destroy the shipping at the New Mole, now and again firing into the town as well, which generated much fear. The garrison found it very difficult to deal with them, and one soldier was frustrated:

I wish we had eighteen or twenty gun-boats, carrying a twenty-four-pounder each, with thirty or forty men; two of these are equal to a frigate in calm weather. If we had a few of these, under an enterprising naval commander, we might have brought in abundance of supplies by seizing neutral vessels and saving many of our own that were taken. I am persuaded too, that with such boats we might cannonade the enemy's camp and enfilade their lines and chandelier, in calm nights, without any risk.[26]

On the morning of 12 November, a small boat was spotted close to the Barbary shore, but when three gunboats set out from Cabrita Point to intercept the vessel, she kept going until the batteries at Europa Point were reached, even though two xebecs fired broadsides. To Captain Price, the episode was heroic:

Captain McLorg ... in a polacca from London fought his way to Europa Point, though a whole swarm of the Enemy's gunboats and other wasps ranged in a chain to intercept him. The Enemy's round and grape shot from a very short distance galled him so severely that, encouraged by appearances, they prepared to board him, but he gave the boats so warm a reception with grape shot and small arms that he obliged them to desist, and the polacca soon after anchored off the new Mole, where the captain soon after was almost suffocated by a croud of admirers who flocked on board to congratulate and guzzle porter.[27]

Ancell said that 'she proves to be the *Young Sabine*, Captain McLorg, from London, in 18 days, with flour and other necessary articles, burthen 200 tons, and ten men. She was greatly damaged, and her sails almost torn to pieces, having received 29 shot which struck her in different parts during the action. She had only one man slightly wounded.'[28] Mrs Green noted that he could not even use all his guns, because he had only nine hands, including boys: 'We had the good fortune to get her safe into the New Mole. Great is the pleasure it affords us all ... Captain McLorg ... has brought a most welcome supply from England, consisting of salt beef and pork, flour, potatoes, sugar, butter, porter, bacon and hams &c, all for the merchants ... what makes this vessel more welcome is ... that it is the first we have had from England since the Hyaena frigate.'[29] The *Hyaena* had arrived in April, and then only with dispatches. The *Young Sabine*'s cargo was soon sold, and Ancell listed some of the prices the goods fetched, including barrels of flour, Cork butter, Gloucester cheese, hams, bacon, herrings, porter, rum, coals and candles. He complained that 'the buyers who retail them again make almost cent. per cent. You may therefore judge how those are situated who are obliged to purchase from the retailers.'[30] What gave them all great hope was the news brought by McLorg that a Grand Convoy was being prepared 'with all expedition', including fifteen thousand troops.

In mid-November, the gunboats came in close and attacked the New Mole area in an attempt to distract the garrison from a great deal of work being done that night on the advance siegeworks. They repeated the same tactic two nights later, but the *Enterprise* spotted the gunboats and made a signal, so that the navy ships fired first. Horsbrugh said that the gunboats responded:

> which, as well as we could judge from the flash of their guns and sound, kept nearly at the distance of two miles and directed their shot principally against the shipping, none of which they struck ... Orders were sent to cease firing from our batteries, unless the boats came nearer, so as they could have a distinct view of them, but before these orders reached the batteries, we had the misfortune to hear that one artilleryman was killed, four others and a soldier of the 12th regiment wounded, by the bursting of one of the Carron guns, a 32-pounder on the King's Bastion.[31]

The artilleryman's head was blown off and several pieces of the gun flew into the centre of the town, but did no further harm. The artillery guards were ordered to remain in readiness, watching for the gunboats, 'till the moon appeared over the Hill and enlightened the Bay'.[32]

Because of the gunboats, Eliott introduced a black-out: 'No lights to appear towards the Bay, in any house, barrack, guard-house, or other building, after seven o'clock at night.'[33] Over the next two nights, the gunboats tried firing again, but their shot fell short, and everyone agreed that they misjudged the distance because no lights were showing. On their next attempt, Horsbrugh thought the gunboats again seemed at a loss: 'Three of the enemy's gun boats paid us a visit at one in the morning, fired all ten shots in different directions, but without seeming to have any determined object, and as none of their shot reached us, neither the garrison nor shipping returned a single shot.' Instead, the upper batteries and Montague's fired their guns all through the night at the isthmus, though that did not prevent another substantial stage of construction: 'at day break we found that they had not been idle, for we then discovered that they had in the night begun a line of communication or approach from the west flank of the Well Battery across the glacis of the Lines, constructed on the surface with fascines, chandeliers, and sand bags, about 8 feet high and ten in breadth, covered in the front with sand'.[34]

It became increasingly difficult to stop the Spanish advance works, because greater protection was constructed for their working parties. 'The enemy have been so very busily employed for sometime past,' Horsbrugh commented, 'that it is said there have been reckoned to the amount of 700 mules employed on different services at the same time.' Mrs Green noted that 'It is now the full moon and we can discover all their motions. We know for a certainty that we have killed a great many of their mules, as we see them lay dead in the neutral ground, and it is not to be doubted but we have also killed men.'[35]

Several more soldiers and seamen tried to desert from Gibraltar to the Spanish side, perhaps because they appeared to have the upper hand, but some fell to their death down the sheer rock face on the eastern and northern sides of the promontory, as Ancell recorded: 'Last night, a soldier attempting to desert to the enemy from Middle-Hill Guard fell from the heights, and was smashed to pieces at the foot of the Rock. One would imagine it to be madness in a person to endeavour to escape that way, as the precipices of the rock are so steep that the very idea to a rational man would deter him from such a proceeding.'[36]

It was not always known what happened to the deserters, though corpses and skeletons were at times found, which Horsbrugh described: 'The body of the soldier of the 12th Regiment who deserted in the night of the 2nd inst was cast on shore opposite the Bomb house and suffered to lie exposed for the rest of the day in terrorem. The skeleton of a soldier supposed a deserter was found at the foot of the rock near to Boyd's quarry, so much broke to pieces and disfigured that there only remained the number on the buttons from which we could distinguish he belonged to the 72nd Regiment.' Mrs Green elaborated:

This morning a coat was first discovered, behind the Rock, belonging to the 72nd, with the remains of some very hard bread and cheese in his pockets; the coat torn all to rags. In the forenoon upon making a close search, the body of a man dreadfully broke to pieces was discovered. He had belonged to the 72nd and was dashed to pieces, it is now seen, in attempting to get away, with 2 others, near a year ago. It was always believed the three had got away safe, but the way this body was found makes it clear he had not been of the lucky ones in escaping.[37]

The days dragged on with no news about the promised convoy to raise the spirits of the people, and December 1780 was marked by appalling weather. There were violent storms at the outset and heavy rain throughout, and on the evening of the 2nd, Mrs Green wrote that

it began to rain very hard and directly came on the most violent storm of hail, rain and thunder that I ever remember, which continued about half an hour, and happy for this garrison it was, that it lasted no longer. As it was, it has done a great deal of harm. Several old houses thrown down and a vast quantity of rubbish came from the mountain. The whole garrison was full

of bustle and hurry. The Colonel was at the Convent when it
began, and could not get away till near 9 o'clock, for though the
violence of the storm was only of a short duration, yet it continued to pour with rain till near 11.[38]

The next morning, there was another torrential downpour, and
similar storms occurred intermittently throughout December,
leaving the Spanish fortifications and camps waterlogged and
destroying the bridge of boats over the Palmones river. Strong
easterly winds in mid-December also caused masses of sand to
drift across the isthmus, smothering the siegeworks.

In spite of the weather, the Spanish guns in the forward batteries looked as if they would soon be ready to hit targets much
further south than previously envisaged, and so even more
street surfaces were removed in early December. 'The Governor
has ordered the pavement of the streets to be dug up as far as
Southport,' Ancell wrote,

[and] one hundred and ten inhabitants (besides the soldiery)
are employed in this work, viz. sixty Roman Catholics, thirty
Jews, and twenty British; the stones are thrown over the line
wall. The intention of this is to prevent the havoc that would
ensue from the explosion of the enemy's shells whenever they
open from their batteries, as the weight with which they fall
buries them under the surface of the ground, and when they
burst, they scatter whatever is near them for seventy or eighty
yards around.[39]

Much more effort was being made to counter the effects of an
enemy attack, and artillery experiments were also happening all
the time. Howitzers had been set up on the Old Mole, and on 9
December they were tried out, which Mrs Green described:

In the forenoon, an experiment was tried from Old Mole to
throw shells from howitzers to the enemy's new battery. It
answered very well for the most part. One shell fell finally into

the front of their work and threw down some fascines, which they instantly repaired. The officer who appeared to command their party behaved remarkably well, with much seeming coolness and conduct and stood upon the front emplacement the whole time and seemed to encourage the men. Our captain upon the batteries was expected to have fired upon the enemy during their working, but did not! The Governor seemed to express a surprise at his not firing. However, it was amply made up by the constant fire to keep up all the evening and night, which it is not to be doubted, did greatly hinder their working.[40]

By late December, there was so much rain that it flooded the batteries at Willis's and even swept away one of the gunners, who broke his leg. Soon after, a cutter arrived after a fierce encounter with a vessel from Ceuta. 'She proves to be a King's Cutter, the Speedwell,' said Mrs Green, 'commanded by Lieutenant Gibson, from Portsmouth; brings dispatches for the Governor. Does not chuse to mention the exact time she has been from England, and the whole seems to be a profound secret.' Gibson was the only person wounded as the *Speedwell* fought off the Spanish ship, and he was brought to the naval hospital the next day. Mrs Green was frustrated by the lack of information, as she normally heard about everything:

all seems to remain a secret, therefore all manner of conjectures are forming as to what the cutter is come out for. It is most certain that it is on business of consequence. We also seem to understand that a frigate came out from England at the same [time]; there has not been one letter for anybody, for not one person on board knew of their destination when they were ordered at a moment's warning to go to sea from Spithead, and Lieutenant Gibson received positive orders not to open his instructions till he arrived at a certain latitude. This is the only King's vessel we have had since the Hyaena frigate in April last. There is not a man on board allowed to come on shore or to answer any questions that are asked of them.[41]

The frigate bringing duplicate dispatches was the *Brilliant*, which had not been seen. Unknown to Eliott, the British government had, for many months, been pursuing secret negotiations to make peace with Spain and even considered ceding Gibraltar and Minorca, but negotiations were going nowhere and would break down in January 1781.[42] One reason why Spain had not started the long-expected bombardment of Gibraltar was that they were hoping for a peace settlement in their favour. As the year progressed, the Spaniards felt more optimistic, buoyed up with the capture of the West Indies convoy, Morocco siding with Spain and the blockade of Gibraltar appearing to be working well.

Christmas Day turned out to be memorable, because, as Horsbrugh related, 'In the night a brig polacre in 30 days from Liverpool arrived and brings us a cargo consisting of flour, butter, cheese, potatoes, beef, pork, hams, white and red herrings, strong beer and a variety of other well chosen articles, on the account of Messieurs Anderson & Company.' Mrs Green said that the polacre had 'no less than 300 casks of flour, which is so much the greater blessing, as it is now openly owned that there is not more than three days flour for the inhabitants in this garrison. This vessel may be placed amongst some of the <u>God Sends</u> that we have experienced since the blockade and has put everybody into spirits.'[43]

Not everyone was happy. 'We are now beginning the year 1781,' wrote one soldier in despair. 'Heaven grant it may bring about a peace, and relieve us from this languid state of inaction and suspense, by a general humiliation of our enemies!'[44] Peace seemed a very remote prospect.

# CHAPTER ELEVEN

———— ·◆· ————

# DARBY'S CONVOY

On the first day of the new year, 1781, many letters were found on board a captured Spanish settee, and in one of them Horsbrugh discovered that 'They acknowledge to have lost some men every night since they began to advance, besides many wounded … Other letters mention that bomb ketches and more gun boats were daily expected from Carthagena; that they intend making more mortar batteries and another line of approach.' Mrs Green saw some of the letters: 'they gave no material account, mostly seemed private family letters, except a couple … but those letters were not signed. There were also some beads and a crucifix and other articles belonging to a priest, who had been too much hurried in getting away. These things are all in Captain Leslie's possession.'[1] Overall, the news was not good, suggesting continued efforts by the Spaniards, in spite of the numerous casualties suffered by the working parties.

There was some fleeting optimism, because carpenters started to erect stagings and temporary cranes, leading everyone to suspect that the *Speedwell* had brought news of an imminent convoy. These wooden structures were being set up well to the south of the New Mole, along the Line Wall and around Rosia and Camp Bays, so as to keep out of range of the new Spanish batteries, but no convoy came. Worse still, the last link with Morocco was severed, because at the end of December around 130 British citizens were expelled from there and handed over to Spain as prisoners-of-war, including the consul Charles Logie and his family. After being held at the Orange Grove, they were now sent to Gibraltar, adding more mouths for the garrison to feed. It was almost a year since Rodney's convoy, and food stocks were once again perilously low and expensive.

While the poorer civilians and rank-and-file were struggling, the higher-ranking families were still able to purchase enough food, albeit at great cost. On 4 January, Mrs Green noted: 'Auctions every day. Sometimes the several articles sold pretty well. The English rounds of beef are very good, but are got up to an amazing price, viz. 7 rials per pound, equal to 3 shillings.' The very next day, a lavish regimental dinner was held, and she heard the details: 'Colonel Ross gives a dinner to the whole of the officers of the 72nd regiment, supposing himself Colonel of that Regiment. It consisted of a very large number, 43. All ended with great harmony, they sat late. Many people wonder that the Colonel should take a step of this kind till he was quite confirmed in his having got the regiment. He is now in very high spirits and seems to have forgot all past circumstances.' During his three months of suspension from duty and pay, Ross had maintained a low profile, with Mrs Green mentioning him only once, in October: 'Colonel Ross was upon Grand Parade at guard mounting this morning for the first time since the court martial. He had his sword on, made several visits afterwards, called upon me in the forenoon; looks well but seems a little agitated.'[2]

Eliott was obviously keen not to lose Ross, because apart from reducing his sentence, he proposed moving him to the 72nd Regiment to replace the late Colonel Mawhood and therefore resolve the friction between him and Boyd. Two weeks before this dinner, the news that Ross had a different regiment was made public in garrison orders, even though formal ratification from London was needed: 'There being the strongest reasons to believe that Colonel Ross is appointed Colonel to the 72nd Regiment or Royal Manchester Volunteers, altho' no official notice has yet been received by the Governor, he is therefore only to do the duty of Colonel in the Garrison and no longer to act Lieutenant Colonel to the 39th Regiment, until further orders.'[3]

In spite of his terrible relationship with Boyd, Ross had many friends and admirers, including Mrs Upton, whose husband John was a lieutenant in the 72nd. To her, he was 'a plain, worthy character', and she published a celebratory poem, starting with a plea for the winds to hasten the arrival of his appointment:

*For once, Aeolus, hear a female Muse,*
*And be propitious—when a* Woman *sues!*
*O speed the Fleet from Britain to this Port,*
*Fill all their Sails, and waft them to this Fort;*
*They bring for Ross, whose Merits well demand*
*His Sov'reign's Mandate for a new Command.*
*Each* Volunteer *will glory to obey,*
*And dare the Foe, when Ross shall lead the Way.*[4]

No news of the promotion came, and eventually Ross had to return to England to sort matters out.

Mrs Upton was not so happy with the English newspapers. Because they reported that Gibraltar had plenty of supplies, she was incensed and complained that what was available was rotten or too expensive:

Four or five small brigs, at different times, got in from Minorca; but how inadequate were their small cargoes to supply so many thousands of people! Besides, what they brought, sold at such an enormous price that few subaltern officers could become purchasers. What ensign or lieutenant could afford to give three pounds twelve shillings for a turkey, two guineas for a pig, half a guinea for a duck, and nine shillings for a very small hen? Eggs were sold for two years past at a *real* a-piece which is almost sixpence English money; cabbages eight-pence a-piece ... old dried pease, one shilling and four-pence a pound; flour, a shilling a pound; Irish butter, half a crown a pound; very bad brown sugar, half a crown a pound; candles, that would not burn three-quarters of an hour, six-pence a piece; biscuits full of maggots, a shilling a pound; the worst tea that ever was used, sixteen shillings a pound; soap, one shilling and two-pence a pound; salt, that was more than half dirt and rubbish, eight-pence a pound; goat's milk, half of which was water, was eight-pence a pint. I have many times paid a shilling for a few herbs to put into my pease soup ... Many people kept pigs in the garrison, but the pork, which was fed on all the filth the place produced, never sold under two shillings a pound.[5]

One soldier thought there was little overall distress, except with the Jews 'who superstitiously abstain from all food that is unclean, viz. pork and salt-beef, which they might get now and then. This dressed up [cooked] with dry beans, rice &c. would keep them in spirits, whereas they are dejected.'[6] The soldier Walter Gordon worried more about the price of alcohol: 'Wine was the cheapest article at this time, being sold at six pence a bottle; the beer was at the exorbitant rate of one shilling and six pence a bottle.' He complained about the treatment of the rank-and-file: 'They who live in ease and affluence at home can form no idea of the hardships to which a common soldier is exposed in the time of war. But the situation of men reduced to such straits, and exposed to such continual toil and dangers, is beyond the powers of description. Did the rich and affluent only experience a little of the hardships of a siege ... it would teach them to feel for others, it would teach them how inhumane it is to treat a soldier with contempt.'[7]

Although an unexpectedly large number of vessels were getting into Gibraltar, Drinkwater made the point that this was of little use to those without money: 'The poor soldiers, and still more the inhabitants, whose finances would not allow them to purchase articles from the Minorquin vessels (the cargoes of which, by the way, were chiefly luxuries) were in intolerable distress.' One such vessel arrived on 19 February, and in a letter to his brother, Ancell sent him the latest news: 'This afternoon a brig arrived from Minorca in four days and a half, with flour, wine, sugar, and brandy ... She brings intelligence that the French had blockaded Minorca.'[8] The original pact between France and Spain included destroying Britain's ability to dominate the Mediterranean by

taking not just Gibraltar but also Minorca. While Gibraltar had
been under siege for a year and a half, French resources had been
helping the American colonies fight the British on the other side
of the Atlantic. A weak blockade of the harbour of Port Mahon
at Minorca was now established by the French navy, which was
effectively an extension of the blockade of Gibraltar by cutting off
an important source of supplies.

The brig from Minorca also brought a letter for Eliott that
had been written on 2 January by Captain Curtis of the 36-gun
frigate *Brilliant* – the warship that the garrison had expected
to arrive at the same time as the *Speedwell*. The son of a farmer
from Wiltshire, Roger Curtis was born in 1746 and was by now an
experienced naval officer who had served as flag captain under
Lord Howe. He explained to Eliott that he had left Portsmouth
with dispatches on 11 November and that duplicates were put on
board the *Speedwell* off the Lizard. The passage to Gibraltar was
plagued by bad weather, but on reaching the coast of Barbary on 1
December, the wind died down, forcing him to wait until the 20th
before he could enter the Straits:

> the wind being from the SW, I came into the Gut with the
> cutter in company. The ensuing night unhappily proved
> uncommonly rainy, dark, and unfavourable for our purpose;
> however, the Brilliant having got under Ape's Hill by midnight
> with the wind strong from the SW, I had the most flattering
> hopes of its continuing until daylight, or that it might be suf-
> ficiently clear during the night for running in for the Rock ...
> The cutter had ... my orders not to pay any attention to me,
> but use his utmost endeavour to get into Gibraltar. We saw him
> beat off a galley at the time I was embarrassed by the enemy's
> ships, and afterwards with a good breeze standing towards the
> Rock, so that I hope your Excellency has received from him the
> duplicates entrusted to my care.[9]

At four in the morning, Curtis said, the wind turned to the
north, and before too long he was becalmed,

when being a few miles to the eastward of Ceuta, I found myself very near two Spanish ships of war, with a third at a greater distance from me towards the Rock of Gibraltar. These ships coming up with me by means of a westerly breeze, one of them was within shot of me while I had not a breath of wind, having my oars out, and my boats ahead towing the ship. The Spaniard shortened sail too soon, and the breeze filling my sails ... I presently was out of his reach, though I was forced to cut adrift two of my boats ... Only one of their shot took effect, and that did no material injury. They continued chase till dark and neared me at the approach of night.[10]

Curtis hoped to have another chance of reaching the Rock the next morning, the 22nd, but the same two warships were spotted, still looking for him, and in the end he was forced to take shelter at Minorca. 'From the information I have collected here, and from my own experience of the Enemy,' he added, 'my return to Gibraltar at present is held impossible.'[11] Other small vessels that reached Gibraltar over the next month also reported that French frigates were closely watching Port Mahon, disrupting communication and supplies.

Unusually, supplies in the Spanish camp were abundant, according to the information brought by one Catalan deserter, who, on 8 February, ran from the Mill Battery (St Carlos) across the remaining gardens and into Landport. Horsbrugh was party to the information he brought:

He confirms the report of their being eight large mortars in the Mill Battery, which he says are kept constantly loaded ... The Guard for the battery consists of a captain, subaltern and forty of the Regiment of Catalonia, eight of the Artillery and sixteen assistants and twenty-four voluntarios de Arragon for the trenches. They have had about one hundred men killed and many more wounded in establishing this battery and the lines of approach to it. Provisions were plenty in camp, but the troops very sickly, and great numbers continued to desert into the country. Knows nothing of any new works being intended and at present they are only repairing the old. Reported in camp that three regiments were going to the West Indies.[12]

Since the new year, work on the Spanish fortifications had been directed towards repairing the constant ravages of the winter weather, with persistent heavy rain and high winds that were waterlogging and eroding the batteries and lines of communications. Huge numbers of mules had to be used to bring in clay to stabilise the embankments. Ominously, the Mill Battery with its mortars appeared to be ready, and the garrison had also observed trials being carried out with a new kind of gunboat – mortar boats, or bomb-boats. Drinkwater watched the first trial:

> some experiments were made at Algeziras, from two new Spanish boats, with mortars on board. We had some time before learned that they were preparing such vessels, and that they intended soon to try them against the Garrison. Their construction was upon a plan similar to that of the gun-boats. The mortars were fixed in a solid bed of timber, in the centre of the boat; and the only apparent distinction was that they had long prows, and braced their yards more athwart the boat when they fired.[13]

Because fewer Spanish working parties were in evidence, firing from the garrison was much reduced, providing a welcome respite from the thunder of the guns. Instead, many more artillery experiments were tried out. Thirteen-inch mortars were set up at sea level on the Old Mole and also, at the other extreme, high up on the Rock Guard battery. One of the trials was described by Horsbrugh: 'we fired two 13-inch shells from the Rock mortar, the first of which burst in the air and the second, which was intended for the Mill Battery, fell short in the gardens. This mortar ... being placed on the summit of the Rock has a most extensive command [and] can be turned to any point, and easily worked by two men, and is probably the most elevated situation of any mortar in the world.'[14]

In March 1781 Ancell summarised the circumstances of everyone creatively applying their minds to slaughtering the enemy:

Art and Ingenuity are with us so perverted from all benevolent exertions that one would be induced to suppose from the
destructive nature of our experiments that the ruin of man was
the sole purpose of their efforts ... Quadrants, spirit-levels,
and instruments of various forms and machinery ... adorn the
batteries for the more exact and certain method of killing.
Everyone seems anxious to find out the safest, quickest, and
surest method of dispatch in the elevation and depression of the
ordnance. I suppose in a few weeks more practice, they will be
so expert in levelling a gun that should a Spaniard raise his head
above the epaulement, it will be immediately severed from his
shoulders; for such an emulative spirit has dispersed itself to
such a pitch among our artists that almost every day produces
some new contrivance for the promotion of slaughter![15]

While some were devising new methods of killing, others were
giving up altogether, and a spate of desertions into Spain occurred
in the first part of 1781, reflecting the anxiety and mood of some
of the soldiers. They included a string of Hanoverian deserters,
the first one in early January: 'In the evening one of the marksmen belonging to General La Motte's Regiment skulked behind
the party on the Queen's Line, from whence he let himself down
by a rope and got off before he was missed by the Corporal who
commanded the party.' At the end of the month, Mrs Green
commented: '2 more men of Hardenbergs deserted last night.
This makes four this week.' Only two days later, two more men
deserted from the same regiment.[16]

Three regiments of Hanoverian troops were based at Gibraltar,
and, unlike the British army troops, these regiments were named,
not numbered – La Motte's, Hardenberg's (which later became
Sydow's) and Reden's.[17] They tended to have a high reputation for
discipline and work, though Horsbrugh was lukewarm when they
first came to Gibraltar five years earlier:

From the trial we have had of the Hanoverian Regiments on
duty here, I may venture to say we carried our ideas of German
troops and their discipline too far. We expected to see them
in the highest order and dress, but this [is] by no means the
case. They are indeed a fine body of men, and in this respect
we must acknowledge their superiority, but when we come to
compare their dress, discipline and other requisite qualities as
soldiers, we cannot help giving the preference to the British
troops. To make amends for their awkwardness, they have
hitherto been very sober, orderly, obedient and attentive, and I
make no doubt will do their business well if called upon.[18]

Men of other regiments also deserted, some in desperate circumstances, and in late January Captain Price tersely reported:
'This morning about 6 o'clock Serjeant John Abercromby of my
company [56th] deserted off his post at Lower Forbes's to the
Enemy.' He was shot at by the sentries and possibly wounded,
because his progress was slow and faltering. Another soldier said
that he 'bore an excellent character, was paymaster to the company, and lately kept a mess for officers; but getting into debt,
was drove to commit that desperate act. He has left behind him a
wife and two children.' A few days later, information was received
that he hanged himself in the Spanish camp the very night he
arrived.[19]

Other soldiers resorted to theft to sort out their problems,
though the level of reported criminality in Gibraltar seems
remarkably small at this stage considering that there were thousands of soldiers. In mid-March, three men also from the 56th
were arrested for robbing a winehouse in Irish Town of about a
thousand cobs. A week later one of them turned King's Evidence,
revealing where he had hidden his share of the loot, so that only
his two comrades, George Hornsby and John Fullingford, were
tried before a General Court Martial. Being found guilty, they
were sentenced to be executed. Quite often, Eliott would intervene and pardon the culprits, but both men were hanged the very
next day.[20]

Officers rarely resorted to desertion or crime to solve their problems, though they were not immune from hardship, and many of
them banded together to present Eliott with a petition, which they
asked him to forward to the king. It stated that their pay would
no longer cover their expenses, because of the exorbitant rate of
exchange and the high cost of everything. They also put the case
that younger officers at home were being promoted, while they
were overlooked. No response was ever received, though when
Boyd submitted a duplicate of the petition to London on behalf
of his own regiment, the 39th, he was told that 'General Eliott has
not transmitted to me any papers on the subject from the other
regiments at Gibraltar and unless matters of this kind are recommended by the Commander in Chief of the Garrison, you must be
sensible that they cannot be taken into consideration.'[21]

One strange incident concerning officers had occurred many
weeks earlier, when Spilsbury noted that 'The officers riot a little,
and break the Jews' doors and windows', though it was overlooked
by everyone else. In mid-March, he recorded another affair:
'Three officers of the 12th Regiment paid smart money, about 30
guineas, for beating and abusing a Jew.'[22] On this occasion, Mrs
Green gave more information: 'Much talk of the bad behaviour of
these officers of the 12th Regiment relating to a Jew in refusing to
pay their debts and ill treatment to the man, &c.'[23] So serious was
the offence that she had expected them to be court-martialled on
the same day as the two men from the 56th, but to her surprise
everything was settled beforehand:

Some papers are to be read tomorrow by the commanding
officers to their respective corps concerning those three young
officers of the 12th and their behaviour to the 2 Jews ... the
offence was of a very serious nature, particularly of one of the
officers, who had sold his provisions more than a year ago to
the Jew, for which he received money down, and the man was
to have the provisions, but he has never been able to draw
them from the Victualling Office, owing to our present circumstances. He therefore wanted his money back, of course, but

instead of that was frequently ill used whenever he made any demand, and it was carried so high as to shut him up and fire – though only with powder – a pistol at him. This disagreeable business ... ended thus quietly, owing to the mildness of the Colonel of the Regiment [Picton] and the Governor. The 2 Jews received the full money and double interest for the time, as he made it appear he could have gained many advantages had he been possessed of the money, and those officers gave ten guineas each to the Jew. It is hoped that this will have a proper effect upon the unthinking young men who make a custom of ill using any tradesman who asks for their money.[24]

Spilsbury was surprised: 'It is the first time they have found protection in this place',[25] but Eliott understood that ill-treating merchants would deter them from bringing in much-needed supplies for the besieged garrison.

Provisions were by now very bad, and Ancell said that 'most of the salt meat is quite rotten, the very smell of it is sufficient for a meal'.[26] Mrs Upton said that flour and fuel for baking bread were extremely scarce:

By this time the stock of flour the bakers had in hand was nearly consumed; a small quantity was baked, and sold at seven o'clock in a morning at one particular place; a guard was obliged to be kept at the door, to keep the people from tearing each other to pieces! A handkerchief was thrown in at the window with the money in it, and no person was suffered to purchase two loaves; these weighed about a pound, and cost five-pence. Happy were they who could get one, for the inhabitants who had no flour left, and officers who had children were in a deplorable situation indeed![27]

According to Thomas Cranfield, who was now promoted to corporal, 'On these occasions a scene of indescribable confusion generally occurred, as several persons would claim the same handkerchief, and violently fight and scramble for its possession.'

In a memoir written by his son, Corporal Cranfield was described as a tall, stout and commanding figure, but during the siege 'was reduced, through scarcity, to a short allowance of provision, and very little could be bought among the inhabitants. Frequently he has been compelled by hunger to eat the flesh of cats and dogs; and even rats have at times afforded him a welcome repast.'[28] Mrs Upton could not bear to witness the dreadful suffering:

I cannot now recollect the distress of a poor woman, without feeling a pang at my heart which gives me a sensible uneasiness. She sat weeping at my door with two children, the one about seven years old, the other an infant which she suckled:– after the former had repeatedly asked her for bread, she laid down her youngest child, and gave her breast to her other son, saying, *Suck me to death at once!* Gracious GOD! how much did I wish, either for the power to relieve her misery, or to be a stranger to the soft pleadings of humanity! However, I desired her to come into my apartment, and gave her part of my own breakfast, though I knew not what to do for bread for the next meal![29]

When a brig tried to reach Gibraltar at the end of March, it was captured by the Spaniards, though the nine crew members managed to escape in a boat. Because he lived on army-issued supplies, Ancell took a close interest in the garrison's stores and the cost of buying food to supplement his rations. He thought that what the crew managed to salvage from their cargo would cover their costs in the short term: 'They brought some poultry in their boat, which will afford them a present supply. The fowls sold for four dollars each, equal to twelve shillings and nine-pence; pigeons, three dollars per couple, equal to nine shillings and seven-pence; ducks, eight dollars four rials per couple, equal to one pound six-shillings and six-pence.' The brig's crew also brought information, but it was bleak – 'the British fleet had twice put to sea, but was forced to return, owing to bad weather, and contrary winds'.[30] Even so, there remained a desperate hope that help would appear soon, and a few days later the longed-for news came, as Ancell witnessed:

The garrison are noisy with tumultuous joy, occasioned by the arrival of a cutter last night from the West. She brings the captivating and enlivening intelligence of the British fleet, for the relief of the garrison, being on their passage. We seem to be another people – no depression of spirits, every countenance is adorned with satisfactory smiles, a social greeting of friends and acquaintances, congratulatory of the happiness about to be experienced.[31]

Two Spanish fireships had just been moved to Cabrita Point from Algeciras, and it was decided to remove this potential hazard so as to prevent them targeting the convoy vessels. Ancell described how a force set out across the bay: 'This evening four armed boats, composed of a detachment of five men from each regiment, under the command of a naval officer, proceeded from the New Mole on an expedition to cut out the two fire-ships which lay at anchor under Cabritta.' Success depended on surprise, but after a promising start their luck ran out: 'It continued rainy and cloudy till they had got within a mile of them, when, on a sudden, the clouds dispersed, and Luna reflected so great a light, that they were under the necessity of returning without accomplishing the business, the enemy having discovered the boats.'[32] In the darkness of a late winter night, the sudden moonlight betrayed the position of the boats long before they were near the fireships, but according to Mrs Green, recriminations later flew back and forth: 'They all came back about three in the morning, not quite so pleasantly, because at their return, everyone concerned seemed to blame each other.'[33]

Although snippets of information about the convoy continued to arrive, definite news was lacking and hope was fading, when suddenly on 11 April the watchtowers along the Spanish coast, out towards the Atlantic, sprang into life, as one soldier witnessed: 'This afternoon two Spanish watch-boats appear from the west, sailing and rowing as fast as they can. Everything seems to be in agitation on the Spanish side; numbers of signals repeating at the towers. Surely our fleet is very near the Streights!'[34] At around midnight, Ancell said that one ship managed to slip into Gibraltar: 'arrived off the Mole Head, the *Kite* cutter. She being challenged by the officer of the Mole guard loudly answered, "From the fleet," which immediately spread like wild-fire through the garrison ... slumber was forgotten; each found sufficient employ and satisfaction in conversing on the interesting subject.'[35]

The convoy was under the protection of the Channel Fleet, which was now commanded by Vice-Admiral George Darby. After a long period of unemployment, he had served in the Channel Fleet under Sir Charles Hardy who was in charge during the crisis weeks of the attempted Franco-Spanish invasion. When Hardy died in May 1780, the command passed to Vice-Admiral Sir Francis Geary, but ill health forced him to resign a few months later. The sixty-year-old Darby then took up the post, and through the winter months of 1780 and into January 1781 his ships were blockading the port of Brest in order to prevent a mass of French warships from sailing. On receiving orders to take a relief convoy to Gibraltar, Darby returned to Portsmouth with the Channel Fleet for repairs and supplies. Realising the blockade was lifted, the French commander, Vice-Admiral Comte de Grasse, was able to slip away from Brest unseen and head for the West Indies and America with twenty battleships, other warships and a large convoy of supplies and troop reinforcements. This French fleet would be the deciding factor in forcing the capitulation of the army under Lord Cornwallis at Yorktown later in the year. While Darby's convoy sailed to save Gibraltar, across the Atlantic Britain lost America.

It took nearly six weeks to prepare the fleet at Portsmouth, and it finally sailed in mid-March. Escorting the large convoy of supply ships were twenty-nine battleships and a collection of smaller warships, led by Darby's flagship, the 100-gun *Britannia*. Among the other large battleships were several from Rodney's relief convoy the previous year, including the *Royal George*, the flagship of Sir

John Lockhart Ross, and the *Prince George*, the flagship of Robert Digby, with Prince William still serving on board as a midshipman. The fleet did not head straight for Gibraltar, but to Cork in Ireland to collect more victuallers, and they were then delayed for another ten days by adverse winds before finally heading for the Mediterranean.

There was a particularly strong naval escort because it was assumed that the Spaniards would make every effort to take the convoy. On 31 March, off Cape Finisterre on the north-west coast of Spain, Sir John Ross in the *Royal George* sent a letter ahead to Eliott, predicting a major battle: 'what is to become of the fleet, [I] cannot at present say ... we are to meet 82 sail of the Spanish fleet off Cape St. Vincent. Inclosed I send you our line of battle, and hope we shall give a good account of them. We left Spithead on the 13th. The convoy from Cork joined us on the 27th.'[36] When George III heard about the likelihood of a battle, he wrote to Lord Sandwich at the Admiralty that he was 'very sanguine that an engagement will ensue between Vice-Admiral Darby and the Spaniards off St. Vincent. I know the justice of our cause; I know the excellence of our fleet; therefore have reason to expect success. Perhaps no country ever had, except near home, an event on which so much depends.'[37] The plan was for the 60-gun battleship HMS *Medway* to continue to Gibraltar with the convoy, carrying dispatches and letters, while the other warships engaged in battle, but, contrary to expectations, the Spanish ships under Cordoba did not stir from Cadiz, and the British fleet had an uneventful voyage to the Rock.

The siege of Gibraltar had so far lasted nearly two years, and although there had been relatively few injuries, the physical and mental health of the soldiers and civilians was greatly affected. Their main enemies were hunger and disease, along with unremitting fear and all the tensions that came from the constant struggle to survive. With the convoy approaching, their suffering now seemed almost at an end. Few people went to bed that night, and many waited excitedly on the quayside. When daylight came, Drinkwater was among those onlookers:

At day-break, on the 12th of April, the much-expected fleet ...
was in sight from our signal-house [top of the Rock], but was
not discernible from below, being obscured by a thick mist in
the Gut. As the sun, however, became more powerful, the fog
gradually rose, like the curtain of a vast theatre, discovering to
the anxious Garrison one of the most beautiful and pleasing
scenes it is possible to conceive. The Convoy, consisting of near
a hundred vessels, were in a compact body, led by several men
of war ... whilst the majority of the line-of-battle ships lay-to
under the Barbary shore, having orders not to enter the Bay, lest
the Enemy should molest them with their fire-ships.[38]

Suddenly, the convoy was attacked by Spanish gunboats in
a well-coordinated plan that was completely unexpected, as
Drinkwater described: 'fifteen gun-boats advanced from Algeziras,
and, forming in regular order under the batteries at Cabritta-point,
began a smart cannonade on the nearest ships, seconded by the
gun and mortar batteries on land. A line-of-battle ship and two
frigates, however, soon obliged them to a precipitate retreat, and,
continuing to pursue them, the crews of several deserted their
boats, and took refuge amongst the rocks.' Considering that the
gunboats would later cause significant damage in the south of
Gibraltar, Drinkwater regretted that Darby's warships did not
attempt to destroy them: 'Had our ships advanced at this critical
juncture, and manned their boats, the whole might probably have
been destroyed, and the Garrison by that means been rid of those
disagreeable neighbours, which afterwards so annoyed us, but the
frigates having dispersed them, thought no more of the *bum-boats*,
as some Naval officers contemptuously called them, and left them
to be repossessed by the fugitives.'[39]

By mid-morning the first of the merchant ships anchored off the
New Mole and Rosia Bay, beyond the reach of the new Spanish
batteries on the isthmus. The cargoes of the long-awaited convoy
began to be unloaded, but not everyone was on the quayside
to welcome the fleet. As the unloading began, in the Roman
Catholic Spanish church Father Messa was conducting a service,

but the building rapidly emptied when 'the Spanish batteries began firing so fiercely that it caused a great panic in all of us, especially the inhabitants of so many nationalities in the city. So that mothers grabbed their younger children in their arms and dragged the others, made their way, crying, away from the imminent danger towards the South Port; the fathers did the same, taking nothing with them apart from what they were wearing.'[40] At the same time, Ancell was writing to his brother, giving a running commentary about the general rejoicing at the arrival of the convoy, but he was forced to finish his letter in a hurry: 'One ship has just dropt anchor. A call to arms prevents my further writing. The enemy have opened all their batteries on the town; confusion and consternation are everywhere to be seen! – Adieu, dear brother, I must hasten to the alarm post.'[41]

# CHAPTER TWELVE

———·◆·———

# BOMBARDMENT

The fateful morning of Thursday 12 April 1781 would be remembered not just for the arrival of Darby's convoy, but also as the start of the Spanish bombardment that had been expected for months. Cannons and mortars unleashed a barrage of exploding shells and solid cannonballs on Gibraltar's military and civilian targets, fired from all the Spanish batteries and forts along the Lines and across the isthmus. This lethal attack was coordinated and well planned, and although private letters had recently warned of a likely attack if another relief convoy appeared, Drinkwater admitted that 'the truth of this intelligence was doubted, it being conceived that no beneficial consequences could arise to them from such a cruel proceeding'.[1] Nobody imagined that the Spaniards, in their obsession to regain the Rock, would attempt to obliterate soldier and civilian alike with such a degree of ferocity, death and destruction.

Panic-stricken, most people fled southwards to escape the Spanish guns: 'The inhabitants exhibit the most impetuous grief and apprehension,' Ancell said, 'precipitately retreating to the southward of the rock for shelter, crowding upon each other like flocks of sheep destined for the slaughter-house, with dread and ghastly amazement pictured on their countenance.'[2] The only way out of the walled town to the south was through the narrow gate at Southport, but the sheer numbers pushing through made everyone's escape slow. Father Messa resolutely continued with

the service in the Spanish church, even though most of his parishioners had gone: 'I was celebrating the service of the Last Supper
and was singing the High Mass, being left almost on my own in
the church; nevertheless, I was able to finish the sacred ceremony
of that day with high spirits and remained calm in the company of
a few devout parishioners.'[3]

Mrs Upton's house at the north end of the town was one of the
most vulnerable, and in terror she seized her two young children
and rushed with their servant along the covered way towards
Montague's Bastion, the closest bombproof fortification. Here
they took shelter with scores of off-duty soldiers in their barracks,
who cheerily declared: 'Never fear, Madam; if the damned Dons
fire to eternity, they will never take the old rock, nor the good
souls that are upon it; and if General Eliott would let us sally out
at Landport Gate, my life to a farthing we would lay the Spanish
camp in ashes.' Montague's Bastion was the very fortification
whose artillery firing had recently kept Mrs Green awake at night,
and now Mrs Upton was directly below the artillery platforms:
'My head was almost distracted with the noise of so many cannon
being fired from the top of the building where I had taken shelter.'
She was very relieved when Lieutenant Upton appeared:

> I had the happiness ... of seeing my husband enter the place;
> luckily for me, he was not on duty that or the day following:
> he procured a curtain, and hung it round one of the soldiers'
> beds for me. I laid down in my clothes, but sleep was out of
> the question; the bursting of shells, and the terrifying sound
> of cannon balls, were sufficient to keep me awake; add to this,
> the disagreeableness of lying amongst near an hundred private
> soldiers: Yet I was thankful to find admittance even here, for
> none know what they will submit to in order to save their lives,
> till they are tried with the near prospect of approaching death.[4]

According to Captain Horsbrugh, the Spanish guns that day
fired cannonballs at the lower military targets at the north end
of the Rock, including the Grand Battery and Landport, with

some reaching as far as the Convent in the town, while shells were aimed at the upper batteries, which also landed in the town. Some shells even reached Southport, while those fired from the St Carlos battery covered the greatest distance, occasionally as far as the New Mole, close to where the supplies were being unloaded. 'It was not imagined that the enemy's shot and shells from their Lines would have reached so far as we find they do,' Horbrugh admitted, 'which has obliged us to make some fresh and unexpected alterations in our arrangements.'[5]

After almost three hours, at around two in the afternoon, the Spaniards ceased their artillery assault for a siesta, but resumed their work two hours later. Captain Price recorded that 'Dinning of Major Hallow's [John Hallowes] company had his head taken off by a cannon shot in his barracks – the first man killed in the garrison.'[6] Men had been killed through accidents, but this was the first soldier killed by incoming shot, and he belonged to the same regiment as Price, the 56th. Corporal Cranfield of the 39th later wrote of his terror: 'I shall never forget the day the Spaniards commenced firing ... I was on duty at the southernmost part of the garrison. Never having heard the whistling of a cannon-shot before, I was filled with horror beyond expression. My old sins, and the roaring of the cannon, produced a very hell in my soul. My regiment lay in barracks in the town; I dreaded to go near them, but duty called, and I was compelled to obey. Paleness was in every face.'[7] Captain George Mackay, who was Eliott's steward, summed it up: 'the Spaniards opened all their batteries on us; they kept up such a shower of shot and shells flying that it appeared impossible for a bird to fly over us unhurt'.[8]

Even though it was Holy Week, the devout Spaniards were not deterred from attacking the British garrison. After conducting the service, Father Messa left his church and returned for a short while to his house in nearby College Lane:

I returned home in order to have some refreshments and later, together with my household, I went to take refuge in the church together with some others, although in fact there were very few devotees, and we sang Matins. However, gradually, they all departed just leaving me and my sacristan, Juan Moreno, and those of my household on our own and there we remained on this most solemn and terrible day, all through the night with His Divine Majesty exposed until 8 o'clock of the following day, which was Good Friday.[9]

Some weeks earlier, Messa had stored many of his household items in the church for safekeeping: 'I was assured by the elders who had experienced the previous siege that the shots and bombs could not reach up to our church. I therefore put all my confidence in the shelter provided by the church, and there I stored some of my more fragile furniture, such as mirrors and pictures, with the hope of being able to transfer the remainder.'[10] The church had so far been spared, but Mrs Upton's house was much closer to the Spanish guns, and when her servant went back in the morning to fetch some clothing, he found a scene of devastation. While there, another shell burst into the kitchen, narrowly missing him but wrecking the house even more. Father Messa, his sister's family and the sacristan were still sheltering in the church: 'a shell came in and hit the floor about two yards away from us. We were so shocked that two gentlemen who had come in to check whether we were alive and well, having observed the blow of the shell, run away without even taking their leave. At that point, pitying the tearful pleas of my sister, the sobbing of my nephews and nieces, who were all so young ... I decided to cut short the celebrations of the sacred ceremonies of the Good Friday.'[11] Much of the silverware was moved into the sacristy, and Messa left the church in the care of Moreno, his sacristan.

By the next day, Easter Saturday, the shells were setting fire to buildings, but at times they failed to explode, giving the garrison a perilous chance to investigate the mixture of gunpowder and flammable material by withdrawing the fuse. With all the dangers, Father Messa decided to return to the church to protect more of the holy objects:

the sacristan and I quickly removed the ciborium with the consecrated Hosts, the reserved Blessed Sacrament and the Holy Oils for the sick and those for baptisms. And leaving the silver objects locked up in the sacristy and others in boxes and chests and several set up with their respective images, the bombardment became so intolerable that the church had to be left completely unattended, apart from an old sick Genoese who stayed behind in order to look after the building, which decision distressed me terribly.[12]

Everything was taken to the hut of another inhabitant: 'There, with tears in my eyes, which I could not stem, I placed the sacred container on a presentable mahogany table, covered with very clean altar cloths. It remained there continuously lit by a lamp, being our best companion day and night until we were able to construct a small shed in a safer location.'[13] During that same day's bombardment, Mrs Upton was ordered to go with the soldiers of the 72nd Regiment as far as the formidable King's Bastion, which was close to the Spanish church, but she could barely move with fright:

I was, if possible, more terrified than before, for I had a much longer way to go, and the Spaniards were firing from all their batteries. To the latest period of my life shall I remember with anguish that dreadful walk! Sometimes I stopt, and I thought I might as well resign myself to die, and with my quivering lips begged of heaven to admit me into its divine abodes! But when I looked on my children, I started up and dragged them forwards, not knowing what I did. Our servant and two soldiers who were with me said all they could to comfort and encourage me.[14]

The removal of the stone surfaces of the streets must have made the journey more difficult, but Mrs Upton reached the King's Bastion safely. She was shown a space to rest, but the room 'smelt very disagreeably; I enquired the cause, and was told, a

man was killed in it, not an hour before, by a ball which entered
in at a hole over the door'. That first night, she could barely sleep:
'This place was so crowded with soldiers, it was impossible to procure either a bed or platform: my servant put me a mattress into
a kind of arch or hole by the door, and in here I and my children
crept ... Though neither shot nor shell could pierce the roof, yet
the enemy kept on so furious a cannonading, that I thought we
must lose numbers of men.'[15] According to Ancell, the incoming
fire was 'computed at about three thousand shot and shells every
twenty-four hours, which probably surpasses the heaviest cannonade in history'. The noise was also unbearable: 'The showers of
shot from the enemy are beyond credibility ... the ear is stunned
with the multiplied sounds.'[16]

The town was now deserted of inhabitants, and more prop-
erties were set alight by shells, including 'a wine-house in the
green market, near the Spanish church; and before the fire could
be extinguished, four or five houses were burnt to the ground'.
Detachments from the regiments were immediately ordered to
quench the flames, but it proved impossible with the constant
bombardment. The difficulties of fire-fighting were described by
the soldier Walter Gordon: 'water engines were employed to extinguish the fires, but had little effect, for while they were applied
to one house, three or four more were also set on fire, while they
were engaged in saving that one'.[17]

When the burning buildings collapsed, the soldiers discovered
the awful truth – while everyone was starving and paying outrageous prices, the civilian merchants had been hoarding supplies.
Straightaway, Drinkwater related, the men went berserk and
started to drink the hidden supplies of spirits, becoming uncon-
trollably drunk:

The extreme distress, to which the soldiers had been reduced
by the mercenary conduct of the hucksters and liquor-dealers
in hoarding, or rather concealing their stocks, to enhance the
price of what was exposed for sale, raised amongst the troops
(when they discovered the great quantities of various articles

in the private stores) a spirit of revenge ... their discipline was overpowered by their inebriation; and from that instant, regardless of punishment, or the intreaties of their officers, they were guilty of many and great excesses.[18]

The soldiers in the King's Bastion were some of those involved in wholesale looting, and at daylight on Easter Sunday, the fourth day of the bombardment, Mrs Upton was startled by the sight of a corpse: 'The first object I beheld in the morning was a man lying dead by the door. He died, I was told, from intoxication.' According to Drinkwater, 'Some died of immediate intoxication, and several were with difficulty recovered, by oils, and tobacco water, from a dangerous state of ebriety.'[19]

The barrage continued on a massive scale, and at noon Mrs Upton witnessed a shell explode just outside the door of her casemate (a vaulted bombproof used as barracks): 'I saw Dr. C—m and Lieutenant B—h fall; they were wounded by the splinters of a shell: the former had his foot shot off, the latter had a dangerous contusion on his head.'[20] The victims were Thomas Chisholm, a surgeon of the 56th regiment, and Lieutenant Joseph Budworth of the 72nd, while Captain Price of the 56th had a lucky escape: 'I had breakfasted with and scarce left poor Chisholm two minutes before the accident. Major Hamilton and Captain Wray were with him. A woman of the Manchester Regiment a little hurt in the leg.'[21]

A few hours later, Lieutenant-Governor Boyd wrote down his thoughts in his journal about the men's behaviour: 'This day the emissaries of wickedness seems to sport with great wantonness, robbery, marauding, housebreaking and shoplifting by the soldiery (a scene never known to be practiced by the besieged, only by the besiegers after a storm, who are generally allowed a small amount of time to plunder).'[22] For besieging troops, if a fort or town did not surrender quickly, or if the place was taken by storm, it was customary for a drunken spree of murder, rape and looting to ensue, before the officers attempted to restore law and order with their soldiers.

The surviving journals of Boyd, written from his headquarters, contain detailed official information, mixed with quirky, humorous, patriotic and prejudiced sentiments, possibly reflecting the character of the deputy governor. However, the handwriting does not match letters that were almost certainly written by him, and so the journals may have been penned by one of his staff and the extent of Boyd's own involvement is uncertain.[23] The journal expressed shock that decent soldiers when drunk took such risks:

> it appears Death is not regarded, and that plunder and all sorts of debauchery are the chief ensigns of glory and fame by the commonality: watches, plate, money and valuables are trod underfoot by people of virtue and integrity, as, being of no value to purchase their lives or safety from the dangerous engines of war! for how shocking have we daily instances of men blown to atoms by shells and dashed in pieces by cannonballs, when ... loaded with robbery and plunder.[24]

Horsbrugh likewise noted that 'Great drunkenness and other irregularities have prevailed among the soldiers since the commencement of the fire ... chiefly owing to the inhabitants having abandoned their houses without taking any precautions for the security of their effects, especially liquors. Patrols were sent out with orders to stave all the spiritous liquors they should find, in every house, particularly the wine houses where there were no proper persons left to take care of it.' Boyd's journal described the chaotic scene: 'The Gentlemen [officers] begin to stave the cellars and stores in order to put a period to drunkenness and recover discipline and good order, so that the streets runs with wines, spirits and other liquors &c. Teas, sugars and all sorts of merchandise are promiscuously mixed together.'[25]

In spite of the Spanish bombardment, the wholesale looting in the town did not stop and was witnessed by Ancell: 'Here a shell blows off the roof of a wine house, the troops haste to partake of the consuming spoil, regardless of life or limb, they drink briefly round, "Destruction to the enemy." Here are parties boiling, baking, roasting, frying, &c. Turkeys, ducks, geese and fowls become the diet of those, who, some days ago, were eagerly soliciting a hard crust of bread. Every pig they meet, receives a ball or bayonet.' In a letter to his brother, he vividly depicted the awful scenes: 'One minute a shot batters a house about your ears, and the next a shell drops at your feet; here you lay prostrate, waiting the mercy of the explosion. If you escape unhurt, you are perfectly stunned, and almost suffocated with an intolerable stench of powder and composition . . . one loses an arm or leg, another [is] cut through the body, a third has his head smashed, and a fourth is blown to pieces, with the bursting of a shell.'[26]

He then related a conversation the previous day in Irish Town with an inebriated soldier by the name of Jack Careless, who was

> singing with uncommon glee (notwithstanding the enemy were firing with prodigious warmth) part of the old song,

> *'A soldier's life is a merry life,*
> *From care and trouble free.'*

> He ran to me with eagerness, and presenting his bottle, cried, 'Damn me, if I don't like fighting. I'd like to be ever tanning the Dons. Plenty of good liquor for carrying away, never was the price so cheap, fine stuff, enough to make a miser quit his gold.' Why, Jack, says I, what have you been about? 'That would puzzle a heathen philosopher, or yearly almanack maker, to unriddle. I scarce know myself. I have been constantly on foot and watch, half starved, and without money, facing a parcel of pitiful Spaniards. I have been fighting, wheeling, marching, and counter-marching; sometimes with a firelock, then a handspike, and now my bottle (brandishing it in the air.) I am so pleased with the melody of great guns that I consider myself as a Roman general, gloriously fighting for my country's honor and liberty.'[27]

At that moment, Ancell said, a shell burst and a splinter
knocked the bottle from Jack's hand:

> with the greatest composure, he replied (having first graved it
> with an oath) 'This is not any loss, I have found a whole cask,
> by good luck,' and brought me to view his treasure. But Jack,
> says I, are you not thankful to God, for your preservation?
> 'How do you mean (he answered) fine talking of God with
> a soldier, whose trade and occupation is cutting throats ...
> Our King is answerable to God for us, I fight for him; my reli-
> gion consists in a fire-lock, open touch-hole, good flint, well
> rammed charge, and seventy rounds of powder and ball. This
> is military creed. Come, comrade, drink success to the British
> arms.'[28]

The 'military creed', as stated by Jack, was his musket (or firelock), kept in good order, with a sound flint and the standard
issue of seventy rounds of ammunition. Rank-and-file soldiers at
this time, particularly new recruits, knew little more than how to
march, how to look after their equipment and how to 'level' their
muskets at the enemy and fire – only the marksmen were taught
to aim. The name Jack Careless may have been the nickname
of a genuine serving soldier or a device used by Ancell to give
an impression of a likeable but hapless soldier. He was probably
acquainted with the character Jack Careless in *Poor Richard's
Almanack*, published by Benjamin Franklin in the American colonies – a kind-hearted person with a fondness for liquor who was
easily led astray, but eventually mended his ways.[29] The verse that
Jack was singing came from an American ballad, known on both
sides of the Atlantic, called 'The Soldier's Life', which seems to
have been newly composed around this time.

Gibraltar was first and foremost a military garrison, but private
merchants, mainly Genoese and Jewish, played a crucial role
in enabling it to function. Many were owners or part-owners
of merchant vessels that until recently brought in cargoes from
Barbary, but now had to operate much further afield. Other

merchants purchased cargoes from vessels that came in from as far away as Ireland and Leghorn, whose owners and crews were willing to risk the dangers of the blockade in return for a reasonable profit. Everyone needed to make a living, or else the cargoes would cease, but nobody ever imagined that the merchants were hoarding immense quantities of goods, particularly alcohol. It was obligatory for civilians and military families to have substantial stores, or else leave the Rock, but by now these stores were severely depleted, and the drunken soldiers targeted every newly discovered cache, unable to distinguish between stores of individual families, fair-minded merchants or unscrupulous traders.

The Jewish merchant Abraham Israel immediately wrote to his brother Moses in London, whose company Moses Israel & Co. he worked for, to acquaint him with their dreadful losses: 'I do not know how to take the pen to write to you. I neither know what I do or what I shall do, but it is necessary that I acquaint you with everything.' After describing the arrival of Darby's convoy and the attack by Spanish gunboats, he said:

> after this the Spaniards opened all their land batteries upon the town and at least 50 mortars and began to throw such fire as was incredible for a human person to believe such destruction and confusion. Consider the state we were in, some dying, some wounded. My first care was to get out and abandon all that we had in the houses and warehouses, and carrying only a handkerchief of cakes not to die with hunger. Thank God we saved our lives and we are now here with such miseries and heartache to see ourselves ruined without knowing how to help ourselves.[30]

By the afternoon, the situation was far worse, and he wrote again to Moses: 'our houses and warehouses are thrown down, and this is not our only misfortune, but thieves at our warehouses robbed all they could and were shot ... I applied immediately at the risk of my life to see if by dint of money I could save anything ... all my goods, furniture, wearing apparel, provisions and everything, all the wearing apparel of our father and mother, and part of nine chests of clothes of my dear Sarah, nothing can be found.'[31] This was his wife Sarah Montefiore, who had died at the start of the siege. Samuel Conquy described the terrible destruction of a private Jewish library: 'My father's house was among those they plundered and despoiled. One of his rooms was filled with books, a library of great value containing a precious collection of Talmud, Midrashim, Turin, Mepharshin of all kinds, etc. The soldiers took these books and threw them out into the street.'[32] Years later, one book from the library was returned to him. It had been picked up during the bombardment by a young boy looking for food in the devastated streets.

Because Father Messa had woken up worrying about all the sacred and precious items that were at risk, he and his sacristan Moreno had spent Easter Sunday going round the wardens and elders of the church, begging for assistance. With no help forthcoming, Messa tried to save what he could on his own the following day:

> I ... found with great difficulty two English soldiers (as others were giving them half of whatever they salvaged). The soldiers, carrying a stretcher ... entered the sacristy and found that all the silver objects that we had taken there on Good Friday, those that had been used especially for the procession of Holy Thursday, such as the cross, processional candlesticks and lanterns, were all broken and buried under the rubble which had fallen from the ceiling. Nevertheless, the soldiers and I removed from under the rubble as many of the pieces and parts of them as we could and placed them on the stretcher and noticing that the tabernacle, or what is termed the monstrance, was still set up on the altar, we lowered it with great difficulty and placed it on the same stretcher.[33]

Messa managed to enlist a young man with a donkey to help him carry the valuables, but when they all reached the Southport

Gate, the guard wanted him to adhere to bureaucratic regulations and obtain written permission from Eliott to remove the
silver from the town. Messa persuaded him that this was folly,
and they continued out of the town, first of all leaving the mon-
strance with Maria Raymundo, the mother of the assistant priest,
Father Raymundo, who lived in a house and tavern behind the
South Barracks.[34] His sacristan now helped shift everything else
to a tent that some sailors – from Minorca, like Messa – had set
up with canvas sails, including one purchased from Lieutenant
Skinner.

Ancell poured out the anguish he felt for everyone harmed by
the bombardment:

It is distressing to humanity to view the situation of the
inhabitants, who have fled from the town to seek shelter
upon the heights of the rock, with only a thin piece of canvas
or sail cloth to screen them from the scorching heat by day,
and excessive dews at night and the inexpressible anguish of
viewing their houses and property in flames: Many of them, in
endeavouring to save part of their effects, have lost their lives,
and others maimed. A corporal had his head shot off as he was
calling from a window to a man in the street. A soldier was so
miserably torn by a shell, that he could not be known – only
by his dress. A Genoese youth, endowed with every grace and
amiable qualification, on the point of nuptial celebration, was
unfortunately killed, to the irremoveable grief of his enam-
oratto. A shot killed two soldiers, one of which was brushing
his shoes for guard.[35]

At Boyd's headquarters, sympathies lay with the marauding
soldiers, not the merchants:

hundreds of these people begun their time with a single shilling, which in the course of time they amassed to thousands of
pounds by avarice, cheat and defraud, I mean petty pedlars that
go under the denomination in this place as capitable merchants.

Those, when the firing began, whether pricked with a guilty
conscience or a cowardly fear I cannot pretend to say, but they
fled to the South as a flock of sheep without a shepherd, and
left their hoarded up little alls ... such is the vicissitudes of this
frail life, one day as a king, the next a beggar.[36]

While Messa was rescuing church property, the military wives
of all ranks and their children were ordered to leave the casemates
in town and take refuge in the far south of the promontory, joining those civilians who had fled there. 'I was again in terrors,' Mrs
Upton confessed,

> but was obliged to obey. My husband carried my little
> Charlotte, while my son Jack ran by my side. We got safe to
> the navy hospital, but when there, found it so crowded with
> wounded soldiers, we could not procure a place to lie down
> in, except an open gallery ... My situation here was painful
> beyond comparison, from hearing the groans of the wounded,
> and from the shrieks of others, whose limbs were undergoing
> the excruciating torture of amputation! If I indulged myself
> with a little fresh air in the gallery, I was often shocked with
> seeing the mangled bodies of my slaughtered countrymen
> brought into the hospital![37]

The naval hospital was overflowing, because the army hospitals
had just been forced to move there from the town. The surgeons were faced with a mass of severe injuries, for which the
only solution in many cases was amputation, such as Surgeon
Chisholm who had just undergone an amputation above the
knee, which Captain Price said he bore 'with the firmest
composure'.[38]

Despite the breakdown of law and order, with the looting and
drunkenness, hundreds of soldiers did remain at their posts, and
so the return of fire from Gibraltar's guns was as vigorous as the
Spanish. Ancell commented that 'we retaliate with equal warmth
upon the foe, who consequently are not exempt from a share in

the direful slaughter'.[39] Most of Darby's warships kept well out of
the way, because the admiral's orders were to return to England as
rapidly as possible in order to defend Britain and try to intercept
French fleets heading west across the Atlantic. For that reason,
as soon as he had reached Gibraltar, Darby advised Eliott that he
needed to keep the fleet in a state of readiness for whenever the
winds shifted to the east. The previous year, during Rodney's
relief convoy, Ross and other officers had enjoyed a round of social
visits, but it was very different this time.

Darby also warned Eliott that he could not leave behind any
large warships and emphasised the gamble in sending the convoy:
'You must be very sensible of the situation everyone is in till the
return [to England] of this squadron and what a great risk it was,
so late in the year of our sailing, even to suffer us to go at all. Of
course they must soon every day wish and expect to hear of our
arrival. I am at the same time very sensible that the Garrison
of Gibraltar is a very grand object or at this season we should
not have been sent.'[40] Because it was April and the weather was
improving, Darby knew that the French and Spanish squadrons
would easily be able to leave port and intercept convoys, reinforce
America and the West Indies or even move into the Channel and
invade England.

In the meantime, Darby told Eliott that he was happy for two
of his frigates and two cutters to patrol the bay to deter the gunboats while the convoy was unloading and that he would allow
the ships' boats to help all they could. He added: 'As to those
with coals, they can no way be so well unloaded as by bringing them ashore by or within the New Mole where it might be
done on stages to the shore. In order to forward this service, I
have directed Rear Admiral Sir John L. Ross in a two decked
ship to anchor in the Bay.'[41] The unloading of thousands of tons
of stores was taking place just beyond the reach of the Spanish
guns, and was now superintended by Ross, after moving from
the *Royal George* to the smaller 74-gun warship *Alexander.*[42]
Ancell was especially impressed with the way Ross treated the
men:

[He] has been indefatigable in landing the provision. His attention to the soldiery evinces the goodness of his heart, both as an officer and a man of feeling. He learned that a soldier was confined for taking a biscuit, he liberated the man with a severe admonishing; then called to a cooper, directed him to open a cask of biscuit, and butter, which he distributed among them: '*My good lads*, (said he) *steal nothing. Your countenances speak the hardships you have suffered, and whilst I command here you shall have plenty to eat.*' He also caused several baskets of cheese to be opened, which he delivered with a countenance expressive of the satisfaction he felt.[43]

Many merchant ships had come with the convoy, but its main purpose was to supply the garrison, and little had been brought to help the inhabitants.

On Tuesday 17th, still living in his makeshift tent, Father Messa was loaned two wooden barrels, enabling him to protect the church silverware better: 'I disassembled the larger pieces [of silver] and once dismantled, I packed all that had been salvaged, half in each barrel, and on top I placed the books that my brother-in-law and some soldiers had also been able to save.'[44] That morning, Horsbrugh reported, 'The Enemy began at day break and continued their fire until noon, during which the Spanish Church was fired and some houses on the Grand Parade burnt down ... before midnight the Spanish Church was again set fire to, and with some other houses lower down the Town totally consumed.'[45] The fire, Messa recorded,

burnt for three continuous days. The choir and organ were burnt, as well as the benches, a new image of the Virgen del Carmen ... The chests and vestments in the sacristy and also part of the sacristy itself were also burnt, as was one of the confessionals and almost all of that in the nave of the Virgen del Rosario ... It was also during those same days that the beautiful painted monument, depicting the mysteries of the Last Supper and the Holy Passion, caught fire and was burnt.[46]

Horsbrugh himself was injured when his own house was hit, and the next morning he noted that 'another shell came into my house, dangerously wounded my servant and did very considerable damage to the furniture'.[47] Many other soldiers were wounded or killed in the casemates of the King's Bastion, and one solution was to stack wooden casks of flour to form temporary traverses. Although intended to protect the soldiers, the men quickly seized the chance to plunder the flour from the lower casks whenever they were hit by shot, as Drinkwater related: 'The contents were soon scooped out and fried into pancakes, a dish which they were very expert in cooking; and the upper casks, wanting support from below, gave way, and the whole came to the ground.' Mrs Upton was thankful to hear that the old casks of rotting salt meat had been destroyed, which would mean using the new supplies from the convoy: 'The provisions which we had in the garrison before the arrival of the fleet were burned, but the army did not esteem this a misfortune; we rather rejoiced at it, for some of them were so bad, there was no bearing to be within the smell of them.'[48]

The situation was critical, and Eliott was expecting the Spanish troops to storm the garrison at any moment. According to Ancell, nearly all the inhabitants were now displaced:

Our town is almost become a heap of ruins, and what few houses are left standing, the walls are so shattered, that it is not safe to go into them. The inhabitants are constructing temporary shades, some in the gullies between Buena Vista and Europa, others on Windmill-hill, nor is there scarce any part of the Rock out of reach of the enemy's fire by land, but what is covered over either with marquees, tents, or huts. The regiments whose quarters in town were destroyed are now encamped at the Southward ... Timber is taken from the ruins of the town to answer this necessary business.[49]

A week after the start of the bombardment, Mrs Upton and her children left the overcrowded hospital to live in a marquee tent in the garden of Captain Peter Delhoste of her husband's regiment, but the Spanish gunboats were becoming increasingly bold and effective, approaching at night to attack the refugees and soldiers camped in the south. She described her terrifying first night:

> A woman, whose tent was a little below mine, was cut in two as she was drawing on her stockings! Our servant ran in, and endeavoured to encourage me. He made me a kind of breast-work of beds, trunks, mattrasses, bolsters, and whatever else he could find, and sat me behind them ... when these formi-dable visitants had expended their ammunition, they retired. I resolved to sleep no more in that place; yet, where to find one that was safer, I knew not: for these infernal spit-fires can attack any quarter of the garrison they please.[50]

She was persuaded to stay put, and her situation was made easier by the company of her friend, the wife of Captain Delhoste, who was also nursing a young baby.

Fearing that the fleet would depart any day, Eliott asked for supplies of biscuit and empty casks from the ships, but Darby thought the winds were changing and that he would need to sail without warning. At the end of his reply, Darby wrote: 'I most sincerely wish you all possible success with a happy release from your troublesome neighbours.'[51] The next day, 20 April, the fleet with the vessels from the convoy hurriedly left, taking advan-tage of the wind turning to the east. It had proved impossible to unload the coal from the colliers, so they remained behind and were scuttled, with only the cutter *Speedwell* left for protection. Drinkwater was somewhat critical of Darby: 'The impatience of the British Admiral to disembark the supplies that he might not lose the opportunity of the easterly wind to return from the Mediterranean, had prevented the Garrison from unloading the colliers that had arrived with the fleet: these ships were therefore scuttled in the New mole, to be discharged at leisure. The ord-nance transports were also ordered within the boom for the same purpose.' He added a more surprising aside: 'Many merchantmen, freighted with merchandise, and articles much wanted in the

Garrison, returned with their cargoes; the merchants refusing to take them, on account of the bombardment.'[52]

The fleet was carrying letters, dispatches and passengers to England, and Abraham Israel took the opportunity to write again to his brother Moses in London:

With tears in my eyes I write this to participate you of the destruction that our enemies have made in all our houses, stock, goods ... our soldiers have possessed themselves of our houses, breaking down all doors and robbing all the inhabitants of all they possessed, which they did to me of all my goods that existed in our warehouses, also my clothes, furniture etc. I beg you will not take it too much to heart, for it is a sentence from heaven and all the world ought to pity us.[53]

Eliott had ordered some of the convoy vessels to take to England, free of charge, all those inhabitants who wished to leave, and Abraham Israel warned Moses that family members were on their way: 'Almost all the inhabitants goes away, some to England, others to Mahon. The risk is great and for as much as I find myself obliged to embark my dear father, mother and brother Jacob and my dear Juda [his son] for your place by this ship ... Look after these poor old people as they go at their age upon the seas, and neither of them can move, and to add I always had money enough in cash, and now I wanted it, I have it not.'[54] Boyd's journal was more acerbic: 'the Fleet sailed to the west and left us to defend ourselves, which was no discouragement to the Military, but much so to the inhabitants, for they flock off, by all vessels that sails from hence, as so many disturbed swarms of bees'.[55] As the fleet departed, Price reflected on the terrible state of the town:

The Enemy's fire has continued without intermission day and night. The town makes a melancholy appearance. Scarce a house has escaped. The streets are choked with rubbish. The Barracks at Bedlam are completely burnt and the town has been on fire in different quarters by the Enemy's shells ... The oldest officer here has seen in his course of service nothing equal in warmth and continuance to the fire of the Spaniards. It is calculated that for each 24 hours, they fire at the rate of 4000 shot and shells.[56]

Darby was almost despairing about Gibraltar's wretched situation, and on the journey to England on board the *Britannia*, he wrote to Lord Sandwich:

The town is quite beat down and often set on fire so that it is quite destroyed, many people killed by saving their effects. Sir George Collier [on board the *Canada*], who left the place last, tells me a very fierce fire was burning in the evening; it will be better for the garrison the sooner it is quite destroyed. The inhabitants are put to great difficulties where to place themselves, and the soldiers that are not in casemates [are] encamped near the barracks, which I apprehend will be plagued with these gun- and bomb-boats, of which they have both.[57]

On talking about the gunboats, he was quite pessimistic about the fate of Gibraltar:

There is no dealing with the kind of vessels but with those of the same construction. Should the Spanish fleet (which has kept close since our being on the coast) come out and join in the attack towards Europa Point, they would harrass the garrison beyond their strength and put the place in some danger. I likewise understand there is such a tired discontent among the common people that they are all inclined to desert, for fear of which [Eliott] do not dare make a sally.[58]

When George III heard the news, he too was worried: 'It is pleasing to find that Admiral Darby is so near returning home. His private letter rather has hurt me, as I fear by it that at some hour least expected that garrison may be vanquished. I had always trusted that want of supplies could alone make it fall into the hands of the enemy; now I fear that what we have done will not alone preserve it.'[59] Gibraltar was now left to its own devices. The Spaniards continued their bombardment, and it appeared that thousands of Spanish infantry and cavalry troops camped nearby might easily overwhelm the garrison. Once again, the fate of Gibraltar was on a knife-edge.

# CHAPTER THIRTEEN

---◦◆◦---

# DEVASTATION

The Spaniards maintained their relentless barrage, firing continuously all day and night from their artillery on land. Now that the fleet had gone, their gunboats and mortar boats also ventured in close to many parts of the Rock, often under cover of darkness. In the midst of this chaos, countless soldiers were still out of control, especially when they stumbled across more caches of alcohol and other concealed supplies, and so the harsh garrison orders for 26 April 1781 stipulated that 'any soldier, convicted of being drunk or asleep upon his post, or found marauding, should be immediately executed'.[1] Sleeping while on guard duty was always regarded as a serious military offence, because security was put in jeopardy, though up to now flogging was the usual punishment. In spite of these new orders, a few soldiers were prepared to run the risk of execution whenever they found an opportunity to loot.

The day after these orders were given, on the 27th, another convoy arrived. When Captain Curtis had notified Eliott that he was stuck at Port Mahon in the *Brilliant*, it was decided to use the opportunity to prepare a convoy in complete secrecy, rather than rely on the safe arrival of Darby's fleet. Eliott risked sending the *Enterprise* and *Fortune* to Minorca, and they had slipped away unseen at the end of March, carrying many invalids and inhabitants who were given free passage.[2] At Minorca, twenty storeships of supplies were ready and waiting. The few French frigates lurking near Port Mahon were no longer a worry, because when the convoy set sail for Gibraltar it was escorted by Curtis's *Brilliant*, as well as the *Enterprise, Fortune, Minorca* and *Porcupine*.

When they reached Gibraltar, Ancell remarked that 'Admiral Barcelo, no doubt, was desperately enraged at the arrival of this unexpected convoy.' In fact, Barcelo had been replaced, which they discovered from the newspapers brought by this convoy. 'The gunboats has been commanded by ... Moreno, of the rank of Major General,' wrote Mrs Green; 'this we heard by means of some Spanish Gazettes which came down from Minorca. NB Barcelo has been gone ever since the firing [started].'[3] Suddenly, the garrison was awash with months of supplies, and Drinkwater was impressed by Eliott's actions: 'It now appeared that the Governor did not entirely depend on receiving succours from England, but thought it prudent to obtain supplies from other quarters ... Captain Curtis of the Brilliant frigate had the charge of this valuable convoy, and the success attending the enterprise demonstrates with what secrecy it had been conducted.'[4]

The cargoes from Darby's convoy were still not all safely under cover, because so much also had to be rescued from buildings being destroyed in the town. 'These heavy rains are particularly unfavorable to us at present,' Horsbrugh said, 'all our stores and provisions being exposed to the weather for want of proper store-houses out of the reach of the Enemy's shot and shells, and they must unavoidably suffer from the wet.' This Minorca convoy exacerbated the storage problems, compounded by days of stormy weather. Canvas sails from the scuttled colliers were used to protect many of the supplies, but Drinkwater felt sorry for the soldiers camping in the south, whose tents proved inadequate: 'The rain that poured down in torrents from the face of the hill soon broke the loose banks of earth raised to cover their tents, which, being pitched on the declivity of the hill, were swept away by the force of the stream; and thus the fatigued soldier, who scarcely was one night out of three in bed, was frequently exposed at midnight to a deluge of rain.'[5]

In spite of the weather, the Spaniards maintained their bombardment, and on 29 April an unimaginably fierce and prolonged thunderstorm added to the havoc, which Mrs Upton endured, with no other shelter than her tent:

About eleven o'clock [at night] it began to thunder and lighten exceedingly; the flashes seemed to last several minutes, and the thunder was so uncommonly loud, that the like had never been heard since the great storm which happened thirty years ago [actually 1766]. The rain deluged through our tent, but I did not mind being wet. The glare of the lightening was so great, that my eyes were sensibly affected; and though accustomed to the thunder rattling amongst the rocks at Gibraltar, yet this by far exceeded all I ever heard ... I went to the door of the tent, but the whole hemisphere seemed on fire; and, as if we did not suffer enough from the Spaniards, Heaven's artillery seemed in array against us! They were firing all the time, but we could scarcely hear their cannon, the thunder was so loud![6]

One respite from the shelling was in the middle of each day, when the Spaniards strictly observed the siesta for two hours. 'The cause of the cessation in the Enemy's fire at noon,' Drinkwater explained, 'arose from a custom, pretty general in Spain, and common, I believe, in most warm climates, that of indulging themselves with a meridian nap. This luxury the Spaniards could not refuse themselves, even in war; and it was invariably attended to during all their future operations against Gibraltar.'[7]

Much of the town had been destroyed in just two weeks, and Ancell described the result: 'The streets of the town are like a desert, and almost every house burnt, or torn with shot and shells. In some parts the shot and broken pieces of shells are so thick, that in walking your feet does not touch the ground.'[8] Abraham Israel, until so recently a prosperous merchant, told his brother in London that he tried to salvage his belongings: 'The town is already destroyed and burnt ... when it is possible to go into the town, I shall try to save what is not burnt', but five days later: 'I did not save you may reckon nothing out of my house.'[9] He had lost everything. Drinkwater commented that 'The buildings in town, at this time, exhibited a most dreadful picture of the effects of so animated a bombardment. Scarce a house, north of the Grand Parade, was tenantable; all of them were deserted. Some few, near South-port, continued to be inhabited by soldiers' families; but in general the floors and roofs were destroyed, and the bare shell only was left standing.'[10]

Many of the shells fired into Gibraltar failed to explode and were discovered to contain 'a vast quantity of sand mixed with the powder', but other shells caused devastating fires in buildings, including the synagogue and Bedlam Barracks. When Lieutenant James Cuninghame of the 39th Regiment was trying to douse flames amongst some fascines on the wharf at Waterport, he received a head injury from a shell splinter. Price related what happened to him: 'for several days after the accident, appearances were very favourable, and very sanguine, and hopes of his recovery formed, but some symptoms of a fracture afterwards appearing, he was trepanned, but did not survive the operation above two or three days. On examination the fracture extended from the crown of his head quite under his ear. He was not quite 19.'[11]

Fires spread rapidly in the ruined buildings, and so Eliott issued an order that 'all inhabitants to remove timber and other combustible matter from their houses within 24 hours'.[12] Much of the timber was used to build huts in the south, particularly at the rear of the naval hospital and South Barracks, and the encampment of huts and tents established by the inhabitants became known as Black Town or Hardy's Town. Father Messa was living in a tent that became extremely crowded whenever the gunboats approached, so he was relieved when the convoy storeships returned to Minorca, because Eliott offered a free passage to any inhabitant. Others chose to go to England with the *Enterprise* at the end of May: 'Many men and women with their sons and daughters, Roman Catholics, Protestants and Jews, took advantage of this opportunity and embarked ... leaving me as the one and only priest with the small flock that remained, which numbered six hundred, more or less.'[13] A few weeks later, a list of names of Jews living in Hardy's Town had to be submitted, 204 people in total. Even allowing for inhabitants scattered elsewhere across Gibraltar, it is clear that their numbers were greatly depleted, with perhaps fewer than a thousand Gibraltarians remaining.[14]

Boyd's journal expressed bitterness towards those merchants who took refuge in the south of the promontory, describing them 'as lost sheep obliged to browse upon the rocks under the shelter of huts, caves, cliffs and tents at a place the military call Cowards retreat, which lies out of the line of land-fire. But when the gun-boats appear, it is shocking to behold them, half naked running to creeks and corners to save their lives, such is the desolation of these unhappy inhabitants.' By contrast, the courageous behaviour of Boyd himself was highlighted:

> One general has another narrow escape from a shell, but his undaunted courage and wise conduct from long experience and trial, renders him bomb-proof from danger of shot or shells, for he wisely at the fall of a shell stands fast, whilst others shiver most strangely aghast, and as soon as the shell explodes, he, with his unalterable serenity in the midst of danger, holds up his hands as if going to catch the pieces, and cries look up! to see the pieces fall. Such is the magnanimity of General Boyd, besieged.[15]

These words were written half in jest, half with feeling, but he did act courageously throughout. One of the inhabitants, who would leave his native Gibraltar the following year, said that 'General Boyd, the Lieutenant-Governor, is a brave and vigilant officer . . . he has remained in a small casemate at his quarters in town ever since the bombardment.' His headquarters, known as 'number 10', was hit by shells time and again. Eliott also continued to live at the Convent, and Drinkwater said that both had 'parties constantly employed in repairing the damage. Both had bomb-proofs, and the former [Eliott] afterwards had a large tent, pitched on a rising situation south of the Red Sands, where, with his suite, he generally remained during the day, returning at night to town; but the Lieutenant Governor constantly resided in town, having accommodations in the Kings bastion.'[16]

As the plunder became scarce, it was recorded in Boyd's journal that the soldiers resorted to other outrages: 'Searching the Spanish Church they met with the effigy of the Virgin Mary with the child in her arms, which they took out, and carried to the foot of the Grand Parade, where they put her in the whirligig, a place of punishment for lewd women guilty of capital crimes; and there mocked the image by putting in provisions in place, and desiring her to breakfast thereon (such is the wickedness of many in this awful time of trial).'[17] The whirligig was a wooden cage that could be turned on a pivot to punish inhabitants, particularly women, for minor offences. It stood in Whirligig Lane (now City Mill Lane), at one corner of the Grand Parade, and a description appeared in a diary from the previous siege of 1727:

A poor lady by name Chidley was ... formally conducted to a pretty whim or whirligig, in form of a bird-cage ... It contains room enough for one person, and though in length it be ten feet, yet it is not as broad as it is long. It is fixed between two swivels, so is turned round till it makes the person (if not used very gently) a little giddy and landsick. This office was performed by two of the private gentlemen of the garrison for the space of an hour in the market-place, being well attended.[18]

Half a century on, attitudes in Gibraltar would have changed little, and they were mirrored in Britain, where hangings and other brutal punishments attracted crowds of enthusiastic spectators. By 'lewd women', bad or ignorant may simply have been meant, or else prostitutes, especially if they combined their trade with theft and robbery. Wherever soldiers were present, prostitutes congregated. Naval ports like Portsmouth were a magnet, and Gibraltar would have been no exception, with many girls and women willing to sell their services. While the soldiers struggled to prevent their families from starving, it was not unknown for wives to resort to prostitution in exchange for food, though with prices for food and fuel rising sharply during the siege, soldiers would have had little spare money, and so most prostitutes may already have left Gibraltar. As for the effigy in the whirligig, Drinkwater said that Eliott ordered her to be moved to a safer place, 'where, by the bye, she was by no means exempt from further insult and disgrace. If a bigoted Spaniard could have beheld this transaction, he probably would have thought the English worse than heretics; and would have concluded, that their impiety could not fail to attract the special vengeance of Heaven.'[19]

By mid-May, Mrs Upton and her children had moved into a small tent at Europa, further to the south, but found it no safer. 'Every time the gun-boats came,' she said, 'I dragged my poor children out of bed, and stood leaning with them against a rock ... It would have melted the hardest heart to see the women and children run from the camp, without a rag to cover them, whenever the gun-boats approached. I was so harassed for want of rest, that I thought fatigue would kill me, if the Spaniards did not.' Later that month, they suffered their worst night:

> About one o'clock in the morning, our old disturbers the gun-boats began to fire upon us. I wrapped a blanket about myself and children, and ran to the side of a rock; but they directed their fire in a different manner from what they had ever done before. They had the temerity to advance so near, that the people in our ships could hear them say, *Guarda Angloise!*, which is, *Take care, English!* Mrs. Tourale [Taurel], a handsome and agreeable lady, was blown almost to atoms! Nothing was found of her but one arm. Her brother, who sat by her, and his clerk, both shared the same fate.[20]

Boyd's journal lamented: 'We have suffered more this morning than any one day since the bombardment began; 8 killed and a great many wounded ... legs, arms and pieces of broken bodies (none whole) of men, women and children are gathered up and interred in their Mother Earth. A dismal catastrophe to behold.'[21]

The three Jewish civilians mentioned by Mrs Upton were in a hut they had built in Black Town. One of them was Abraham Israel. Having first lost his fortune, he had now lost his life. His sister was Mrs Taurel, and the clerk was Abraham Benider, whose own father Jacob was in London.[22] A splinter of the shell that killed them was kept and later put on display in Sir Ashton Lever's museum in London.[23] In their camp, the officers had large tents or marquees, and during the same attack Captain Price remarked that the 'marquee belonging to Hamilton [Captain Henry Hamilton] shot through, his bureau broke to pieces together with some plate in the drawers. The shot entered a lumber tent we had near the marquee, and after damaging the bottom of a trunk belonging to him and another of mine, lodged in the bottom of a third. It was a 26-pounder.'[24]

The following day, one soldier was killed in circumstances that, Boyd's journal stated, showed 'death in all its ghastly forms, a cannonball shot him through the middle, dashed his privities against the wall, with part of his bowels; his legs thighs and hips laid dead before his eyes, yet the body retained life and sense for 20 minutes, during which time he begged for prayers, after which he entreated the bystanders to take the ball that lay by him and with it knock out his brains.' He then mercifully died, but by chance his wife arrived on the scene moments later and 'assists in gathering together the mashed remains of her husband for interment'. Yet it was often impossible to retrieve the remains of the dead, and for those who had a body or body parts that could be buried, Ancell deplored the lack of dignity: 'Your body, which once was costly arrayed in fashionable attire, is denied the form of a Christian burial, rich and poor, without discrimination, are tumbled into a hole or ditch, a prey for worms and crawling insects.'[25]

This latest atrocity was the catalyst that forced Mrs Upton to embark on the hazardous journey to England. Her love for her two children had in the end outweighed that for her husband: 'After what I had seen and suffered, I was of opinion it was not *courage*, but *madness* to stay. As a parent, I considered I had no right to expose the lives of my children.'[26] She therefore requested permission to return to England by the next available ship and embarked on board the *Hope* ordnance storeship on 27 May, along with other exhausted civilians, such as the mother and sister of the clerk Abraham Benider, as well as nineteen invalids from various regiments who were unfit for service.[27]

With the ships about to leave for England, Eliott prepared various reports and dispatches, including a letter to Lord Amherst, his commander-in-chief in London, in which he admitted to the breakdown in law and order: 'I must not conceal from you the scandalous irregularity of the British Regiments composing this Garrison, ever since the Enemy opened his batteries; except rapes and murders, there is no one crime but what they have been repeatedly guilty of, and that in the most daring manner: altho' many have been tried and convicted before General Courts Martial.'[28] He added: 'I shall persevere with the assistance of the most active [officers] in my endeavours to restore military obedience. I have no reason to suspect that any care is wanting at the posts next the enemy. The Soldier is wakeful when the fumes of liquor are evaporated.' Although other eyewitnesses used terms like debauchery and licentiousness, Eliott's assurance that no rapes were committed may have been true, as most women had fled 2 miles to the south, away from the town where the soldiers were largely out of control. Even so, one soldier commented in sorrow: 'It were to be wished, indeed, that a veil could for ever be thrown over the conduct of the troops at this period.'[29] Eliott always held the German troops in high regard and told Amherst that they had given him no cause for complaint: 'I must declare that the Hanoverians have committed no public outrage, and I believe but few private, having maintained apparent good order despite of the most dissolute examples.'[30]

Punishments continued to be severe, and because the ships did not sail straightaway, Eliott quickly wrote a further short note to Amherst about two soldiers who were sentenced to death: 'I think it my duty to inform your Lordship that two of the British soldiers are this day found guilty of robbing the naval stores; they are condemned and will be executed tomorrow. I wish these examples may have any effect, but at this hour, there remains many for trial full as criminal in all appearance.' The two condemned soldiers were from the artificer company and were duly hanged the next day, the 29th, outside the White Convent naval stores in Irish Town, which they had robbed, and Ancell said that the 'town-guards, by order of the Governor, marched past while they were hanging'.[31]

On the 29th, the *Enterprise* sailed with fifteen other vessels and two hundred inhabitants, including Mrs Upton and her family. Her misery at leaving behind her husband was all too apparent to her small son Jack, who ran to her, declaring: 'Don't cry, Mamma; the good roast beef we shall get in England will soon make me a man, and then I will return to Gibraltar, sink the gun-boats, and kill all the Spaniards.' He was too young to fulfil his promise, and those left behind had nearly two more years of the deadly game of the Great Siege to suffer. As the wife of a commissioned offi-cer, she was afforded special treatment, but poorer inhabitants were placed in the hold, as she described when they encountered enemy warships less than a week later. 'The ship is cleared for action,' she wrote. 'Captain Walker has desired me to take my children down into the hold. I have been there, but above twenty Jews and Jewesses, with their children, have lived in that part of the ship during the voyage, and the place smells so disagreeable and unwholesome, I could not stay.'[32] Being below the waterline, the Jews were actually in a far safer place. Two ships of their convoy were captured, but their own vessel, the *Hope*, saw no action, and they reached England safely.

On Gibraltar, the attacks continued. The gunboats came every night at around 1 a.m. and fired until about 3.30 a.m., when rockets were fired as a signal to leave. There was a monotonous cycle of deaths, injuries, drunkenness, thieving, desertions, punishments and suicides. Many soldiers remained desperate for alcohol, and diaries are full of incidents. Spilsbury said that 'One of 58th punished, and another hung, for stealing rum, which is buried all over the Garrison, and in the Hospital Garden.' The particular man who was executed was thirty-five-year-old James Ward, a former blacksmith from Suffolk, who had been thirteen years in the army. Ancell agreed with the punishment: 'the General is a very humane man, but cannot overlook so great an infringement of martial law. It is amazing that men should sport away their existence for the gratification of their sensual appetites, as the crimes for which they all suffered were for plundering the king's stores of provisions and liquor. I hope these examples will be sufficient to deter the unthinking part from committing the same acts.'[33]

Before he returned to his quarters, one soldier tried to hide his stolen goods, consisting of watches, purses and other valuable items, down the barrel of a gun on the King's Bastion. 'In times of peace,' Drinkwater said, 'he could not have devised a better repository, but unfortunately the gun-boats came in the evening, whilst he was fast asleep in his casemate . . . this richly-loaded gun was one of the first that was discharged; and the foundation of his future greatness was dispersed in an instant.' Boyd heard that more than one soldier was involved and that they used two guns to hide 'their ill begotten spoils; but what must the Spaniards say, that we are very scarce of ammunition, or otherwise they must think that the garrison is very rich to fire gold and silver at them in place of balls'.[34]

Civilian women were also subject to military law and could not escape justice. Eliott's diary recorded: 'The soldiers wives, Mrs Drake, Mrs Mitchell and Mrs Clarke, having been convicted of receiving stolen goods were severally sentenced to be whipped by the hangman which was accordingly executed today between 12 and 1.'[35] Boyd's journal gave more details:

> Three women was flogged through the camp for buying and receiving stolen goods from the plunderers. One of them was an honest midwife who will be of great loss to the Garrison if she is sent out, as ordered. For, in general, we marry and breed faster than ever known in peacable times. The second was an Highland woman without a word of English and the third an Irish-woman who had enough to spare for her two fellow sufferers, without leaving herself short of Blarney in the least.

The hangman was very favourable to them, as their shoulders showed few marks of violence, further than the scandal of so disagreeable a procession.[36]

The latest intelligence from deserters was that the besieging troops now had scaling ladders and were expecting to storm the garrison any day. This increased everyone's anxiety, and on the night of 3 June they were further troubled by a particularly serious gunboat attack, which Price personally experienced:

At two this morning, gun and mortar boats again, their fire chiefly confined to the naval hospital and the adjoining encampment. Serjeant Brookes of the 12th torn limb from limb by a shell in front of the hospital and Drum Major Jennings wounded in the arm. Hamilton, Hallows and myself obliged to fly for it, being very near to the above unfortunate objects, and myself speaking to Jennings a moment before the accident. Brook's watch blown to pieces in his fob.[37]

At Boyd's headquarters there was general sympathy towards the plight of the ordinary soldiers and their families, even when committing crimes, but this attack provoked bitter condemnation of the Spaniards: 'the gun-boats bombarded us this morning from 1 till half past 2 o'clock. The garrison returned the fire with spirit, but the boats being such small objects, it is hard to conceive the damage done [to] them. The Spaniards fight more like Turks than Christian enemies, in bombarding the camp of poor inoffensive inhabitants, a thing quite inconsistent with the honours of war. And not only that, but they fire double headed shot of 33 pounds weight.'[38]

Mrs Green's house on the hillside beyond the town, The Mount, was one of the few that had not been damaged or destroyed, but at night, the most dangerous time, she was often forced to take refuge in the bombproof shelter in the garden, a source of great discomfort, as she was constantly troubled by illness. On Tuesday 5 June, after fifty-four days of constant bombardment, she recorded:

'When the family were going to bed, between 11 and 12, an alarm was given from the guard boats, and instantly the whole camps went up, and the artillery went to the batteries &c. I went down to the bombproof instead of going to bed; had the child [Charlotte] taken up, a fire made in [the] bombproof, and every thing made as comfortable as it could be, every moment expecting the gunboats.' The next day, she said: 'A good deal of firing as usual. Could not make myself easy in the evening, therefore went again to bomb-proof – all quiet.'[39]

She was not so lucky the next night: 'Find myself growing very tired and indisposed in the evening. Therefore went to bed before 10. A little before 11, an alarm was given of vessels being coming very near our batteries. It was supposed it was either fireships or bomb ketches ... I was obliged to be taken out of bed and away again to bombproof. This disagreed with me more than I can express. Our suspense continued till past 12.' The following day, Friday the 8th, she felt much worse: 'All has remained quiet. I find myself exceedingly ill, the whole day, indeed uncommonly so – obliged to go to bed after dinner, and dreadfully alarmed lest the gunboats should come this night, as I am really too bad to bear the moving. However they luckily did not, and we all got a good nights sleep.'[40] Saturday brought her more cheering news, because the Spanish troops accidentally blew up their main factory for the manufacture of shells, which had been housed in a huge tent:

> Westerly wind; cold and blowing hard. About 11 a very loud explosion was heard, and a very heavy discharge of shells, with the utmost rapidity from the enemy's camp. It was instantly seen to proceed from an accident amongst themselves. Their principal laboratory tent, under the Queen of Spains chair, near the Catalan Camp, blew up; also a building next to it. The fire was violent; and extended to a large heap of live shells, which blew up in a most furious manner.[41]

The fire spread rapidly to the fuses of the shells, with no way of stopping them from exploding within the laboratory, and Mrs

Green watched the pandemonium within the Spanish camp: 'Nothing could equal the confusion the enemy were in. This tent is about four thousand five hundred yards [around 2½ miles] from Landport ... I plainly saw the poor men running from the flames. It continued burning an hour and half and the bursting of the shells more than half an hour. This accident must have done them most essential hurt; and of course lowered the ammunition greatly.' The garrison gained some useful information about the strength of the besieging force: 'They beat to arms,' Mrs Green said. 'Their whole line turned out under arms. It enabled our officers to form some idea of the number of troops, which, by observing the number of battalions, seems by all accounts to amount to 10,000 men.'[42]

This explosion did not stop hostilities, and the terrible routine continued on Sunday the 10th, with Mrs Green writing: 'The enemy fired a good deal this day. Went as usual to bombproof.' After going to bed on Monday night, she was woken only a little later by the gunboats:

This morning at half past one, the gun and mortar boats came as usual. There seemed to be a good number. They were fired at from every part that bore upon them. The shipping also gave them a warm reception. Several of their shells burst in the air, one over our house, and the fuzee [fuse] remains upon the top of it. They stayed a little better than an hour. An unlucky accident happened in a tent belonging to a soldier of the 56th. His wife, a very good young woman, and a young child of three months were blown out of the tent by a shell. They were thrown into a deep gully, and [the] child torn to pieces and the woman much burnt and otherwise wounded.[43]

On that same day, the 12th, Eliott's diary says simply: 'Travelling pass granted Mrs Green.'[44] She had made a decision to return to England and wrote one final diary entry, for Wednesday 13 June 1781: 'Westerly wind; all quiet from gunboats.'[45] At that point, she abandoned her diary for good.

The next day, 14 June, was Corpus Christi, which caused much fear. 'On this great holy day,' Horsbrugh declared, 'we expected a general salute of shot and shells from their land batteries in return for the one we gave them on our King's birthday, but they made no alteration in their usual mode of firing.'[46] Instead, it was celebrated in Spain by decorations, customary salutes and the normal murderous volley from the Lines, killing and wounding several people in the garrison.

The distances the Spanish guns were achieving from land and sea increased all the time, and indiscriminate attacks at night from the gunboats and mortar boats continued. The fear of attacks and of being hit was ever-present, and civilians and soldiers alike could barely sleep. On 28 June, the gunboats and mortar boats came as usual at about half past midnight, and although they could not be seen Horsbrugh said their distance was calculated: 'we counted at four seconds, which, allowing 1142 feet to a second gives a distance of 1522 yards 2 feet'.[47] The garrison returned fire, and as usual the gunboats ceased. The artillerymen were then dismissed, and the soldiers started to go back to their tents and barracks, when something totally unexpected happened, as Price reported: 'after a pretty long interval it was discovered to be a new device of the Enemy to lull us into security. Two of their mortar boats had continued on their station and renewed the fire. By this unexpected stratagem, nine men of the 39th Regiment who had escaped the first attack were badly wounded by the Enemy's shells. Our total loss in this dirty business – a man of the artillery killed and (including the 39th) eleven or twelve wounded. This little finesse of the Enemy owed its success entirely to novelty and will never do on repetition. The Artillery are now ordered to remain on the batteries until day break.'[48] Horsbrugh gave more details:

One private of the artillery killed, 9 rank and file of the 39th regiment, 2 of the 73rd and one of La Motte's wounded, two of which dangerously. One shell fell into the cooperage within the enclosure of the magazine near the New Mole, broke and did some damage. One went through the roof of the South Barracks, pierced the two upper floors, wounded two men of the 73rd Regiment, broke five casks of pease in the lower room, went out of the window and burst in the yard. One went through the roof of the chapel in the Navy Hospital, broke in its fall and damaged some furniture. We compute that their fire amounted to about 219 shot and 76 shells exclusive of the land batteries which also fired briskly upon the town all the time, but added little to the damage they had already done amongst the ruined houses.[49]

The garrison had long been grumbling that little retaliation for the gunboat attacks was being made against the enemy, but on this same day they did try firing from the Old Mole towards the Spanish camp for the first time with sea mortars, as well as with cannons that were set into the ground and elevated at almost 45 degrees. Sea mortars were a very heavy type of mortar, often used at sea in bomb vessels, and they usually fired a shell weighing 200 pounds or more.[50] Some of the shells went beyond the wharf at the Orange Grove and some went into their camp, as much as 3900 yards – just over 2 miles away. Horsbrugh noticed that 'there appeared a good deal of confusion in the Enemy's camp. The Quarter Guards got under arms, and several women moved off towards St Roque. And soon after we observed them busy removing stores from the nearest of their fixed laboratory huts, under the Queen of Spain's Chair to one of the tents lately pitched at a greater distance.'[51] The experiments were so successful that the garrison began to retaliate using these guns, firing right into the Spanish camp, particularly at siesta time. Eliott had earlier ordered two brigs to be cut down into large gunboats or prames fitted with four or five guns, and the first one, the *Vanguard*, was now ready and also began to confront the gunboats.

Mrs Green had to endure the constant bombardments for nearly six more weeks, until a small convoy was ready. She was worn out by illness, dispirited by the news that her daughter Susanna, born on Gibraltar eleven years earlier, had died in London, and fearful for herself and her daughter Charlotte. She set out for England in the evening of 22 July with Charlotte and their maids, and at the same time Colonel Ross sailed in another vessel for Portugal. For over two decades Mrs Green had lived on Gibraltar with her husband William, who she now left behind. They would never see each other again.[52]

# CHAPTER FOURTEEN

—— ·◆· ——

# SURRENDER

The siege was affecting the wildlife, not just the domesticated horses and dogs that had to be culled. Gibraltar is important for birds migrating across the Straits, and although they may not have been deterred, on a local level the constant firing and the destruction of habitats were having an impact: 'A 13-inch shell fell in the picquet yard after day-going [dusk] near some poplar trees, and by the explosion killed a great number of sparrows that were in the trees at roost. 150 were taken up, but it is thought that there must have been 300 killed at least.' The firing continued to be indiscriminate, and a week later: 'A favourite cat ... belonging to the Artillery on Willis's district, came out of the casemate in the night to air herself, but unlucky for poor puss, she sat upon a large rock, when a Spanish ball came and cut off poor puss's head and left her body behind ... The above cat was a great favourite, which gave her a military burying (thrown into a hole and covered over).'[1]

What proved unexpected in July 1781 was a reduction in the amount of firing from the Spanish Lines, but a great deal was changing in their camp, with tents taken down, troops marching off, others replacing them, and huge numbers of gabions and fascines being loaded on boats. Nobody knew where the men and equipment were heading, but many militia troops had replaced the regular ones. The main focus of their work was now on repairing and improving all their fortifications, and Captain Price wrote: 'the Spaniards did not fire above half a dozen shells in 24 hours. Oh wonderful!'[2] Horsbrugh also mentioned this lack of firing: 'The enemy have been unusually moderate in their fire through the night and all this morning except from 7 to 8 o'clock when being teased with some shot and shells from our upper batteries, they fired pretty briskly and threw some long shells, one of which fell and exploded on the New Mole Parade opposite Prince William's Battery, and is reckoned the longest they have yet thrown from San Carlos.' Two days later he said: 'from twelve o'clock yesterday until twelve this day they only threw seven shells, five from the Mill Battery [St Carlos] and two from the first mortar battery to the east of Fort [St] Philip.'[3]

Nobody realised that the numerous troops besieging the Rock had actually been withdrawn to take part in a combined French-Spanish expedition to Minorca. In Britain, though, the early warning signs were misinterpreted, because when the huge combined fleet left Cadiz, it initially sailed westwards in order to make it appear they were off to America or even planning a new invasion of England. After successfully reaching the Mediterranean unopposed, the fleet ran into bad weather and was delayed, giving time for reports to reach London, which were then sent to Minorca. On Gibraltar, the news was received on 10 August: 'They say by reports from England ... by an information from Marseilles by a spy, they expect Minorca to be besieged very shortly by the French and Spaniards in conjunction.'[4]

The invasion force was under the overall command of the sixty-four-year-old Duc Louis de Berton des Balbes de Crillon. Born in Avignon, France, he was a highly experienced officer who had joined the French army in 1730 and transferred to the service of Spain in 1762, with the rank of lieutenant-general. A surprise attack on Minorca was now impossible, and the combined fleet was spotted as soon as it reached the island on the morning of 19 August, as one British officer noted in his diary: 'About 10 o'clock the signal for an Enemy's fleet was hoisted at the signal house of Cape Mola. About 12, one division of the fleet was off the harbour and went round towards Sandy Bay, where they landed a large detachment and in the evening took possession of Mahon.'[5]

Crillon had hoped his invasion force would be mistaken for a friendly convoy so that they could sail straight into Port Mahon harbour, but the garrison blocked the entrance with a chain and retreated within Fort St Philip. The invasion fleet was forced to sail further round the coast and land the French and Spanish troops at Sandy Bay, not far from the town of Mahon. From here, they quickly took control of the island, with only the fort holding out against them, where many citizens and British soldiers took refuge. This citadel was now besieged, and there was little prospect of assistance from Britain.

The island of Minorca, a far larger territory than Gibraltar, had a fine, sheltered, deep-water anchorage at Port Mahon, where for almost two decades the Royal Navy had established a substantial base for repairing and overhauling warships. British newspapers took a keen interest in the siege, with regular reports, including a description that highlighted its immense value to Gibraltar:

> Minorca is situated almost opposite the port of Barcelona, at about 30 leagues distance. It is of a very irregular form, about 30 miles long in its extremest length, and about 16 broad. Port Mahon and Citadelle are the chiefest places in the island, which in the interior parts is very hilly, and some very excellent sheep, whose wool is equal to that of Spain, are bred upon them. There are several vineyards, and a prodigious number of mulberry trees, which favour the culture of silk. Its other productions are fruits, oil, and fish, which are caught in every bay round the island.[6]

At Port Mahon, the newspapers said, was 'the castle of St. Philip, which stands on a rock, [with] six forts, several redoubts, and some strong lunette batteries. The harbour which it commands will hold 150 sail of large shipping conveniently.'[7] On Gibraltar, there were fears that if the French and Spaniards took over Minorca, another important supply line would be lost. Even worse, thousands of reinforcements from their combined army might be subsequently moved from Minorca to reinforce

the siege of the Rock. In the short term, though, firing from the
isthmus had dwindled to a few shots each night, something that
Drinkwater commented on:

> The Enemy's bombardment, if we may call it by that name,
> scarcely exceeded, at this time, three shells in the twenty-four
> hours, which the soldiers ... profanely termed, *Father*, *Son*,
> and *Holy Ghost*. It is not indeed altogether improbable, that the
> Spaniards might entertain some bigoted respect for that mysti-
> cal number, and, considering the British in the light of heretics,
> might apprehend some efficacy from it, in the great work of con-
> verting the Garrison to the Catholic faith. At least it is difficult,
> on any more reasonable ground, to account for their exactly con-
> tinuing to fire neither more nor less for so considerable a period.[8]

Every now and again, more vigorous firing took place from the
batteries, particularly if they had been provoked by the British
firing at their working parties, while periodic attacks still occurred
from the gunboats and mortar boats. In the middle of August,
Boyd's journal recorded a particularly fierce bombardment:

> The Enemy's gun and mortar-boats paid us a visit at half past
> 11 o'clock last night, when they begun the heaviest and hottest
> fire with shot and shells that has been as yet, which our batter-
> ies returned with equal spirit and vigour. The old mole opened
> upon their camp with 14 rounds of 13-inch shells and 6 rounds
> from the guns of shot and small shells to satisfy the cowardly
> Dons of their coming like a thief in the night to massacre our
> women and children in camp, which drew on us a very heavy
> fire from their land batteries that continued until 2 o'clock this
> morning. We have one man killed, 1 died suddenly, 3 men and
> 4 children wounded, and by all appearance the Enemy must
> have suffered considerably both by sea and land. ... A shell fell
> in the Seamans Hospital, set on fire some loose sails and pease
> bags, but was timely extinguished before it done any further
> damage.[9]

Being in the southern part of the promontory, near Rosia Bay, the hospital was well clear of firing from the Spanish artillery on land, but the gunboats were concentrating on the encampment and naval hospital. At the end of August, Drinkwater was upset by the death of an artillery gunner when a shell fell on his hospital bed:

> The circumstances attending this man's case are so melancholy and affecting, that I cannot pass over them in silence. Some time previous to this event, he had been so unlucky as to break his thigh: being a man of great spirits, he ill brooked the confinement ... and exerted himself to get abroad, that he might enjoy the benefit of fresh air in the court of the hospital: unfortunately, in one of his playful moments, he fell, and was obliged to take to his bed again ... when a shell from the mortar-boats fell into the ward, and rebounding lodged upon him. The convalescents and sick, in the same room, instantly summed up strength to crawl out on hands and knees, whilst the fuse was burning; but this wretched victim was kept down by the weight of the shell, which after some seconds burst, took off both his legs, and scorched him in a dreadful manner; but, what was still more horrid, he survived the explosion, and was sensible to the very moment that death relieved him from his misery. His last words were expressive of regret that he had not been killed on the batteries.[10]

He was unlucky, because dozens of Spanish shells did not explode, and it was found that they 'were filled chiefly of earth blackened with powder ... it is supposed that their laboratory workers must sell the powder to the country bores for fowling, as they are vastly fond of that amusement'.[11]

Although the hospital was long established, Spilsbury could not help finding fault with the army surgeons working there. In the early hours of 18 September, a shell splinter took off both legs of a soldier from the 12th Regiment. He was taken to the naval hospital where, according to Spilsbury, 'he lay two hours and a quarter before the Surgeons would venture out of their bomb-proof to dress him, so that the loss of blood would have killed him of itself'.[12] His criticism may have been unjust, because a fierce bombardment from the batteries, gunboats and mortar boats took place that night, mainly directed towards the King's Bastion and adjacent fortifications in order to divert attention from a considerable amount of work being done on the isthmus. Another casualty of the same attack was thirty-nine-year-old Donald Ross, a former labourer from Tain in Ross-shire, who had joined the 73rd Regiment three years earlier. That night he had been a sentry at the King's Lines, and his regimental surgeon, Andrew Cairncross, did everything possible to save his life after he was injured:

> Donald Ross ... was knocked down by the wind of a thirteen inch shell, which fell close by him. The shock and fear had such an effect upon him, that he was rendered entirely incapable of making any efforts to save himself by running away. The fuze burnt only a few seconds, when the shell exploded. He was soon after taken up senseless by some of the guards, in a miserable mangled condition by the splinters of the shell and pieces of stone thrown about; and he was conveyed in a litter to the hospital of the 73d [at the naval hospital]. When brought there, his appearance was so shocking, that I really was almost at a loss what part of his body to pay attention to first.[13]

On examining him, Cairncross saw that the bone above his right eye was exposed and fractured, and he had severe fractures of his left arm and leg. In addition, he recorded, 'A great part of the skin and muscles were lacerated from three of his fingers of the right hand, and the bone of the middle one was shattered to pieces. His body was contused all over; the scrotum and penis particularly so. The British regimental surgeons assisted me; and indeed we were all of opinion, that the unfortunate man could not live.' He decided to look first at the cranium fracture: 'On laying the bone bare, I found a fracture running about an inch and a half upwards in the direction of the wound; and there was a particular *dint* in the lower part of the bone, which seemed to be the point struck. No time was lost; the trephine [small circular saw to remove part of the skull] was immediately applied on the part; it cut well; the sawing was complete, without injuring the dura mater.' He realised a sliver of bone was missing, and on wiping away some blood, 'the bit of bone was found drove through the membranes into the brain, and sticking fast. It was immediately removed; on which a pretty considerable haemorrhage ensued.'[14] After a while, they stopped the bleeding, and Ross showed signs of recognising those around him. Cairncross and his colleagues agreed it was best to dress his other wounds lightly and let him sleep, only undertaking further surgery if he lived.

At this time there was no concept of hygiene, so the surgeon's instruments were not sterilised beforehand, and the conditions in which operations took place were basic. Infections were common, and gangrene and tetanus were frequent killers. A further difficulty with Donald Ross was that the trepanning was carried out by the light of candles and lanterns, with the danger that the hospital might be hit at any moment. A few hours later, Cairncross was surprised that his patient was still alive, that he had slept well and his pulse was fine. For many days, he was carefully monitored, but on the fourteenth day Ross complained of an acute pain in his fractured leg. 'I expected nothing but gangrene and its consequences to follow,' Cairncross recorded; 'and this now appeared to be the critical time to remove the limb entirely, as the only probable chance of saving the patient's life. On consulting with my brother surgeons, they all agreed with me in opinion ... and as no time was to be lost, it was determined to be done immediately.'[15]

Speed was essential because there were no effective anaesthetics, only alcohol and opium to dull the pain. A surgeon would try to perform an amputation in minutes to minimise blood loss and prevent the overwhelming pain causing shock. The patient was usually held down on a table, given a leather gag to bite on, while a tourniquet was placed on the limb above the incision.

The surgeon was now ready to cut through the flesh, muscle and sinews in a circle down to the bone, and this soft tissue was pulled back, enabling him to saw through the bone higher up. The damaged limb was removed, and the flap of flesh was folded over the end of the bone. By loosening the tourniquet slightly, bleeding revealed the position of the blood vessels so that they could be tied with thread or silk ligatures. The tourniquet was released, and the stump was sealed with something like spirits of turpentine or pitch and then bandaged. The ends of the ligatures were left long to help drain the fluids as the stump healed.

Cairncross described the operation on Ross: 'As soon as the necessary apparatus was got ready, that I might not disturb my patient by placing him on a table, I took off the limb in the usual place below the knee, whilst he lay in bed in the hospital cradle. He bore the operation exceedingly well, all circumstances considered, and soon after fell fast asleep ... Next morning, I found him in good spirits, without any quickness of pulse.' On the fifth day, the dressings were removed, and all looked well, but Ross wanted his damaged middle finger to be removed, because it 'gave a good deal of pain all up the arm, and was very offensive to the smell'.[16] Ten weeks after his near-fatal accident, Cairncross was very pleased to report that 'he was perfectly well, but weakly'.[17] Ross was soon sent home and accepted for a pension, though his records suggest that his recovery was interrupted by complications, because he also had an arm amputated.[18]

Ross was lucky to have been in the care of Cairncross, somebody who greatly impressed Eliott: 'the very many sick and wounded, whether officers or soldiers, whom the climate or the chance of war was committed to his care, were treated with such equal attention, humanity and skill by him, as to merit my highest approbation and place his professional abilities in a very high point of view throughout the Garrison ... his behavior always becoming a Gentleman'.[19] Spilsbury nevertheless continued to vent his anger against the medical staff: 'The Regiment doctors are little better than butchers, and ours are not trusted with medicines. When Major B— was wounded, no proper dressings were at the Main Guard, where a [surgeon's] mate attends; the Director, being accused of it next morning, answered they were, having sent them just before, at daylight.'[20] He was referring to a shell that had smashed through a house opposite the King's Bastion only a few hours after Ross was injured. Remarkably, the house had been little damaged up to now, but this time Edward Burke, the Town-Major, was killed, which shocked everyone, including Captain Price:

> About 8 o'clock this night, a shell fell through the roof [of] Major Vignole's quarters, on the Lines near the King's Bastion, upon Captain Burke's leg, which it shattered above the knee and wounded Majors Mercier and Vignoles who were sitting at table with him. While the fuze continued burning, the two gentlemen ... rushed out of the house, the shell in the meantime exploding, blew Captain Burke up to the ceiling, as is supposed from the quantity of blood sprinkled all over it. He was carried to the hospital and an amputation performed above the knee. When I saw him he was in agonies of death and survived only a few minutes after I reached the hospital. The universal dejection visible in the countenances of the whole parade [in] the morning regarding the accident did that justice to his abilities and which no words are able to convey. He was Town Major to the Garrison and was scarce 30 years old. He was equally regretted by the inhabitants to whom his amicable qualities had generally endeared him.[21]

The next evening, Price said, Burke's funeral took place: 'the remains of poor worthy Burke were privately interred at South Port. The Governor was too deeply affected to be able to attend.'[22] This was an unusual sign of frailty in Eliott. Today, there is an impressive monument to Burke in the King's Chapel.

Spilsbury continued complaining about the hospital: 'It seems cradles [for carrying the sick and wounded] are not sufficiently provided for the hospitals, nor places to perform surgical operations in; the wards where the sick are, are all they have, the others being inhabited by families, &c.'[23] A few weeks later, the overcrowding was addressed by turning out many people, but too many wounded soldiers continued to die through loss of blood, and Drinkwater said that the death of one soldier at the end of September made Eliott intervene:

> A soldier of the 72d lost his legs by a shot from Fort Barbara, from which they continued occasionally to fire. He bore amputation with prodigious firmness, but died soon after, through the loss of blood previous to his being brought to the Hospital. This fact being represented to the Governor, the serjeants of the different regiments were ordered to attend the Hospital, to be taught by the surgeons how to apply the tourniquets, which was afterwards productive of very beneficial consequences. Tourniquets were also distributed to the different guards, to be at hand in case of necessity.[24]

This was one of the earliest instances of organised first aid amongst the rank-and-file soldiers, and it undoubtedly gave the wounded a better chance of survival.

By now, the firing from the Spanish gunboats and batteries had increased once more, resulting in a catalogue of injuries. At the start of October, fierce firing from both sides lasted all night long, and Price, who was on guard duty at Waterport, recorded that from six in the evening to six the next morning the Spaniards fired 1385 shells and 231 cannonballs. One of those injured was Private Elsegood, one of his recruits, who was 'supposed mortally wounded, having his skull frightfully shattered'.[25] Everyone was astonished that, through the dedicated skill of the surgeon of the 56th Regiment, the soldier recovered. Thomas Chisholm was the surgeon, back at work saving others after he himself had a leg amputated in April.

Some of the soldiers and seamen on Gibraltar were feeling dispirited, and a mutiny was even planned on board the *Speedwell* cutter, but the potential mutineers were arrested after it was reported. A trickle of deserters also continued. Some were successful, but others were caught or died in the attempt. While on guard duty at Waterport, Price found some clothes on the Old Mole belonging to someone from the 12th Regiment. Two nights later, Drinkwater reported, 'the body of a soldier of the 12th regiment, who attempted to swim to the Enemy from Waterport, was discovered floating near the Repulse prame [another new gunboat converted from a brig]. The sailors on watch, imagining some large fish had got foul of their cable, darted a harpoon into the body, but soon found out their mistake.'[26] The drowned man was taken on shore and buried.

Ancell remained defiant in tone when writing to his brother, despite the relentless shelling:

> The enemy ... have bombarded us now near six months, and General Alvarez is as far from taking possession of the garrison as he was at first, although they have discharged from their batteries, according to the nearest calculation, between thirty and forty thousand rounds of shot and shells. He may view the rock with his perspective from the camp of St. Roque, but if he wishes to examine the workmanship of the walls, and the strength of the fortification, he must come much nearer, or return without the gratification of his curiosity.[27]

This was exactly what the Spaniards were doing, inexorably spreading their siegeworks across the sand dunes of the isthmus towards the Rock, with more gun and mortar batteries in the area of St Carlos battery, as well as new communication lines. They included an eastern parallel that was already halfway to the Mediterranean, where it looked as if another battery was being laid out. The work was done mostly at night, and, with the huge defences covered in sand, the garrison could only disrupt the work, not stop it. From the Rock, it was difficult to determine exactly what was happening, and virtually nobody had deserted to Gibraltar over the last few months. Each morning, something new and substantial was visible, and on one occasion in mid-November Horsbrugh recorded:

The Enemy have in the night thrown up more sand to cover
the front face of the first six-gun battery and have made an
addition of about 100 feet to the eastern branch, which seems
now to incline towards the burying ground. This branch is constructed with two rows of casks lined and capped with fascines
and banked up with sand. A number of men have been at work
through the day in the two new gun batteries, which they are
both strengthening and raising, and we think they are laying
the platforms of the first. There is the appearance of much
hurry and business in the artillery fascine and picketting parks,
where they have collected a prodigious quantity of brushwood
and have this day brought forward from thence many mule and
cart loads of timber, long and short fascines.[28]

The next morning, he said, 'they threw two shells from San
Carlos much further than any they have yet thrown. One fell
close by the wine house betwixt the South Barracks and Picardos
Garden, the other burst in the air and some of the splinters went
as far as Mr Wards, which is above 4000 yards from San Carlos.'
He was worried that they 'have of late totally changed their mode
of firing – are quiet through the night and only fire in the day,
directing their fire at particular objects and with greater judgment than heretofore'.[29] In particular, the Spanish gunners tried
to aim at the garrison working parties, and because they had also
recently adopted Mercier's technique of cutting the fuses of their
shells, many more casualties were caused when the shells burst
overhead.

Earlier in the week, some information had been received
from Portugal: 'Grievances innumerable among the Enemy's
troops – Don Alvarez a tyrant, bread scarce, duty hard, and water
execrable!'[30] Two disaffected Walloon Guards, a corporal and a
private, also managed to escape into Gibraltar on 20 November,
bringing in first-hand information. Horsbrugh said they were
examined separately, to ensure they were genuine deserters, and
the corporal in particular gave valuable information, including a
complete picture of the state of the Spanish fortifications. His

description of their new St Paschal's (or Pascual's) battery, on the south-west side of the St Carlos battery, highlighted the massive scale of construction:

> There are six cannon fixed behind the epaulment of the new battery next to San Carlos at a very great elevation and on the same principle with ours behind the old mole, with the intention to disturb our encampment and quarters at the southward. There are also two large and heavy mortars placed in the same battery. Their beds are strongly fixed down on the platforms which are sunk in the ground, and laid upon several thick piles of cork tree wood, of about twelve feet long, resting on large stones that are laid down in the bottom of pits dug for that purpose, and the vacant space between the piles is filled with clay or binding soil well rammed.[31]

The corporal then talked about the two batteries of St Martin's, on the north-west side of St Carlos: 'The first of the two six-gun batteries is finished, the guns mounted and placed under cover of the merlons. They are very busy laying the platforms in the second gun battery and constructing square traverses for magazines and covering their men. The guns for this battery lie ready behind the first return of their new approaches.' He confirmed that another battery was planned much further out, in an exposed position: 'A battery for eight or twelve guns is marked out at the extremity of the eastern branch or parallel. It is said the Chief Engineer disapproves of this battery and had only undertaken it by positive orders from the General.'[32] This information, along with observations from the Rock, showed that the new batteries were designed to fire right over the northern defences and bombard the southern part of Gibraltar that had previously been reached only by gunboats. They were obviously so strongly built that the garrison was unlikely to destroy them by artillery fire alone.

The corporal also said that in the camp were about nine thousand troops, though two-thirds of them were militia, that there was much sickness, and that 'the men were much dissatisfied with their situation, and greatly harrassed in raising the additional batteries; that they had suffered lately very severe losses from our fire'.[33] This was probably the weakest force facing the Rock since the siege began.

In London on Sunday 25 November 1781, dispatches reached Lord George Germain, Secretary of the American Department, with the shocking information that the British had surrendered at Yorktown some five weeks earlier.[34] He immediately forwarded the news to the king. Having led a major expedition to the southern colonies, General Charles Cornwallis had occupied Yorktown, where he and his army of over 7600 men were besieged by American and French troops under General George Washington and by a French fleet commanded by Vice-Admiral Comte de Grasse – the fleet that had slipped away unseen from Brest a few months earlier. The surrender of General Lord Cornwallis (nephew of Edward Cornwallis, Gibraltar's former governor) marked the last great encounter of the American War of Independence, although the conflict would drag on for another year. That America had been sacrificed for Gibraltar was a view vigorously debated in Britain, for many believed that if the army and navy had not been involved in Gibraltar, the colonies might indeed have been saved. Ultimately, King George III had wanted both America and Gibraltar, but successive governments had diminished Britain's armed forces, particularly the navy, to the point where they were not able to fulfil his wishes.

# CHAPTER FIFTEEN

◆

# COUNTERSIGN STEADY

With America lost, all hope inevitably turned to Gibraltar. Eliott would not hear about the disaster there for some time, but on 26 November 1781, the day after the Yorktown news reached London, he issued orders for the winehouses to shut immediately and for all the soldiers to go to their quarters. His evening garrison orders began: 'Countersign, STEADY. All the grenadiers and light-infantry of the Garrison, and all the men of the 12th and Hardenberg's regiments, officers, and non-commissioned officers now on duty, to be immediately relieved, and join their regiments.'[1]

It was now six in the evening, and Walter Gordon of the 73rd Regiment was on guard duty: 'the 12th regiment and Hardenburgh regiment of Hanoverians were relieved off guard and picquet ... I was on picquet the same evening in the picquet guard, when a call came about eight o'clock for the grenadiers and light infantry's picquet of the 73rd regiment to turn out. When I came to the door of the picquet room, C.B. of the royal artillery bid me adieu!' His friend Charles Bell, an artillery matross, had already got wind of what was about to happen, but Gordon found his words strange: 'I asked him in haste, what he meant? he told me he did not know whether or not he should ever see me again. I then enquired if he knew where we were to be sent, or upon what business? says he, you are going to burn the Mill Battery [St Carlos].'[2]

This was astounding news, because it meant that for the first time in two years of being besieged, he and other soldiers were about to embark on a sally or sortie – going into enemy territory to attempt to destroy the huge St Carlos battery that they persisted in calling the Mill battery, as well as the nearby batteries of St Martin's and St Paschal's. Eliott had been watching the siegeworks get closer and closer, and he knew that the Spanish troops could soon be reinforced with thousands more men from Minorca. It was a case of 'now or never' for such an attack, and it was useful to hear from the two recent deserters about the discord between senior officers, and that everything was lax in the camp. There had been no gunboat attacks of late, and as the Spanish gunners had recently gone over to firing only at particular targets in the daytime, there was every chance that their guns were not properly manned by night. The deserters had also given Eliott information about the guards, and when he took them to Willis's they pointed out everything to him. Since then, he had kept them closely confined at the Convent to prevent communication with anyone else.[3]

Eliott formed his plans in secret. Nobody else knew until he told his officers on the evening of the 26th and gave them their orders, but there was no doubt this was a dangerous operation with the likelihood of numerous casualties and men taken prisoner. Charles Bell obviously expected the worst, and Gordon duly made his farewells: 'I took my leave of my friend, desired him if I did not return, to write my friends in Aberdeenshire, and recommended myself to the care of providence.'[4]

Large numbers of the garrison's forces were ordered to assemble at midnight on the Red Sands – the big parade ground just outside the town walls at Southport. Those involved were the entire 12th Regiment and Hardenberg's Regiment, as well as all the grenadiers and light infantry from every other regiment. Traditionally, land battles were fought with lines of infantry facing each other as cannon fodder – much like warships fought in opposing lines, giving rise to the term line-of-battle ship, which was abbreviated to battleship. The grenadiers were elite foot soldiers whose normal fighting position was on the right, and they tended to be the tallest of the men, armed with hand grenades – small shells. The light infantry, placed on the left, were agile skirmishers. The sortie would not be a set-piece battle, and the grenadiers and light infantry were to lead the way, dealing with any resistance.

In addition, there were various officers, artillerymen, naval seamen, engineers and artificers, as well as workmen drawn from the rank-and-file of different regiments. The whole lot was to be commanded by Charles Ross, which was itself extraordinary after all the trouble he had caused in his earlier feud with Boyd. He had returned to Gibraltar only two weeks previously, after being on leave since July and having at last been confirmed as colonel of the 72nd Regiment. He had already proved awkward when looking for suitable accommodation, with Spilsbury commenting: 'Ross, not being satisfied with having turned a major, a captain and sub out of the house on Scud Hill, has now changed to Windmill Hill and there turned out a captain and 5 subs.'⁵ Even so, Eliott trusted Ross implicitly as the best person to be put in charge of this mission.

The orders were for 'Each man to carry thirty-six rounds or more, a good flint in his piece [musket], and another in his pocket. No drums, excepting two with the 12th, and two with Hardenberg's. No swords ... No volunteers will be allowed.'⁶ At midnight, everyone was assembled on the Red Sands parade ground, forming three columns two deep. Also at midnight, the remaining troops of the 39th and 58th regiments were told to assemble on the Grand Parade under the command of Colonel Picton, ready to help out if required. 'It was with much satisfaction remarked that the greatest silence and regularity was preserved,' Horsbrugh wrote, 'and not a single man in liquor seen on the Parade.'⁷ They waited almost three hours for the moon to set, giving them the cover of darkness, and during that time the officers were given precise instructions about the task ahead.

At quarter to three in the morning, the right column (at the far end of the Red Sands parade ground) started to march off, followed by the centre column and finally the left column – around 2200 men and officers in all. The workmen, engineers, artillerymen and seamen were in the rear of each column, all carrying specialist tools. They moved steadily and silently through the Southport Gate, down Main Street past Eliott's headquarters at the Convent on their left, then the burnt-out Spanish church on the right, navigating round the traverses. They would have maintained their silence as the 39th and 58th regiments came into view, waiting as reserves on the Grand Parade. The troops continued in the darkness as far as the Landport Gate – almost a mile's march from where they started. It was, Horsbrugh noted, 'a pleasant morning with a gentle breeze from the west'.[8] For days, there had been no rain, though it was rather cold, as the winds had been mainly from the north and north-west.

Hanoverian troops formed the bulk of the right (or east) column, and their orders were to keep to the eastern side of the inundation, pass through Forbes's barrier and then cross the sand dunes as far as the new eastern parallel that led from St Carlos battery to the site of a newly planned battery. The centre column was to follow the path known as the Strand alongside the Bay of Gibraltar, pass through the Bayside barrier and veer across the old market gardens towards St Carlos battery. The left column was to travel the furthest, along the Strand until they reached the St Martin's and St Paschal's batteries – a distance of over half a mile from the safety of Landport. The plan was for the light infantry and grenadier troops to move ahead swiftly and attack and defeat any guards, after which they were to form a defensive line while the Spanish works and guns were destroyed.

Just as the centre column was approaching the gardens, they were unexpectedly spotted by alert Spanish guards who, perhaps in the act of gathering vegetables, were taken completely by surprise and started firing before fleeing. Musket shots fired at deserters trying to reach Gibraltar was routine, and so they were ignored. In the centre column was Walter Gordon, who explained how they found their way in the dark: 'A Spanish deserter was our guide; he did his part exceedingly well, yet we could have looked on with pleasure, and seen the traitor to his country hanged on a gibbet. Tho' these rascals are necessary to their employers, and are well paid for their services, their very employers detest them, and every honest heart holds them in utter contempt.'[9]

The right column pushed on towards the parallel and took possession with virtually no resistance. Despite such guides, Hardenberg's regiment from the right column then mistook their route and veered too far westwards, ending up at the formidable St Carlos battery. 'In this dilemma,' Drinkwater said, 'no other alternative offered but pressing forwards, which they gallantly did, after receiving the Enemy's fire. Upon mounting the parapet, the Enemy precipitately retreated, and with great difficulty they descended the stupendous work.'[10] The front of the battery was a huge mound of sand, but the interior was a formidable timber structure measuring about 18 feet from the parapet to the bottom, and the Spaniards had already removed the ladders. Once the grenadiers from the centre column reached this battery, Hardenberg's troops were mistaken for the enemy. Several were wounded, and it was only by shouting out the countersign 'Steady' that further friendly fire was prevented. When the centre column stormed another section of this battery, the Spanish captain of artillery was encountered, and he fought with a soldier from the 73rd Regiment until both were badly wounded. As the British troops attacked, Horsbrugh said, the gunners left behind on Gibraltar fired at the Spanish Lines and the two forts at each end: 'The fire of upper batteries was during the attack laid on with great judgment on Fort Philip, the Barrier, and Sta. Barbara, supported with much vivacity.'[11]

Eliott had broken several rules of warfare. Not only did he remove over one-third of his men from the garrison to attack the enemy positions, but they also advanced well beyond an acceptable distance. He broke a further rule by taking part himself, which Horsbrugh witnessed: 'The Governor went out at the head of the 12th Regiment, having ordered me as soon as the rear of that column [the left one] had passed Landport, to return and acquaint the Lieutenant Governor [Boyd] of his intention to go out a little way with the detachment.'[12] If the Spaniards had organised a counterattack, the situation could have been perilous, leaving

Gibraltar highly vulnerable, but the sortie was not a spur-of-the-moment decision. It was a carefully calculated risk based on all the intelligence at Eliott's disposal.

As soon as each gun battery and fortification was taken and the Spanish guards killed or captured, the light infantry, grenadiers and other troops took up defensive positions to repel any attackers, while workmen, artificers and seamen from the *Brilliant* and *Porcupine* frigates rapidly set about the demolition process with axes, tomahawks, crowbars, hammers and other equipment. The men from the artillery regiment also embarked on their work, for which they were likewise well equipped, as one of their officers described:

Each non-commissioned officer was provided with a lighted slow [match] and paper match, and two portfires (which were carried in a 3-pounder empty cartridge, pricked in holes to give air). The portfires were lighted after the combustibles were fixed; one hammer and 6 spikes to spike up the ordnance; each private was provided with a fire faggot and 10 devils (or hand lights) which he carried in a bag slung across his shoulder; and also had two portfires each.[13]

Their first task was to spike all the ordnance, which was an effective and quick way of putting the guns out of action. It was done by driving a metal spike into the touch-hole, making it impossible to ignite a powder charge. In total, the men wrecked ten mortars and eighteen 26-pounder cannons, all made of brass. Already, the vast fortifications that had been watched for so long from the vantage point of the Rock were being destroyed, and their immense scale and engineering were highlighted by the same artillery officer, who first of all described the most recently constructed batteries:

Six pieces of brass ordnance were found in each of the two gun batteries [St Martin's], which they term 24 pounders, mounted on new garrison truck carriages, with spunges, rammers etc.

complete. The guns were above 9 feet in length, carriages high, and seemingly constructed to allow great elevation. Batteries complete, and ready for immediate service; platforms short; plank laid parallel to the sill of the embrasure; a great slope to diminish the recoil, merlons about 10 feet high with fascines, and filled with sand-bags, etc. The western mortar battery [St Paschal's] was about 60 yards long, and from 12 to 15 feet high, divided into 3 parts, lined with fascines, well made, and strongly picketted together. In the right division of the battery were two large brass 13-inch mortars, their beds were in frames of strong timber, sunk in the ground, so that their direction was invariable ... The center and left divisions of the battery had each 3 brass 26-pounders, fixed in frames of strong timber, their breech sunk about 2 feet below the surface ... they were all laid in the direction of our camp, apparently at about 40 degrees of elevation.[14]

He next outlined the appearance of the St Carlos battery, which had caused such devastation on Gibraltar since the bombardment started in April:

7 mortars of 13 inch and one of 11 [inch], all brass, whose beds were seated in the same manner ... One grand powder magazine situated at about 150 yards in the rear of the eastern angle, and another on the western angle for fixed ammunition ... There was also a capacious bomb-proof in the rear, nearly central, with a number of splinter-proofs of less note. The epaulment on face of the works, about 14 feet in height, well faced with fascines, and a space in front of the mortars, lined with a strong oak plank, at least 7 inches thick, which they had braced together by strong iron work. The battery was well provided with traverses of about 10 feet square, and nothing seemingly wanting to render it as complete as could be wished.[15]

In short, all the batteries had been designed to give the maximum range to their guns, combined with a strong defence against bombardment. They were massive works that had required a vast amount of labour and materials, and had cost a great deal in expenditure and lives.

Once the workmen had dismantled everything, preparations were made for lighting fires to destroy the timber construction of all the batteries and approaches, as well as the gun carriages:

> the Artillery Officers instantly ordered their people to fix their faggots and devils, to the different parts where the materials were collected, and on the signal given at St. Carlos every man set fire to his faggot and devil, and the wind springing up, about that time, made it communicate very rapidly and successfully to the whole, soon after which Captn. Whitham reported to ... Ross that the business was perfectly completed, and that the blowing up of the magazines might soon be expected.[16]

Devils, Ancell said, were incendiary devices, comprising an 'inflammable composition bound in small bundles, which, after the bands of the fascines are cut, are stuck in between the openings'.[17]

By now, Eliott had arrived at St Carlos battery, and John Heriot, in a report he later published to accompany a painting of the sortie, said that Eliott was seen ensuring that those wounded on both sides were cared for, including the Spanish captain of artillery:

> Amongst them, and almost expiring, he found an elegant young man, who was known by his uniform to be a Captain of the Spanish Artillery. The General spoke to him with the tenderness which such a scene naturally inspires in a brave mind, and assuring him of all possible assistance, ordered him to be removed, as the fire was spreading rapidly to the spot where he lay. The Spaniard endeavoured to raise himself from the ground, and with the most expressive action, feebly articulated, '*No, Sir, no—leave me—Let me perish amidst the ruins of my post.*' An officer remained near him a few minutes, until he expired.[18]

The Spanish officer's name was Don Joseph Barboza, and Heriot said that 'he had commanded the guard of the St. Carlos Battery, and gallantly maintained his ground, until his men, finding themselves overpowered, threw down their arms, and deserted him. He reproached their baseness, and exclaiming, *"at least one Spaniard shall die honourably"*—rushed down from the top of his work amongst the attacking column, and fell where he was found, at the foot, and in front of the battery which he guarded.'[19]

The soldiers were so buoyed up by their success that they desperately wanted to attack the Spanish Lines next, but this was too risky, as Spanish reinforcements might arrive any moment from their camp. Instead, the men were ordered to return to Gibraltar, particularly as the fires were taking hold and gunpowder trails were being laid to the magazines. Although Ross was in command, he was not aware that Eliott was present until accosted by him as the troops were preparing to retreat. Eliott asked him what he thought of the business and 'if it was not something extraordinary that they should have gained the enemy's works so easily?' Heriot recorded that Ross, in his astonishment, could only reply that 'the most extraordinary thing was to see *him* there'.[20]

The fortifications were burning fiercely and illuminating the Rock. Ancell said that 'in a few minutes the isthmus appeared an entire blaze, from the fire of their consuming batteries, and the reflection of the light was so great, that a person could have read upon our batteries. Thus successful, the whole body gave three huzzas, which consequently must sensibly aggravate and vex the foe.'[21] Having given Boyd the message that Eliott had gone out with the troops, Horsbrugh was waiting to find out what was happening, and at last the fires shed light on the events in the distance:

The grandeur of this morning's scene cannot possibly be described, when the blaze of the works all on fire first presented to our view the parties busily employed in that important service. The troops under arms regularly formed in excellent order to support the advanced Corps and working parties and ready to march on any other service they might be ordered, which being contrasted with a variety of other objects – grand of themselves – but heightened by the noise of the cannon and mortar on both sides, mingled with the explosions of the magazines of powder and shells blowing up at different times, rendered the whole truly great and magnificent and much exceeds my power of description.[22]

While they marched back to Gibraltar, Eliott shouted out excitedly: 'Look round, my boys, and view how beautiful the rock appears, by the light of this glorious fire.' Boyd's journal was also enthusiastic with praise: 'At half past 4 o'clock our troops returned to the Garrison, with the trophies of honour and victory, which they had with an undaunted courage so nobly obtained as true Britons for their king and country, at the utmost hazard of their lives.' The troops themselves may have regarded the produce in the gardens as more tangible trophies, because 'almost every man was seen with a cabbage or cauliflower, taken from the Land-Port Gardens'.[23]

The return to the garrison should have been hazardous, the artillery officer reflected, because the Spanish forces had a real opportunity to fire on them from Fort St Philip: 'in our retreat they fired but very little, and that little very ill directed, when they must know ... that we had a very narrow pass into the Garrison, particularly from our advanced barriers [Bayside and Forbes] to Landport, and where they might have directed all the fire of their guns and mortars'. Heriot even recorded that 'by some over-sight, the barrier at Forbes was locked after the flank companies had returned, which might have proved of serious consequences to Hardenberg's Regiment had the enemy attempted to annoy the retreat, as the Hanoverians were obliged ... to follow the 12th Regiment through Bay-side.'[24]

The Spaniards had been so certain that an attack was impossible that the commanding officer had even written his report for the guard the next day: 'nothing extraordinary has happened'.[25] Nevertheless, the Royal Artillery officer found it difficult to explain why the British troops were not fired on from the nearby forts:

the enemy had been lulled into security, for the works were not only weakly guarded, but ill defended, their surprize was so great, that, instead of attempting to repulse us, they thought of nothing but securing themselves by flight, for they totally abandoned their Lines, and retired into the two Forts [St Philip and St Barbara], and even in them they did not think themselves secured, so great must be their consternation, otherwise how is it to be accounted for their not firing upon us, even from their forts? Fort Philip particularly was only at 600 yards distance, nay much nearer to the Grenadier and Light Infantry Companies of the 72nd regiment [left column], that was posted betwixt the works and the Fort.[26]

In his dispatches to London, Eliott mentioned casualty figures: 'Many of the enemy were killed upon the spot; but owing to the darkness and other circumstances, I am not enabled to inform your Lordship either of the exact number, or their particular quality.'[27] The numbers were a continued topic of speculation, and Horsbrugh admitted: 'The number of the Enemy killed is not known but cannot be considerable as it is confidently reported there were not more than 150 men in these advanced works. It is however certain that a captain of artillery and about sixteen men were killed and we suppose the rest fled to the Lines.'[28] The captured Spaniards were brought back to the garrison as prisoners-of-war, including two officers, Don Vicente Vasquez Freire, a lieutenant of artillery, and a twenty-two-year-old lieutenant of the Walloon Guards, Baron von Helmstadt, who was from the Palatinate of the Rhine and had only recently joined the Spanish army. Wounded in one knee by a musket shot, he was found on the platform of St Carlos battery, and Heriot described his rescue by two artillerymen:

They took him up in their arms, and carried him out of the battery, where he must soon have perished in the flames. Unwilling to leave him upon the sands in his helpless state, they determined upon carrying him into the Garrison. They were executing their noble purpose, when they met with Lieutenant Cuppage of their own Corps, who ... himself assisted ... With every possible tenderness they conveyed the wounded prisoner to the barriers, where they did not arrive till two hours after the whole detachment had arrived. During this time they had been exposed to the fire of the Enemy's Lines, and had been reported in the Garrison as lost. Having presented themselves at the barrier, and being admitted, they passed through the different Guards amidst the mingled admiration and applause of the whole; till they reached the Garrison Hospital.[29]

Heriot thought that the two soldiers should be remembered for risking their lives:

To the feelings of a British officer, any eulogium upon an exercise of his humanity would wear the appearance of an insult. Generosity to a conquered Enemy is a distinguishing feature in the military character of this country ... To the two soldiers, the same considerations of delicacy do not so strongly apply as to their Officer, and it becomes the peculiar duty of the Historian to snatch from oblivion the names of two men, whose feelings were equally an honour to their profession and their species. They were named Campbell and Paton, two privates in the second Battalion of the Royal Regiment of Artillery.[30]

The losses on the British side were four killed, one man missing and about two dozen wounded, mainly those Hanoverians wounded by friendly fire at St Carlos battery. The missing man, Heriot related, was the soldier from the 73rd who had mortally wounded the captain of artillery. He had fallen 'upon the top of the battery, and when the troops were ordered to retire, the flames spread with such rapidity to the spot where he lay, that it was impossible to save him. It is to be regretted that the name of this gallant soldier cannot now be ascertained.'[31] Drinkwater thought it was commendable that no tools or weapons were lost, though a soldier of the 73rd did lose his plaid.

A greater loss was that of Colonel Abraham Tovey, who commanded the Royal Artillery, but died of illness on the day his men were doing their duty in the sortie. Almost a century later, Captain Duncan, historian of the Royal Artillery, wrote:

> It was the last order issued in Colonel Tovey's name ... and as his men were parading for the sortie, and the moon was running her nightly course—his was running fast too. Before his men returned, he was dead. For nearly half a century he had served in the Royal Artillery—beginning his career as a matross in 1734, and ending it as a Lieutenant-Colonel in 1781. He died in harness—died in the command of a force of Garrison Artillery, which has never been surpassed nor equalled, save by the great and famous siege-train in the Crimea.[32]

Before the end of the year, his daughter Augusta Tovey, who had been left a fortune by him, married Martin Eccles Lindsay of the 73rd Regiment, by special licence issued by Eliott.[33]

It was only when the last of the troops were returning to the garrison that the Spaniards began to beat to arms, and at that time a massive explosion shook Gibraltar, described in Boyd's journal: 'at half past 5 we had the pleasure to see their grand magazine in the new works blow up in the air, by which explosion some of our shattered buildings near Landport fell, but done no further damage, our soldiers on the batteries giving 3 huzzas at [the] same time to mortify the enemy with our success.'[34] At daybreak, Horsbrugh recorded,

> we discovered the Lines filled with troops ... but none appeared to be advanced, nor was any attempt made by the enemy to extinguish the fire. Some few stragglers only now and then approached it, seemingly with great caution ... The fire continued to burn briskly for the greatest part of the day, with repeated explosions of powder and shots ... In the afternoon it was reported that the Commander in Chief had come down to the Lines and that one or two officers had advanced separately at different times to survey the damage, and soon afterwards retired.[35]

It was thought that 'the cowardly Spaniards are so confused that they dare not attempt the least assistance to put out the fire',[36] but the real reason was surely due to the intensity of the fires.

The following morning, the 28th, the General Orders gave the countersign as 'St Roque', in a mocking reference to the Spanish headquarters, whose forward batteries were still burning.[37] Before daybreak, Horsbrugh was woken by the pounding of heavy guns. Arriving at the Grand Battery, he was informed that a considerable explosion in one of the burning batteries had been followed by small-arms fire from the Spanish Lines. The fires had obviously ignited a store of shells, but the nervous Spaniards had assumed they were being attacked by yet another sortie. As dawn broke, the thick plumes of smoke and occasional bursts of flame showed that fires were still consuming the works over a wide area. That afternoon, Horsbrugh watched as one high-ranking Spaniard acknowledged the catastrophe: 'several officers came from the camp and some few of them singly ventured forward to reconnoitre the demolished works. One of them after attentively surveying the general ruin, looked up to Willis's, pulled off his hat, and made a low bow to the officers who were looking out from thence, and afterwards walked deliberately back to the Lines.'[38]

While the exchange of cannon fire between the garrison and Spanish Lines continued, the fires still burned, even though the next day brought wind and rain. 'By the consuming of the wooden materials with which the batteries were constructed,' Horsbrugh noted, 'the sand has already sunk so considerably that we can now see some of the mortars and guns fallen from their beds, which we are persuaded are totally burnt, and as the fire blazed out at different times in the night and still sends out a great deal of smoke, it is imagined it may continue burning for some time longer.' It took a week for the fires to die down, and to their disappointment the garrison could see that part of St Carlos battery was less badly damaged than they had hoped. Even so, Horsbrugh noted, 'we only see one of the guns standing and one mortar on its bed, the wooden work being in all probability consumed'.[39]

The sortie was an incredible achievement. It had lasted only an hour and a half, but in that time countless months of work had been destroyed. One soldier who took part remarked: 'The work of the enemy, thus destroyed, has cost them immense labour and expence, as it was most completely finished – it is supposed it must have stood them in fifteen millions of dollars.' Ancell was of the opinion that the garrison had destroyed 'in fifteen minutes, a work estimated at three million of dollars', while a decade later Heriot wrote: 'It is known as a fact, by the acknowledgment of several persons of distinction in the Spanish army, that the construction and materials of these works, destroyed by the fire, cost the enormous sum of thirteen millions of large piastres (equal to three millions sterling).'[40]

The report penned by the artillery officer contained his own opinion:

This is barely credible at the first view, that the ... detachment should march out, attack, and completely destroy the enemy's advanced works, spike all their ordnance, blow up the magazines, works that had taken them 14 months in erecting, with a very great expence and loss of men, exclusive of 16 months previous to that, in preparing the materials; those works at 1200 yards distance from the Garrison, covered and flanked by a number of pieces of cannon and mortars at only 600 yards distance [Fort St Philip], and in the front of an encampment of 10 or 12000 men, with so small a loss, but no plan could be better constructed, and the event shews it was well executed.[41]

Eliott's own steward, Captain Mackay, commented: 'thus our brave troops has executed an arduous task which all Europe will remember to the Honour of Great Britain.'[42] He was not overstating the significance of the sortie, because it is still regarded as one of the most famous in military history.

# CHAPTER SIXTEEN

———— ·◆· ————

# MINORCA FALLS

After Baron von Helmstadt was carried to the naval hospital, the surgeons found that his shattered leg needed amputating, but he resisted. Not only was such surgery rarely successful in Spain, but this young good-looking man was betrothed to be married and 'would rather risk his life than present himself before her with only one leg'.[1] Yet amputation was the only viable treatment for a badly broken leg, as John Bell, an eminent Edinburgh surgeon, advised: 'In besieged cities, or in the trenches before a besieged city, most of the wounds are with great shot, or by bombs, or by great splinters of stone, and in such wounds, the limbs are so miserably broken, that in most of the cases, amputation is necessary.'[2] The sooner the operation was performed, the better the chance of a successful outcome, limiting the time for infections to set in.

The reluctance of von Helmstadt to have his leg amputated was understandable, but Eliott was concerned and ordered several convalescent amputees into his room to show off the surgeons' skill. Von Helmstadt relented and recovered well from the operation until a month later, on 28 December 1781, when he died of fever. Everybody on Gibraltar was upset, and the next day his body 'was put into a coffin, covered with black cloth, and decorated with elegant white furniture, the corpse dressed in full uniform, according to the custom of Spain'.[3] At noon, he was taken from the naval hospital down to the New Mole in an elaborate procession:

The Grenadiers of the 12th Regiment in caps and arms reversed. Band of music and two drummers beating the dead march. Town Major and Secretary. Two lights, crucifix, Roman Priest [Father Messa] in robes and mitre. The corpse borne by the 39th Grenadiers, and six officers the pall bearers. The Governor, Lieutenant-General de la Motte, General Picton and Commodore Curtis with a numerous train of officers, soldiers and inhabitants. Thus went the procession to the ... New Mole, where two barges waited under cartel flags to receive him, with the Governor's secretary and Town Major, and his baggage in the other barge. The Grenadiers being drawn up on the Wharf, they fired three vollies in the air over the corpse ... The barges proceeding into the Bay until they met the Spanish cartel ... and both parties returned to their respective shores.[4]

With the shock of having their advance works so badly damaged in the sortie, the Spaniards were initially in a state of torpor. For some weeks, the ruins had smouldered, bursting into flames now and again. 'They contented themselves with venting their revenge by a brisk cannonade upon the Garrison,' Heriot said, 'and by hanging in their Camp some of the unfortunate soldiers who had been driven from their works and escaped into their Lines.'[5] On the last day of 1781, one officer calculated the cost to Spain of their shot and shells over the past year: 'According to judges, the lowest estimate of the Enemy's ... firings for metal and powder only, at the rate of £3 per shell, and £1 per shot, will amount to £188,721 sterling, which divide by 127, the number they have killed us, and it will appear that each man's death will stand on their books to cost £1,486 sterling; besides adding to our magazines about 80,000 shot and shells that we have gathered up fit for service.'[6]

It did not take long, after the courtesies and solemnity of the funeral procession, for the Spaniards to resume their customary bombardments, and as soon as the sun came up over the Rock on New Year's Day, 1 January 1782, an especially fierce attack led to one act of heroism that impressed Captain Price:

Lieutenant [John] Rogers of the Royal Artillery had a very narrow escape at Princess Anne's Battery, Willis's. A shell fell close beside him, and he tumbled into the hole which it had made, where he was wedged up by the earth to his middle, while the fuze of the shell continued burning. In this alarming situation, Corporal Martin of the same corps with an uncommon intrepidity and presence of mind came to his assistance, but finding Mr. Rogers hemmed in, in such a manner that he could not disengage him, he called to all mattrosses at some distance. By their joint assistance and the blessing of providence, he was rescued from the very jaws of death, and they had scarce reached a traverse close at hand when the shell exploded. When it is considered that poor Martin had a wife and children depending on him for support, there will be found something even beyond intrepidity to admire in him. The Governor, when he heard the story, ordered both the brave fellows concerned a handsome present [5 guineas] and gave them his particular thanks.[7]

Although the town was already a scene of devastation, Walter Gordon described the outcome of the continued bombardment: 'The destruction of the town was now completed. The Spanish Church, which was a beautiful edifice, was entirely destroyed; the few houses which had escaped the former devastation, were now beat to the ground, and not one stone left standing upon another. Gardens were plowed up by the bursting of bombs and the falling of balls, fruit trees tore up by the roots, the bodies of the dead tore up from their graves, and streets filled with the ruins of houses.'[8]

On 4 January the *St Philip's Castle* cutter reached Gibraltar from Leghorn in Italy, having slipped away from Minorca in November. The siege of the citadel had been going on since August 1781, and the news they brought was that the small British garrison was completely outnumbered by the Duc de Crillon's besieging forces – which would eventually amount to some fifteen thousand men. Fort St Philip (which they also called St Philip's Castle) was strong, but not well supplied, particularly where food was concerned. The garrison could surrender or attempt to hold off the attackers until a convoy came with supplies and reinforcements. Newspapers in Britain were clamouring for such a convoy, and speculation was rife that one was on its way, but Minorca's officers knew there was little likelihood of a convoy in the near future. The garrison was strong enough to hold out against most attacks, and so Eliott's decision not to allow the 73rd Regiment to proceed to Minorca was a blessing, because it would have meant more men to feed.

After invading Minorca in August, the French and Spaniards had embarked on building batteries, which the garrison fired at from Fort St Philip. In September, Lieutenant-General James Murray, the governor, had seen an opportunity for a daring sortie against Crillon's headquarters, during which one battery was destroyed and a hundred prisoners captured.[9] The fort maintained its bombardment of the siegeworks, backed up by more sorties, which led the Comte de Crillon, one of the French army officers, to admit his gloom: 'I think absolutely like you, my friend, on the impossibility of taking Fort St Philip with the forces that we have. But what can we do – if the King of Spain has got it into his head, it will be necessary to attack it. I don't believe that we could extend the siegeworks from here in a month ... and I understand less the possibility of remaining all winter under canvas.'[10] He also thought that if they did stay there all winter, half the men would be in hospital within four months. Born at Paris in 1748, Félix-François-Dorothée des Balbes de Berton, comte de Crillon, was a younger son of the overall commander, Duc de Crillon. He had formerly served in the Spanish army and later moved to the French army, becoming colonel of the Bretagne Regiment in 1778.

The *St Philip's Castle* cutter had brought twenty-two of the prisoners-of-war to Gibraltar, as well as dispatches and many letters written six weeks earlier, which Horsbrugh said 'are in a style of confidence and cheerfulness which give us reason to hope the Enemy will not find that so easy a conquest as they give out. Some of the letters mention ... that the Duke de Crillon had made an attempt to bribe the Governor General Murray with the offer of a million dollars.'[11] Boyd's journal reported that Murray was outraged and replied that he never expected Crillon to think he could turn traitor to his King and Country, 'and that he would defend the Garrison against all the powers of France and Spain while he has a man left that was able to fire a gun, and ... he would advise the Duke to take care of himself, for he might be assured that wherever he met him, at the Courts of France or in any other place, that he would cane him like a scoundrel that he was, for he was neither a soldier nor a gentleman by his behaviour.'[12]

After a few days, on 10 January, the *St Philip's Castle* headed back to Port Mahon, but Captain William Wilson, one of Boyd's aides-de-camp and possibly the author of his journals, was unhappy with Eliott: 'A certain great Captain (W.— W.—n) here has procured 3 dozen [bottles] of wine to send to a brother in St Philips Castle at Mahon by the above vessel, but once, nay twice, he applied for a permit to put it on board the ship, but was refused by the Governor of so small a favour to a Gentleman.'[13] The following week, the *Henry* and *Mercury* ordnance ships sailed for England, taking with them more invalids, inhabitants and soldiers' wives, as well as the prisoners-of-war from Minorca and those captured in the November sortie, including Don Vicente Freire.

By now, the Spaniards felt reinvigorated and were starting to replenish their materials and rebuild their devastated fortifications. By late February the work was well under way, as Corporal Cranfield told his parents in London:

The Spaniards are renewing their advanced works with a ten-gun battery and two mortar batteries; but all in vain; we never were better prepared for them than we are at this time. Our works and fortifications are firm and strong, so that no Spaniard dare face us within musket-shot. They still hold on the siege with great vigour, and have now been firing upon us night and day for eleven months. The like was never known in the memory of man ... I have actually counted, when upon guard, eighty shells in one hour; but the name of an Englishman frightens the stoutest hearts in Spain, in spite of Anthony, their great saint.[14]

He was right to say that the garrison's works were strong, because following the sortie, all the defences on the Rock were being improved, and Drinkwater admired the engineers who 'were indefatigable in repairing the splinter-proofs, magazines, traverses, and communications, along the north front, which were damaged by the Enemy's fire. The King's, Queen's, and Prince's lines had likewise a share in their attention.'[15]

As the Spanish siegeworks on the isthmus were extended, many of them could only be targeted from high up on the Rock, and then only by aiming the cannons downwards at a steep angle. In these conditions it was difficult to load the guns, and the violent recoil often destroyed the mountings. This major problem was now overcome when Lieutenant George Koehler of the Royal Artillery devised a mechanism known as the depressing gun carriage. Koehler was born in London in 1758 to an English mother and a German father serving in the Royal Artillery. Soon after his arrival in Gibraltar with Darby's convoy in April 1781, he was noticed by Eliott, who thought so highly of him that he appointed him his aide-de-camp later that year.

Koehler solved the problem of firing cannons downwards by fixing a gun barrel to a plank that was laid on top of another plank. The underside of the upper plank had a spindle that ran in a groove in the lower plank. The downwards tilt of the gun was achieved by attaching the front end of the lower plank by a hinge to a gun carriage, and the gun was pointed downwards by propping up the other end of the plank. When the gun was fired, the recoil was absorbed by the upper plank sliding over the lower one, rather than wrecking the carriage. This system also allowed the gun barrel to be lowered, swivelled to one side, cleaned out and reloaded behind the safety of the defences, before being pointed downwards again.

From mid-February, the first of several depressing gun carriages was moved to the highest part of the Rock, overlooking the isthmus, and experiments proved very effective: 'As to the accuracy of the depressing shot, no farther proof need be adduced, than that out of thirty rounds, twenty-eight shot took place in one traverse in the St. Carlos's battery, at the distance of near one thousand four hundred yards.'[16] Koehler's invention was the forerunner of later artillery recoil systems.

Towards the end of February, a ship successfully ran the blockade, bringing much-needed provisions from Portugal – as well as many distressed passengers. This was the *Mercury* that had left Gibraltar six weeks earlier, ostensibly for England. The passengers were unaware that Eliott had secretly instructed Captain Heighington to go to Lisbon, load up with wine, oranges and lemons and return to Gibraltar. With Minorca being besieged, Portugal was Gibraltar's nearest ally, and lemons were desperately needed, since even before the sortie scurvy had once again been affecting every regiment. The numbers of those afflicted had recently dropped, probably because several small vessels had of late brought cargoes to Gibraltar, but at the end of February 162 people were still suffering from scurvy, and 155 of those were in hospital.[17] In his latest letter to his brother, Ancell expressed his horror at their plight:

> Our garrison are pretty healthy, considering the hardships, dangers, and scarcity of fresh diet, which at present prevails; but of late, they have been very much afflicted with the most inveterate scurvy, which deprived a great many of the use of their limbs, by rendering them stiff and swelled. The flesh of the sufferers, I assure you, was almost black, and you would pity, were you a spectator, to view them limping to their post to partake of a share of their comrades, in opposing the foe.[18]

Attempts had been made at Lisbon to persuade the passengers of the *Mercury* to disembark, but they refused, and nobody there was told about the plan, for fear of spies. Drinkwater recorded that 'to their great mortification, they found, on their entrance into the Straits, the unpleasant shores of Spain and Barbary, instead of the exhilarating coast of Britain'.[19]

That afternoon, Drinkwater noted that 'the Enemy fired a grand feu-de-joie in camp, commencing with a salute from the lines. They repeated the fire a fourth time, which led us to imagine they had gained some advantage at Minorca.'[20] It was later learned that the *feu de joie* was indeed in celebration of the surrender of the besieged Fort St Philip a few days earlier. Although a few privateers and supply vessels had managed to evade the French and Spanish ships, it was never enough to sustain the British garrison, especially when the Duc de Crillon tightened the blockade. Nowhere in Fort St Philip could vegetables be grown, and in late December the first cases of scurvy had appeared. Soon they were all suffering. The garrison was also affected by constant disagreements between Murray and his deputy governor, Sir William Draper, who was highly critical of his methods of defence. Draper thought that the bombardment was not sufficiently heavy to hinder the enemy's siegeworks, a situation made even worse back in October when, one British officer recorded, 'The Governor by this day's orders has thought proper to put a stop to all firing whatever without his or the commanding officer of Artillery's orders.'[21]

As the winter dragged on, the health of the men in Fort St Philip deteriorated, and while the French and Spanish troops also suffered, they managed to push forward their siegeworks and set up gun batteries. Over Christmas, the same British officer wrote: 'Very fine weather. The Enemy lucky in having such [weather] to carry on their works, but more so as the Governor being so saving of his powder. The Garrison might fire a great deal more, but no one dare do it without orders',[22] while on 4 January 1782 (when the *St Philip's Castle* had reached Gibraltar), he noted: 'Capt. Squires daughter sent into the fort by the Duc (a child on account of some family disagreement). She says the batteries are to be opened on Sunday. If this intelligence proves true we think it very extraordinary the Duke should let us have such information of his intentions.'[23]

Two days later, the French and Spanish guns did indeed start firing, as Captain Dixon of the artillery witnessed: 'A little before seven o'clock this morning they gave three cheers and fired a feu de joie, then all their batteries fired upon us with great fury, which was equally returned by our brave Artillery. Our General declared he had never seen guns and mortars better served than ours were.' The next day, he commented: 'such a terrible fire, night and day, from both sides, never has been seen at any siege', followed by: 'All last night and this day they never ceased firing, and we as well returned it. You would have thought the elements were in a blaze. It has been observed they fire about 750 shot and shell every hour. Who in the name of God is able to stand it?'[24]

The bombardment was relentless, day after day, and on the 10th Dixon wrote: 'The enemy had 36 shells in flight at the same time. God has been with us in preserving our people: they are in high spirits, and behave as Englishmen. Considering our small garrison, they do wonders.' But by the 20th it was obvious the garrison could not hold out much longer: 'This night shells meet shells in the air. We have a great many sick and wounded and those that have died of their wounds ... Our sentries have hardly time to call out "A shell!" and "Down!" before others are at their heels.' Four days later he added: 'The Artillery have hard duty and are greatly fatigued. The scurvy rages among our men.'[25]

Between the scurvy and the bombardment, the garrison was whittled away, and Dixon admitted that Fort St Philip was a battered ruin: 'They fire shot and shell every minute. The poor Castle is in a tattered and rotten condition, as indeed are all the works in general ... The Castle and every battery round it are so filled by the excavations made by the enemy's shells, that he must be a nimble young man who can go from one battery to another without danger. The Castle, their grand mark, as well as the rest of the works, are in a most shocking plight.'[26] A week later, on 4 February 1782, the garrison raised a white flag for a parley and negotiated terms for a surrender.

The fort may have been wrecked, but it was scurvy that had forced the surrender. According to Murray, the garrison surgeon had considered that 'Three days further obstinacy on my part must have inevitably destroyed the brave remains of this Garrison, as they declare there was no remedy for the men in the hospitals, but vegetables, and that of the six hundred and sixty able to do duty, five hundred and sixty were actually tainted with the scurvy, and, in all likelihood, would be in the hospitals in four days time.' Generous terms of surrender were negotiated, and the garrison was allowed to leave the fort with their arms and colours, before laying them down, which Murray described: 'Perhaps a more noble, nor more tragical scene, was never exhibited than that of the march of the Garrison of St. Philip's through the Spanish and French armies ... Such was the distressing figures of our men that many of the Spanish and French troops are said to have shed tears as they passed them ... The Spanish as well as the French surgeons attend our hospitals.'[27]

Hardly a fit man was left in the garrison, and they were allowed to be taken to England, technically remaining prisoners-of-war, on condition that they did not serve again until officially exchanged. This was an unusual instance of parole terms for officers being extended to all ranks, and Murray expressed his gratitude, in particular to the Comte de Crillon: 'We owe infinite obligations to the Count de Crillon; they can never be forgot by any of us. I hope this young man never will command an army against my sovereign, for his military talents are as conspicuous as the goodness of his heart.'[28] Less happily, Draper continued his complaints against Murray and forced a court-martial. Of all the charges against him, Murray was found guilty of only two, for which he was reprimanded, but it did not affect his subsequent career.

Civilians in the fort, other than the families of soldiers, had included 'Twenty Corsicans, and twenty-five Greeks, Turks, Moors, Jews &c.' They were expelled from the island to Leghorn and left to their own devices. Some of the Jews had earlier fled to Minorca to escape the siege at Gibraltar, but they were not allowed to return, and thirteen of them eventually arrived in London, by then in a wretched state, to be taken in by the Jewish community.[29] For Gibraltar, the fall of Fort St Philip had serious consequences. An important source of supplies was now completely cut off, the French and Spaniards had proved they could overwhelm a strong fortress, so they were buoyed up by success, and it was expected that their massive army on Minorca would soon join those besieging the Rock.

On 24 February, the day after the *feu de joie* around the Bay of Gibraltar in celebration of Minorca's fall, the *St Ann* ordnance ship arrived with gunpowder and two gunboats, similar to those used by the Spaniards to such deadly effect. They were supplied in pieces, which the navy carpenters began to assemble. The *St Ann* also brought news that the *Vernon* would soon arrive with ten more gunboats. Four weeks later, the *Vernon* and *Success* were approaching the Straits when they encountered the Spanish 32-gun frigate *Santa Catalina*. After a long battle, the severely damaged *Santa Catalina* surrendered to the *Success*, but when other Spanish ships were sighted in the distance all the valuables and prisoners were taken off, and the prize-ship was set on fire, subsequently blowing up. The ships in the distance may actually have been the Royal Navy frigates *Cerberus* and *Apollo*, escorting a small convoy of four transports with troop reinforcements, primarily seven hundred men from a new regiment, the 97th. This convoy, along with the *Vernon* and the *Success*, reached Gibraltar at intervals on 24 March.

The paperwork salvaged from the *Santa Catalina* had evidence of a spy network, as Drinkwater recounted: 'On board the prize were found papers describing the Vernon, to the most minute part of her rigging, at the same time mentioning the officers' names, who were passengers, and every particular article of her cargo.'[30] Drinkwater also heard that several enemy ships had been specifically looking for the *Vernon*. These papers demonstrated the important role of espionage in European warfare. Before being allowed to be sent, all letters from Gibraltar were vetted, and every care was taken to safeguard dispatches to Britain, as seen in the sailing orders issued by Eliott to the *St Ann*:

You are hereby directed and required ... to make the best of your way to England, and on no account to deviate from your course to go in chace, nor are you to speak with any vessel, but use your best endeavours to make your passage with the utmost expedition. You are to receive and give passage to all such persons as shall be sent on board by Capt. Curtis's order, or by mine thro' the Quarter Master General, and no other passengers whomsoever. The dispatches which will be committed to your care you are to deliver to the post master of the first port at which you may arrive, to whom you are to give directions to forward them to London by express. And in the mean time you are to keep a sufficient weight constantly affixt to them, that in case you should be attacked by an Enemy and no probability of escaping, they may, previous to your striking, be thrown overboard and sunk.[31]

On the Rock, it was the deserters who provided more information than spies about what was happening within the besieging forces, and the Spaniards also made good use of deserters from the Rock, but occasionally men suspected of being spies were arrested in Gibraltar. They were interrogated, tried and usually sentenced to death if found guilty, and a few weeks earlier Antonio Juanico, a mariner, had been tried on the charge of being employed as a spy by the Spanish general Don Martin Alvarez.[32] After being found guilty, Eliott ordered him to be hanged, declaring that 'in regard to spies and traitors, it has ever been an established maxim amongst all nations that as their crimes are of the most enormous kind, for as much as the mischief they may occasion is of the most alarming nature, so their punishment should be capital'. Two weeks later, he was granted a stay of execution, and in early March Eliott pardoned him from 'a motive of compassion for the miserable situation of the Convict's family'. There was one condition – Juanico should atone for this serious offence by 'constantly serving on board His Majesty's Ships during the present war, and that he never attempts to put his foot on shore again in this Fortress'.[33] He was lucky to escape with his life.

Just five days after arriving with the *Cerberus* and *Apollo*, most of the 97th Regiment fell ill, and the hospital became extremely crowded. A few weeks later, Spilsbury wrote disparagingly: 'A picquet was demanded from the 97th, but they could not furnish it. So much for young Regiments', but after a few days he was more sympathetic: 'The 97th still sickly and dying fast; their fever is contagious, and others of the Garrison have it.'[34] Seventy men died of the fever, possibly typhus, and the remainder of the regiment would be of little use for several months.

The artillery firing continued on both sides regardless, bringing with it yet more injuries and deaths, and after one severe thunderstorm Boyd's journal noted that it was impossible to distinguish thunder and lightning from the awesome artillery fire: 'how amazed we stand and cry, that's the report of a gun, nay a second says it is a shell, and a third it's thunder, so confused we stand aghast not knowing which way to look for safety, from sulphur, smoke and fire! If this is not a representation of the worlds expiring in flames, I do not know what is.'[35] Because of their burning fuses, it was easier to spot incoming shells rather than cannonballs, but many people found themselves transfixed, unable to move out of the way.

Even in good light in the daytime, with calm weather, it was often difficult to spot incoming fire, but some of the very young soldiers possessed this uncanny skill and were employed to keep a look-out. At Willis's on 25 March, the day after the ordnance convoy arrived, Drinkwater recorded: 'The boy who was usually stationed on the works where a large party was employed, to inform the men when the Enemy's fire was directed to that place, had been reproving them for their carelessness in not attending to him; and had just turned his head toward the Enemy, when he observed this shot, and instantly called for them to take care: his caution was however too late; the shot entered the embrasure.' This one shot alone 'took off the legs of two men belonging to the 72d and 73d regiments, one leg of a soldier of the 73d, and wounded another man in both legs: thus *four* men had *seven* legs taken off and wounded by one shot.'[36] He added:

It is somewhat singular, that this boy should be possessed of such uncommon quickness of sight, as to see the Enemy's shot almost immediately after they quitted the guns. He was not, however, the only one in the Garrison possessing this qualification; another boy of about the same age was as celebrated, if not his superior. Both of them belonged to the Artificer company, and were constantly placed on some part of the works to observe the Enemy's fire: their names were Richardson and Brand; the former was reputed to have the best eye.[37]

They were actually called Thomas Richmond, a carpenter, and John Brand, a mason, whose fathers were sergeants in the company, and they had the nicknames of 'Shell' and 'Shot'. Another artificer boy, Joseph Parsons, was said to be equally talented.[38]

The bombardment was so constant that almost every entry in Boyd's journal around this time begins with the words 'Firing continues'. On 10 April, during a particularly fierce bombardment, Ancell mentioned the death of one young officer who was leading the guard uphill to the Spur battery: 'a shell which fell in Landport Ditch [a covered way], just as the new guard came to relieve the old one, killed Lieutenant [Thomas] Whetham, of the 12th Regiment, wounded his servant who was on the right of the guard, and blew the drummer's drum in pieces. He was an amiable officer, and well respected; the loss of him is much regretted by all ranks.'[39]

Two days later, on 12 April 1782, everyone was expecting a massive assault because it was the first anniversary of the bombardment that had started when Darby's convoy arrived. Instead, the Spaniards behaved strangely, firing a single gun every two or three minutes, and, according to Drinkwater, 'Some jocular person in the Garrison remarked, that perhaps they were commemorating the day with fasting and prayer, and by their *minute-guns* expressing their sorrow, that so many thousand barrels of powder, and rounds of ammunition, should have been expended to so little purpose.'[40] The Spaniards, though, were not giving up, but were actually laying out more camps for troops and extending their fortifications, in expectation of reinforcements.[41] Now and again, the gunners on the Rock managed to set fire to parts of the siege-works, with everyone admitting that the Spaniards behaved with particular courage in extinguishing the fires, but it was obvious that after the success of Minorca, the Duc de Crillon was now going to take charge of operations, with France joining forces for a final assault on Gibraltar.

This was a bleak prospect for the garrison, and more soldiers chose to desert, while others committed a series of crimes, with brutal punishments inflicted on anyone who was caught. In mid-April, Horsbrugh related: 'Edward Hammerton, soldier in the 12th Regiment, was tried by a General Court Martial for attempting to commit sodomy with a drummer of the same regiment and sentenced to receive five hundred lashes on his bare back and backside, with a Cat of Nine Tails from the hands of the common hangman under the gallows, and to stand in a pillory for the space of two hours at such time or times as the Governor shall appoint.'[42] This was lenient, because he could have been hanged for sodomy. Another journal recorded a soldier by the name of Atkins who decided to desert rather than await punishment for robbing a soldier of the 72nd of his watch and money: 'The batteries fired very heavy upon him, and it's thought he is deadly wounded by the bursting of a small shell, as he was carried into the enemy's works by 3 or 4 men. The loss of this man (being an old offender in bad practices) is better lost than found, and as to intelligence, he can give none of any consequence.'[43]

The Spaniards already knew that the garrison had received artillery supplies and gunboats, so it was only details of the defences on the Rock that deserters could offer. Trials of the new gunboats now took place, with one soldier commenting: 'We promise ourselves great things from these gun-boats, during the summer.'[44] They were put under the command of Captain Roger Curtis, but were hardly used at first, because the following few weeks proved strangely quiet, with the amount of firing greatly diminished. The Spaniards were instead concentrating on increasing their troop numbers and improving their fortifications. Even more remarkable was a period of silence from seven o'clock in the evening of 4 May to seven in the evening of the following day, when no firing whatsoever took place from the Spanish artillery and the garrison. It was, as Drinkwater noted, 'the first *twenty-four hours* in which there had been no firing for the space of nearly THIRTEEN MONTHS'.[45] This lull in firing was not to last, and the siege was about to change direction.

# CHAPTER SEVENTEEN

—— •◆• ——

# FRENCH INGENUITY

An outline of a new plan for attacking Gibraltar appeared in the French press in the spring of 1782 and was soon translated and published in British newspapers:

LETTER *from* PARIS, *March* 15.

The officer who has planned the attack of Gibraltar is Monsieur D'Arcon, Sub Brigadier of the French corps of Engineers. The Duc de Crillon, who was well acquainted with that gentleman's abilities, had called him to Spain ... Mons. de Arcon, on his arrival at Cadiz, some time in August [1781] was much surprised to hear that he was to proceed to Minorca, a place of which he had not the least knowledge. He requested leave to return to France, but was desired to stay at Cadiz, in order to bring to perfection his plan, by surveying Gibraltar on every side. He thus spent six months in going backwards and forwards to St. Roch [San Roque], Algeciras, Ceuta &c.[1]

At the start of the siege in 1779, King Carlos III had asked for ideas on capturing Gibraltar. Of the sixty-nine replies, most were too outlandish to consider seriously. One that came to the fore was presented by Pedro Pablo Abarca de Bolea, the Count of Aranda, who proposed a massive Franco-Spanish invasion of England in order to force the British government to concede to various demands, including Spain taking possession of Gibraltar. This plan was received favourably, but shrank in size and scope after being discussed, amended and agreed with the French, resulting in the invasion attempt that had failed so dismally.[2]

When the sustained bombardment of Gibraltar also failed to bring the garrison to its knees, the other plans were considered once again, and in July 1781 that of the forty-seven-year-old French military engineer, Jean-Claude-Eléonor Le Michaud d'Arçon, was chosen. His suggestion was for a combined attack from land and sea, relying especially on a bombardment from formidable floating gun batteries. There had been few previous attempts to build and use such vessels, and d'Arçon's planned attack against Gibraltar would be the first to employ elaborately designed and constructed floating batteries as the main thrust of an attack. Warships were effectively floating batteries, because their main purpose was to carry as many cannons as possible to counter enemy warships, but they did not have a great deal of protection against cannonballs fired at them. At close range, solid shot could smash through both sides of a warship, and they were particularly vulnerable to red-hot shot, which might burn right through the bottom of a ship, set it on fire or ignite the gunpowder magazines. They could not withstand prolonged artillery fire from batteries on land and had no chance of making a dent in strongly built masonry defences, such as those on Gibraltar. D'Arçon therefore wanted to create gun batteries that floated on the sea, but had the resilience and firepower of land batteries.

By April 1782 he had been working on his plan for several months and had spent a considerable time surveying the coastline and defences of Gibraltar. From time to time suspicious activity was noticed, as on one occasion when Horsbrugh recorded: 'At five in the morning the Vanguard and Repulse prames fired each a shot at a small boat they supposed to be sounding or reconnoitring.'[3] Using such a small boat in the dead of night, d'Arçon avoided being wounded or captured while he took soundings close to Gibraltar, but the surveying was only the beginning, because the major work was in the preparation of the floating batteries, which started in Cadiz and then shifted to Algeciras.

British newspapers also published other details they had learned about d'Arçon:

His plan has been adopted, and requires only 18,000 men. He is now at Algesiras, busy in the construction of boats, which are so formed as not to be overset or burnt. It is supposed that the principal attack will be made by sea, towards the New Mole ... and the advanced works, which are daily encreasing, will unite in the general onset, the success of which, if not beyond doubt, appears at least very probable to those who are acquainted with the abilities of the engineer.[4]

The attack on the Rock would be a battle between engineers: d'Arçon and his staff, who were devising novel methods of assault, pitted against William Green and his engineers, who were doing everything they could think of to defend Gibraltar.

News of d'Arçon's scheme soon reached the garrison, and on 11 April one soldier wrote in his diary:

By letters from Portugal, by a boat this morning, we learn that the enemy are fitting up a number of ships, at Cadiz, intended for floating batteries to come against the walls: it is said they are to be lined with cork and oakum, and rendered shot and shell proof; that the Duke de Crillon is to have the command of the army in camp, and that, as soon as he arrives with the conquering troops from Minorca, the regular siege against this place will commence.[5]

Having suffered so much for nearly three years, the soldier was appalled by the arrogance of the suggestion that, up to now, it had not been a proper siege. 'In the name of all that is horrible in war,' he raged, 'what is meant by a siege, if bombarding, cannonading, and blockading on all sides ... is not one?'[6] The idea that the French would now start a 'regular siege' probably emanated from their disdain for the Spanish military effort.

D'Arçon's plan was to convert a number of merchant ships into floating batteries. The work had already begun at Cadiz, where the internal frames of each ship were strengthened and the hull covered with cork and oakum. The unpicked fibres from lengths of old rope were called 'oakum', while 'junk' was the old rope itself. On Gibraltar, the floating batteries were not only referred to as battering ships, but also as 'junk ships' because of the old rope used in their construction. Over this flexible layer of cork and oakum, a complete hull was built of new timber, resulting in a triple-thickness hull designed to absorb the impact of cannonballs, in the same way that worn-out rope made into mats was used by the garrison to absorb the impact of cannonballs fired at their gun batteries. In March one batch of ships had been brought to Algeciras for the next stage of conversion into floating batteries, and more arrived in early May, but Ancell heard that onlookers were not impressed: 'The eight large ships that arrived over the way the 9th instant [9 May] are hauled close to the shore, and are unrigging, and those that arrived on the 24th March have proceeded to the Orange Grove. It is currently reported that they are lined with cork, and are to be converted into batteries, but most people think that they are more fit for fire-wood, than attacking a fortress.'[7]

This work was taking place within sight of Gibraltar, and the progress of the ships was a subject of constant interest, with Horsbrugh recording what was happening only a few days later: 'in the Bay of Algaziras they are begun to cut down the quarter deck and poops of the two ships lately hauled in shore, on which work a number of boats and men appear to be employed'. They were being prepared for one or two specially strengthened gun decks within the hull that could support large cannons. Towards the end of May, it became obvious that the ships were also being given additional protection. 'This forenoon we had a tolerable good view of the Enemy at work on their shipping at Algaziras,' wrote Horsbrugh. 'They are covering their larboard [port] sides with timber or planks, which is no doubt intended as a defence against our shot &c.'[8] Speculation was rife, and another soldier commented: 'The enemy have been fully employed these ten days past on two very large ships at Algesiras, thickening the larboard side with light materials. They have cut out eleven or twelve ports between decks, and shortened the larboard waist. I suppose they intend to make the upper deck splinter proof, as well as the sides shot proof. From every appearance, they will be snug batteries on the water.'[9]

Because the starboard side was not being reinforced, the assumption was that the floating batteries were intended to fire only from their port side towards the garrison. They would therefore need to be towed into position by boats and be securely anchored, which would make them stationary targets. There was widespread scepticism, and Ancell remarked that 'most of the garrison are of opinion, from their construction, that they will be found of very little use when they attack our walls, as they never will be able to tow them near enough to do any material execution, for should they daringly come on, their boats will be inevitably cut off by the grape shot from the garrison'.[10]

Progress on the siegeworks slowed down while every effort was concentrated on the floating batteries. The Spanish firing also began to be aimed much more at the garrison's upper batteries – including Koehler's guns – that overlooked the isthmus, as Drinkwater saw: 'The cannonade from the Enemy was now principally directed at our upper batteries. The rock-gun, mounted on the summit of the northern front, was become as warm, if not warmer than any other battery, and scarcely a day passed without some casuals [casualties] at that post.'[11] Most of the guns at the northern front were positioned on a series of terraces at the western side of the Rock, allowing gun batteries to be ranged in lines to face Spain. On the eastern side of Gibraltar at the north front, the terrain was too steep to establish many gun batteries. Although the sheer cliff face made an assault impossible, the lack of guns able to cover the eastern approach meant that the Spaniards could get very close this way. One legend is constantly repeated about the search for a solution:

the Governor, attended by the Chief Engineer [William Green] and staff made an inspection of the batteries at the north front. Great havoc had been made in some of them by the enemy's fire, and for the present they were abandoned whilst the artificers were restoring them. Meditating for a few moments over the ruins, he said aloud, 'I will give a thousand dollars to anyone who can suggest how I am to get a flanking fire upon the enemy's works.'[12]

At this point, Sergeant Major Henry Ince apparently proposed a tunnel, though there is no evidence that a reward was ever paid or even offered. After discussing such an idea in detail with Colonel Green, Eliott had in fact issued official orders for a tunnel a few days earlier than this supposed conversation, on 1 May: 'To carry on a cannon communication by means of a souterrain gallery six feet high and 6 feet broad cut thro' the solid rock beginning ... above Farrington's Battery, proceeding round towards the North East to a very favourable Notche in the Rock, nearly under the Royal Battery, in a commanding situation, being about 640 feet above the Isthmus, and will admit to form a level for a well shouldered establishment of two guns at least.'[13]

The plan was to drive a tunnel eastwards, behind the cliff face, emerging at what they called 'the Notch' or 'the Hook', a projecting part of the rock face that was topped by an inaccessible platform nearly halfway up the cliff face, which it was hoped would be suitable as a gun emplacement, rather like a bastion, giving a wide field of fire over the area that they were currently unable to reach. It would then be possible, Eliott said in his orders, to respond to 'any attack or approaches the Enemy may endeavour to push from the Devil's Tower towards the pass of the Inundation at Lower Forbes, and will flank in an eminent degree any works they may advance towards the outer line ... and may also command the access to, as well as the anchorage behind the mountain, all between the north east and south east quarters'.[14]

It took until 25 May to start the tunnel: 'This morning Sergt. Major Ince of the Artificer Company with 12 miners and labourers begun a new work at Greens Lodge above Willis's to cut a dreft or subterraneous passage through the Rock to a declivity where a battery is to be made to annoy the enemy.'[15] Gibraltar nowadays has over 30 miles of tunnels and chambers,[16] but tunnelling had never been attempted before Ince began his work. The mining was done using basic hand tools, with gunpowder for blasting, and the resulting debris was cleared away by hand. It would be a slow process, and time was pressing considering that an assault on the Rock was imminent.

D'Arçon's plan was that after the floating batteries, gunboats and some warships had battered the garrison into submission, backed up by the gun batteries of the Spanish Lines and the advance works, thousands of troops would invade the Rock in several places, rather than a single massive assault against the strongest defences at the north end of Gibraltar. The attack would be supported by numerous warships of the combined French and Spanish fleet, as well as by every available smaller boat from the locality. Many of the troops were to be transported in small landing craft that had been specially designed by him so that they could attack weaker points in the defences to the south.

The build-up of forces ranged against Gibraltar was increasing daily, and just as the tunnelling started, one soldier noted: 'above ninety sail of Spanish transports arrived this evening, with a bomb-ketch, from the east, with troops and stores for the camp'. A few days later, he observed: 'the number of vessels that have arrived at Algesiras exceeds a hundred: about ten battalions of troops have been landed from them'.[17] Horsbrugh was more precise: 'the enemy are pitching tents for a regiment in white to the right of the Catalan Camp on the south west face of the Queen of Spains Chair, and for the regiment in blue uniform on the west of Bona Vista Barracks'.[18] This was a massive reinforcement of French forces who were no longer needed on Minorca.

The floating batteries were being monitored from Gibraltar, with increasing concern as more and more of the old merchant ships were converted. Although the garrison now had gunboats – some completed, others nearly so – to cope with the menace of

the Spanish gunboats, it was difficult to see how they could withstand an attack by floating batteries. Spain was pouring everything
into the scheme, and in Boyd's journal it was acknowledged that
Gibraltar's inhabitants were in a state of terror: 'The Enemy have
now, about two hundred sail of vessels between Algaziers and the
Orange Grove . . . This show of shipping before us puts our inhabitants and women in a great panic. They are hourly gathering up
the little remains that devastation has left them, and carries it to
caves, creeks and corners in the Rock, in order to save what they
can of their remaining substances, as we daily expect a very heavy
attack and storm both by sea and land.'[19] The inhabitants were
still in makeshift huts and tents in the south, as were many of the
soldiers, and after coming off guard duty, William Maddin from
the 12th Regiment raised his musket, 'making believe to shoot
a girl in camp'. He had forgotten to unload his weapon and shot
nine-year-old Maria Palerano, an inhabitant, through the head.
She died instantly. Towards the end of May, Maddin was put on
trial for murder and acquitted.[20]

In spite of the anxiety of waiting for the attack, unexpectedly
good health was recorded within the garrison at the start of June:
'The Doctors reports does not show one man in the scurvy, and
the fever brought here by the 97th Regiment is almost spent (as
the men recovers very fast), neither has it been very fatal, so that
we are at present, in general, in a much better state of health
through the Garrison than we've been in since the Siege begun.'[21]
It probably helped that supplies were managing to reach the garrison from Leghorn, Algiers and Portugal, and one Portuguese boat
recently obtained thirty thousand oranges and a few casks of oil
at Tetuan by the captain claiming the cargo was for Cadiz, then
bringing it undetected to Gibraltar. Although the most effective
remedy for scurvy was known to be fruit and vegetables, other
ideas were still being pursued, and the Garrison Orders in early
June said: 'One quarter and half of a pint of vinegar to be issued
to every ration, till further orders. The surgeons of the different
corps are of opinion that this will be a great preventative in the sad
effects of the scurvy.'[22]

One asset to the garrison was the completion of the gunboats, with the final one being launched on 4 June, the king's birthday. There were twelve in all, bearing suitable names such as *Dreadnought* and *Vengeance*. The day was celebrated with a royal salute of forty-four guns, the age of the king, all directed towards the Spanish siegeworks, while the 'Governor honoured himself this morning with a captain's guard and a standard of colours of the 73rd Regiment of Highlanders dressed in their tartan plaids'.[23] There was also another glimmer of hope – that red-hot shot or heated cannonballs might deal with the floating batteries. Although known for decades as a theoretical technique, this dangerous procedure had until now been rarely used. It also required a great deal of fuel, which was in short supply. Solid cast-iron cannonballs were heated in a furnace and were fired by placing a cartridge into the gun, ramming down a well-soaked wad, followed by a heated cannonball. Another wet wad was rammed in on top of the red-hot shot if the cannon was to be fired while pointed downwards. Experiments at the beginning of the siege had established that a cannonball took about twenty-five minutes to heat and was still hot enough to ignite gunpowder after fifty minutes.[24] On hitting the target, the intense heat made red-hot shot extremely difficult to deal with, and it set fire to anything combustible.

The technique of using red-hot shot was difficult to master. Early on, some equipment for heating shot had been set up, with Captain Paterson noting that 'a detachment of artillery ordered to practise the motions of firing red hot shot daily'.[25] These 'motions' were probably done with cold shot, but now that an attack was imminent, the gunners needed to be able to use the real thing. The red-hot shot furnaces, sometimes called grates or forges, comprised a strong iron framework to support a grid or rack to hold the cannonballs, with a fire of wood, coal and coke underneath. The heated shot was manhandled with specially made tools such as tongs and two-handled shot carriers, which were all made on Gibraltar by blacksmiths from the artificers.

The loaded cannons had to be aimed and fired quickly before

the shot burned through the wad and fired the gun prematurely, which is what occurred at a practice session in early June: 'On the 7th, our artillery practised from the King's Bastion with red-hot shot against the Irishman's brig.' A few weeks earlier, this brig had sailed towards the Old Mole, but ran aground when fired on by the Spaniards. After being rescued, the captain was severely rebuked, but he explained that before leaving Cork in Ireland he had heard about the successful sortie and was told that the Old Mole, his old anchoring place in peacetime, was open. The garrison gunners were now using his vessel for red-hot shot practice: 'In the first round, one of the artillery-men putting in the shot, the fire by some means immediately communicated to the cartridge, and the unfortunate man was blown from the embrasure in some hundred pieces. Two others were also slightly wounded with the unexpected recoil of the carriage.'[26]

By now, the tunnel being cut by Ince was progressing steadily, but on the same day as this accident, Horsbrugh said that two miners were injured: 'two men of the 72nd Regiment had the misfortune to lose each a leg by the blowing up of a mine in the communication we are making through the Rock to get at the Notch on the North Front, and one of them died soon after being carried to the Hospital.'[27] Because they were mercifully rare, such accidents were more newsworthy than the commonplace casualties caused by the Spanish bombardment, but an incident a few days later, on 11 June, turned out to be the worst single day for casualties in the last three years. Garrison working parties were making considerable improvements and repairs to the defences while the Spaniards were focused on the floating batteries and their guns remained fairly quiet, but during a random episode of firing, a single shot caused havoc. An emotional description was set down in Boyd's journal:

Between 10 and 11 o'clock this forenoon a large shell from the enemy fell in the door of one of the small magazines at Willis's, on Princess Ann's Battery (where a great working party were repairing the fortification there); the shell on its explosion blew up the magazine which contained about 96 barrels, or, 9,600 pounds of powder, killing 13 men and wounding 12 more. This has been the most fatal day since the beginning of the siege. How horrid and dreadful to behold the terrible blast and explosion! To feel the town and the Rock tremble, and to see men, stones, timber, casks, mortar and earth flying promiscuously in the dark smoky cloud far above the surface, in the air; and on their coming down are dashed to pieces on the craggy rocks, some thrown headlong down the dreadful precipice into the Lines, a most shocking exit! having not time to offer up to God a single prayer preparatory to their acceptance in an everlasting state.[28]

The huge explosion was clearly visible to those at the Spanish Lines, who were heard cheering at the sight of the disaster. Their firing continued to concentrate on the same spot, in the hopes of another spectacular hit: 'The enemy poured in shot and shells upon that part as thick as hail, so that it was night before all the killed and wounded were gathered up.'[29] Because a mixture of soldiers had been drafted into the working party doing the repairs, the final casualty list was thirteen rank-and-file soldiers and one drummer killed, with many more injured.

Over at Algeciras, tents were now visible for the workmen who were converting the old warships into floating batteries. Even with powerful telescopes, though, observations from the Rock could yield only a limited amount of information about what the Spaniards and French were preparing, and all kinds of rumours circulated. Definite information at last arrived on 21 June from two former Genoese inhabitants, who had been captured when bringing a cargo to Gibraltar from Algiers. They had been taken to Algeciras, from where they had just managed to escape in the prison-ship's boat. From them, it was learned that French reinforcements had indeed arrived, that ten ships were being converted into floating batteries, though a shortage of carpenters was causing delays, and that the Spaniards were in high spirits.[30]

On the same day, the French troops finished landing, and it was said that there were now thirty thousand men in the camp. The commander of the Minorca siege, the Duc de Crillon, had also arrived to take over command of the siege of Gibraltar, and the two Genoese, Drinkwater said, 'informed us that the grand attack was fixed to be in September, but that all, both sailors and soldiers, were much averse to the enterprise'.[31] If they were correct, then the garrison still had at least two more months to prepare.

# CHAPTER EIGHTEEN

———— • ✦ • ————

# TUNNELS

Ince's tunnel was slow and dangerous work, with further injuries and fatalities, but on 4 July 1782 Spilsbury said: 'Serjt Ince's gallery going on well; 13 men, in about 5 weeks, have cut about 82 feet long by 8 feet high and broad, in the solid rock.'[1] He also mentioned that the numbers of workmen were depleted, no doubt suffering from influenza. Eliott had already mentioned influenza in his dispatches to England, and in early July the *Newcastle Journal* reported that he was very concerned: 'There is late news from Gibraltar, of the most alarming kind for the safety of that garrison. Governor Eliott having been promised succours under the convoy of the Grand Fleet, by the latter end of March writes that he is in great distress for almost every article; and that the influenza having been there prevalent, though not fatal, the spirits of his troops begin to droop, especially as there is no prospect of relief from Britain.'[2]

Work now began on a new tunnel between the King's and Queen's Lines. Improving the natural defences of this area had been one of the earliest tasks of the siege, including the formation of the Queen's Lines, which had led to the discovery of another cave. The King's and Queen's Lines ran along a terrace facing north-west, providing flanking fire across the approach to the Landport Gate. They were the lowest of the hillside gun batteries, situated below the Prince's Lines and well below Willis's, and the Queen's Lines were probably the most exposed of all. Covered access from the King's Lines was badly needed, but a solid mass of rock was in the way. In his formal orders to William Green, Eliott specified that he should

> carry on a cannon communication by means of a souterain gallery, to be cut through the Rock 6 feet broad and 6 feet high between the cave at the head of the King's Lines and the cave lately discovered, being now the shelter and protection for the Guard in the new constructed Queen's Lines, for the easier and safer communication of those two important posts, particularly to and from the Queen's Lines, being at present unavoidably difficult and troublesome, and, to speak in a military way, rather hazardous.[3]

With the threat of an imminent assault, the tunnelling needed to be done rapidly, as Boyd's journal recorded: 'The miners are divided into two watches, relieving every 6 hours night and day, having their provisions dressed [prepared] by labourers at the place of work, and Mr. Ince's party on the Hill at the Notch is ordered to follow the same method [of operating]. These works when completed ... will render the Garrison the strongest by art and nature in the known world, and may be looked upon [as] impregnable.'[4]

Part of the strengthening of defences was the storage of ammunition and gunpowder where it was needed. All kinds of shot, shells, cartridges and gunpowder were being distributed to small service magazines near the gun batteries, supplied from the larger magazines that were sited in places less vulnerable to Spanish gun fire. Even so, Spilsbury moaned that 'Our great mortars are placed at a great distance from the magazines, and makes the labour very great in carrying shells of 200 weight, and ammunition, to them.'[5] The garrison was reasonably well stocked with ammunition because in mid-May three storeships from England had managed to slip past the Spanish gunboats by flying French flags and pretending to sail eastwards into the Mediterranean. At the last minute, they had hauled down the flags, hoisted English colours and changed course for Gibraltar before the gunboats could catch them. These ships had brought various ordnance stores, including shells and 1900 barrels of gunpowder.[6]

Solid shot, such as cannonballs, came from England by ship, as did the cast-iron components of shells, which had to be filled with gunpowder and fitted with fuses at Gibraltar. This highly dangerous work was carried out in buildings called 'laboratories', and Drinkwater admired the bravery of one artilleryman when an accident occurred: 'The afternoon of the 8th [July], an extraordinary instance of gallantry and presence of mind occurred at the laboratory adjoining the South Bastion. An artillery-man (named Hartley) was employed in the laboratory, filling shells with carcass [incendiary] composition, and driving fuses into five and a half, and six-inch shells. One of them, by some unaccountable accident, took fire in the operation.'[7] Under such circumstances, men usually shouted a warning and fled in panic, hoping to get far enough away to avoid the massive blast, but not Corporal Caleb Hartley:

> Although he was surrounded with unfixed fuses, loaded shells, composition, &c., with the most astonishing coolness, he carried out the lighted shell, and threw it where it could do little or no harm, and two seconds had scarcely passed before it disploded. If the shell had burst in the laboratory, it is almost certain the whole would have been blown up, when the loss in fixed ammunition, fuses, &c. &c. would have been irreparable, exclusive of the damage which the fortifications would have suffered from the explosion, and the lives that might have been lost. He was handsomely rewarded by the Governor.

For his quick-thinking and heroism, Hartley was actually given an award of twenty dollars.[8]

Preparations also continued for firing red-hot shot, and in mid-July Drinkwater noted that 'about this period, additional forges for heating shots were established in different parts of the Garrison, with all the proper apparatus' – by which he probably meant the specialised tools. Recent deserters confirmed that the Duc de Crillon was now in charge, that a massive army had been assembled and that the floating batteries might be ready by the end of August, but Ancell was certain that they could be destroyed: 'there is not the least doubt but our red hot pills will effectually answer our purpose. They must be of an amazing construction if blazing twenty-four and thirty-two pounders will not burn them.'[9]

One setback occurred with Ince's tunnel, because, with shifts of miners working round the clock, the build-up of smoke and dust was making the work extremely difficult. It was therefore decided to blast a ventilation hole through the cliff face itself, though in doing so, Drinkwater said, the miners overestimated the amount of gunpowder needed:

> The mine was loaded with an unusual quantity of powder, and the explosion was so amazingly loud, that almost the whole of the Enemy's camp turned out at the report: but what must their surprise be, when they observed from where the smoke issued [halfway up the cliff face]! The original intention of this opening was to communicate air to the workmen, who before were almost suffocated with the smoke which remained after blowing the different mines, but, on examining the aperture more closely, an idea was conceived of mounting a gun to bear on all the Enemy's batteries, excepting Fort Barbara. Accordingly orders were given to enlarge the inner part for the recoil, and when finished a twenty-four pounder was mounted.[10]

From this fortunate accident it was realised that there was no necessity to wait until the tunnel had been driven as far as the Notch. It could be used as a gun battery now, with cannons set up in embrasures through the cliff face. This discovery was very welcome, because the work was particularly gruelling in the intense summer heat, and there was a shortage of water. Spilsbury noted: 'Soldiers forbid to run or heat themselves ... Thermometer 88°.' Shortly afterwards, a new order specified: 'No one to bathe at the New Mole for dysentery's sake.' Much of the shipping was anchored at the New Mole, with the crews living on board, so that all kinds of waste emptied into the surrounding water, potentially making it very unhealthy. The food was also harmful, as Spilsbury described: 'Sour crout served to the Hanoverians, but it is nearly spoilt', while 'Our flour is so full of weevils, &c, that a plum pudding has the appearance of a currant one.'[11]

In late July, two ships came from Italy with supplies and news. 'Arrived the St Philip's Castle and General Murray sloop of war from Leghorn; they have brought provision for the garrison, with five officers and seventy-five Corsicans,' wrote Ancell. 'They bring the agreeable intelligence of Admiral Rodney having defeated the French, and taken the Ville de Paris of 100 guns, with four other line of battleships.'[12] After delivering the convoy to Gibraltar in January 1780, Rodney had taken up his post as commander-in-chief of the Leeward Islands in the Caribbean in a continuing struggle with the French. In April 1782, a fleet of battleships commanded by the Comte de Grasse had been reinforced by a massive convoy carrying nine thousand troops, intended for an assault on Jamaica. Rodney, with a fleet of similar size, caught up with the French near a group of islands called the Saintes, between Guadeloupe and Dominica. The French were so comprehensively beaten that Rodney wrote to Sandwich at the Admiralty: 'My Dear Lord, You may now despise all your enemies. The British fleet, under your Lordship's auspices, has proved itself superior to that of the enemy, and given them such a blow as they will not recover.'[13]

For Gibraltar, this was wonderful news. Not only was such a massive British victory a boost to morale, but any reduction in the power of the French and Spanish navies might help diminish the blockade of the Rock. Eliott decided to celebrate by bombarding the Spaniards during their siesta. 'At one o'clock all the ordnance was made to bear upon the enemy from the Royal Battery to Princess Carolina Battery,' Walter Gordon said. 'Our new gun boats formed the line along the New Mole booms, and fired one round each, and were answered by all the shipping in the bay, thus these expressions of joy answered also the purpose of distressing the enemy, who knew the cause of our joy, and severely felt the effects of our rejoicing. Every heart blessed the gallant Rodney; a more sincere feu de joie was never observed.'[14]

Amongst the private letters brought by the ships was one for William Green, telling him the devastating news that his wife Miriam had died in London a month previously, on 21 June 1782, at the age of forty-six, and had been buried in St Margaret's, Westminster.[15] Although Mrs Green had left for England eleven months earlier, she never recovered, but suffered one final tragedy – the death of her own mother in March. As Chief Engineer with a crisis looming, Green was unable to leave Gibraltar to rejoin his family.

The Corsicans who came as passengers on board the two ships to offer their services to Eliott were described by Drinkwater as 'Signor Leonetti, nephew to Pascal Paoli, the celebrated Corsican General, with two officers, a chaplain, and sixty-eight volunteers'. Twelve Corsicans had arrived in May and been distributed amongst some of the regiments, though by the time the rest arrived a fight between two of them had already ended in a fatal stabbing. In a letter to Eliott, Sir Thomas Mann, the British envoy to Florence, explained that following the fall of Minorca to the French, he had been directed to divert to Gibraltar any provisions or supplies, including a party of Corsicans who had wanted to join the British at Minorca. He drew attention to five of them: 'I beg leave on this occasion to recommend to your protection the following persons. Monsieur Leonetti, General Paoli's nephew, who quitted the Great Duke's [Grand Duke of Tuscany] service by his uncle's order, to shew his zeal in that of His Majesty [George III]. Monsieur Catti, a very ingenious and resolute young man. Monsieur Lioncourt, Micheli and Masseria, who are all very deserving and may be of great use at the head of the Corsicans.'[16]

In the early eighteenth century, Corsica was ruled by the Genoese, but an independence movement had developed in opposition. In 1755, Pascale Paoli led a group of guerrillas that forced the Genoese out of the mountains and then drove them from the lowlands. France later took control of Corsica, and after

losing a battle against the French in 1769, Paoli was forced to flee
and went into exile in England. Consequently, many Corsicans
hated the French and wanted revenge. One of the families associated with Paoli was that of the Bonapartes, who had remained in
Corsica. Their son Napoleon, the future emperor of the French,
was a pupil at the military school at Brienne Le Château in central
France from 1779 to 1784 and must have been well aware of the
siege of Gibraltar that was being talked about across Europe. Yet
he was bullied as a despised Corsican by the French boys, and,
although he would later lead the armies of France, as a young man
he was a fervent Corsican nationalist.

On Gibraltar nobody seemed to know what to do with the
Corsican volunteers, but after a few days they were formed into an
independent corps under the command of Antonio Leonetti and
sent to Windmill Hill, as Drinkwater related: 'They were armed
with a firelock and bayonet, each with a horse-pistol slung on the
left side, and two cartridge boxes. The Governor quartered them
on Wind-mill hill, and committed that post to their charge.' This
small report highlights Drinkwater as an accurate eyewitness,
because it mirrors almost exactly the official record of the stores
issued to the Corsican Company: 'Firelocks 78, pistols 78, car-
touch boxes with straps and frogs 168, carbines 6, bayonets with
scabbards.'[17]

Windmill Hill was well away from much of the bombardment,
and although the garrison was maintaining an almost daily shelling of the fortifications on the isthmus, only occasional retaliation
had occurred from the Spanish batteries and gunboats since late
June. Instead, the besieging troops continued to prepare for a
massive assault with the floating batteries. On the day after the
arrival of the news of Rodney's victory, two vessels from Faro in
Portugal brought letters containing intelligence that troops were
already at Cadiz waiting for embarkation, that all the boats in the
vicinity were held in readiness, that the floating batteries were
nearing completion and, worse still, that an attack was planned for
the middle of August.[18] One letter said that the attackers 'were to
have forty thousand men in camp, and the principal attack was to

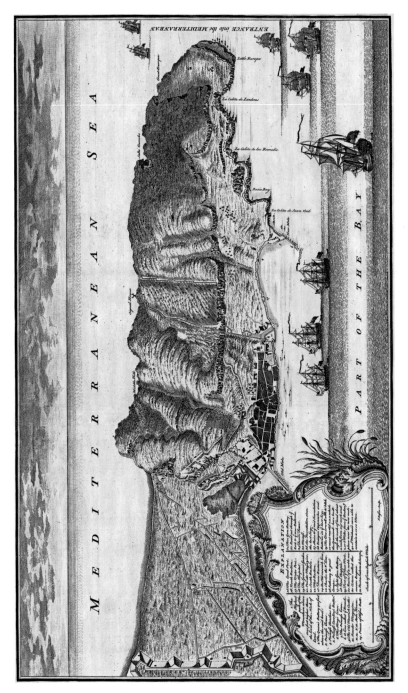

A 1738 map of Gibraltar showing the isthmus fortifications from the 1727 siege, the inundation, the Old Mole, Gibraltar town and a schematic, but effective, view of the Rock

The west side of Gibraltar viewed from the bay. The isthmus is beyond the picture (far left). Behind the red tanker is Camp Bay and the Windmill Hill plateau, and on the far right is the Europa plateau

Looking to Gibraltar from close to Fort St Philip, with the Old Mole projecting into the Bay of Gibraltar, the Barbary coast in the distance and Cabrita Point on the far right. On the isthmus is the old tower around which St Carlos battery was built. Illustration by Captain John Drinkwater

The Strait of Gibraltar viewed from the Line Wall. Much of the coastline is that of Barbary, and on the far right is Cabrita Point. Illustration by Captain John Drinkwater

Gibraltar viewed from across part of the isthmus, with the typical cloud caused by easterly winds, shrouding the site of the Rock Gun

The ruins of the Spanish Fort St Barbara, looking south towards the eastern and northern sides of Gibraltar

Looking from the hills above Algeciras to Gibraltar in a print of 1840. The town of Algeciras is just beyond the aqueduct and the Green Island lies to the right

San Roque viewed from the Governor's Palace. In the distance, on the left, is Gibraltar and on the right is the Spanish coast with Cabrita Point and Algeciras. Ape's Hill in Barbary rises above the layer of mist. The chimneys of an oil refinery (right) mark the site of the Carteia Roman ruins

The Governor's Palace at San Roque, the headquarters of the Spanish military campaign during the siege

Barbary macaques largely inhabited the inaccessible eastern side of Gibraltar

A view northwards to Spain from Signal Hill towards Middle Hill and the site of the Rock Gun. On the right is the sheer eastern side and the Mediterranean

*Left:* Looking from Willis's battery (now with World War Two structures) towards the north front of the Rock. The protruding rock on the left is 'the Notch', towards which Ince was mining a tunnel in 1782

*Bottom left:* The Landport gate and tunnel through which the soldiers passed during the sortie of November 1781. The stone bridge was demolished a few months later, and the sally port in the ditch (bottom left) was used instead

*Bottom right:* Looking through the original Southport gate from the town

One of the larger floating batteries moving into position

A brass cannon on a wooden gun carriage, made by Bowen in 1758, now in the Alameda Gardens, in front of the Wellington monument

A brass howitzer, made by the Verbruggens at Woolwich in 1778, looking at the muzzle down which gunpowder and ammunition were loaded. It now forms part of a large monument in the Alameda Gardens dedicated to Eliott

British officers, one with a telescope, watching the floating batteries burn. In the distance are white tents of the French and Spanish camp

Obverse of a halfpenny token showing the head of General Eliott (spelled Elliot). The reverse has a fleur-de-lys with the words 'Birmingham Halfpenny 1792'

A Dutch medal commemorating (left) the sinking of the *Royal George* and the loss of Admiral Kempenfelt and (right) the floating batteries attacking Gibraltar be made by sea, to be covered by a squadron of men of war with bomb-ketches, floating-batteries, gun and mortar-boats, &c and that the Comte d'Artois, brother to the King of France, with other great personages, was to be present at the attack'.

The letters brought additional information about the construction of the floating batteries: 'Ten ships were to be fortified six or seven feet thick, on the larboard side, with green timber bolted with iron, cork, junk, and raw hides, which were to carry guns of heavy metal, and be bomb-proof on the top, with a descent [sloping roof] for the shells to slide off: that these vessels, which they supposed would be impregnable, were to be moored within half gun-shot of the walls with iron chains.'[19] D'Arçon's design was intended to make the vessels unsinkable, impossible to hole with cannonballs and impossible to set on fire with red-hot shot.

On top of the reinforced hull, extra layers of protection were added, including a layer of wet sand to quench the heat of any red-hot shot that managed to penetrate the outer layers. To keep the whole of this armour wet, a network of pipes was threaded between the layers, through which water was pumped. If any red-hot shot managed to break one or more pipes, the leaking water would help douse the shot. The sloping roof was designed to deflect cannonballs and protect the gun crews. Intended to sail only as far as Gibraltar, they would have a lop-sided appearance, with one heavily armoured side designed to face Gibraltar and a less well-protected side facing the bay.

Depending on the size of the particular vessel, the floating batteries had one or two gun decks and between six and twenty-one brand-new brass guns, which were mounted on one side only – the side facing Gibraltar's defences. The weight of the guns was balanced by ballast on the opposite side of the vessel. They were to be fully rigged with masts and sails in order to sail across the bay, but were unlikely to be very manoeuvrable and so would need to be towed into position by smaller boats. Because they were not meant to move again, the masts and sails were expendable. Once anchored, the floating batteries were designed to pound the garrison into submission, while remaining unscathed by everything fired at them. Looking back a century later, one newspaper in the shipbuilding port of Belfast commented: 'The vessels may be said to have been in a sense unwieldy predecessors of ironclads.'[20]

Unknown to those on Gibraltar, the influenza they were suffering from was a widespread epidemic that was raging across Europe. In Britain, entire families had been wiped out, especially in south-east England. It now had a more serious impact on the garrison and was made more unbearable by the intense summer heat. Countless people fell ill, though Gibraltar was lucky that sufferers recovered fairly quickly. 'Its general symptoms,' Drinkwater related, 'were sudden pains, accompanied with a dizziness in the head; though others were affected in a different manner. For several days near a hundred were daily taken to the Hospital; but bleeding, and a night's rest, usually removed it. It was attributed at that time to the extraordinary heat of the atmosphere, which was unusually warm, owing to the prodigious fires made by the Spaniards on the neighbouring hills, and the stagnant state of the air.'[21]

Influenza was affecting the French and Spaniards at least as much as the garrison, and, like the soldiers on the Rock, they struggled on with their tasks. Among them, twenty-eight-year-old François-Silvain-Denis Houdan-Deslandes was a second lieutenant in the Bretagne Regiment. Born at Vernou, near Tours, in France, he had previously studied at military college and had been part of the successful besieging force at Minorca. According to him, they were now waiting for the arrival of two princes from the Court of Versailles before the next major stage of work on the isthmus – a new line stretching from the Mahon battery to the Mediterranean. The Comte d'Artois arrived in the evening of 12 August and the following day was guided round the Spanish Lines by the Duc de Crillon and other officers. D'Artois was the younger brother of Louis XVI of France and, in 1824, would become Charles X after the French monarchy was restored following Napoleon's final defeat. Houdan-Deslandes said that d'Artois 'was struck by the beauty of those great and formidable works ... The Prince made a tour of the Lines under fire from the fortress, without fear or conceit.'[22] During the inspection of the Lines, fourteen-year-old Pierre Dumont was working in the stables of d'Artois in the nearby camp and recorded a near miss from a shell:

> all lay flat on the ground, to shun the effects of a bomb that fell near part of the barracks where a French woman had a canteen. The woman, with two children on her arm, rushes forth, sits with the utmost sang froid on the bomb-shell, puts out the match [actually the fuse], and thus extricates from danger all that were around her. Numbers were witnesses of this incident, and his highness granted her a pension of three francs a day, and promised to promote her husband after the siege. The Duc de Crillon imitated the prince's generosity, and ensured to her, likewise, a payment of five francs a day.[23]

The arrival of d'Artois was the signal to push on with the siege-works, and at daybreak on 16 August everybody on Gibraltar was astounded to see that a vast extension had been constructed overnight, in just six hours of darkness, using casks and sandbags, only 800 yards from the garrison's batteries. Writing to General Charles Cornwallis, William Picton, colonel of the 12th, said that 'the enemy had accomplished a most arduous task ... having carried on their advanced work, or parallel, about seven hundred yards in length, and about twelve feet in height, composed principally of sandbags, from near the Mahon battery almost to the eastern shore, with sixty-four masked embrasures in it, and two mortar batteries at the extremities'. He admitted that it was all carried out with complete secrecy and silence: 'Although there must have been at least twelve or fifteen thousand men employed in effecting this very extensive and laborious operation ... yet the plan was ... executed with so much silence, assiduity and regularity that not even the smallest suspicion, it is believed, was entertained of any such work.'[24]

Houdan-Deslandes explained that on the previous evening, more than 7000 Spaniards and 2300 French converged upon different parts of the isthmus. Although there was much confusion with so many people involved, by four in the morning the French soldiers in particular had performed miracles. 'The work of that memorable night,' he declared, 'is perhaps the most astonishing ever to have been done since fortresses were besieged. We built with sandbags and casks filled with sand a line that was ... a minimum height of 9 feet, whose thickness was almost everywhere 12 feet.'[25] What he found most extraordinary was the absence of firing from the Rock, so that they retired in the morning with no losses. That evening saw the arrival of the Duc de Bourbon, the cousin of the Comte d'Artois.

At this critical time, one young Jewish inhabitant had already decided to join a regiment to help defend Gibraltar. The muster lists show that Abraham Hassan enlisted with the 58th Regiment on 16 August 1782. He was described as a labourer by trade, 5 feet 5 inches tall, with a brown complexion, black eyes, black hair and a long face. Up to then, he had been living in Hardy's Town with the rest of the Jewish inhabitants. His mother Hannah later declared that he was 'the only inhabitant who voluntarily took arms in defence of this important fortress ... and cheerfully and gratuitously did the duty and shared the dangers of a private soldier as a volunteer in the 58th'.[26] Everything appeared so dire that on the 18th Spilsbury remarked: 'The parsons exhort all to do their duty.'[27] That same day, Eliott recorded in his diary an unusual sequence of events: 'About 11 o'clock this forenoon six or seven barges with crimson awnings proceeded from Algaziras to Orange Grove attended by twelve gun boats. Soon after, the barges put off with the gun boats and steered back to Algaziras. The ship of the line at Orange Grove saluted them as they passed with 24 guns.' The barges were then saluted by all the other ships and boats, and Eliott guessed that 'this salvo ... is on account of the arrival of a Prince'.[28]

What happened next was the first trial of a floating battery, in front of the Duc de Crillon, the Comte d'Artois and the Duc de Bourbon. The barges had picked up the royal party at the Orange Grove and took them to Algeciras for the event, which Drinkwater watched: 'The barges then proceeded to the battering-ship which was anchored apart from the rest, where they remained some time, and on the company's quitting the ship, she fired a salute of eight guns.' In the afternoon, though, the sailing trial of the float-ing battery did not appear entirely successful to those watching from the Rock: 'about three [3 p.m.], the battering-ship got under way, and sailed to the northward, past the flag-ship. She endeav-oured to sail back, but in vain, and was obliged to be towed to her station by ten gun-boats.'[29]

There had been no attempt to hide this demonstration, which took place in full view of the garrison. So confident were the French and Spanish royal courts about the plan to destroy Gibraltar that, far from being kept secret, details were being publicised all over Europe. Gibraltar became so famous that imaginative theatrical productions were staged in Paris showing how the end would come. News of the impending attack also reached America, and Abigail Adams wrote to her husband, the future President John Adams, who was at that time a diplomat in Holland: 'We are hoping for the fall of Gibraltar, because we imagine that will facilitate a peace; and who is not weary of the war?'[30] Even more incredible was the fact that thousands of people were making their way across France and Spain, hoping to witness this wonderful spectacle personally. The exceptions were the Comte d'Artois and the Duc de Bourbon, who had come – in theory at least – as military volunteers. In this official capacity, they anticipated sharing in the glory of the capture of Gibraltar.

That evening, thousands of soldiers once again worked on the isthmus, but this time they were fired on by the garrison, as Houdan-Deslandes described:

Around 10 in the evening, the silence [from firing] that was so favourable to our operations was disturbed by the most lively firing that had occurred since the start of the siege. The Rock was spewing out cannonballs at every instant, and their dread-ful whistling echoed around the rocks and brought terror to the hearts of everyone who was not in a trench ... That night was less bloody than we had feared. Thirteen men killed or wounded were the only victims of that night-time firing that could have been a lot more deadly.[31]

In the morning, the 19th, Houdan-Deslandes recorded how they then caused their own misfortune: 'Daylight brought tranquillity, the workers had returned to camp, the fortress was quiet. Suddenly, we heard, not far from the camp, a dreadful noise; it was the explosion of several barrels of gunpowder ... A spark fallen from a [tobacco] pipe had set fire to some saltpetre and caused 21 shells to explode. Four Spaniards were blown to bits, 12 were burned but had the misfortune to survive. This was all due to the incurable habit that the Spaniards have, of smoking everywhere, without taking any care, which caused this fatal accident.'[32] At noon, a boat approached Gibraltar under a flag of truce, carrying a letter from the Duc de Crillon to Eliott that began:

Sir, His Royal Highness Comte d'Artois, who has received permission from the King his brother to assist at the siege, as a volunteer in the Combined Army, of which their Most Christian and Catholic Majesties have honoured me with the command, arrived in this camp the 15th instant. This young Prince has been pleased, in passing through Madrid, to take charge of some letters which had been sent to that capital from this place, and which are addressed to persons belonging to your Garrison.[33]

Crillon said that he was also using this opportunity 'to offer a few trifles for your table, of which I am sure you must stand in need, as I know you live entirely upon vegetables. I should be glad to know what kind you like best. I shall add a few partridges for the Gentlemen of your household, and some ice, which I presume will not be disagreeable in the excessive heat of this climate at this season of the year.'[34]

In fulsome diplomatic language, Eliott sent a reply:

I find myself honoured by your obliging letter of yesterday, in which your Excellency was so kind as to inform me of the arrival in your camp of his Royal Highness the Comte d'Artois, and the Duc de Bourbon, to serve as volunteers in the siege. These Princes have shewn their judgement in making choice of a master in the art of war, whose abilities cannot fail to form great warriors. I am overpowered with the condescension of His Royal Highness, in suffering some letters for persons in this town to be conveyed from Madrid in his carriages. I flatter myself that your Excellency will give my most profound respect to His Royal Highness, and to the Duc de Bourbon, for the expressions of esteem with which they have been pleased to honour so insignificant a person as I am.[35]

Eliott underlined his ironic response by thanking Crillon for the very kind gifts, though he pointed out that everything coming into the garrison was publicly sold:

the private soldier, if he has money, can become a purchaser, as well as the Governor. I confess, I make it a point of honour to partake both of plenty and scarcity in common with the lowest of my brave soldiers. This furnishes me with an excuse for the liberty I now take, of entreating your Excellency not to heap any more favours on me of this kind, as in future I cannot convert your presents to my own private use. Indeed, to be plain with your Excellency, though vegetables at this season are scarce with us, every man has got a quantity proportioned to the labour which he has bestowed in raising them. The English are naturally fond of gardening and cultivation; and here we find our amusement in it, during the intervals of rest from public duty.[36]

As a final graceful insult, Eliott responded with a more lavish gift of his own. 'I am confidently told,' Ancell said, 'it consisted of a cask of beef, pork, and butter, a cheese, a puncheon of rum, a sheep and a goat, some poultry, and a quantity of potatoes.'[37]

Boyd likewise sent a gift to his adversaries, which was recorded as 'Melons, callabash, parsley, greenbeats [probably green beans], tomatesses, berryhoness's [aubergines – 'berenjenas' in Spanish], onions, pears, apples, 3 sorts of plums, lemons, 2 sorts of figgs, kidney beans, grapes, peaches, 2 rabbets and 3 brace of partridges'. In addition, there were two hampers of ice, which must have been stored in an ice house all summer.[38] These lavish gifts were sheer bravado, and everyone in the garrison knew it to be so, with Ancell commenting: 'This was policy to make the enemy believe that our situation was not so deplorable as they imagined.'[39]

That night, a great deal more work was done to the new battery and the eastern approach, and although Houdan-Deslandes said that the firing from the garrison was very brisk, no French were killed, only a few Spaniards. 'The Spanish troops are composed of sturdy men, accustomed from the cradle to a life of poverty,' he said. '... These men, almost savages, taken from their huts in order to become soldiers, have the strength so necessary for a career in arms, the patience that makes them used to suffering, and the spirit of subservience.'[40] What they lacked, he felt, was an ability to think for themselves, and so they walked into danger and had many more casualties than the French soldiers.

Late in the afternoon of 21 August, loose fascines in their eastern approach were set alight by a carcass fired from Willis's, and Drinkwater saw the fire take hold rapidly: 'On the appearance of the smoke our lower batteries immediately opened, and a most animated cannonade was directed from the Garrison. A party of the Enemy endeavoured to extinguish the fire; but finding their efforts to stop its progress in vain, they gallantly pulled down the line on each side to prevent the flames from spreading; which they at length effected, but not without considerable loss from our artillery.'[41] According to Houdan-Deslandes, 'The enemy had numerous shot raining down on us to prevent us extinguishing this fire that was going to consume a work that was raised with so much strain and good cheer. Several guards ... got up on the blazing line. Without axes, they used sabres to cut the burning fascines to stop the flames. The English fired with rage on the workers they could see from their elevated batteries.[42]

Since the arrival of Crillon, Houdan-Deslandes said, the Spanish artillery had kept a respectful silence, but for the first time in two months the Spanish guns bombarded the garrison in retaliation: 'This was without doubt a beautiful spectacle for those who had never yet been witness to the grand operations of a siege. On the one side, Gibraltar raging against the Spanish Lines, and on the other, these Lines, feeble work of man, firing at this majestic mountain, whose clouds of smoke were enveloping the summit.'[43] On Gibraltar, Drinkwater felt that 'Our fire was so brisk, and so well served, that it exceeded theirs by four to one.' Around two thousand men were involved in extinguishing the blaze, and their losses must have been severe, because the garrison fired the entire time.[44]

Everyone on Gibraltar was expecting an attack from the floating batteries at any time now, because a deserter had disclosed that it was planned for 25 August, the feast day of St Louis – Louis IX of France who died in 1270 and was the only French monarch to be declared a saint. When the day dawned, the Spaniards marked the occasion by decorating their ships and firing from them – but the feared attack never came. The following evening, a deserter who swam from Fort St Philip explained that Crillon had intended to attack then, but had suffered too much damage in the blaze. The anxious waiting continued, and the Rock appeared more vulnerable than ever.

————— ·◆· —————

# CHAPTER NINETEEN

# WAITING

Admiral Lord Richard Howe had been appointed commander-in-chief of the Royal Navy's Channel Fleet in April 1782, and almost immediately speculation was rife that he would lead a convoy for the relief of Gibraltar. The *Newcastle Courant* was wildly optimistic: 'there will be ready for sea at the end of this month, a fleet of 25 sail of the line under Lord Howe, and Admirals Campbell and Kempenfelt. Their first operation is to throw a body of troops and other supplies into Gibraltar.'[1] News subsequently reached Britain that a major attack was being prepared; the Rock was now in danger of being taken by storm, not slowly starved into submission. The government started to act, but it dismissed the idea of a small convoy that could be assembled with relative speed, because only a weak and vulnerable naval escort would be available. Instead, a massive convoy protected by the entire Channel Fleet was planned, though it would not be ready to sail before September.

George III was opposed to a lengthy wait and voiced his concerns to Lord Shelburne, who was now Prime Minister following the unexpected death on 1 July of Rockingham, who had taken over when Lord North resigned after the Yorktown disaster: 'the relief of Gibraltar ought not to be delayed till September; the way to keep up the spirits of the men is to shew they are not neglected; the Enemy avow that is the time they mean to make their attack, therefore our succours ought to be there before that time.'[2] To collect together all the supplies, the transport and merchant ships and the warships was a formidable task, but by early August preparations were well advanced, as the *Kentish Gazette* learned: 'A letter from Gosport, dated August 5, says, "A cutter is said to be arrived from Lord Howe, with an account that the fleet under his command was coming up Channel, and would arrive at Spithead in a few days; and that orders are given to prepare beef, beer &c.".'[3]

Unseasonably strong winds in August then prevented the small boats from taking supplies to the ships, but by 29 August, after a period of calm, it looked as if they might sail within two or three days. Frantic, last-minute tasks were being carried out on most vessels, which were crowded with many more people than normal, including traders from Portsmouth and Gosport who had rowed out with their wares, hoping to persuade the seamen to part with their wages, especially those recently paid. Many wives, some with their children, were bidding farewell to their husbands, while hordes of prostitutes were vying for business.

The *Royal George* was no exception and was packed with prostitutes and traders, while a procession of small craft brought more supplies to be hauled aboard. This was the third time the *Royal George* had been involved in a convoy to relieve Gibraltar, though no longer as the flagship of Sir John Lockhart Ross, but of Rear-Admiral Kempenfelt, with Martin Waghorn as captain, because Ross had resigned his command a few months earlier. On board the warship, several workmen from Portsmouth Dockyard were carrying out repairs, one of which involved heeling the ship in order to expose a damaged pipe just below the waterline. Tilting a vessel sideways for repairs was not uncommon, and the relatively calm weather and sea that day provided good conditions. There were several ways to heel a ship, and the quickest, though most dangerous, method was chosen. Because the damaged pipe was on the starboard side, all the gunports on the port side were opened and the guns run out as far as possible through the side of the ship. The ropes securing the starboard guns were eased, enabling them to be rolled towards the centre of the ship, which moved the weight towards the port side and lifted the starboard side slightly out of the water.

Because the dockyard plumbers were still unable to reach the pipe, cannonballs were next shifted to the port side to tilt the ship further. By now, the sea was almost level with the open gunports, and small waves lapped over the sills into the ship. This might not have proved fatal but for the barrels of rum being hauled up from the *Lark* lighter on the port side. Normally, each barrel was lowered into the hold, but for speed they were temporarily stacked on the upper deck.

Some crew members were ashore, though Richard Searle, the sailing master, was at that moment being rowed back to his ship: 'As they neared to the Royal George, the master suddenly exclaimed, She will sink! Give way! The boatman, turning his head, saw that the ship was in a position of extreme peril, and began to back.' It was immediately obvious that the ship was about to topple over, and his reaction was to flee from danger, but Searle urged him on: 'Give way, man! Give way! shrieked the master; and a few strokes of the oars enabled him to spring upon the companion ladder. The boatman said that he could just see him rush up and appear to fall into the now almost horizontal entry-port. It was only by the greatest exertion that the waterman pulled his boat beyond the vortex.'[4] Searle was just in time to see his ship in peril, but too late to avert the calamity, and he was drowned, along with most of the crew.

As the *Royal George* tipped over, the lighter was pushed beneath the waves. Entangled together, both filled rapidly with water and sank, giving few people on board any chance to escape. A few hours later, Richard Cumberland wrote hurriedly to his brother about what he had so far learned of the reasons for the tragedy:

The cock which communicates with the pump wanting repair, they had hove all her guns out on the opposite side to careen, when a slight squall of wind taking her, the sea rushed in at her lower tier and she went down instantly. A victualling cutter alongside went with her, the master of which saved himself and the captain [of the *Royal George*] on a hencoop, the latter leaping out of the stern gallery into the sea. The tide was strong and most of the boats to leeward, or more might have been picked up.[5]

John Ker, a surgeon on board the *Queen*, saw the disaster:

I ran to the entry port on hearing the alarm just as the ship was going down ... Hundreds of poor souls were standing on it when she sank from below them and left them struggling with the merciless elements ... For some days afterwards the three towns of Portsmouth, Gosport and [Portsmouth] Common were in a commotion. Almost everyone had lost some relation, friend or acquaintance. Every hour corpses were coming ashore on the beach, every hour the bell was tolling and the long procession winding along the streets. Every tide brought the dead bodies past the ships at Spithead, and it was many days before they could all be interred. Above all, everybody laments the good old Admiral. One of the best and bravest in the service.[6]

The body of Rear-Admiral Kempenfelt was never found.

It was a terrible blow to wartime morale that such a ship, anchored at the main British naval base, could roll over and sink with such loss of life – around three-quarters of those on board. The loss of any warship automatically triggered a naval court-martial to ascertain whether the captain was responsible. With such an important ship and with the convoy about to sail, it was politically expedient to carry out the court-martial as soon as possible. It took place in Portsmouth Harbour on board HMS *Warspite* on 7 September – nine days after the disaster. By the standards of the time, when important courts-martial were often swayed by political or financial considerations rather than facts, this one was not particularly rushed or corrupt. Nevertheless, the verdict was a whitewash. Despite clear evidence to the contrary, the court decided that there was no negligence or mismanagement by Captain Waghorn and his officers and that the ship had sunk because decayed timbers in the hull gave way and let in the water. This neatly passed the blame to Plymouth dockyard, which had undertaken the ship's recent refit. With the conclusive evidence – the wreck itself – safely out of sight, the court-martial was quickly concluded.

Amid increasingly anxious newspaper reports about the impending attack on Gibraltar, the convoy finally set sail from Spithead four days later, on 11 September, led by Howe in his flagship, HMS *Victory*. Poor weather meant the voyage would be a struggle against the elements, and there was the prospect of a more desperate battle with the enemy's fleet at the journey's end.

A few days earlier, at the beginning of September, William Marsden and two friends had sailed from Dover across the Channel to Calais. Although Britain and France were at war, they found themselves welcome visitors, and in their accommodation Marsden said he noticed 'a large coloured print of "le fameux vaisseau Anglois le Royal George" [the famous English ship, the *Royal George*]'. He therefore 'took the occasion of communicating the intelligence of that ship's melancholy loss, which had taken place at Spithead a few days before ... The event had not been previously known at Calais, and I must do our enemies ... the justice to observe, that they expressed what appeared to be genuine feelings of horror at such a loss of English lives.'[7]

The tourists next headed towards Paris, where they saw many members of the royal family, including Louis XVI and Marie-Antoinette (who would both be guillotined in just over a decade, during the French Revolution). At a few theatre productions, the three men witnessed the excitement of the French people, who were anticipating a victory at Gibraltar:

Great preparations were making at one of them for a magnificent representation of the surrender of Gibraltar by the united French and Spanish forces, and one evening when we were in the *coulisses* [backstage], a report was spread of the long expected event having actually taken place. It caused an enthusiastic sensation, particularly among *mesdames les danseuses*, who vociferated, clapping their hands, 'la bonne nouvelle, Gibraltar est prise' [great news, Gibraltar is taken].[8]

On Gibraltar itself, everyone could see the huge forces being massed against them on land and at sea, while in the French and Spanish camps confidence was riding high. The end was in sight, and it appeared as if nothing could stop them. The cream of society was filling the camps of the besieging army, and thousands of spectators were gathering on the surrounding hills to watch the promised spectacle of the magnificent triumph over Gibraltar. The whole of Europe was waiting with interest, expecting an easy victory for France and Spain.

News that they were the centre of attention across the Continent filtered into Gibraltar, causing Ancell to sum up his feelings in a few lines of verse:

> *But as we're actors – Europe the spectators,*
> *I trust we shall perform in this great cause,*
> *As men determined to maintain the right*
> *Of George our King, and Britain's fame and welfare.*
> *Although the foe has made a hectoring boast,*
> *That each discharge from land and sea we'll find,*
> *Two thousand shot and shells from guns and mortars,*
> *Will constantly be show'ring on the garrison.*[9]

Towards the end of August, much of Gibraltar's shipping was gathered inside the New Mole, protected by a boom, and the seamen were busy removing the stores from each vessel, taking down masts and rigging, removing the guns and setting up a camp at Europa. Now that they were living ashore, the seamen were formed into a Marine Brigade, numbering around nine hundred men, under Captain Roger Curtis, who was given the rank of brigadier. Ancell described the men in a letter to his brother:

The seamen are in good spirits, and swear bitterly against the Dons … You would smile to view the tars handling their firelocks, and march fully accoutred; the boatswain's pipe, all hands aloft, brace the yards, tacks and sheets, &c. are no longer heard. The glittering beauties of the parade engage the attention, while whistling winds, and roaring billows are forgotten. Thus military equipped, they long for battle to perform their evolutions and manoeuvres, which on a parade might excite laughter, but amidst blazing cannon, and clouds of smoke, every awkward appearance will be hid.[10]

Including officers and the Marine Brigade, the garrison had about 7500 men, of whom more than 400 were in the hospital, even though the influenza epidemic had died out. Eliott estimated that nearly forty thousand French and Spanish troops were waiting to invade, and Ancell, whose estimate was even higher, reckoned that the opposing force was not just greater in numbers, but in health: 'In the camp of Santa Roque is an army of 50,000 men, not worn out with the heavy toils of war, but healthful and vigorous, while our garrison deprived of all nourishment, and almost as feeble as old age for want of succour, can muster very few more than 5000 men and boys, including sick, wounded and disabled, to repulse the efforts of such a superior force.'[11] The pace of preparations was being pushed to the limit, and over a thousand men were employed night and day at Willis's, reinforcing all the batteries.

From the French camp, Houdan-Deslandes could see that 'the English were working relentlessly on an epaulement that they wanted to withstand the firing from our new parallel. Every day we could hear the explosion of mines that they were carrying out in order to open up refuges in the interior of the mountain.' On 2 September, he mentioned a religious service that took place in the presence of the Comte d'Artois and Duc de Bourbon:

a grand mass was celebrated at the Spanish hospital for the prosperity of our armies. The princes, the generals and a number of designated officers from the Spanish and French regiments assisted in this holy ceremony. A philosophical writer might be permitted to reflect on the spirit of the nations of Europe that wanted to interest the Supreme Being in their quarrels and vengeances. God is the father of everyone; everyone has an equal right to his goodness.[12]

After the mass, Houdan-Deslandes said, 'their Royal Highnesses went to see the wounded Spaniards, who they treated with the sweetest affability'. Two days later, they visited the French invalids in the hospital at St Roque, and that same evening they must have watched as seven of the floating batteries sailed, with the assistance of sweeps, from Algeciras to the Orange Grove. Houdan-Deslandes thought that 'they appeared to move perfectly, confounding their critics, and undoubtedly impressed the English, who saw them move with so much ease'.[13] Ancell, though, was not impressed: 'they had a very stiff breeze from S.W. but were two hours in performing the distance of four miles. They look very unwieldy, and lay deep in the water; three of them have two tier of guns.'[14] As a precaution, the decision was taken to scuttle some of the shipping at the New Mole to help its survival during an attack.

The next day, 5 September, Drinkwater watched as the floating batteries began to take on supplies, ammunition and crews: 'towards evening, about five hundred men, escorted by a body of cavalry, embarked from the pier, on board the battering ships. The singular mode of conducting them to the beach could not fail to attract our notice, and to cause in us some degree of surprise.' Some were volunteers, but most were Spanish regular troops who may have needed some encouragement. The day after, Ancell noticed that 'The tenth [and final] floating battery is roofed, and they have begun to rig her; a few days more, and then we shall fall to it *ding-dong*.'[15]

The officers for the floating batteries were now chosen, and Houdan-Deslandes said that they all envied them:

The Spanish and French officers whose duty it was to go on board were named and applauded. Each one had its captain, its staff, its crew. Forty gunboats and twenty mortar boats were completed and armed. Everything was ready for this day, which was already famous, when Gibraltar would finally be attacked by sea and by land, within sight of two Bourbons, under the orders of the conqueror of Minorca, and with new machines whose inventor ... must be added to those rare geniuses who add to discoveries each century ... Everyone was saying that Gibraltar would be forced to capitulate before the end of September; everyone believed it; and if there were any unbelievers, they didn't dare show it.[16]

This was, he said, the biggest army that had ever gathered in Europe, and the attack would take place 'in the presence of several famous admirals, and in the sight of more than 80,000 spectators'.[17] These war tourists, who now outnumbered the French and Spanish soldiers, were jostling for viewing positions on the Spanish hills, and Picton described them in a letter to General Cornwallis as 'multitudes of spectators of all ranks, and from various parts, as seemed to form, as it were, an endless succession of promiscuous groups, extending over all the adjacent eminences'.[18]

In the afternoon of 7 September, while the soldiers of the besieging army continued toiling on the advance works on the isthmus and the crews were stuck inside the floating batteries, the high-ranking French and Spanish officers, along with the royalty, were invited to a dinner hosted by the Comte de Crillon, the son of the Duc de Crillon:

Monsieur the Comte d'Artois and Monsieur the Duc de Bourbon came to dine with me in the French camp. After eating, the afternoon was filled in the most merry way, with a parade done very cheerily, and dances as well as singing rounds and verses by our grenadiers. For my own part, I was greatly entertained, and I believe that M. the Comte d'Artois has never laughed so much. The cheerfulness of our soldiers had spread to him, and there was something frivolous about it.[19]

Drinkwater was of the opinion that the Duc de Crillon was so engrossed in completing the alterations and repairs to the gun and mortar batteries on the isthmus that he had neglected to take precautions for their defence. They were piled high with construction materials, some guns were obstructed and others had been removed. Boyd suggested to Eliott that they should seize the opportunity to attack the Spanish positions with red-hot shot, and Ancell described how he took charge: 'This morning [the 8th], Lieutenant-General Boyd took post on the grand-battery (having command of all the batteries) and the necessary arrangements being made from the rock-gun to the Old-Mole-Head, we began a furious cannonade of red-hot balls upon the enemy's Mahon-battery (mounted with six pieces of ordnance) and other lines of approach, together with a supply of shells and carcasses.'[20] The results were spectacular, as Drinkwater related: 'The effect of the red-hot shot and carcasses exceeds our most sanguine expectations. In a few hours, the Mahon battery of six guns with the battery of two guns on its flank, and great parts of the adjoining parallel, were on fire; and the flames, notwithstanding the Enemy's exertions to extinguish them, burnt so rapidly that the whole of those works before night were consumed.'[21]

Houdan-Deslandes said that the Comte de Crillon gave orders in every direction, and officers and soldiers alike tried to tear down and cut the fascines or fetch sea water, but the Rock kept firing:

> Nothing could make them relent. Neither the sight of the dying, nor the groans of the wounded, nor the constant firing which became so fierce that we counted 20 shots per minute ... The firing of the besieged ... was inflamed by rage; it could not be extinguished by bravery. Red-hot shot increased the fire ... We saw several officers in shirt-sleeves, their bare arms black with smoke, their fronts covered with ash, who worked for hours on the blazing fortification and encouraged the men by this rare and powerful example.[22]

Boyd's journal expressed admiration for the enemy's valour: '[the red-hot shot] had the desired and glorious effect to set on fire their different advanced batteries, which was repeatedly put out by them, for braver men was never seen than the enemy were on the batteries that was on fire. They never flinched from shot or shells which fell among them as thick as hail.'[23] Ancell likewise admired them:

The foe withstood our fire with intrepidity, until most of their works, and the thirteen-gun battery next the bay, were blazing in several places, and strewed over with mangled limbs and dead bodies. Several parties appeared upon the glacis, and in an undaunted manner, tore up the fascines. Some kept pouring of baskets of sand upon the parts that were on fire, and others running to the sea for buckets of water. Thus they stood, while showers of balls fell on every side, and many were observed to be knocked off the works. I assure you, it was a horrid scene of slaughter.[24]

The garrison's gunners relished being able to take decisive action, particularly in defiance of the hostile crowd watching from a safe distance, and managed to destroy the new Mahon battery and badly damaged two batteries that had been rebuilt since the sortie – St Carlos and St Martin's. Ancell could barely contain his excitement: 'The most intoxicating joy gained possession of the soldiery, and every heart and hand was cheerfully employed; and while gazing crowds, who had taken post upon Andalusia's hills, beheld the vollies of destruction that flew in showers, and the sad effects that were productive of the red-flaming balls, our men rejoiced, and made a pastime of the dire employ.'[25] This was certainly not the magnificent spectacle that the tourists had come to see.

The Spanish guns retaliated furiously, and some casualties were inflicted on the British side. Drinkwater mentioned Major Philip Martin of the artillery, who had 'a very fortunate escape from a twenty-six pounder, which shot away the cock of his hat close to the crown. I insert this anecdote, because it is commonly believed, that if a cannon-ball of this diameter pass so near the head of a person, it is generally fatal. The Major was considerably stunned with the wind of the shot, but experienced little further injury.'[26]

The French and Spanish forces immediately set about a rapid repair of the devastation, to the surprise and disappointment of the garrison. From sunrise the next day, a huge retaliatory attack was launched against the northern fortifications of the Rock, particularly Willis's, which astonished Ancell: 'Their sixty-four gun battery was an incessant volley the whole time, which lasted most of the day, and the distance being so short, their shot reached the walls almost as soon as you perceived the flash; the discharge was so quick that the balls rolled along the streets by dozens.'[27] From the French side, Houdan-Deslandes commented: 'Ever since sieges have taken place, nobody had ever carried out such a formidable bombardment against a fortress, in such an awesome manner ... The English did not reply with a single cannon shot. This mountain, which the previous day had rung out with the noise of cannonballs that were constantly belched out, kept a deathly silence and seemed uninhabited.'[28]

The garrison was preserving its ammunition, assuming that an attack by the floating batteries would come next. Instead, they were restocking the magazines and carrying out repairs, which were summarised in Boyd's journal: 'Our batteries at Willis's, Prince's, Kings and Queens Lines, suffers much by the enemies shot striking against the rocks above, which throws down such heaps of stones that the Lines &c. are almost daily choked up, for which we have about 600 men nightly employed to clear them and keep the avenues open, with necessary repairs.'[29] Later on, battleships sailed from the Orange Grove and fired at the west side of the Rock, all the way down to Europa, and then returned, still firing. The next morning, 10 September, they repeated the process, but this time the garrison fired back and they suddenly withdrew. 'We were afterwards informed,' Drinkwater said, 'that the discovery of a red-hot shot on board one of the ships was the immediate cause of this hasty manoeuvre.'[30] This was a salutary lesson why warships were of limited use when attacking land fortifications.

The inhabitants were terrified, and Drinkwater watched them trying to protect their property and themselves: 'Affairs seemed now drawing to a crisis, and as every appearance indicated that the attack would not long be deferred, the inhabitants, apprehensive of the consequences, were wonderfully active in securing themselves and their property.'[31] Those who had homes or improvised accommodation in the town fled to the south and took refuge in caves, 'which opportunity the soldiers do not miss, or let slip them,' Boyd's journal related, 'for they rob, plunder, steal, break open houses and marauds in the same manner, though not with so much success, as they did at the begining of the siege'. Dennis Murray, a soldier in the 39th, seized the opportunity, but was caught. At his court-martial, he was found guilty of breaking into the Red Lion Wine House of Damian Stericho, a Genoese inhabitant, in order to steal a cask of brandy and other goods. Murray was hanged for the crime.[32] There was certainly no heroic alliance between the civilians and military against a common enemy, but a basic instinct for self-preservation.

Orders had been given to the French and Spanish army detachments to be ready as soon as the wind changed, because a westerly or north-westerly wind was needed to propel the floating batteries towards Gibraltar. At about midday on the 11th, Houdan-Deslandes said, when 'everyone was unhappy at the contrary winds, and all eyes were fixed on the weather vanes of the tents, everyone making heartfelt wishes for a change in the weather, the wind changed to the west'.[33] Drums started beating in the camps, sounding the signal to go on board. While they waited their turn, in the French camp there was huge excitement, with dancing, singing and drinking everyone's health.

When the garrison spotted what seemed to be signals for the start of the attack, orders were given for the furnaces to be lit for red-hot shot, but as the afternoon gave way to evening, Drinkwater thought that the first move would be made under the cover of darkness: 'Thus prepared, we waited their appearance (for it seemed to be the general opinion, that the battering-ships would advance, and be moored in the night, and open with greater effect together at day-break).'[34] What happened instead was that, during the night, soldiers came in close to the approaches to Landport and set fire to the wooden barricades at Bayside and Forbes, causing them to burn right down to the water's edge. The intruders were driven off by musket fire, but it looked as if a ground assault was to coincide with the floating batteries, though Houdan-Deslandes later revealed that the reason for burning the barricades was to facilitate soldiers deserting from Gibraltar. In the distance, bands of music were heard playing all night, so the camp was obviously in high spirits, while the Spanish artillery bombardment also continued. The gunboats joined in after midnight, but only a few retaliatory shots were fired from the Rock. Instead, everyone was waiting for daylight, convinced that this would be the day for the grand assault.

Almost four weeks earlier, a letter from a soldier in Gibraltar to his father in London was published in the *Newcastle Journal*, saying that Eliott was sending dispatches to England to ask for urgent assistance:

The Spaniards are preparing to attack us in form with a numerous army and a large train of heavy artillery, and our men are greatly harassed and fatigued with hard duty, and dispirited by being so long cooped up. Our brave Governor does all he can to encourage them to persevere, and to defend the place to the last moment. We are able I believe to hold out to the middle of September, but if we are not relieved by that time we must surrender ... I think that if we are effectually relieved by the 12th of September, the united force of France and Spain will not be able to take the place.[35]

It was now 12 September, and as daylight came there was both relief and disappointment that the expected array of floating batteries before the Line Wall had not materialised overnight.

According to Houdan-Deslandes, there was similar disappointment in the French camp: 'The wind was still favourable for
mooring the floating batteries that everyone thought they would
see in place in the morning ... There was grumbling. Impatience
led to the rise of suspicions, undoubtedly false.'[36] Instead, the
Spanish batteries maintained their bombardment, concentrating
on the Landport area, from where Ancell came off guard duty that
morning:

> crossing the Esplanade, I observed a soldier before me, lying on
> the ground, and his head somewhat raised; I ran to him, imagin-
> ing the man had life, and lifted him up, when such a sight was
> displayed to my view that I think I shall never forget: a twenty-
> six pound ball had gone through his body, and his entrails as
> they hung out from the orifice were of a most disagreeable
> resemblance. The shot from the enemy was dropping on every
> side, and as I found his life was gone, I left him on the same
> spot ... A party of men buried him soon afterwards.[37]

Everything appeared ready for the attack by the floating batteries, so it was strange that it had still not happened. Peering
through a telescope, Ancell could even see that the 'enemy have
erected stands or booths around the shore, lined with crimson or
scarlet, where the nobles and grandees will take their seats'.[38] In a
letter to his son-in-law Oliver Nicolls, William Green wrote:

> Their ten great floating batteries ... seemed to be got all per-
> fectly ready about the 1st of September, as was every other
> preparation by sea, including 3 bomb ketches, 16 gun boats, 8
> mortar boats, 16 large boats with mantelets across their bow,
> to let down with a hinge for the easier disembarking of troops,
> besides about 2 or 300 boats brought from the adjacent coasts
> to assist in throwing troops ashore ... The whole of this sea
> attack, as we thought, was to be supported by 9 line of battle
> ships (7 Spanish and 2 French) and which had been in the Bay
> for some time.[39]

At about 8 o'clock in the morning of the 12th, a huge fleet appeared, which was initially thought to be the relief convoy from England, as nobody knew that Howe's ships had only set sail from England on the previous day, the 11th. This was the enemy's Grand Fleet from Cadiz, which had been prepared in the greatest secrecy. The garrison was completely taken aback. Captain Colin Lindsay of the 73rd Highlanders described the scene to his brother Alexander, the Earl of Balcarres: 'a large fleet appeared in the Streights from the West, but the morning being hazy, it was not till they approached very near, that we discovered them to be the combined fleet of France and Spain ... It must not now be denied that their arrival, which was totally unexpected, had some effect upon the spirits of the garrison.'[40]

Green also admitted to Nicolls that the fleet's arrival was completely unforeseen: 'to our great astonishment in come their Grand combined fleet, and anchored at the head of the Bay, consisting of 41 large ships, 7 of which are three deckers ... A formidable fleet, you'll say, and commanded by eight Admirals.'[41] On the Rock, the overall effect was demoralisation: 'This great accumulation of force could not fail to surprise, if not alarm the Garrison. It appeared as if they meant, previous to their final efforts, to strike, if possible, a terror through their opponents, by displaying before us a more powerful armament than had probably ever been brought against any fortress ... Such a naval and military spectacle most certainly is not to be equalled in the annals of war.'[42] This was the largest concentration of military force ever known, and the odds were overwhelming, which Houdan-Deslandes commented on:

The heavens seemed to want to favour our efforts and crown them with victory. The wind from the west ... hadn't changed. Forty-eight warships were anchored in front of Gibraltar and must have brought consternation to the English garrison, for whom their presence must have removed all hope of help. The Bay of Algeciras was covered with vessels of all kinds, destined for a maritime attack on this besieged fortress. The weather was beautiful, the wind was good, the floating batteries were ready, the two armies full of confidence. The firing from our Lines was continuous. Gibraltar was quiet. Everything promised us a triumph.[43]

Under such circumstances, it was natural to clutch at any straw of hope, as Drinkwater noticed: 'When the van of the Combined Fleet had entered the Bay, the soldiers in the town were attentively viewing the ships, alleging, amongst other reasons for their arrival, that the British fleet must undoubtedly be in pursuit. On a sudden, a general huzza was given, and all, to a man, cried out, the British Admiral was certainly in their rear, as a flag for a fleet was hoisted upon our signal-house [flag]pole.' They were disappointed to learn that it was not a flag, but an eagle perched on top of the pole for a few minutes. Eagles from Africa flew into Gibraltar from time to time, while some bred in remote places at the top of the Rock, so they were not such an unusual sight. Those officers and soldiers who knew some classical history were happy to view the eagle as a symbol of victory, and Drinkwater added: 'Though less superstitious than the ancient Romans, many could not help fancying it a favourable omen to the Garrison.'[44]

# CHAPTER TWENTY

—————— · ✦ · ——————

# MASS ATTACK

As dawn broke the next day, Friday 13 September, everyone on Gibraltar expected the floating batteries to have moved into position under cover of darkness. Instead, it looked to be another day of waiting, though each day brought the hope of a relief convoy arriving from England. As usual, everyone kept a close watch on what the enemy was doing, including Drinkwater: 'we observed the Combined Fleet had made some new arrangements in their position, or moorings and that the remaining two battering-ships had joined the others at the Orange-grove, where their whole force seemed to be assembled'. At around quarter to seven in the morning, some movements were spotted amongst their shipping, 'and soon after, the battering-ships got under way, with a gentle breeze from the north-west, standing to the southward, to clear the men of war, and were attended by a number of boats'.[1]

Because the other warships were showing no signs of setting sail, Drinkwater said it took some time to realise what was happening, in broad daylight, with the floating batteries:

As our Navy were constantly of the opinion that the [battering] ships would be brought before the Garrison in the night, few suspected that the present manoeuvres were preparatory to their finally entering on the interesting enterprise. But observing a crowd of spectators on the beach, near Point Mala, and upon the neighbouring eminences, and the ships edging down towards the Garrison, the Governor thought it would be imprudent any longer to doubt it. The Town-batteries were accordingly manned, and the grates and furnaces for heating shot ordered to be lighted.[2]

The spectators on the distant shores were expecting something dramatic to take place, while Ancell's excitable words imply that on Gibraltar they were all galvanised at the prospect of action:

To arms! to arms! is all the cry. The enemy's floating batteries have weighed anchor, and are now under sail with a fine breeze at N.W. Their colours wanton in the wind, with gaudy decorations for the battle, while thousands of spectators from yon glittering shore impatiently wait to triumph in their success. They have now tacked with their head towards the garrison, and what is remarkable, they work them without a man being exposed or seen.[3]

That morning, Houdan-Deslandes had seen the signals: 'The floating batteries spread their sails and steered towards Gibraltar ... in a moment the news spread all round the camp. No news had ever spread so quickly. Officers, soldiers, servants, all climbed on the most elevated rocks from where they might see the new and daring operation that was going to take place in full daylight.'[4] Unprepared for a daytime attack, the garrison was caught by surprise when the ten floating batteries set off, not least because it was an inauspicious day of the week. Sailors generally did not like setting sail on a Friday, and one French traveller confirmed that it was also a widely held superstition in Spain: 'The Spanish are convinced that Fridays are unlucky, and that although there are orders in all the ports to allow the King's ships to leave on any day of the week, most captains avoid setting sail on Fridays, perhaps out of consideration for their crew, or perhaps they themselves fear a malign influence on Fridays.'[5]

French sailors held the same view, and it was generally believed, both on land and at sea, that it was bad luck to start anything new on a Friday. Since the numeral thirteen was also considered unlucky, this Friday the 13th may have seemed particularly unlucky, though for which side was unclear. Faced with such an overwhelming force, some on Gibraltar took comfort that this day was the anniversary of the victory in 1759 at the Battle of Quebec. Even though General Wolfe, the British commander, did not survive the battle, the victory over the French was periodically celebrated by those who had served in North America, including members of Gibraltar's American Club, such as William Green.

There might have been slightly more optimism if it had been realised that none of the commanders of the French and Spanish forces agreed with one another. The Duc de Crillon, who was in overall command, and Admiral Cordoba, who was in command of the combined fleet, were both sceptical about the plan to use floating batteries, while d'Arçon, who had designed them, wanted to carry out more tests. Early on, he had insisted that the effects of red-hot shot on the floating batteries should be tried out by firing from the Spanish batteries, but it was now too late.[6] With the pressure of so many impatient spectators, including two French princes and other aristocrats and dignitaries, Crillon was not willing to wait any longer, and so he overruled d'Arçon's protests and gave the order for the attack.

Under the command of Admiral Buenaventura Moreno, who was on board his flagship *Pastora*, the floating batteries sailed from the Orange Grove to the shoreline defences on the west side of Gibraltar town, a journey of some three miles that took three hours.[7] Captain Colin Lindsay was amazed at how well they sailed, even though the wind had increased in strength: 'We ... saw, what we could not have believed, that these unwieldy looking machines sailed and steered with as much quickness and precision as the lightest ships'.[8] Eliott watched their manoeuvres as they came into position:

all the battering ships came forward to the several stations previously determined they should take up: the Admiral

being placed upon the capital of [opposite] the King's Bastion,
the other ships extending three to the southward of the flag
[flagship], as far as the church battery; five to the northward
about the height of the Old Mole; and one a very little to the
westward of the Admiral. By a quarter before ten, they were
anchored in line, at the distance of a thousand to twelve hundred yards.[9]

Other eyewitnesses reported them as slightly closer, 800 to 1000
yards. Houdan-Deslandes heard that the original plan was for
the larger floating batteries to anchor from the King's Bastion as
far south as the New Mole, spaced out sufficiently to allow the
smaller ones to form a line behind and fire through the gaps.
D'Arçon himself had done many soundings of the sea-bed and
later claimed he wanted the main attack to be concentrated on
the Old Mole, allowing the floating batteries to be more easily
withdrawn if the need arose.[10] In the end, two of them anchored
opposite the King's Bastion – Moreno's flagship *Pastora* and the
*Talla Piedra*, which had d'Arçon on board and was commanded
by the French naval officer Prince of Nassau, who had only just
arrived with the combined fleet. Two others were stationed south
of the King's Bastion, while the rest were to the north, as far as the
Old Mole, and there were reports of several of them grounding on
the sea-bed, unable to advance any closer.

The King's Bastion was the strongest part of the Line Wall,
with at least twenty-five guns. William Green was astonished and
baffled at their decision to anchor there, as he had been responsible for improving this whole stretch of fortification, including
the design and construction of the King's Bastion. In 1773, years
before Eliott became governor, Green and other officers had
attended a ceremony in which Boyd laid the foundation stone,
with the words: 'This is the first stone of a work which I name
the King's Bastion: may it be as gallantly defended, as I know it
will be ably executed, and may I live to see it resist the united
efforts of France and Spain!'[11] For the floating batteries to focus
on this part of the Line Wall was, Green said to his son-in-law,

rather like 'taking the Bull by the Horns, viz. the King's, the Prince of Orange's, and the Montague Bastions ... universally acknowledged to be very conspicuous and efficacious, particularly the King's Bastion, opposite to which the Spanish Admiral and Commander of the Armada drew up.'[12]

In all, the floating batteries carried just over five thousand men and around 142 guns ready to fire at Gibraltar – fewer guns than if three large warships were firing broadsides at the fortifications, though warships were not built to withstand fierce bombardments and red-hot shot. The number of guns varied in different reports – Drinkwater gave 142, d'Arçon 152 and Houdan-Deslandes 153, while Boyd's journal said that a boatswain specified 166. As a minimum, the *Pastora* had twenty-one brass guns on the port side and a crew of around 760 men, almost the size of the crew of a 100-gun warship. The *Talla Piedra* and *Paula Prima* were roughly the same size, while the *Rosario* was slightly smaller, with nineteen guns and 700 men. The *San Cristobal* was smaller again, with eighteen guns and 650 men, and the *Principe Carlos* had eleven guns and 400 men. The remaining four vessels had far fewer guns – the *San Juan* and *Paula Secunda* nine guns each and crews of 340 men, the *Santa Ana* seven guns and 300 men, and the *Dolores* only six guns and 250 men. The brass guns were all specially cast, and the bigger vessels carried ten spares and the smaller ones four to six spares.

Within ten minutes, both sides began a devastating barrage of shot and shells, which Drinkwater tried to describe:

The cannonade then became in a high degree tremendous. The showers of shot and shells which were directed from their land-batteries, the battering ships, and on the other hand, from the various works of the Garrison, exhibited a scene, of which perhaps neither the pen nor pencil can furnish a competent idea. It is sufficient to say, that *four hundred pieces* of the heaviest artillery were playing at the same moment: an instance which has scarcely occurred in any siege since the invention of those wonderful engines of destruction.[13]

Boyd took up position on the South Bastion to watch, while Eliott was on the King's Bastion, at the heart of the action. Walter Gordon of the 73rd, who was helping with the guns there, was greatly impressed: 'With what amazing coolness does he issue his orders! His looks express settled contempt of their boasted batteries: His air is truly magnetic ... undiscomposed he stands, during the time of action, which was for many hours.'[14] Most of the regiments remained in the south, ready to take part if there was an invasion by French and Spanish troops, but some of the officers, Lindsay said, chose to ignore orders 'and to be eye-witnesses of the gallantry of the artillery, or to animate, by their presence, the men of their respective corps employed on the batteries, or on duty in the ruins of the town'.[15]

The furnaces were still not sufficiently hot to heat cannonballs, and so the artillerymen did what they could with cold shot, though Ancell and others were dismayed at the results: 'the artillery ... directed the ordnance on these wonderful ships of destruction. Our astonishment was raised to the highest pitch on beholding our heaviest shot rebound from their sides, and an unusual anxiety seemed to possess the mind of all ranks, when a thirteen-inch shell, which dropped on the roof of the Admiral's ship, resisted penetration!'[16] With shot and shells bouncing off their roofs, the floating batteries were proving resilient to everything.

From his viewpoint in the French camp, Houdan-Deslandes remarked: 'We saw then what has only been seen that once and what will probably never be seen again – ten monstrous vessels striking Gibraltar with artillery ... and that Rock deploying all means of defence ... firing at its attackers in the most astonishing way since the invention of gunpowder.'[17] However, he thought that 'all the moored floating batteries were ... too close to each other and nearly all opposite the same rampart',[18] though he could not help being impressed: 'No spectacle has ever been more beautiful; never has genius and valour had as many judges and never could they have hoped for as many admirers.'[19] Boyd's journal mentioned that from Gibraltar they could see thousands of spectators all round the bay: 'the Queen's Chair, the hills and mountains round to Cabrito Point, we plainly saw with our glasses [telescopes] crowded, and by report, with people of both sexes and of all ranks, of people assembled from every village, town and city, far and near; even proud Madrid Dons brings up the promiscuous crowd to behold the reduction of Gibraltar.'[20]

The exchange of fire continued furiously, with little apparent effect on either side. The floating batteries were designed to pound Gibraltar's fortifications, knock out the guns and create breaches to enable soldiers to land, but the sea swell was affecting the aim of their gunners, so that they had trouble concentrating their fire on a single point. More seriously, most of the vessels were too far from the defences. The fiercest battle was taking place between the King's Bastion and the *Pastora* and *Talla Piedra*. The other floating batteries were unable to elevate their guns in order to increase their range, and d'Arçon reckoned that only sixty guns in all were capable of reaching their target.

On the Rock, the gunners had the problem of trying to hit relatively small targets that were becoming rapidly obscured by smoke from the gun fire. Although the garrison guns were pouring out cold shot and shells, nothing appeared to be effective against the floating batteries. 'Our balls seemed to rebound into the sea,' Lindsay admitted,

and even such shells from the thirteen inch mortars as struck, glanced off the shelving roofs, composed of logs, and did them not the least apparent injury; yet shells of this nature, when loaded, weigh above two hundred pounds upon the ground, and where they fall from their elevation, as that weight increases every instant of the fall, we might suppose the shock to be irresistible; accordingly, wherever they fall on our most solid fortifications, they never fail to make such havoc as requires time and prodigious labour to repair. Of what sort of materials, it was then naturally asked, can these formidable engines be made, to possess a repelling and elastic power to so very wonderful a degree?[21]

The gunners kept persevering in the hopes of some success or a lucky shot striking home, and they enjoyed one freak accident: 'A shot from one of the enemy's junk ships came into one of our howitzers on the King's Bastion, which fired her off, and the ball returned with the howitzer shell to its own ship again, through one of the portholes, and the shell exploding between decks, killed and wounded about 40 men.'[22] Conditions for the crews of the floating batteries were terrible, with very little air except through the deep embrasures or gunports. These embrasures were actually a weakness because shells did occasionally get through, causing carnage. The plan was for the crew members to work in shifts: 'Two-thirds of each crew were below, under the surface of the water,' Lindsay related, 'and relieved the decks alternately; they were there almost suffocated for want of air ... several of our shells entered at the ports or embrasures, and killed and wounded between thirty and forty men each time. A frigate cruised behind as a hospital ship.'[23]

In spite of their plight, the crews fought on, and Ancell thought he knew why:

> previous to the attack, an aid-de-camp to the Duc de Crillon was sent aboard each vessel, who after examining her condition, represented to the crew the glorious undertaking they were about to launch into, and promising in the King's name, the highest regard for their bravery. Each soldier and sailor was to be exempt from all further service, to have a gratuity of fifty dollars and full pay for the remainder of his life. The widows and children of the killed were to enjoy the same benefit.[24]

What nobody realised was that the fierce bombardment was actually weakening the structure of the floating batteries, preparing the way for red-hot shot to penetrate. From around midday, red-hot shot was at last available – relatively few at first, but a plentiful supply after another hour. The long distance to the floating batteries was now an advantage, because the guns needed to be elevated, with the barrels pointing upwards, to reach their target. This allowed the gunners to tip the red-hot shot down the muzzle and dispense with a wet wad to hold it in place. They soon learned that they could also abandon the wet wad between the cartridge and the shot. Instead, they simply loaded the gunpowder cartridge in the barrel, aimed the gun and tipped in the red-hot shot, which ignited the cartridge and fired the gun. This method produced an extremely fast rate of fire, such that the furnaces could not keep up with demand. Makeshift methods were devised, and Drinkwater described shot being heated 'by piling them in a corner of some old house adjoining the batteries ... and surrounding them with faggots, pieces of timber, and small-coal. By those means, the artificers were enabled to supply the Artillery with a constant succession for the ordnance.'[25]

The way the red-hot shot was carried from the furnaces to the guns now proved too slow, and Ancell said that while the blacksmiths among the artificers were busy at the forges heating the shot, 'others were allotted to carry the blazing balls on an iron instrument made for that purpose, but as these did not furnish sufficient [shot] for the vast supply required at the batteries, wheel-barrows were procured, lined with wet sand, and half a dozen thirty-two pound balls thrown into each'.[26] Because they were wooden wheelbarrows, the wet sand was essential to stop them catching fire. Gradually, the supply of red-hot shot increased to such an extent that a rate of fire was achieved similar to that for cold shot. On board the floating batteries, conditions had improved because the sea was now calmer, but the volleys of red-hot shot were a shock to the crews, because they had been told it would be slow and inaccurate. Lindsay even heard that the crews 'were all made to believe that we could not fire above one red shot in an hour from a gun, and that it was against the rules of war'.[27]

The gunners were being struck down by shot coming in from the Spanish land batteries, but instead of being distracted and turning some of their guns to retaliate, Drinkwater said that they increased their bombardment of the floating batteries: 'A fire, more tremendous if possible than ever, was therefore directed from the Garrison. Incessant showers of hot balls, carcasses, and shells of every species, flew from all quarters, and as the masts of several of the ships were shot away, and the rigging of all in great confusion, our hopes of a favourable and speedy decision began to revive.' Although they managed to destroy some of the masts and rigging, Drinkwater gloomily thought that they were achieving little else: 'For some hours, the attack and defence were so equally well supported, as scarcely to admit any appearance of superiority in the cannonade on either side. The wonderful construction of the ships seemed to bid defiance to the powers of the heaviest ordnance.'[28]

William Green told his son-in-law Nicolls that in the early afternoon he became aware of smoke seeping from some of the floating batteries: 'we could perceive some of them, by the issues of smoke, [and they] seemed internally to be on fire, and as if some lurking embryos of fire were labouring to burst forth'.[29] With the *Pastora* and *Talla Piedra* taking the brunt of the bombardment, conditions on board were worse than anyone on Gibraltar imagined. According to Houdan-Deslandes, a message was sent from the *Talla Piedra* to the French camp behind the Lines: 'The Prince of Nassau has asked for another captain and 25 soldiers to replace the dead and wounded. He has added, so we were told, that the enemy has sent him a great deal of red-hot shot, but that they have easily extinguished the fires.' The soldiers who delivered the message may well have been responsible for the subsequent speculation: 'the rumour was spreading in the Spanish camp that the Pastora had lost an infinite number of people, that fire had taken hold several times and that they hadn't managed to completely extinguish it, and Moreno had come to inform the Comte d'Artois of these disasters'.[30]

On Gibraltar, the effort to keep the guns firing at such a rate, hour after hour in the intense summer sunshine, was utterly exhausting, and by late afternoon the men were parched, hungry and thoroughly blackened by the dirty gunpowder smoke. Ancell described their predicament:

The fatigue attending conveyance of shot to the cannon was very great, from the heat which issued from such large bodies of hot iron, together with wheeling the barrows up the ascent to the line wall. What with the arduousness of the work, the warmth of the weather, the scorching heat of the furnaces, forges, and piles of blazing balls, besides the clouds of smoke from the ordnance, a universal thirst prevailed, and a drink of water (which was all the allowance for the day) could scarcely be procured.[31]

Lindsay was also worried that the huge combined fleet would shortly be able to join in: 'It occurred to many that our artillery-men must soon be exhausted with mere bodily fatigue, and now that the wind had subsided to a breeze, and the sea was smooth, their whole train of gun and mortar-boats, and all their ships of war, were every hour expected ... the men [gunners] declared that had they but a short refreshment, they could stand to the guns for eight and forty hours, whatever might be apprehended.' At this point, Eliott decided to bring in a hundred men from the Marine Brigade. Being naval seamen, they were accustomed to working guns, and so it did not take long to show them how to deal with the red-hot shot, while the artillerymen were able to have 'a draught of water from the fountain, and such salt provisions as could be brought'.[32]

No support came to the floating batteries from the French and Spanish fleet, though it could easily have upset the balance of the battle. One reason was that the floating batteries had been loaded with provisions, including plentiful brandy and wine, intended to last ten to twelve days, and the plan was for the bombardment of Gibraltar's defences to take at least a week, with more ammunition supplied by boat if the garrison did not surrender within twenty-four hours.[33] But according to d'Arçon, they should have been supported from the outset by the gunboats and mortar boats, and although the wind did strengthen through the day, causing a swell, he felt that conditions were perfectly adequate: 'thirty gunboats, which were supposed to operate together, behind the shelter of the floating batteries, never appeared. Thirty mortar boats were also supposed to operate in the rear, on the flanks of the attack. Their purpose was (at the same time as all the mortars on land) not to let the enemy have one moment of safety ... it had been asked for in writing, agreed and promised.'[34]

He was not alone in bemoaning the lack of support. Houdan-Deslandes was equally perplexed: 'The galiots, the mortar boats, the gunboats that were supposed to help the floating batteries, and which should have added their firing to this powerful attack, made no move at all. Only one galiot fired. Nobody questions ... why all the armed ships didn't advance at the same time as the floating batteries, but remained immobile.'[35]

At long last the garrison gunners began to see some results for all their exertions, as Lindsay explained:

A little before dark, the enemy hoisted a chequered flag, which inspired some hopes that all might not be quite so well with them on board. Some lucky shot entering their embrasures, were heard to ring against their cannon, and several ten-inch shells, sent with a fortunate horizontal direction from our how-itzers were seen to enter in the same manner, and some at last stick in their sides, and afterwards explode. A considerable and increasing smoke was seen to issue from the vessel of their admiral [*Pastora*], but was soon extinguished.[36]

The smouldering fire was in fact far from extinguished, and Houdan-Deslandes later learned that conditions were intolerable on board the two floating batteries closest to the Rock:

Already, fire took hold eleven times in the Talla Piedra, and perhaps the Pastora as well. After the greatest efforts of valour, they succeeded in extinguishing it in several places. But the red-hot shot lodged in the thick side of the vessel ... starting a fire inside that was not suspected, that spread without being noticed, and only showed when it had become impossible to extinguish. More than 100 men have been killed on board the Pastora. The Talla Piedra has lost as many.[37]

On board the *Pastora* and *Talla Piedra*, Walter Gordon said, 'Men were perceived to be using fire engines, and pouring water into the holes, endeavouring to extinguish the fire; this was found to be the case repeatedly during the day.'[38]

At around eight in the evening of Friday the 13th, firing from virtually all of the floating batteries stopped, but the gunners on the Rock never let up. It was now decided that the infantry soldiers, who had been waiting all day, should get some rest. As Lindsay said, they would need to put up a determined resistance once the final assault came, because 'the Duc de Crillon had often publicly declared, that one half of his army should be sacrificed, were it necessary ... and that in such a case, no quarter should be given to the garrison'.[39] Everyone was apprehensive, as there were still many uncertainties. They had been attacked by the floating batteries and suffered a furious barrage from the guns on the Lines, but there had been no ground assault from the isthmus, no attempted invasions by troops in boats, and the powerful combined French and Spanish fleet had remained at anchor all day. What was the French and Spanish plan, and what would they do next?

# CHAPTER TWENTY-ONE

## EXPLOSION

In the evening darkness, Houdan-Deslandes climbed to the top of a signal tower near the French camp to try to make out what was happening, in the hopes that the fires he had heard about on board the floating batteries were extinguished. Flashes of guns firing could be seen, but as far as he was concerned, 'everything was calm and appeared to have been so for a long time. The floating batteries were hardly firing, but I was far from suspecting the reason. I returned to camp. I went towards my tent, and I said adieu to one of my friends.' The news he then received was shocking: 'Another heard me, called me, and told me everything was lost. He advised me that Monsieur de la Tour had retreated from the French floating battery that was being consumed by a fire which was impossible to put out, that Monsieur du Berard had lost an arm, and that Monsieur de Myring had a broken thigh.'[1]

When it was obvious that fires had taken hold in two of the floating batteries, with no significant breach in Gibraltar's defences, Admiral Moreno had sent word to Admiral Cordoba. As later recorded by the Duc de Crillon, at a council-of-war he and the Prince of Nassau then asked Cordoba to send frigates from the combined fleet 'to try to tow some floating batteries stuck on sandbanks ... which the enemy hadn't been able to reach with gunfire. The admiral refused them, saying it would expose the frigates to the dangers of being burned, with the certainty of not bringing back anything.'[2] On board the *Talla Piedra* and *Pastora*, the heat and smoke became so bad that rockets were fired in distress. At that moment Crillon decided to issue orders to send boats to take the men off the floating batteries, and he also ordered all of them to be set alight so that the British could not capture any. Because Cordoba was refusing to tow away the floating batteries that were unscathed – the majority of them – Crillon had no other option.

While the council-of-war was still taking place, the reinforcements that had been earlier requested by the Prince of Nassau were still trying to reach the floating batteries – a dangerous undertaking because the garrison was constantly firing shells and red-hot shot. Eighty men were crammed in one boat, which was overturned by a shot as they reached the *Talla Piedra*. Most of the men drowned, while others managed to cling to wreckage. By now, d'Arçon had abandoned the *Talla Piedra* so that he himself could go to Cordoba's flagship to beg for help, but it was too late: 'He [d'Arçon] hurried to ask for help from the first flagship, from where they sent him to the General of the Land Forces, who had to decide on everything, they said, with the Commander of the Batteries. He rushed there. He couldn't find anyone, but learned that the order had been given – and set in train – to set fire to all the [floating] batteries.'[3]

Finding it too difficult to snatch some sleep, Captain Lindsay was soon back on the Line Wall, just as the men clinging to the wreckage of their boat were detected: 'About eleven at night a boat was seen approaching to the shore, which, on its coming nearer, was discovered to be floating on its side, with twelve French soldiers and a Spanish officer upon it. The assistance they implored was sent to them, and they were received into the garrison.' This windfall of prisoners was interrogated and provided the first real information:

> We learnt that the slaughter of the enemy on board had been so great, that a reinforcement had been necessary; that they had been volunteers for that purpose, and had almost reached the vessel they were destined for, which was manned entirely by the French, when a shot from the garrison overset the

boat, which had fourscore men on board; that they had floated above four hours in the water … that the tide had driven them beneath our walls.[4]

Despite their own predicament, Lindsay said that these prisoners were adamant the garrison could not hold out: 'if we thought to destroy the battering ships by our artillery, or by fire, we might spare ourselves the trouble of making the attempt; that whatever numbers we might kill on board … their whole army and their fleet would eagerly crowd to supply the places of the slain, well knowing that it could not require any great length of time to make a sufficient breach'. He thought that these were not the words of bravado or defiance, but 'nothing more than the creed with which the enemy were universally inspired'.[5] The officers on board the floating batteries, not sharing the same enthusiasm, were the first to take advantage of the rescue boats. The *Pastora* and *Talla Piedra* were smouldering fiercely, and red-hot shot seems to have caused fires in a few other floating batteries, while the rest were being deliberately set on fire, with assurances given to the crews that further boats would rescue them in time.[6]

It was now approaching midnight, and in the French camp Houdan-Deslandes watched the disaster unfolding: 'We glanced towards the floating batteries. Two balls of fire erupted and terrified us. All our friends got up. Everyone looked eagerly towards these awful and terrible objects. Soldiers returned to the camp, all were still appalled at the dangers they had just run. We questioned them. "Two floating batteries are burning," they said, "ours [*Talla Piedra*] and that of Moreno."'[7] These were the ones closest to the King's Bastion, and they were no longer smouldering but completely ablaze. Drinkwater saw the fire spread: 'About an hour after midnight [on the 14th], the battering-ship which had suffered the greatest injury, and which had been frequently on fire the preceding day, was completely in flames, and by two o'clock, she appeared as one continued blaze from stem to stern. The ship to the southward [*Pastora*] was also on fire, but did not burn with so much rapidity.'[8]

To Colonel Picton, the fire consuming the *Pastora* 'exhibited one of the most magnificent illuminations that the most fertile imagination could form an idea of, and resembled, from its apparent symmetry and uniformity, a most perfect artificial firework'. As the fire increased, so did the dramatic scene: 'her guns, which had been left loaded, went off irregularly, and the flames were almost immediately after seen blazing. At the same instant, out of all the different ports and the entire roof or covering over the gun decks, seemed to be one continued sheet of vivid fire, from stem to stern.'[9]

Several more floating batteries were now obviously on fire, and their crews were in a state of panic, especially as few could swim. 'We could plainly perceive the ships were on fire,' one soldier said; 'soon after we heard violent screamings on board them, rockets thrown up, and innumerable boats from the fleet coming to their assistance.'[10] Lindsay also heard 'the shrieks of horror, of agony, and despair, rendered more striking from the perfect stillness of the night, the scene illuminated to a distance and at hand as bright as day, closed in the back-ground with the rugged declivity of Gibraltar, towering to the sky'.[11] Houdan-Deslandes and his fellow officers could only watch helplessly, after being so confident of glorious victory: 'The shot and shells were thundering towards these machines that the fire was consuming. The boats of several vessels advanced towards the storm of shot, going to look for and rescue the crews. We were all at once moved, desperate, indignant. We abandoned ourselves to our blackest thoughts. We cried for our brave and unlucky soldiers who were trapped in these burning prisons.'[12]

Their despondency was in marked contrast to the mood of the exhausted, smoke-blackened soldiers on the Rock, who had a new hope that they might prevail. As Drinkwater said, 'the approaching day now promised us one of the completest defensive victories on record'.[13] Walter Gordon was trying to snatch some sleep after an arduous session at the guns, when 'a short time after, one of my companions came to the place where I lay, pulled me by the arm and woke me with these words, "get up, says he, and behold the most glorious sight ever was to be beheld, the floating batteries are at last done for. You'll see the French and Spaniards flying in the air like rooks." Though no doubt their defeat was a joyful sight, yet I confess their melancholy fate gave me no pleasure.'[14]

At around three in the morning, Captain Curtis took another detachment of the Marine Brigade to the New Mole, from where they set off in gunboats to fire at the small boats that were approaching, so as to prevent any of the floating batteries being towed away and to stop them rescuing the crews. 'I thought this a fit opportunity to employ my gun-boats,' he explained,

> and I advanced with the whole, (twelve in number, each carrying a twenty-four or eighteen pounder [gun]), and drew them up so as to flank the line of the enemy's battering ships, while they were annoyed extremely by an excessive heavy and well-directed fire from the garrison. The fire from the gun-boats was kept up with great vigour and effect. The boats of the enemy durst not approach; they abandoned their ships [the floating batteries], and the men left in them, to our mercy, or to the flames.[15]

When Curtis captured two of the rescue boats, he learned that many of their comrades were still on board, so he decided to save as many as he could, even though nearly all the floating batteries were on fire: 'The scene at this time before me was dreadful to a high degree, numbers of men crying from amidst the flames, some upon pieces of wood in the water, others appearing in the ships where the fire had as yet made but little progress, all expressing by speech and gesture the deepest distress, and all imploring assistance.'[16]

Watching from afar, Houdan-Deslandes appreciated their humane rescue efforts, but was shocked when the flames reached one of the gunpowder magazines, and it 'was blown sky high at 5 o'clock with a terrible explosion'.[17] Others then blew up, one after another, but not the *Pastora* and *Talla Piedra*, whose gunpowder had been waterlogged or hurled overboard. These unpredictable

explosions made the work of rescuing the crews particularly hazardous, and the rescue efforts were not helped by the Spanish
guns firing at them from the isthmus. Curtis sent his boats and
men to virtually every burning vessel, and Lindsay said that he
'even ransacked the holds of several, and removed the wounded.
Some infatuated wretches were employed in drinking spirits,
and in search of plunder, losing thereby the opportunity of being
saved.'[18]

One explosion engulfed Curtis's own gunboat in burning
debris, which horrified Eliott:

> For some time I felt the utmost anguish, seeing his pinnace
> [small boat] close to one of the largest ships at the instant she
> blew up, and spread her wreck to a vast extent all round. The
> black cloud of smoke being dispersed, I was again revived by
> the sight of the pinnace, little apprehending that the Brigadier
> was in the utmost danger of sinking, some pieces of timber
> having fallen into and pierced the boat (killing the coxswain,
> and wounding others of the men), scarce any hope left of
> reaching the shore. Providentially he was saved by stopping
> the hole with the seamen's jackets, until boats arrived to their
> relief.[19]

At the same time, another of Gibraltar's gunboats was sunk, but
its crew was saved, and there were other lucky escapes while the
rescue effort continued. Ancell related one story:

> A young boy on board one of the floating batteries (which
> was almost in an entire blaze), observing our boats making
> for the shore, got upon the head, wept and cried, and in the
> Spanish tongue called for help. His entreaties prevailed, and
> one of our boats, notwithstanding the immense danger which
> threatened, rowed towards him, which he perceiving, jumped
> into the sea, and at that very instant the ship exploded, with
> the greatest part of the hands on board. The boat soon after
> took the boy up.[20]

With the danger of further explosions, the gunboats rowed back to the New Mole, rescuing a few more people on the way. The remaining floating batteries continued to burn, and Spilsbury said that 'numbers of Spaniards were blown up in the vessels, some that would not leave them, and others that were so wounded they could not be got out'.[21]

The garrison hoped to save two of the vessels near the Old Mole as trophies, but unexpectedly one of them exploded with great violence, vividly described by Lindsay:

> After it had burnt almost an hour, we felt everything near us tremble; there was a thunder from it which was dreadful; but the cloud which it formed was beyond all description, rolling its prodigious volumes one over another, mixed with fire, with earth, with smoke, and heavy bodies innumerable, on which the fancy formed various conjectures while they rose and fell; till the whole arriving at its height in a gradual progress of near ten minutes, the top rolled downwards, forming the capital of a column of prodigious architecture, which the first-rate painter must have been eager, though perhaps unequal to have imitated.[22]

This massive explosion broke glass window panes and blew open doors of buildings. It also threw up a mushroom cloud that dominated the scene for some time, before dispersing, which Picton also described:

> The explosion was tremendous, and the innumerable particles of the wreck that were thrown up perceptibly into the air fell down in a kind of circular shower, as it were, with that degree of violence as caused such prodigious agitation in the water for some short continuance, as if produced by the most extreme subterranean heat, but the enormous column of smoke of variegated colours which ascended at the same time, expanding itself gradually to an immense height, was really most astonishing.[23]

Once the smoke cleared, Picton said, there was virtually no vestige of the floating battery. Because of the danger of further loss of life, it was decided to set fire to the very last one. In all, seven of the floating batteries exploded and three burned down to the waterline, after being bombarded by about five thousand red-hot shot. Picton was disappointed that the garrison did not save any of the floating batteries, thinking they would have been a great asset moored between the South Bastion and New Mole. 'I suppose there were sufficient reasons for not making any such attempt,' he wrote, 'although I am perfectly unacquainted with them.'[24]

Curtis and his men managed to drag from the burning wrecks ten officers, three priests and 354 soldiers and sailors, who were all landed at the New Mole as prisoners-of-war.[25] During their rescue efforts, his seamen also liberated what they could grab from the floating batteries, and at 8 o'clock in the morning they brought their spoils on shore. It was now the turn of the spectators on Gibraltar to revel in the scene, as Ancell observed:

one [seaman] has just landed with the royal standard of Spain which was intended by the foe to be hoisted on these battle-ments. The hills and heights were covered with spectators when the tars began their procession, incessant shouts and repeated acclamations continued from the Mole to the South Parade, where the governor and principal officers were .... to whom they carried the colours, which sensibly pleased our gallant Chief, who joined the crowd in three cheers, and presented the tars with some gold as a reward.[26]

Later on, Ancell said, 'Our Governor, to please the soldiery and inhabitants, has directed the Spanish standard to be reversed and tied to a gun on the South Parade. It must be a galling vexation to our foes to behold their royal flag so ignobly displayed, and made the sport of the multitude.'[27]

That morning, at around 9 o'clock, the prisoners-of-war were escorted to Windmill Hill, where they were to be guarded in a camp by the Corsican Volunteers. Drinkwater was struck by their advanced age:

> it was observed, with no small surprise, by many who were present when the prisoners were landed, that the majority of them seemed to be past that age when the vital powers are supposed to be in their greatest vigour ... The Spaniards, from their dark complexion and scanty diet, have naturally, even when young, an aged look: and yet our observations seemed confirmed by other indubitable facts. Several bodies were thrown ashore, all of which seemed advanced in years; and one in particular appeared, from his grey beard and lean visage, past sixty.[28]

Many other prisoners were taken to the naval hospital with dreadful injuries and burns. 'Some of them were most horrid spectacles,' Ancell remarked,

> one in particular I must mention, who was carried by four men on a handbarrow. He had received a wound on his face, so that his nose and eyes were separated from his head, hanging by a piece of skin, and the motion of the men that carried him occasioned its flapping backwards and forwards, much resembling a mask. Though he must have felt the most sensible agony, yet he looked round him with great complacency, as he passed the numerous crowds of people.[29]

It was estimated that one-third or more of the French and Spaniards on board the floating batteries must have perished – between 1600 and 2000 men. Houdan-Deslandes reckoned the death toll numbered 1400 to 1500 men, as well as many officers. Eliott interrogated the prisoners and could only establish that 'a great number of officers and men serving on board were either killed, wounded or burnt in the ships'.[30] A Spanish officer wrote shortly afterwards to a friend:

There will be horror and astonishment throughout the whole world at the news of the burning and destruction of the much-vaunted floating batteries; dismay at the thought of the sacrifice of close to 1480 valiant soldiers, dead, wounded or taken prisoner in this fatal enterprise; and surprise that in the short space of two hours, these contrivances were set on fire, even though they were proved by their inventor as incombustible and unsinkable and adopted by the two ministers in Madrid and at Versailles.[31]

Within the garrison only seventeen men died and eighty-six were wounded, and many of those were due to the fiercest ever bombardment from the batteries along the Spanish Lines, in which over eleven thousand shot and shells were fired. Walter Gordon gave a succinct assessment: 'The officers and seamen deserve immortal praise; even I whose name will soon sink in oblivion ... exerted my utmost efforts.'[32]

The joy of those men saved 'was next to being frantic', and the heroism of Curtis and his men became legendary. Houdan-Deslandes, who had watched everything from the camp, was full of praise: 'This feeling of humanity, the generous devotedness of Curtis, the rescue, the consideration that the Spanish and French prisoners received at Gibraltar, are noble monuments of the greatness of the soul of our enemy, and will be much more of a credit to Eliott in the eyes of posterity.'[33] Flags of truce went between Eliott and the Duc de Crillon, and some of the uninjured prisoners-of-war were returned to Spain within a few days. While being escorted to the transport boats by a guard of Corsican soldiers, Boyd's journal related that some prisoners 'were greatly astonished on seeing one of our large forges at the new mole, with a frame of 50 red hot balls on the fire; the Corsican guard very funningly [wittily] told them these were English roasted potatoes, which were preparing for all uncivil strangers that came this way for a refreshment, at the sight of which the priests with the Dons crossed themselves, and with uplifted eyes of wonder, craved a bless from heaven for themselves and their country.'[34]

The whole bay was covered in wreckage, and debris was brought in on successive tides, aided by the westerly winds. All manner of detritus washed up along Gibraltar's shore, as Gordon described: 'The wreck under our walls, formed a scene truly horrible. Dead bodies were floating upon the water, heads, legs, arms, wood, wool, cork, oakum, casks, and boxes, were washed ashore by the sea, and lay in heaps together.'[35] Gibraltar was still being blockaded, and so, in spite of the horrific mix, anything of use was eagerly salvaged, and Drinkwater recounted that the wind blew on shore

many trifling curiosities, and some things of value, which had floated on the surface of the Bay, after the battering-ships had blown up. Large wax candles, such as are usually burnt by the Romish priests before their altars, salt provisions, and a great number of ammunition-boxes, containing ten rounds of powder in linen cartridges, were collected by the Garrison ... Considerable pieces of mahogany, and some cedar, were saved from the wrecks ... and these were afterwards converted into various useful articles, serving as memorials of our victory. The Governor had a handsome set of tables made for the Convent.[36]

Friday 13 September had proved to be unlucky for the French and Spaniards, but Lindsay heard that some blamed their misfortune on one of the priests: 'They had a priest on board of every ship; one of whom, according to the French reports, was so frightened a little before coming on, that he let the Bon Dieu fall into the water, and that many attributed their failure to that piece of unintended sacrilege.'[37] For the garrison it was a propitious day, a victory to add to that of Quebec twenty-three years earlier. In Boyd's headquarters they were jubilant: 'Thus ended the unexpected and dismal fate of these 10 battering ships, the boast of Spain. The tragic scene was not in private, neither, but to the publick view and mortifying sight of their combined fleet of 50 sail of C—ds [Cowards] of the Line and above 200 sail of other vessel ... and their great land army of between forty and fifty thousand ... the crowd with shame and remorse turns their eyes from the tragic scene, and with heavy steps returns to their distant dwellings, there to condole and bemoan with their neighbours.'[38]

While the gunboats and mortar boats had failed to support the floating batteries, Houdan-Deslandes also blamed the guns on land for not doing their job, because they were supposed to attack Gibraltar at the same time:

> The floating batteries were exposed all alone to the fire from the fortress and were not supported by anything. The Lines, it is true, fired ... in a fairly courageous and praiseworthy way, from 8 in the morning to 5 in the evening. But then they went silent ... I haven't sought to find out why the land batteries lacked ammunition on this most important occasion of the siege; why they didn't send any shot or shells throughout this disastrous night; why 60 armed vessels let the floating batteries burn without helping them.[39]

Curtis's rescue efforts had been fired on late in the night from the land batteries, but for the most part insufficient ammunition had been prepared for the Spanish Lines and the batteries of the advance siegeworks. Houdan-Deslandes also failed to comprehend why the floating batteries were not towed away, why the undamaged ones were ordered to be burnt, why more effort was not put into saving the men and why, at the outset, they were moored too close to each other. 'Why, in short,' he lamented, 'was this superb project carried out without proper intelligence, preparation and in a manner that sunk its inventor and the respectable and courageous General [Crillon] who commanded the combined army?'[40] The French and Spaniards were also bitter about each other, and Lindsay was certain that 'The antipathy between the two nations is infinite: the Spaniard hates from the bottom of his soul the Frenchman, who in turn only does the other the honour to hold him in supreme contempt.'[41]

Houdan-Deslandes, a French officer, felt more compassion: 'I will never forget, and not even the hardest heart could forget, the horrible night when the floating batteries burned. That bloody scene will always remain in my memory; and all my life I will weep for my friends and soldiers who perished in such a horrifying way.' Nevertheless, he added:

> I cannot hide the fact that the attack was badly conducted. I will not accuse the Engineer d'Arçon for all the accumulated misfortunes of that night. I will accuse the discord and the unknown reason that prevented the simultaneous deployment of everything in our means ... and I will say with all the boldness of a truthful and impartial man: 'The floating batteries were not fireproof; they weren't supposed to be; but the immense artillery which should, all at the same time, have struck Gibraltar by land and sea, should have prevented the English from burning them within fourteen hours.'[42]

In Madrid, King Carlos III received the news with disbelief, while in Paris one visitor repeatedly heard the French talk about

> that constant and uniform hatred, which subsists between themselves and the Spaniards, notwithstanding their forced and unnatural alliance ... With the assistance of the French ... they entertained the warmest hope that the fortress must yield. Hope did I say:– They were morally certain of it ... The managers of one of the public places had prepared scenes, at a great expence, to exhibit the storming and capture of Gibraltar. The ballad writers too had been indefatigable; and all were ready at two hours warning. The news therefore of the destruction of these famous batteries was like a thunderclap!

A courier arrived in Paris with an account of the battle from the Comte d'Artois, who summed up his view of the attack as: 'All is lost but Honour.'[43]

# CHAPTER TWENTY-TWO

———•◆•———

# HURRICANE

The total destruction of the floating batteries caused general rejoicing in Gibraltar, which was matched by despondency among the French and Spaniards, but soon the garrison began to wonder what would happen next. All movements in and behind the Lines were keenly observed, and Drinkwater was not alone in expecting a renewed attack:

> The afternoon of the 14th [September 1782], several thousand men marched with colours from the Enemy's camp to their lines, and many ships in the Combined Fleet loosed their topsails. These motions, and the circumstance of many of their boats being manned, caused various speculations within the Garrison ... The furnaces for heating shot [were ordered] to be continued lighted, lest the Enemy should be prompted to put all to the stake, and attempt the Garrison by a general attack. It was indeed afterwards rumoured that such a design had been in contemplation, but was over-ruled by the Duke [de Crillon], who was of opinion it would be exposing the fleet and army to immediate destruction.[1]

The combined fleet fired a grand salute the following day, as if they had just achieved a victory. They may have been beaten, but the siege was not at an end, as Houdan-Deslandes remarked: 'Crillon did not give up the enterprise [but] ordered the continuation of firing from the lines, and had a new mortar battery set up. The Court of Madrid thought like him. Charles III extended his powers and ordered him to continue the siege.'[2]

On Gibraltar life was returning to what passed for normal. The main focus of work was on repairs to all the defences, which was constantly interrupted by firing from the isthmus, and the engineers decided to erect many more purpose-built kilns for heating red-hot shot all round the garrison, similar to limekilns, but smaller.[3] The gunboat that had sunk in one of the explosions was salvaged, and efforts were also made to raise the *Porcupine* and *Brilliant* frigates that had been deliberately scuttled, though this was not so easy and took several days. A week after the disaster of the floating batteries, the Spanish mortar boats returned, along with a few gunboats, though their initial attacks seemed half-hearted, as Boyd's journal related: 'At half past one o'clock this morning [20 September] the enemy's mortar boats attacked us, at a very great distance, so that one shell in 10 did not reach the shore but fell in the sea. One of their shells fell in Southport ditch, wounded 2 men and the fountain or aqueduct pipe that leads through the ditch. One man of the Artillery had his head shot off as he sat on the business of nature, near the south Line Wall Guard.'[4] Doubtless the possibility of being fired on with red-hot shot kept the mortar boats at a distance.

The firing from the isthmus was intermittent, though quite intense at times, and the mortar boats and gunboats kept returning at night, even attacking the naval hospital and Windmill Hill, where their own prisoners-of-war were held. Instead of pressing home an immediate attack as everyone on the Rock feared, the French and Spaniards reverted to extending their siegeworks, but first they held a review, which Drinkwater watched: 'The evening of the 26th of September, the whole of the Combined Army were under arms, formed in one line (which extended about four miles and a half) from the river Guadaranque to very near Fort Tunara [Atunara]. Some persons of high rank, attended by a numerous suite of cavalry, passed along the front; and they were not dismissed until after sun-set.'[5]

Crillon still planned to take the Rock and so now had scaling ladders made and iron grappling hooks forged for an assault. Houdan-Deslandes described a new and daring communication line a quarter of a mile long that was constructed overnight with sandbags, from the burnt Mahon battery to the shore at Bayside, cutting across a corner of the gardens at Landport: 'It was on the night of 5 to 6 October that 6000 men, including 480 French, began the new communication ... The besieged were outwitted ... we didn't lose one man, but we should have lost at least 300.'[6] The next day, many of the prisoners-of-war rescued from the floating batteries were returned to Spain, apart from those too severely injured and fifty-nine who wanted to remain and were therefore distributed amongst the regiments. Bodies were still floating in with each tide, and Drinkwater noted that 'the corpse of a Spanish officer was washed ashore under our walls. A purse of pistoles [gold coins], and a gold watch, were found in his pockets. He was buried with respect, two navy officers attending the funeral; and the following day a flag of truce delivered the watch and money, to be returned to his friends.'[7]

Even though the floating batteries had failed, Houdan-Deslandes thought that Crillon should continue bombarding the garrison vigorously, tighten the blockade and make all efforts to prevent the garrison being revictualled by a convoy:

That fortress hadn't received any general supplies since that of Darby in April 1781. The Garrison therefore must be lacking in several essential ordnance supplies. They might last several months, but a longer period of privation would be unbearable and impossible to sustain. It was virtually certain that the besieged lacked shells, had little powder, and every day suffered small losses which, when multiplied, exhaust a garrison, add to the weariness of service, and end by completely wearing them down.[8]

Gibraltar could only wait, but there was renewed hope because the prisoners-of-war had disclosed that Lord Howe was preparing to sail from England with a relief convoy. The only worry was that the powerful combined French and Spanish fleet was unscathed, still controlled the bay and was also waiting for the convoy. The fate of Gibraltar hung in the balance, because nobody knew if the naval escort would be strong enough to ensure that essential supplies reached the Rock. Everything depended on Lord Howe and his fleet.

After sailing from Spithead on 11 September, Admiral Lord Richard Howe's convoy had been disrupted by bad weather. Four days later, the wind changed direction but continued blowing a gale for almost the rest of the month. Several vessels in the convoy were badly damaged and were forced to turn back, as recorded by Henry Duncan, captain of HMS *Victory*: 'The Duchess of Richmond, a large ordnance transport, lost her topmasts, made the signal of distress, and quitted the fleet in the night; several of the vessels loaded with wood and coals returned to England; others threw over-board part of their cargoes.'[9] One newspaper reported the *Duchess of Richmond* limping back to Plymouth on the 19th, the same day as another ordnance vessel came in: 'the Lord Holland, late an old East-Indiaman, but now an ordnance store-ship; she parted company with the fleet last Monday morning, having sprung a leak, and carried away her three top-masts, in the gale of wind last Saturday. Lord Howe took 200 matrosses from on board her, and distributed them on board the men of war ... The Lord Holland had a valuable cargo of ordnance stores, and will be a loss to the garrison.'[10]

Other ships from the convoy straggled into smaller ports, including Waterford in Ireland, according to *Lloyd's List*:

Arrived the Jenny, Capt. Jacks, from London and Portsmouth for Gibraltar; she parted Lord Howe's fleet in a gale of wind the 22d inst. ... The Captain says two East-India ships parted the day before, and two ships made signals of distress before he left them. The Mary, Wolf [the captain], from London for Tortola, parted the 23rd, is also arrived here; both these vessels are leaky, and had very bad weather, southerly winds, and are afraid most of the fleet are separated, and will be under the disagree-able necessity of returning into port.[11]

Close followers of the story in the newspapers could be forgiven for concluding that the entire convoy was broken and scattered, but most of the ships were able to continue their voyage. Once the West Indies and Oporto convoys parted company, Duncan noted that only 'twelve or thirteen' ships were missing from those intended for Gibraltar. A week later, the convoy arrived off Faro on the southern coast of Portugal, and a cutter was sent in which brought back the news of the overwhelming defeat of the French and Spanish floating batteries, though at the same time Howe received the ominous intelligence that the formidable combined fleet was lying in wait.[12]

While the convoy continued towards Gibraltar, pushed on at long last by favourable winds, in the Bay of Gibraltar the weather was rapidly deteriorating, with fierce winds increasing to what was described as a hurricane, as Drinkwater narrated: 'The wind blew fresh westerly on the 10th [October] ... After sun-set the gale increased, and at Midnight it blew a hurricane, with smart showers of rain. Signal-guns were repeatedly fired by the Combined Fleet; and from their continuance, and the violence of the wind, we concluded some of them were in distress. At day-break, a Spanish two-decker was discovered in a crippled state, close in shore off Orange's bastion.' With Howe's fleet expected any moment, Cordoba had ordered his own ships 'to lie at single anchor, and prepare to weigh at the shortest notice'.[13] This was a disastrous decision, because Houdan-Deslandes said that during the night, 'the storm ripped up tents, broke down huts and flooded the camp ... it was horrible; officers and soldiers without shelter or bread, drenched, demoralised, vessels without cables, without anchors ... a great number of little boats sunk, 26 gunboats capsized on the riverbank, their guns stuck in the sand, corpses washed down to the beach and tossed by the waves'.[14]

The hurricane had caused the French and Spanish warships to drag their anchors, and many were in distress and fired guns to call for help. Some were forced on to the Spanish shore or were badly damaged, but the *San Miguel* (*St Michael*) two-decker had been driven relatively unscathed right across the bay. This was one of the best and newest Spanish warships, the leading vessel in the attempted invasion of Britain three years earlier. Eliott noted how the warship surrendered:

Friday 11th October. S:W [wind] — blew a storm before day light, with heavy rain. The St. Michael Spanish 70 gun ship of war ... having been driven from her anchors, drove down under our walls: a few shot being fired at her she hoisted an English Jack over her Spanish ensign and surrendered; Brigadier Curtis thereupon went on board her and took possession sending the prisoners ashore to the amount of 700 men including officers, the rest of the combined fleet suffered much by the storm.[15]

That evening, in all this chaos, Howe's convoy suddenly arrived, and Eliott noted in his diary that 'the British Fleet and Convoy appeared; about 6 p.m. the Latona frigate arrived and anchored off Bonavista and four storeships [arrived] in the evening'.[16] The long-awaited convoy had taken one month to sail from Spithead to Gibraltar, after suffering the sinking of the *Royal George* and the loss of part of the convoy in storms. It now came into view at an ideal time – just as the hurricane was subsiding and when the combined fleet was in disarray. Only a few vessels actually made it into the bay, as a midshipman on board HMS *Cambridge* described:

On the afternoon of the 11th we entered the Gut or Straits, formed in a line of battle a-head, the Buffalo and Panther going on before with the convoy. The wind, which till now had been to the westward, chopped round to the north, just as we got a-breast of the Bay, so that we were compelled to stand on a little farther to the eastward. About ten o'clock at night, the whole fleet brought to, and we amused ourselves with observing a very heavy cannonade which was this evening carrying on betwixt the rock and the lines. Next morning the 12th, we found ourselves rather farther to the eastward than desirable, having been drove thither by the current, which always sets in to the Mediterranean.[17]

This was incredibly disappointing to those watching from Gibraltar, because with contrary winds it would be difficult for the convoy to return from the Mediterranean. Captain Curtis sailed from Gibraltar to HMS *Victory* to acquaint Howe with a complete picture of the situation, but the French and Spanish fleet was working hard to make good the storm damage, and the next day was ready to sail. 'About nine o'clock a.m. the Spanish Admiral made the signal for the Combined Fleets to weigh anchor,' Drinkwater wrote,

and by one o'clock the whole were under way. At three, a French Rear-Admiral, which was the last of the rear division, cleared the Bay. Their number in all amounted to eighty sail ... When the Combined Fleet had cleared the Bay, they stood some time to the southward, and leaving a line-of-battle ship and two frigates to prevent the Panther [at Gibraltar] from joining her Admiral, drove with the current some leagues to the eastward. They then appeared to edge down towards the British Fleet, which was in close line of battle upon a wind, with their heads to the southward.[18]

A major naval battle was now anticipated, and because Howe's fleet was significantly outnumbered, it could prove disastrous for Gibraltar. There was huge excitement in the French and Spanish camps, as Houdan-Deslandes related: 'Nothing without doubt offered or will ever offer a more superb sight than the strong combined fleet with 46 warships of the line, leaving Algesiras in magnificent weather, under the gaze of the army of San Roque and the garrison of Gibraltar, from which it was only separated by this mountain, the object of such a great quarrel, which, at this moment, was firing ferociously on those vessels that were forced to approach its batteries.' He then added: 'We believed in the camp that the battle was inevitable; our comrades ... wanted to avenge the burning of the floating batteries through the capture or sinking of some enemy vessels. Princes, generals, the curious, everyone made their way to high vantage points where they could see the two fleets. The enemy were near Estepona. We saw them, but night made us lose sight of them.'[19]

By the time darkness fell, the two fleets had still not reached each other. 'As our observations on the manoeuvres of the fleet were interrupted soon after sun-set,' Drinkwater remarked, 'we impatiently waited for the succeeding day to be spectators of the action, which was now considered as impossible to be avoided; and orders were therefore given for preparing several wards in the Navy Hospital for the reception of the wounded.'[20] The piper John Macdonald of the 73rd still helped at the hospital and had himself been injured when bringing in a wounded soldier during the floating battery attack. He was one of many looking forward to watching this contest in view of Gibraltar: 'A great concourse of people of all ranks and denominations assembled on the different eminences expecting a general engagement'.[21] The Spanish prisoners-of-war from the *St Michael*, who were being guarded in their Windmill Hill camp by the Corsican Volunteers, were so overjoyed on seeing the two fleets 'that they could not forebear expressing their ecstacies in so riotous a manner, as to call for some severity, to confine them within the limits of their camp'.[22]

At first light the next day, 14 October, there was incredulity on all sides that the two fleets were far apart, but after the initial shock, the opinion on Gibraltar was that the combined fleet had decided against an engagement, while Howe was right to avoid one, considering that his primary aim was to ensure that the convoy of supplies reached Gibraltar. This was the view of the midshipman on board the *Cambridge*:

> we discovered the enemy's fleet [on the 13th] ... They were close in with the Barbary shore, near the east end of the Gut. We immediately prepared for action, tacked, and stood to the southward, being close aboard of the Spanish shore, near the town of Marvella [Marbella]. They showed no inclination to come down to us, and it was out of our power to go to them; neither was it our duty, could we have done it, because we had not

effected the purpose for which we came thither; and it would have been imprudent to leave that to the issue of an engagement, whilst it could be avoided.[23]

Commanded by the overly cautious Admiral Cordoba, who had already failed to support the attack by the floating batteries, the French and Spaniards did not take advantage of the overwhelming odds in their favour, but kept away from the smaller British fleet.

Over the next few days, while at the mercy of changeable winds, Howe's fleet manoeuvred to ensure it was not caught at a disadvantage, while the larger, slower and more unwieldy combined fleet failed to engage. The convoy came into Gibraltar piecemeal, a few ships at a time, avoiding the enemy ships and gunboats. Stores and ammunition were landed, as well as reinforcements, most notably sixteen hundred men from the 25th and 59th regiments. The garrison also safely received three boxes containing £20,000 in gold and silver that Curtis brought back in a boat from the *Victory*.[24] It would have been a valuable prize, but for all the efforts of the French and Spanish ships, and despite some near misses, only one transport ship, the *Minerva*, was captured, which was carrying the baggage, wives and children of the men of the 25th and 59th regiments. Drinkwater said that the last convoy ships to unload delivered that wretched news: 'The missing vessel, they informed us, had been taken by the Enemy some days before, off Malaga; and having on board, the wives and baggage of the two regiments which were on board the Fleet, and were intended for our reinforcement, her capture greatly distressed those corps, and the Garrison heartily condoled with them.'[25]

Admiral Howe had now accomplished his mission and was preparing to sail for England, but first of all he dispatched the *Tisiphone* fireship with a further supply of powder collected from the fleet. Although the combined fleet was visible, the British fleet departed on the 19th, with Howe apparently refusing battle. Lieutenant Charles Wale of the 97th Regiment implied in a letter to his father that it did look as if he was running away:

The two Fleets are now going through the Straits at about 1½ league distant from each other. I am sorry to say our Fleet lead the way; however, Lord Howe knows what is best to be done. The Combined Fleets are upwards of ten sail superior to ours. But it is here supposed that our Fleet wish to avoid an action so near the enemy's harbours, and wish to get them out into open sea, and there perhaps risk an engagement. There is this satisfaction for us, that their fleet is very badly manned. Ours was never better.[26]

Being dependent on the wind for both power and direction of sailing, large fleets needed room to manoeuvre in battles, and the Strait of Gibraltar was not ideal, as Captain Duncan of the *Victory* explained: 'At 6 a.m. saw the enemy's fleet. They were standing to the southward and we to the northward; [they] thus had the wind of us, and we found upon trial that the space between Europa and Ceuta was not sufficient to draw up our line.' Instead, Duncan said, they continued through the Straits into the Atlantic until there was more room to manoeuvre, and the next day prepared for battle:

We were under an easy sail and hauled to the southward, in hope that the enemy would run right through and we might get the weather-gauge ... Our fleet was brought to, and formed a line ahead, with the wind upon the beam. The enemy kept bearing down upon us, but were so long in dressing their line that it was exactly sunset before a shot was fired. The action began in the van, and then the rear, and lastly in the centre; it ceased in the van and then commenced again there, and went through the line as at first ... the ships opposed to us kept up a heavy fire, but, being in the moonlight and at such a distance, we received little or no damage.[27]

Major Henry Stanhope, a passenger on board HMS *Courageuse*, thought that 'The combined fleet behaved in the most scandalous manner. They engaged us – with a superiority of 12 sail of the

line, and continued firing for six hours without approaching ...
It was not in Lord Howe's power to continue the engagement,
or to come nearer to the enemy, as he could not get windward of
them.'[28] Duncan's ship, the *Victory*, had only minor damage and
did not even fire a shot in what became known as the Battle of
Cape Spartel. His account of the erratic battle was terse:

> The English fleet consisted of 34 sail of the line, being 11
> three-deckers and 23 of two decks. A return of their loss in
> the action gives 70 killed, 132 wounded. The combined fleet
> consisted of 46 sail of the line, being –
> French, 4 three-deckers, 8 two-deckers
> Spanish, 3 three-deckers, 31 two-deckers.[29]

He also noted that 'We lay all next day, 21st, to leeward of them
and in sight; but they made no attempt to come near us, although
they had the wind.'[30]

Howe's fleet then continued to England, but Duncan was
sent ahead with dispatches in the *Latona* frigate, which also had
Captain Curtis on board carrying Governor Eliott's dispatches
about the floating batteries. Even before the *Latona* had left
Gibraltar, news of the complete failure of the attack by the floating
batteries had made its way overland through Europe, and garbled
reports of the encounter between Howe's and the Franco-Spanish
fleets were soon to follow. By a curious coincidence, newspapers
in Britain published a letter from Gibraltar on 14 September, the
day after the attack by the floating batteries. It described an attack
by the floating batteries and a land bombardment, all of which
had been supposedly repulsed on 25 August.[31] Shortly afterwards,
it was exposed as a fictitious account – just one of the multitude
of myths that were circulating, this one no doubt deliberately
spread to tie in with the date originally planned for the attack – 25
August.

The *Latona* frigate did not arrive at Plymouth until 6 November, and the next day the dispatches carried by Curtis and Duncan
reached the Admiralty. The news spread across the country, with

newspapers publishing extracts from these dispatches and from private letters. The saving of Gibraltar was acclaimed as a triumph in Britain, and having travelled there and back with Howe's fleet, Major Stanhope reported: 'I landed at Gibraltar for a few hours, but could not stay ... General Elliott has acquired immortal honour by his gallant and very able defence. He speaks very confidently of the security of Gibraltar.'[32]

Informing Madrid of the latest events, Admiral Cordoba effectively claimed victory over Howe: 'one should form a fair judgement of the combat, by reckoning 32 of our ships against 34 of the enemy's, who withdrew, and took flight ... they did not chuse to trust to the event of an obstinate engagement, by which we might have been enabled to display all our forces, and improve the advantage of our superiority.'[33] It is doubtful if this satisfied anybody, and reports reached Britain that some Spanish people thought the whole attack on Gibraltar had been betrayed or sabotaged: 'They write from Madrid of the 25th of Oct. that the revictualling of Gibraltar, the passage of Admiral Howe's fleet from the ocean into the Mediterranean, and its easy return into the waters of the Streights, excite great murmurs among the people. Four persons are accused of betraying the State, and of keeping a secret correspondence with Lord Grantham, to conspire against Spain.'[34]

The Comte de Crillon, who was still in the camp at San Roque, summed up the feelings of many: 'The work of several months by thousands of men which has cost millions lasted scarcely more than fireworks. We are waiting for orders from the Court of Spain before knowing what should be done. I don't doubt that they will, in the end, decide to give up this place that cannot be taken by land or blockaded by sea.'[35]

# CHAPTER TWENTY-THREE

## PEACE AND PLENTY

On Gibraltar there was a feeling that it was the end of the siege, especially now that Howe's convoy had brought supplies. Most officers thought it was high time to control prices, and in various locations a message was displayed:

> This is to give notice to all whom it may concern, that the officers of every Regiment in the Garrison have signed an agreement upon Honour and have lodged the same, that they will not purchase from any person whatsoever, either at auction or by retail any of the following articles at a higher price than which is here set down, as fixed by a committee, consisting of an officer from each corps when met for that purpose on Wednesday 23rd October 1782.[1]

There followed a long list, from beef to tobacco, with the prices they hoped to fix, but it was doomed to failure, because, without huge profits at Gibraltar, ships from England took their cargoes to sell in Lisbon. The price fixing lasted barely a fortnight before it was cancelled.

The month of November seemed lacking in purpose, with desultory attacks by gunboats and some bombardment by land, which Drinkwater described:

After the departure of the fleets, little attention was paid by the Enemy to the blockade. Not one cruiser was now to be seen in the Straits ... The idea of gaining Gibraltar either by force or stratagem, seemed, at length, to be relinquished. Their cannonade from the land nevertheless continued, but as it gradually diminished, and scarce exceeded at this time two hundred and fifty rounds in the twenty four hours, we imagined it would in a short time totally cease.[2]

The Spanish prisoners-of-war from the *St Michael* were allowed to return to their camp, which was getting smaller, because French and Spanish troops were being withdrawn, while guns and ammunition from the artillery park were also being removed. On the isthmus, the Spaniards were nevertheless pushing on with the advance works, though what they hoped to achieve was not readily apparent. On the Rock, defences were being repaired and strengthened, and Drinkwater was particularly impressed by one project: 'The rebuilding of the whole flank of the Prince of Orange's bastion, a hundred and twenty feet in length, with solid masonry ... in the face of such powerful Artillery, can scarcely be paralleled in any siege.'[3]

Behind the scenes, negotiations for peace were being conducted between Britain and Spain. The British had been prepared to exchange Gibraltar for, preferably, Puerto Rico, but negotiations had stalled until the result of the floating batteries attack was clear, after which Britain's bargaining position was strengthened. Spain still hoped to exchange some territory for Gibraltar, but peace negotiations dragged on. At the opening of Parliament on 5 December 1782, a heated debate erupted over surrendering Gibraltar, and Charles James Fox blamed the previous ministry for not stationing a naval fleet there. If they had done so, he argued, 'perhaps all the calamities of this war might have been prevented. If a fleet had been stationed there in time to watch the Mediterranean, comte d'Estaing never could have got to America, to give that assistance to the colonies, which had since secured to them their independence.'[4] Not only that, he said, but Britain would lose all influence in Europe:

a sagacious ministry would always employ Gibraltar in dividing France from France, Spain from Spain, and the one nation from the other ... The fortress of Gibraltar was to be ranked among the most important possessions of this country; it was that which gave us respect in the eyes of nations; it manifested our superiority, and gave us the means of obliging them by protection. Give up to Spain the fortress of Gibraltar, and the Mediterranean becomes to them a pool, a pond in which they can navigate at pleasure, and act without control or check. Deprive yourselves of this station, and the states of Europe, who border on the Mediterranean, will no longer look to you for the maintenance of the free navigation of that sea; and having it no longer in your power to be useful, you cannot expect alliances.[5]

A week later, in another parliamentary debate, it was resolved to give thanks to Eliott for his brave and gallant behaviour in defending Gibraltar, and also to 'Generals Boyd and Green, to Sir Roger Curtis, and to the officers, seamen, and soldiers of the garrison'.[6] General Charles Ross, now the Scottish Member of Parliament for Tain Burghs, was fiercely opposed:

Gen. Ross wished Gen. Boyd's name to be struck out of the motion, and contended, that voting the thanks of the House to him would disgrace the dignity of the House ... Mr Burke endeavoured to persuade Gen. Ross not to disturb the harmony and good humour of the House, but to let the vote pass unanimously ... Gen. Ross persisted, and moved, that Lt. Gen. Boyd's name be left out of the motion. No member seconding it, the amendment could not be put. Ross walked out alone, when the Speaker put the original motion, which passed *nem. com.*[7]

Ross had left Gibraltar the year before, not long after commanding his successful sortie, but such was his deep loathing of Boyd that he continued to wage war against him.

On Gibraltar, Eliott was preparing for renewed aggression. The tunnel through the face of the north front of the Rock progressed steadily and now had five embrasures from which cannons could fire over the isthmus. Within a few more weeks, and after further fatal accidents, the tunnel would be a formidable battery 600 feet long, with ten embrasures.[8] New experiments with guns were also conducted, with Spilsbury reporting on 9 December: 'About noon a 32-pounder gun on a new carriage, elevated at 45°, fired shells, and [went] ⅓ over the bay, or about 5,000 yards', while ten days later the results were more impressive: 'This forenoon Lieutenant Colonel Williams' new constructed gun was fired for experiments 18 times in a minute and half, with canister shot and shells at 45 degrees of elevation.' Griffith Williams of the Royal Artillery had developed a new gun carriage capable of a 45-degree elevation for maximum range. It was later installed on the Old Mole, ready to retaliate in any renewed bombardment.[9]

The Spaniards were trying a different tactic: 'A German deserted to us from the Walloon guards,' reported Drinkwater. 'He informed us that the Enemy stationed every evening a guard of three hundred men near the Devil's tower, where they had miners at work in a cave, hoping to form a mine to blow up the north part of the Rock.'[10] At first nobody believed him, though it made sense of some strange activity they had seen. A tunnel was actually being mined into the rock, intended to be filled with a vast amount of gunpowder that would cause a massive explosion. The Spaniards hoped it would bring about a catastrophic collapse of the north front of the Rock, including the gun batteries, creating a breach through which the invaders would pour.

Soon sounds of blasting and other signs of mining were detected, and it was the task of Sergeant Thomas Jackson of the artificers to investigate, who 'descended the steep and rugged rock by means of ropes and ladders. The attempt was as bold as it was hazardous. Stopped by an opening very near to the base of the cliff he explored the entrance, and hearing the hum of voices and the strokes of hammers and picks he was well assured of their purpose. Climbing the steep again, he reported what he had discovered.'[11] In mid-December, Boyd's journal noted: 'this morning Sergt. Major Ince, having discovered the enemy's working parties, under the Rock near the Devils Tower, he took up a party of miners to a declivity above them unobserved.' They found a suitable place for explosives in the rock and 'blew it down upon them, supposed to have killed an officer, 3 men and a great many wounded'.[12] Another deserter said there were twenty miners with a strong guard, and they had suffered many casualties, so the attacks on them were increased.

Flags of truce, leading to meetings between representatives of the garrison and the Spaniards, were frequent at this time, and it was learned that Spain expected the preliminaries for a peace treaty to be signed very soon. Even so, men still deserted from both sides, and late at night on 12 December there was a mass desertion of seven seamen from the *St Michael*, when they seized control of a guard boat.[13] Hostilities also did not stop, and five days later Boyd's journal mentioned that 'Reed, soldier of 58th Regiment, had his leg shot off this morning; his son a drummer had both legs shot off the 13th September, so that father and son only have one leg between them, but are in a fair way of recovery.'[14] This incident was obviously worth noting as a curiosity, but it encapsulated the everyday tragedies of families on both sides. John Read was 'born in the regiment' and became a drummer after joining the 58th at the age of twelve in November 1778, before the siege began. During the attack by the floating batteries, he lost both his legs. Now his father George had been hit, probably during a gunboat attack in the early hours. One leg was amputated, but it was not enough to save his life, and he died the same day, putting paid to the novelty of the story.[15]

Only a few days after the sailors deserted, Drinkwater reported a well-planned daytime attack, probably resulting from information that those men had supplied:

> twenty-nine gun and mortar-boats commenced a spirited attack upon the St. Michael, and other ships, at anchor off Buena-Vista ... The mortar-boats composed the centre division, and

a division of gun-boats was arranged on each flank, their line-of-battle extending about two miles. They got their distance the first round, and retained it with such precision that almost every shell fell within fifty yards of the St. Michael, which was the chief object of their attack. The seventy-fourth shell fell on board, about midship, pierced the first [deck] and broke on the lower deck, killed four, and wounded eleven sailors, three of them mortally.[16]

The shore batteries fired back, and the garrison gunboats tried to get involved, but the Spanish vessels retreated after running out of ammunition.

This was not the *St Michael*'s only misfortune, because on 21 December she was driven halfway across the bay by a severe storm, which also ripped up the tents of the 59th Regiment on Windmill Hill, who were ordered to camp instead at Southport Ditch. The next day, under a flag of truce, a boat brought in around a hundred women with their children belonging to the 25th and 59th regiments. They were forced to undergo examination for venereal disease when they landed: 'the Governor sent a guard to conduct them to a room in the South Barracks, there to be examined by the doctors, in respect to their health or any disorders they might have'. Spilsbury reported that there were '17 of the women disordered. Gibraltar has been free of it several months, before these two regiments came.'[17]

From some of the women it was learned that the Spaniards were going to concentrate on attacking with gunboats and mortar boats and that more crews were being raised and the numbers of vessels increased, which to Drinkwater was a 'dishonourable and cruel mode of prosecuting the war', but Eliott pre-empted their attacks by ordering a sustained bombardment against the Spaniards. 'Although the Enemy's fire from the isthmus was almost discontinued,' Drinkwater said, 'the Governor, towards the conclusion of December, made up for their deficiency by a more animated discharge than usual. Every night the whole north front appeared a continual line of fire. The Devil's Tower chiefly engaged his attention.'[18]

By now everyone was heartily sick of the war, and not just the soldiers facing each other across the isthmus at Gibraltar. In America, Abigail Adams yearned for her husband to return home from Europe, writing to him two days before Christmas: 'It is now, my dear friend, a long, long time, since I had a line from you. The fate of Gibraltar leads me to fear, that a peace is far distant, and that I shall not see you,—God only knows when.'[19] In fact, John Adams was in Paris as one of the participants negotiating peace between America, Britain, France, Spain and Holland.

Despite the promised peace, the firing continued, and in the afternoon of 25 December the gunboats and mortar boats came across the bay, hoping to destroy the *St Michael*, but the garrison gunboats resisted them so well that they bombarded targets in the south instead, including William Green's house, where 'they threw a great many shells ashore, one to General Green's at Mount Pleasant, wounding two of his servants'.[20] Walter Gordon recorded the attack: 'Upon Christmas Day, 1782, our dinner was as good as the place could afford, our supper was bomb-shells mixed with cannon balls, spiced with powder, from the enemy's gun and mortar boats.'[21] The hospital was also hit, as Drinkwater recounted: 'Seven or eight shells fell within the hospital-wall: one disploded in a ward and killed and wounded several of the sick. One was killed and seven wounded in the camp. Several houses and sheds were also destroyed, and others considerably injured. In short, it was thought to be the warmest attack we had ever experienced from these boats; and our men, being mostly in spirits after their Christmas dinner, were consequently less upon their guard.'[22]

On the last day of the year, the navy fished up a 26-pounder gun from one of the floating battery wrecks, which Spilsbury described as 'a very plain iron 26 pounder, 9 feet 6 inches long', even though eyewitnesses had described all the guns as brass. To celebrate New Year's Day, it was 'drawn in procession by the British tars, with a Spanish ensign which had been taken from on board one of the ships, displayed over it, and attended by a band of music, playing *God save the King*.' Others were raised over the following days: 'Many more of these guns were afterwards recovered from the wrecks, and most of them, being of brass, were sold, and the sums, with other monies arising from the head-money [for prisoners captured] granted by Parliament for the battering-ships, and the sale of the St. Michael prize, were proportioned in shares to the Garrison and Marine brigade.'[23]

The prospect of being paid prize-money brought only a temporary improvement in morale, and tensions in the garrison surfaced again. On 6 January 1783, a strange episode occurred. 'Some officers have been engaged in a riot among some sergeants of 73rd, at a dance,' Spilsbury recorded, 'and some others in breaking open a ward in the Hospital, and attacking the women there ill of the venereal disorder.' Other officers decided to release their tensions by putting on a theatrical play, the type of entertainment that was commonplace before the siege. On 19 January, Spilsbury said, 'The officers have acted a play, "Cross Purposes," and "True Blue.".'[24] Two days later, Eliott banned their play-acting, with consternation voiced at Boyd's headquarters:

This day the Governor has forbid the continuation of the Dramatic Theatre, or plays performed on the stage by a few young officers, for their own, and their brother officers' amusement, at such intervals of time, as the Garrison duty spared, or admitted of. For which they have been at great expense in fitting up a large room with a stage, seats and scenes for that purpose and had but the pleasure of performing only one night, so austere and strict the governor is in this place, that he will not allow the gentlemen any amusement that he can prevent them of.[25]

The tedious daily round continued, punctuated by petty and more serious crimes, with the inevitable harsh penalties for those convicted. On 25 January, Owen McDonald of the 97th was hanged. His crime was 'stealing a bag of money, the property of Bernardo Piedro, inhabitant [a gardener], out of the shop of Laurence Passiano, also inhabitant, in the evening of the 3rd of December'. In Boyd's journal was written: 'This day was executed on the gallows for robbery one McDonald, a soldier of the 97th Regiment. At this time is discovered the disagreeable circumstances of the last execution, where the prisoner protested innocence to the last, which the guilty person has since confessed to the crime.'[26]

The previous soldier executed had been Murdoch Sutherland, the servant of Captain John Irving. At a court-martial, Sutherland was found guilty of robbery, and Eliott had signed the warrant for his execution, on the grounds that 'Murdoch Sutherland soldier in the 73d Regiment was tried for robbing Captain Irving of the said Regiment thirty-six guineas, two shirts, one handkerchief, one silk stocking and a night cap'.[27] The sentence was duly carried out on 4 November, and Ancell simply commented: 'A criminal was executed this day', though Boyd's journal showed uneasiness: 'This day between the hours of 10 and 1 o'clock a soldier of the 73d Regiment was executed on the gallows for robbing his master of 35 guineas &c but he persisted innocent to the last.'[28] He had been wrongly executed, though it is unclear if McDonald was the culprit, or if somebody else had escaped prosecution.

Day after day, exchanges of fire brought fresh casualties on both sides, and still no news came about the peace that everyone was longing for. Generally, the attacks were from a small group of gunboats under the cover of darkness, but on the afternoon of 29 January, another daylight attack occurred: 'At 3 o'clock P.M. the enemy's gun and mortar boats to the number of 29 came out in the Bay opposite Algaziers; at the same time the St. Michael fired a signal gun and our 12 gun boats were immediately manned and went out half gun shot [about 500 yards] from the Garrison and the red flag hoisted on the south bastion, when all the batteries were manned ready for the enemy.'[29]

Drinkwater described how the battle started: 'They took their stations off Europa and Rosia, apparently determined to avoid the fire from the King's Bastion, (which they had found so *fatal* to their enterprises) and directed their fire principally against the Brilliant frigate, which was then at anchor off Buena-Vista, and the St. Michael in the New mole. Their land-batteries opened at the same time, directing a furious cannonade into the Town, and along our northern front.' Although the alarm was raised at 3 o'clock, it took the Spanish gunboats two hours to form their battle line and open fire, and then 'at 5 they began a very heavy cannonade both by sea and land upon the garrison who returned their fire with great spirit upon their boats, and upon their camp from the old mole with shells and red hot shot'.[30] The gunboats were beaten off and retreated at six in the evening, after killing one man and injuring many more, including ten who lost limbs.

The following day, and for several days afterwards, the exchange of fire continued as before, but on 2 February news was delivered from the Spanish side that peace had been signed and so they had ceased firing. Everyone wanted to believe it, but with no certain evidence the garrison maintained its firing. The next day brought more positive signs that the end of the siege was in sight, and Ancell was jubilant:

This morning we received (by a flag of truce) intelligence of the most joyful and enlivening nature, which for some time, belief appeared doubtful, but after a few hours suspense, we had the happiness of being in possession of the particulars, brought by the *Spanish* flag boat. The *Duc de Crillon* has sent his compliments to General *Elliott*, acquainting him that the different courts had agreed upon a cessation of hostilities, and that the preliminary articles of peace would shortly be signed. The garrison, enraptured with the sound, spread the harmonious tidings, and in the evening all firing ceased on our side, agreeable to an order sent by his Excellency the Governor to the different posts. The enemy's cannonade became silent in the afternoon.[31]

It was not peace yet, but on 5 February everything changed:

A flag of truce came from the enemy this forenoon which informed us for a certainty that the ratifications of peace were signed and that hostilities were now to cease entirely between

Great Britain, France and Spain, and that all ports were open to the British flag; which the Governor confirmed to us by an advertisement and our batteries ceased their fire, so that from this day we may date a peace in Gibraltar, tho' still we stand on the defensive and act in every respect with great precaution.[32]

Nevertheless, Drinkwater observed that 'About noon, an elevated gun was wantonly fired *over* their works, which was the last shot fired in this siege.'[33]

The news was an enormous relief and, as Gordon of the 73rd noted, was received 'with inexpressible joy by every man, woman, and child, in the garrison'.[34] Ancell was greatly moved:

I scarce know how to begin ... Our situation is changed from noise and confusion to calm serenity. The atmosphere that was continually disturbed with flames and smoke, is now illumined with variegated brightness. The stars that have been so long eclipsed, now shine with their wonted splendor and the bes-pangled rays of *Aurora* [dawn], with resplendent lustre again adorn each hill and height, that for upwards of eighteen months has only been distinguishable by the flashing of pieces of ord-nance. Our sudden change from war to peace, the tranquillity that presides over the battered Rock, and Andalusian shore, so powerfully affects all ranks in the garrison.[35]

The emotion was universal, he said, with both sides overjoyed:

Everything wears a different aspect, our very foes jump upon their works and in strong vociferation send forth their congratu-lations, the thundering cannon that so often has spread death around, are now silent. The rapturous sound of peace re-echoes from shore to shore, and every tongue is filled with the blissful melody. The Spanish officers advance towards the garrison, bowing to the guards, and seem sensibly to share in the hap-piness. In every corner greeting crowds are seen, and the most inexpressible pleasure is by all ranks displayed.[36]

The absence of the noise of artillery was strange, and having kept a constant record, Boyd's journal calculated that during the siege of 1323 days, from 21 June 1779 to 2 February 1783, the Spaniards had fired at the Rock for 663 days, while for '1243 days the garrison fired upon the Spaniards, being 3 years and 148 days ... in a long and tedious contest'.[37] It was the sudden calm after the constant roar of the guns that Drinkwater most noticed:

This return of tranquillity, this prospect of plenty, and relief from the daily vexations of so tedious a siege, could not fail to diffuse a general joy throughout the Garrison. Indeed such feelings are seldom experienced; they baffle all attempts to describe them: far beyond the pleasure resulting from private instances of success or good fortune, ours was a social happiness; and the benevolent sentiments acted upon the heart with additional energy, on the prospect of meeting those as friends, with whom we had been so long engaged in a succession of hostilities.[38]

Aware that this might be an elaborate trick to break into the fortress by stealth, Eliott was more cautious and prevented any direct contact with Spain. 'This intercourse was ... forbidden by the Governor,' Drinkwater said, 'who ordered the guards to inform those who approached our works, that all correspondence of this nature was to be suspended till official accounts were received from England of the peace.' There was the added anxiety that peace might have been achieved by Britain giving Gibraltar to Spain, ignoring the three-and-a-half years of desperate sacrifice that everyone had endured. A message from the Duc de Crillon greatly reduced this worry: 'The Duke, on the 6th [February], informed the Governor that preliminaries had been signed the 20th of January at Paris, and that Gibraltar was to remain in the possession of Great Britain. From this period, operations on both sides were suspended, each party anxiously waiting official accounts from England of the Peace.'[39]

The port of Gibraltar was declared open, and almost immediately provisions reached the Rock unhindered, improving the situation rapidly, so that by 11 February: 'The best green tea selling for four dollars per lb., and everything fallen to half price except wearing apparel. No more wood to be burnt by the soldiers, coals being in plenty, and, the inhabitants' houses not to be inhabited but by their permission', and four days later: 'Things now very cheap', though 'Houses begin to be let very high in town.'[40]

What everyone wanted most was confirmation of peace from England, without which the return to normality could not properly begin. Days dragged into weeks, with the Spaniards and everyone on Gibraltar becoming increasingly concerned, until at last a British ship appeared. 'Their patience as well as ours was nearly exhausted,' Drinkwater recounted,

> when the long-expected frigate arrived on the 10 March, but for some time, even when she had got into the Bay, she kept us in suspense, by steering close along the Spanish shore, and showing no colours. At length, however, the British ensign was displayed, and the anxious Garrison saluted her with a *general huzza*. She was the Thetis frigate, Captain Blankett, and soon after she anchored, Sir Roger Curtis (who had been knighted for his conduct on the 14th of September) landed with dispatches for the Governor.[41]

At long last, confirmation of the peace had arrived, and two days later, on 12 March, the Duc de Crillon with his retinue came right down to the western approach on the isthmus and sent an aide-de-camp to inform Eliott of his arrival there. Drinkwater described their meeting: 'General Eliott soon afterwards rode out by Lower Forbes's, and was met by the Duke on the beach, half-way between the works and Bay-side barrier. Both instantly dismounted and embraced. When the salutations were over, they conversed about half an hour, and then returned to their respective commands.'[42] Nearly a week later, Crillon sent Eliott a fine Andalusian horse as a gift, and a few days afterwards he showed Eliott and William Green round all their works on the isthmus, including the Devil's Tower tunnel. Eliott then went to San

Roque to dine with him, the first time he had been in Spain for almost four years.

With grand celebrations planned for April, a great deal of work was done to spruce up the garrison, which also proved useful preparation for a visit by the Duc de Crillon. Some rebuilding began, and Spilsbury said that for sawing wood, 'The Church Alley, where several of the old inhabitants have been buried, is dug up and made a sawpit of.' One major task was the cleaning up of streets, including the removal of the traverses, but by the morning of Crillon's visit much had been completed: 'The streets and lanes having all been cleaned and put in good order, the water engines are sprinkling them for the reception of the Duke de Crillon'.[43] At about ten in the morning on 31 March, the Duc de Crillon arrived, attended by various officers and servants: 'When the Duke appeared within the walls, the soldiers saluted him with a general huzza; which being unexpected, it was said, greatly confused him. The reason however being explained, he seemed highly pleased with the old English custom; and, as he passed up the main street, where the ruinous and desolate appearance of the town attracted a good deal of his observation, his Grace behaved with great affability.'[44]

All the men were dressed as if for Sunday, the 73rd wore their plaids, and the streets were so crowded that he could hardly pass, with the soldiers cheering him as he went. At the Convent, he was introduced to the officers, including Boyd, who, suffering from gout, had been carried in a sedan chair to meet Crillon. The artillery officers were also presented. 'Gentlemen,' Crillon said, 'I would rather see you here as friends, than on your batteries as enemies, where you never spared me.' Eliott next conducted him round Willis's batteries and then into Ince's tunnel, which astonished him. 'These Works,' he exclaimed, 'are worthy of the Romans.' Turning to Eliott, he declared: 'General Eliott, I have done all that I could do, but yet, you have done more.'[45]

During the conversation over dinner at the Convent, Crillon asked Eliott what he thought of his mine at the foot of the Rock, but seeing him smile, he continued: 'Is it not true, General, that that mine was a farce? But in war, as in everything else, we must have amusement, and on that account it was I [who] ordered that gallery to be made, merely to amuse my soldiers.'[46]

Such were the vagaries of war that Barbary was once again a friend of Britain. At the start of March, a schooner had come from Barbary with a present of bullocks for Eliott, along with a letter. 'We were ignorant of the contents of the letter,' Drinkwater said; 'but it was imagined the subject was to request a renewal of our friendship.' On board the schooner were several Corsicans, who had been held prisoner there, and from them he heard that 'upon the commencement of the attack of the battering-ships on the preceding 13th of September, the Moors at Tangier repaired to their mosques, imploring Heaven on behalf of their *old allies*; and that, on receiving accounts of the defeat of the Enemy, they made public rejoicing, and gave every demonstration of their affection for the English nation.'[47] It was therefore fitting that, in mid-April, the first diplomatic move to the emperor of Morocco at Tangier was by Sir Roger Curtis in the *Brilliant* frigate with a present of four brass 26-pounder guns salvaged from the floating batteries, along with field carriages and ammunition.

On 23 April 1783, St George's Day, a lavish ceremony was held at which George Augustus Eliott, the governor, was invested with the Order of the Bath. He himself gave a speech in which he passed on to all the troops the heartfelt gratitude of King George III, after which he said:

No army has ever been rewarded by higher national honours, and it is well known how great, universal, and spontaneous were the rejoicings throughout the kingdom, upon the news of your success. These must not only give you inexpressible pleasure, but afford matter of triumph to your dearest friends and latest posterity. As a farther proof how just your title is to such flattering distinctions at home, rest assured, from undoubted authority, that the Nations in Europe, and other parts, are struck with admiration of your gallant behaviour: even our late resolute and determined antagonists do not scruple to bestow the commendations due to such valour and perseverance.[48]

He then expressed his own gratitude:

> I must now warmly congratulate you on these united and
> brilliant testimonies of approbation, amidst such numerous,
> such exalted tokens of applause: and forgive me, faithful
> companions, if I humbly crave your acceptance of my grateful
> acknowledgements. I only presume to ask this favour as having
> been a constant witness of your cheerful submission to the
> greatest hardships, your matchless spirit and exertions, and on
> all occasions, your heroic contempt of every danger.[49]

After the ceremony, the soldiers were each given a bottle of
wine and a pound of fresh beef, while the senior officers dined
at the Convent. True to form, Captain John Spilsbury could not
help being critical, particularly of anything to do with the artillery. 'At about dusk the lamps were lighted in the colonnade,'
he said, 'except those in the center arch, and, there being no
musick, all seemed extremely dull ... At 9 p.m. the fireworks
were exhibited, but it rained at times very hard ... but they were
too much of a sameness to have been good at any rate, except the
sun and the rockets that answered very well ... Never was a worse
salute performed by the Artillery ... a worse feu de joye fired by
troops, worse weather, worse music, worse fireworks, or worse
entertainment.'[50]

# CHAPTER TWENTY-FOUR

# AFTERMATH

*Remember friends if war should spare,*
*My life, I shall expect to share,*
*At my return each dainty dish,*
*Fowls, beef, mutton, veal or fish,*
*A jug of the best home brewed beer,*
*To quench my thirst, my spirits clear,*
*A pipe provide tobacco good,*
*A cheering fire of coal or wood,*
*The corner it must be my seat,*
*And then my wishes are complete.*

Written by a soldier in Gibraltar
during the Great Siege[1]

In July 1785, Midshipman Francis Vernon was back at Gibraltar. It was five years since he had returned to England with Admiral Digby's ships, and two years had passed since the ending of the siege. He was now curious to see what had changed:

The havoc caused by the siege was discernable from the ruined situation of the town and the innumerable cannon balls and bursted bumb-shells that almost covered the northern surface of the rock. The attention of General Eliott was now directed to restore the works to their former perfection, and to encrease the strength of a fortress that had so brilliantly shewn itself impregnable. To the very summit of the rock, an excellent road whereon two could ride a-breast was completed, and towards Europa Point, an extensive place of parade was nearly finished. A vessel with a diving bell was employed in searching for guns, &c. that had been sunk in the Spanish floating batteries, and many were found half melted by the conflagration.[2]

At the turn of the century, fifteen years later, Midshipman William Lovell sailed to Gibraltar:

I was much pleased to see the celebrated rock, so well defended by the gallant Elliot in 1782, and to read, on the spot, Colonel Drinkwater's most amusing story of that famous siege. As late as the year 1801, the greater part of the garrison was still covered with shot and broken shells, thrown by the Spaniards at that period. They have since been collected, and sold to be melted down for various purposes, some probably to be again converted into missiles of destruction.[3]

Although salvage of the guns from the sunken floating batteries had begun almost straightaway, it was now the turn of the debris from the bombardments to be cleared. The salvage work was mirrored in Britain, where the contract for raising the *Royal George* at Spithead was won by William Tracey, who started work in the spring of 1783. By mid-July the newspapers were reporting that 'the victualling hoy, which was sunk with the Royal George, was yesterday weighed, and in a few days it is expected they will begin their attempt to raise the Royal George'.[4] The victualling hoy was the *Lark* sloop, but the much larger *Royal George* presented a more difficult challenge. Portsmouth Naval Dockyard was instructed to assist Tracey, but instead deliberately obstructed his work. The money ran out, and Tracey went bankrupt.

Apart from marking the site as a hazard to shipping, little more was done until 1834, when Charles Deane with his brother John started to salvage items from the wreck, including brass and iron cannons, using a new diving helmet. Similar in form to later helmets of diving suits, this one operated as a form of diving bell, because it was fixed to a jacket that was open, like a bell, at the bottom. It was the pressure of air pumped into the helmet that prevented water getting in, so long as the diver remained upright. The helmet was made to a design of Charles Deane's by Augustus Siebe, a German engineer, who went on to found a business making diving equipment, while the Deane brothers made a career of diving for salvage.[5]

Newspapers had for some years been carrying stories about those believed to be the last survivors from the *Royal George*. The only woman definitely known to have survived, Betty Horn, was awarded £50 by William IV in 1836, when she was eighty-six years old and living in Wivenhoe in Essex.[6] Doubtless the king remembered that, as a midshipman in the *Prince George*, he had twice sailed alongside the *Royal George* in convoys to Gibraltar. The wreck still posed a hazard to shipping in the busy naval anchorage at Spithead, but in 1839 Colonel Charles William Pasley of the Royal Engineers employed a team using diving suits developed by Siebe. He placed a series of explosives on the wreck to blow it apart, and occasionally large pieces of the ship floated to the surface that could be salvaged, while other items were lifted off the seabed. It took Pasley until November 1843 to finish clearing the site, and after he had finished, the wreck was obliterated and the site forgotten.

Bringing a semblance of normality back to Gibraltar took less time than clearing the wreck of the *Royal George*. The town of Gibraltar was reduced to ruins and would take years to clear and rebuild, but already by September 1783 Eliott was able to issue a proclamation that 'the butchers are at liberty to erect stalls for selling their meat in the new market place'.[7] George Cockburn served as an ensign and an aide-de-camp to Eliott, and on returning to Gibraltar in 1810 he recalled its appearance in the last year of the siege:

a dismantled town, a large garrison, and scarcely any other inhabitants, no shops. Shot and shells flying about, and lying in all directions, traverses of barrels, and many of the works,

in particular the old Mole, almost in ruins from fire, no merchant vessels in the bay – no appearance of trade. The isthmus
between Gibraltar and St Roque covered with works, camps, and
all the implements of war. Fort Barbara on the Mediterranean,
and St. Philip on the west, with their flags proudly flying: no
living creature between the advanced posts of the two armies.[8]

At the time of his visit, the Peninsular War was raging in Spain,
but in spite of the fighting against the French Napoleonic forces
in the north, southern Spain was friendly to Britain. Although
improvements were visible at Gibraltar, with some rebuilding,
Cockburn was not entirely complimentary:

the town of Gibraltar is very poor and miserable in appearance:
I never saw worse shops, and yet there is a great trade here.
The Moles and Bay are now full of ships, and the view, taking
in the Spanish mountains, Apes-hill, and Ceuta in Africa, is as
beautiful as can be conceived ... The inns are the worst, and
the innkeepers the most imposing in the world. Such imposi-
tion is very intolerable, for the necessaries of life are at present
cheap. This place was always remarkable for drunkenness, and
from what I see, it keeps up its character.[9]

The defences and other official buildings formed the most
impressive part of the garrison, which were renovated before anything else:

They have all been repaired since the famous siege, and are
in the most complete order. The convent where the governor
lives, is also in good order, and well calculated to resist the
heat, which this day is very great. The gardens have been much
improved. A large handsome building [Garrison Library] has
been erected by subscription in the town. The lower room contains a library, and the upper is used for the garrison assemblies,
though I should think dancing in such a climate, anything but
pleasure.[10]

To Cockburn, Gibraltar gave the impression of being on a peacetime footing, with a small garrison and little sign of the Spanish siegeworks that had once threatened the Rock. The only evidence that all the major European powers were fighting a world war was on the isthmus: 'The neutral space about the Devil's Tower is at present covered with miserable men, women, and children, who are half naked, and half starved, but who are encamped like gipsies all round the tower, and under the rock. On enquiry, I found these people had come from St. Roque and the neighbouring towns and valleys for fear of the French.'[11] Some of those people fleeing the French also took refuge around the east side of Gibraltar, in the area known now as Catalan Bay, which they could reach without having to try to gain access to the fortress, something that was likely to be refused.

One innovation had been the establishment in May 1801 of the *Gibraltar Chronicle* newspaper. The year after Cockburn's visit, in 1811, it translated and published an intercepted letter from an anonymous French officer to a friend in France, demonstrating why Spanish refugees had fled to Gibraltar:

We have been pursuing an Enemy who kept constantly flying before us. And yet, upon reaching St. Roch, two short leagues from Gibraltar, he offered some resistance, but seeing himself on the point of being overpowered, he retired under the walls of Gibraltar, protected by the land and sea batteries. As to us, we took up a position before St. Roch, in the presence of the English and Spanish troops, expecting every moment to be attacked, but although we remained full six days there, there was only trifling skirmishing.[12]

The officer went on to explain that, as they made their way south towards the Spanish coast, the French troops found the villages deserted, but were fired on in the mountain passes. They stopped for a few days at San Roque, the Spanish headquarters during the siege, and left it in a ruinous state: 'We at length reached St. Roch, after driving the Enemy from it, but we did not find a soul in the houses, all of them having been abandoned. It is a pretty well-built town, of a regular size, but at present a heap of ruins because, the Division having encamped before it, the houses have been stripped and considerably damaged to furnish the camp.' Unable to find anyone to fight, the French troops ran short of provisions and were forced to retreat. The officer complained that he had lost his baggage and was 'without clothes and penniless', though he was pleased to have had an opportunity to see Gibraltar from San Roque and considered it a very difficult fortress to attack – 'all batteries over batteries'.[13]

Although the war continued outside, behind its defences Gibraltar was slowly returning to a peacetime existence. The signing of the peace in 1783 had brought an end to the devastation of the buildings and defences, and it also brought great changes to lives that had been shaped by conflict. In the years following the siege, soldiers had left to be replaced by others, and gradually the inhabitants returned from the various places where they had taken refuge. At first, Eliott remained as governor, very much in charge of everything, dealing with both military and civilian issues on a daily basis. In the months before Vernon's arrival in 1785, Eliott had permitted various people to settle in the town itself, such as 'Andreas Fluter, late of the Gibraltar Hanoverian Brigade', who had come to Gibraltar in 1775 with his regiment. In the 1791 census, he is listed as Andrew Flewter, working as a shoemaker, and living with his wife from Ireland and their two young daughters. Eliott also allowed John Martin Baker, a forty-seven-year-old Protestant originally from London, to 'establish himself as inhabitant and merchant taylor in this garrison', but some were refused, like 'Antonio Bayon, Spanish Deserter,' who wanted to set up a school.[14]

Many soldiers disappeared back into civilian life once their regiments were disbanded, but others re-enlisted. Samuel Ancell was one of those who left the army, opening a military commission agency in Dublin, where he died in 1802. William Green returned to England and continued his army career, becoming chief military engineer of Great Britain. Despite the failure of his floating batteries, the French engineer Michaud d'Arçon also found employment for many years on other sieges. The conquest of Minorca and his involvement in the siege of Gibraltar made the Duc de Crillon famous, and he was given the title of Duc de Mahon. He continued in the Spanish army until his death at Madrid in 1796 at the age of seventy-nine. Ten years later, the Spanish Admiral Don Juan Langara also died at Madrid, but had not accumulated wealth for a lavish funeral, as the *Annual Register* reported:

> In consequence of his disregard of his private interest, he died poor, and his widow was in the greatest embarrassment how to provide a funeral adequate to his rank. The prince of peace [Manuel Godoy], being informed of this, wrote a letter to Madame De L. in which he expressed his regret at the decease of such a meritorious officer, and at the same time informed her that he would defray the expences of the funeral, which was performed with the utmost magnificence and splendour.[15]

The following year, in 1807, Houdan-Deslandes died suddenly at the age of fifty-three. By the time of the French Revolution, he was a captain, but because he did not support the principles of the revolution, he managed to leave the army and lived quietly with his family at Chinon, devoting himself to literature.[16]

At Gibraltar, Corporal Thomas Cranfield remained with his regiment, the 39th, for a few months after the siege, and at the King's Chapel in October 1783 'he was married to a most amiable young woman, who had only just entered upon her sixteenth year. So great was the estimation in which the parties were held, that Lieutenant-General Boyd was present at the marriage, and gave away the bride.'[17] She had been raised on Gibraltar, but they now left for England, and Cranfield wrote to his parents on reaching Southampton:

> We had a long and tedious voyage. You must know, that since my last [letter] I have entered into a new state of life; that is marriage ... My wife's name is Sarah Connolley, the daughter

of a corporal in the [same] regiment, and bears an excellent character. Her father and mother have been very good to me; and before I left Gibraltar, gave me a house in the town, which at one time was worth fifty pounds; but when I came away, I could obtain no more than six guineas and a half for it. My wife is not yet arrived in England; for all the women are on board a transport ... My father and mother-in-law desire to be remembered to you both, and would be glad to carry on a correspondence with you. They hope that their daughter will be a credit to your family.[18]

Cranfield was reunited with his parents in London, where he discovered that his father had become fervently religious. He was persuaded to follow the same path and devoted the rest of his life to charitable works and establishing schools and Sunday schools for the poor. He died at the age of eighty in 1838 and was buried in the chapel graveyard at Collier's Rents in Southwark. Having touched so many lives, his funeral procession was attended by hundreds of mourners, mainly teachers, former pupils and neighbours.

John Macdonald decided not return to Scotland at the end of the siege, but as his regiment, the 73rd Highlanders, was being disbanded, he joined the 25th. With the reduction of troops stationed on Gibraltar, he was subsequently discharged, but before sailing home his good friend George Mackay, who was Eliott's steward, told him there was a vacancy for a butler. On Mackay's recommendation, Eliott gave him the job, but because he had been injured Macdonald needed to return to England first of all to arrange his pension (as an out-pensioner) with the Chelsea Hospital Board. In March 1786 he was back in Gibraltar and then, the following year, sailed for England again with Eliott.

In London, Macdonald's role was to prepare Eliott's house in Charles Street, near Berkeley Square, the same house that another renowned general – Sir Henry Creswicke Rawlinson – would own some eighty years later.[19] The reason for Eliott's homecoming was to receive his peerage in July as Lord Heathfield, Baron Gibraltar, named after the village of Heathfield in Sussex, where almost two decades earlier he had purchased the Bailey (or Bayley) Park estate using his Havana prize-money. A year later, in July 1788 and now living in Great Marlborough Street, the once fit and resilient governor of Gibraltar suffered a stroke, as Macdonald described: 'His lordship ... was suddenly seized with a paralytic stroke which almost immediately deprived him of the use of his left side, from the top of his head to the sole of his foot.'[20]

Two months later, Eliott drew up his will, no doubt fearing that he was beyond recovery. It took several months before he showed signs of improvement, and in March 1789, perhaps wanting to escape from the city, he 'bought a large house with a garden and about twelve acres of pleasure grounds at Turnham Green, five miles from Hyde Park Corner'. Turnham Green was then a small rural village west of London, on the main coaching route. Unfortunately, Eliott suffered another stroke and was advised to go to the healing spa at Bath to take the waters. Macdonald and another servant stayed with him there until he was well enough to return to Turnham Green, though still affected down his left side, quite lame and relying on an invalid chair.[21]

A mile-and-a-half away, at Kew Palace, George III had also been very ill, and so in April his recovery was marked with huge celebrations across the country, particularly in the form of illuminations. At Turnham Green, Eliott put on a magnificent display and joined the procession from Kew Palace to St Paul's Cathedral for a service of rejoicing. George Thomas Landmann, one of the guests, described the intricate fireworks and other incendiary devices that Eliott's military colleagues prepared:

a party of the Royal Artillery, selected as the best firework makers, were employed in arranging the rockets and disposing of a collection of wheels, maroons, &c., but more particularly in manufacturing a large fire-ball to be erected on a strong iron pole, and placed on the top of the house. This fire-ball was in every respect similar to those used at Gibraltar during the last siege ... These men were also occupied in making

various experiments for lighting all the lamps for some large
and well-executed transparent paintings ... cotton-wicks
dipped in spirits of turpentine leading from lamp to lamp, were
cleverly arranged; ultimately communicating with the grand
fire-ball which was three to four foot in diameter. Much care
was required amongst so much fire to guard against the danger
of destroying the premises; in consequence of which two fire-
engines were procured, and kept in constant readiness to act in
case of need.[22]

The celebrations lasted all day, a huge ox filled with potatoes
was roasted on the green in front of the house, and Eliott also supplied casks of beer for the local people. Everyone then waited for
the return of the king:

Between five and six of the evening of the day, whilst we were
at dinner, the King passed along the high road on the opposite
side of the green, on his return to Kew; upon which, as had
been previously arranged, a royal salute was commenced on the
top of the house with maroons. The loud reports called us all
to the stone platform at the front of the house; and whilst Lord
Heathfield, who had been wheeled in his chair to the door, was
waving his hat to his Majesty, who had ordered his carriage to
be stopped, and was leaning out of the carriage window, bowing
and waving his hat in acknowledgement of the compliment,
a large piece of the parapet-wall coping was thrown down by
the repeated explosions: it fell to the ground with great force,
grazing the left arm of his Lordship, but doing him no further
injury. On returning to the dinner-table, he seized a bottle of
port wine, filled a bumper, and standing up, enthusiastically
exclaimed, 'Here's to the health of my beloved King—George
the Third, God bless him!'[23]

Because Eliott was by now much improved, he decided to
travel to Germany to try the waters at the spa of Aix-la-Chapelle
(Aachen), where he arrived in mid-June. 'Soon after he took a

country house at a place called Kalkhofen [Schloss Kalkhofen],'
Macdonald said, 'about a mile from the town, to have the purer
air. And from this place his lordship came every morning to town
to bathe and drink the water. We stayed there until October and
then returned to his lordship's house at Turnham Green, where we
spent the winter at home.'[24]

As a military commander, loved by some and loathed by
others, Eliott had successfully guided Gibraltar through the
years of siege and still held the office of governor. He decided
that the Rock was where he wanted to end his days, so he
obtained permission from the king to return. Because he was not
well enough to embark on a long sea voyage, and because France
was now in the turmoil of revolution, a circuitous overland route
was chosen. He therefore set off for Aix-la-Chapelle, arriving in
May. Here he took the waters for several weeks, but suffered
another stroke and died the next day, 6 July 1790, at the age
of seventy-two. Rumour and gossip then erupted about a possible marriage, though Macdonald – who would have witnessed
everything – remained loyal as a discreet butler and revealed
nothing. The *Gentleman's Magazine* reported conflicting gossip
that Eliott had been due to marry on the day he died, but on the
other hand they had heard his pension of £2000 per year was left
to 'his long-beloved Irish mistress, to whom, it is said, he was
married at Aix-la-Chapelle, a short time before his decease', and
also that 'he was married, and that he has settled a jointure of
400l. on his lady'.[25]

*The Times* sounded more authoritative: 'The Lady to whom
his Lordship meant to be united, and who would certainly have
been his wife had not death stepped in, is the sister of a Lady of
whom his Lordship was extremely fond, but she dying about ten
years ago, he transferred his affections to the other who is about
thirty-five years of age. His Lordship had for a long series of years
been acquainted with the family.'[26] Colonel Landmann and his
family had been very close to Eliott, and his analysis is probably
the most accurate: 'At Aix-la-Chapelle, his Lordship met with a
lady towards whom, in earlier days, he had felt much esteem, and

probably sentiments of a more tender nature. Feeling himself rapidly sinking, and being anxious to provide for her future comforts, he offered to marry her, but died before the ceremony could be performed.' Eliott's will finally put an end to such speculation, because his estate passed to his descendants, apart from two specific bequests – £600 to Lieutenant George Frederick Koehler and £400 to George Mackay.[27]

Eliott's body was embalmed and conveyed from Aix-la-Chapelle to Heathfield, which was an unusual decision because most people were buried close to where they died, given the absence of refrigeration, the cost of embalming and the difficulties of transport. Fifteen years later, the arrival of Nelson's body in London after the Battle of Trafalgar would be a massive event. Eliott had acquired a similar heroic status, but his was not a public funeral in London. Nevertheless, the procession to Heathfield was accompanied by much pomp, as one newspaper described:

By a letter from Dover, dated the 30th instant [July], we are informed, that the remains of the late Lord Heathfield arrived there in the Racehorse packet, from Ostend, and were received on shore in a hearse and six, preceded by two porters, and eight men on foot, with wands, and followed by his Lordship's servants to the inn, where they remained that day, and on Saturday morning, the 31st, the body went out of Dover for Heathfield, in the following procession, viz.

The undertaker,

A party of troops quartered in Dover,

Two beadles of the port,

Two porters on horseback,

Six mutes ditto,

Two porters ditto,

The coronet and cushion carried by a person uncovered, his
horse, in a black caparison, led by two grooms,

A hearse and six, with feathers, velvets, and escutcheons,

Two coaches and six, with the like,

His Lordship's carriage.

At Bailey Park, his Lordship's funeral procession will be joined
by a number of tenants and other inhabitants, and this day his
remains will be deposited at Heathfield, in a vault built for that
purpose, over which a handsome monument is preparing to be
erected.[28]

At Gibraltar, Eliott's memory has never been forgotten, and
after the Battle of Trafalgar in 1805 a wooden statue of Eliott
was even carved out of the bowsprit of the captured Spanish
warship *San Juan Nepomuceno*.[29] In Britain, his memory was honoured over the years, including several pubs taking his name. His
long-standing and elderly deputy, Robert Boyd, became the new
governor of Gibraltar and did a great deal to continue the rebuilding of the town. On his death in 1794, at the age of eighty-four, he
was buried in a tomb within the King's Bastion, whose foundation
stone he had himself laid over two decades earlier. His adversary
Charles Ross died three years later.

Turnham Green, to the west of London, where Eliott had
lived, also became home to Lieutenant John Upton. His wife,
Catherine, had returned to London with their two children in
mid-1781, and two years later her husband was back in England.
His regiment, the 72nd, was disbanded, and he spent the rest of
his life on half-pay, dying at Turnham Green in 1815 at the age of
sixty-four. In 1784 Mrs Upton paid to have published a small book
entitled *Miscellaneous Pieces in Verse and Prose*, and in its preface
she declared: 'I have but little time to write, or *correct* what I write,
and shall ingenuously confess, that I send the following sheets
into the world, with a view to *support my children*, not to extend

my own fame.'[30] She described herself as the Governess of the
Ladies Academy at 43 Bartholomew Close in London, and for a
married woman with two young children such a role was highly
unusual, perhaps suggesting that she was estranged from her husband. Her short essay 'Thoughts on Love and Marriage' certainly
railed against the injustice of women being expected to tolerate
their husband's infidelity, which may have been based on her own
experience.

In *Miscellaneous Pieces in Verse and Prose*, one poem was 'The
Siege of Gibraltar', in which Mrs Upton complained that the suffering of the soldiers was little appreciated, to which she added
the poignant lines:

> *If a maim'd soldier meets thy wand'ring eye,*
> *Ne'er turn disgusted, but his wants supply;*
> *Think how he lost his limbs, his health, his home;*
> *Perhaps his children, to secure thy own!*
> *Could there be found on earth a soul so poor*
> *To turn the crippled vet'ran from his door;*
> *Or think a tear of gratitude too much,*
> *I'd blush that armies ever bled for such.*[31]

By the end of the eighteenth century, the Rock of Gibraltar
was considered by Britain as a valuable asset, but immediately
after the siege there had been a vociferous debate about whether
or not Gibraltar should be kept. In 1783 the Scottish politician
and prolific writer Sir John Sinclair anonymously published a
booklet in which he expressed the opinion that Spain had only
supported America's bid for independence in the expectation of
gaining Gibraltar: 'the possession of America has been sacrificed
to the retention of Gibraltar. That darling object could alone
have induced Spain to countenance the independence of our
Colonies, and without her assistance that event could never have
taken place.' He went on to argue that there was no good reason
for keeping Gibraltar, especially when considering trade: 'For the
trade of the Mediterranean, of which Gibraltar is boasted of as the

key, becomes every day of less importance in proportion to the commerce of the rest of the world. There was a time ... when the trade of Europe in a manner centred in that sea ... but how many other channels of commerce are open.'[32]

In his view, Spain should have been kept as an ally, which might have saved America: 'Gibraltar ... ought to be restored to Spain provided full and adequate compensation is received. He [Sinclair] dislikes a possession that is principally retained out of spite to a neighbour, whose feelings on the subject we may judge of by putting this question to ourselves: What would England say to a treaty of peace that surrendered Portsmouth to the Spaniards?'[33] Had Spain not been so intent on recovering Gibraltar, several thousand additional British soldiers might have been spared for the war in America, and British warships might have concentrated on American waters, rather than being diverted to Gibraltar. Equally, if Britain had simply ceded Gibraltar to Spain, the American colonies might have been retained, but British influence in the Mediterranean would have been significantly diminished. The Great Siege of Gibraltar proved to be a major pivotal point in world history.

With the loss of the American colonies, Gibraltar became a national symbol for Britain, without which the course of history would have been very different, for while Gibraltar remained a British possession, it provided a crucial naval base between the Atlantic and Mediterranean. Without Gibraltar, there might not have been the remarkable naval victories such as occurred at the Battles of the Nile and Trafalgar, which led to British naval supremacy, and without this naval advantage Britain may have found it impossible to defeat Napoleon. With the opening of the Suez Canal several decades on, Gibraltar became not just the key to the Mediterranean and the Levant but to countries far beyond, forming an essential element in the growth of the British Empire.

Although Eliott was rewarded with a peerage for his service during the siege, there were no medals routinely awarded to soldiers or sailors at this time, but he obtained George III's permission to issue medals to the Hanoverian officers and men at his own expense. Consequently, twelve hundred large silver medals were struck with a picture of Gibraltar and the floating batteries on one side and the words 'Reden, La Motte, Sydow and Eliott' encircled by a wreath on the other.[34] The king also decided to honour the Hanoverian regiments:

> [He] ordered a donation to be presented [to] every soldier belonging to the several corps. It consisted of a scarf, to be worn on their arms, with a motto, descriptive of the glorious service for which it was bestowed. His majesty further ordered, that all the men ... when they shall come to the situation of pensioners, shall receive double the allowance permitted to ordinary soldiers. The grenadiers belonging to the same body are to bear upon their caps a silver plate given by his majesty with the word GIBRALTAR inscribed upon it in large letters.[35]

In France in August 1914, the first month of the First World War, the British Expeditionary Force was retreating in the face of an overwhelming German invasion. At Le Cateau on the 26th, Lieutenant-General Sir Horace Smith-Dorrien ordered his Corps to halt and fight the Germans, to slow down their advance. Those involved in this epic battle included the 2nd Battalion of Suffolks, the 1st Dorsetshires and the 2nd Essex, three of the regiments that had fought together during the Great Siege (as the 12th, 39th and 56th) and were entitled to Gibraltar battle-honours. This coincidence was magnified when they encountered German soldiers with 'Gibraltar' embroidered on their right sleeves – successors to the Hanoverians they had fought alongside during the Great Siege.[36] In another twist, Smith-Dorrien was appointed as governor and commander-in-chief of Gibraltar in 1918, a position that he held until his retirement in 1923.

The special recognition of the Hanoverians created ill feeling among officers and men of other regiments, and Colonel William Picton decided to issue a medal to his own regiment, the 12th, at his own expense. Unfortunately the die cracked after only about sixty of the medals were made, and although a few of them were issued, he let the project drop. A few unofficial memorial medals were made by soldiers in the garrison, and the siege featured on commemorative medals struck by other countries.[37] A Dutch medal of 1783 shows the attack of the floating batteries on one side and the sinking of the *Royal George* on the other, while another medal made the same year for the Treaty of Paris, which ended the American War of Independence, portrays on the obverse the sieges of Gibraltar and Minorca in the background.

Even before that treaty was signed, George III confessed himself very disappointed when Spain finally gave up the claim to Gibraltar, accepting Minorca and Florida instead: 'I should have liked Minorca, the two Floridas and Guadeloupe better than this *proud Fortress*, and in my opinion source of another War, or at least of a constant lurking enmity.'[38] His assessment was accurate, because even now the territory remains an issue of great contention between Britain and Spain. Over two centuries after the siege, Spain is still demanding the return of Gibraltar. For their part, the inhabitants of Gibraltar are the staunchest of Britons, fiercely opposed to becoming Spanish, but they are also proud Europeans. After more than three centuries as a British possession, the conflict underlying the Great Siege has still not been resolved.

George III had in mind the revenue and trade value of places like Guadeloupe, whereas the value of the Rock was always its strategic position at the gateway to the Mediterranean, which later became the gateway to the Suez Canal as well. In the Second World War, Gibraltar was again of especial strategic importance to Britain and her allies, and Winston Churchill became worried about the dwindling Barbary macaque population, mindful of the effect on people's fighting spirit because of the legend that if the apes (actually monkeys) left the Rock, so would the British.[39] Some people went further and said that if the apes left the Rock, then Britain itself was doomed, so they were especially important for wartime morale.

Their numbers seem to have dwindled since the Great Siege,

because by 1939, there were only a dozen apes, and in September 1944 Churchill sent a directive on the subject to the Colonial Secretary: 'The establishment of the apes should be twenty-four, and every effort should be made to reach this number as soon as possible and maintain it thereafter.'[40] The solution was to bring in more macaques from Morocco, and they are now a key attraction for the mass of tourists who visit the Rock, which has become an essential stopover for cruise ships. Many people from around the world feel drawn to Gibraltar, in particular anyone who has served in the Royal Navy or allied navies, because they would have all put in at its dockyard on numerous occasions.

The most famous instance of a fleet visiting Gibraltar was when the shattered remains of Nelson's victorious ships arrived for refitting in the days following the Battle of Trafalgar that took place on 21 October 1805. Sailing ahead, the *Flying Fish* schooner arrived on the 23rd, bringing the news of the battle and the death of Nelson, and the next day the *Gibraltar Chronicle* had one of the biggest scoops in the history of newspapers when it published, in English and French, the first report about Trafalgar.[41] The ships were rapidly repaired with the aid of the dockyard under the direction of the new Superintendent of the Navy Yard, Captain Robert Gambier Middleton, who had arrived with his wife Susanna only a few weeks earlier.[42] Their official residence was The Mount, which had been the home of Colonel and Mrs Green during the siege. Captain Middleton held his post on Gibraltar for three years, during which time he and his wife enjoyed the social life of the garrison, and she occupied part of her time reading. In the summer of 1806, she wrote to her sister in England that she was currently enjoying reading Drinkwater's account of the Great Siege, but was annoyed that it had been recalled by the Garrison Library when she was only halfway through.[43]

John Drinkwater was one of the most interesting characters of the Great Siege. He had joined the 72nd Regiment at a very young age and towards the end of the conflict was promoted to captain. He returned to England when his regiment was disbanded, and in 1785 he published the detailed record of events that he had kept during the siege, as *A History of the Late Siege of Gibraltar*. It went through several editions and became a military classic. A few years later, he purchased a commission in the 1st Regiment of Foot, which was stationed at Gibraltar, and while serving there he established the Gibraltar Garrison Library that survives to the present day. His own son, Admiral Charles Ramsay Drinkwater Bethune, said of Drinkwater: 'Although his son, I may say that he did not take, owing to his retiring disposition, that place in the public eye to which he was entitled. He was content to do his duty quietly, and was one among that class to which our country is much indebted.'[44]

Drinkwater had a long career in the army, including twenty-five years as comptroller of accounts, but apart from his journal of the Great Siege, he is probably best known for an account of the Battle of St Vincent in 1797, at which he himself was present. He published it anonymously that same year in order to draw attention to the role of one man who had been overlooked in dispatches – Horatio Nelson.[45] When Drinkwater died at the age of eighty-one in 1844, he was claimed as the last known survivor of Gibraltar's Great Siege.[46] The names of Drinkwater, Nelson and Gibraltar have been closely linked ever since.

# WEIGHTS, MEASUREMENTS AND MONEY

On Gibraltar, all weights and measurements used were imperial ones, and so for those better acquainted with a metric system, the following may be useful:

## Linear
12 inches (in.) = 1 foot (ft)
3 feet = 1 yard (yd)
6 feet = 1 fathom
22 yards = 1 chain
10 chains = 1 furlong
1760 yards = 1 mile
8 furlongs = 1 mile

## Capacity
2 pints = 1 quart
4 quarts = 1 gallon
36 gallons = 1 barrel
54 gallons = 1 hogshead

## Weight
16 ounces (oz) = 1 pound (lb)
14 pounds = 1 stone
8 stone = 1 hundredweight (cwt)
20 hundredweight = 1 ton

## Some metric equivalents:
1 inch = 2.54 centimetres
1 foot = 30.48 centimetres
1 yard = 0.91 metres
1 mile = 1.61 kilometres
1 pint = 0.568 litres
1 gallon = 4.54 litres
1 ounce = 28.35 grams
1 pound = 0.45 kilograms

## Money
¼ penny = 1 farthing
½ penny = 1 halfpenny
12 pence or pennies (12d.) = 1 shilling (1s.)
2 shillings and sixpence (2s. 6d.) = half a crown
20 shillings = £1 (one pound)
£1 1s. = 1 guinea

Approximate equivalents in decimal coinage are one guinea = £1.05; one pound = £1.00; one shilling = 5p; sixpence = 2.5p, and one penny = 0.416p. In terms of purchasing power, a penny at that time was worth about 26p today, a shilling (1s.) was worth about £3, and one pound about £62 (using The National Archives currency converter, which translates prices in 1780 to values in 2005). See also Chapter 5 for the local currency used on Gibraltar.

# CHRONOLOGICAL OVERVIEW

———— •◆• ————

This list of dates is a summary of a few key events relating to the Great Siege and other selected episodes in Britain's history.

| | | |
|---|---|---|
| 1713 | March | Treaty of Utrecht |
| 1760 | 25 October | George III becomes king |
| 1771 | March | Nelson joins the Royal Navy |
| 1773 | 16 December | Boston Tea Party, when American colonists protest against the unjust taxation of tea imports |
| 1774 | 10 May | Accession of Louis XVI as King of France |
| 1775 | 19 April | American War of Independence (American Revolutionary War) begins, with the British defeat at Lexington |
| | 16 December | Jane Austen is born |
| 1776 | 4 July | American Declaration of Independence |
| 1778 | 6 February | The French become allies of America |
| | 10 July | France declares war on Britain |
| 1779 | 16 June | Spain declares war on Britain |
| | 21 June | The Great Siege of Gibraltar begins with a Spanish blockade |
| | 11 July | The first shot of the Great Siege is fired from Fort St Barbara |
| | August to September | Attempted invasion of Britain by a combined French and Spanish fleet |
| | 12 September | The first shot is fired from the garrison of Gibraltar |
| | 30 October | The *Peace and Plenty* is destroyed |
| | 14 November | The *Buck* arrives |

| | | |
|---|---|---|
| 1780 | 16–17 January | Moonlight Battle |
| | 18 January | Rodney's fleet and relief convoy arrive |
| | 7 June | Fireship attack |
| | 2–9 June | Gordon Riots in London |
| | October | Spanish siegeworks start on the isthmus |
| | 20 December | Britain declares war on the Netherlands |
| 1781 | 12 April | Darby's fleet and relief convoy arrive; the Spanish bombardment begins |
| | 22 July | Mrs Green returns to England |
| | 19 August | Invasion of Minorca; the siege of Fort St Philip begins |
| | 19 October | Surrender at Yorktown |
| | 27 November | The Great Sortie |
| 1782 | 4 February | On Minorca, Fort St Philip surrenders |
| | 12 April | Battle of the Saintes |
| | 25 May | The first tunnel in the Rock is started |
| | 12 August | Comte d'Artois arrives |
| | 29 August | The *Royal George* sinks |
| | 12 September | The combined fleet arrives in the Bay of Gibraltar |
| | 13 September | Attack by floating batteries |
| | 11 October | Hurricane; the *San Miguel* surrenders |
| | | Howe's relief convoy arrives |
| 1783 | 2 February | The Great Siege of Gibraltar ends |
| | 12 March | Eliott and Crillon meet |
| | 31 March | Crillon visits Gibraltar |
| | 23 April | Celebrations on St George's Day |
| | 3 September | Peace of Versailles between Britain, France, Spain and America. Britain, France and Spain each recover lost territories. Britain recognises American independence |
| 1790 | 6 July | George Augustus Eliott dies |

# NOTES

———— ·◆· ————

ABBREVIATIONS

| | |
|---|---|
| BL | British Library, London |
| BL Add MS | British Library Additional Manuscripts |
| DALSS | Devon Archives and Local Studies Service |
| NMM | National Maritime Museum (Royal Museums, Greenwich) |
| GNA | Gibraltar National Archives |
| REM | Royal Engineers Museum, Gillingham |
| TNA | The National Archives, Kew |

The spelling in eyewitness accounts has occasionally been corrected, since the way words were spelled at that time was often fluid, such as 'robbery and marauding' spelled as 'robery and moroding'. Punctuation and style have sometimes been modernised as well, particularly the tendency to use dashes instead of full-stops, ampersands (&) instead of 'and', and upper-case letters for the start of many words. Most quotations have been only slightly altered, if at all, and the words and meaning have not been changed. For further background on this book, see www.adkinshistory.com.

## PROLOGUE: DISASTER

1. TNA ADM 34/365, which says 'Complement 867 men'.
2. Payn 1885, pp. 29–30. He also says: 'In a letter which Miss Martineau once showed me, from a relative of hers, long dead, addressed to her great-niece from Southsea, near Portsmouth, and dated August 9, 1782'. The date '9' should be '29'. Many thanks to members of the Martineau Society for trying to identify the letter writer and recipient.

3. *United Services Magazine* (1839), pp. 419–20.
4. Anon 1834, p. 175. TNA ADM 34/365 says 'Jas. Ingram ~~Ord~~ AB'. He was discharged to the *Ruby* on 29 August 1782.
5. Anon 1834, p. 175. Ned Carrell was presumed drowned, but TNA ADM 34/365 has a 'Hez. Carroll AB', who survived.
6. Anon 1834, pp. 175–6.
7. Anon 1834, p. 176.
8. Anon 1834, p. 176.
9. BL Add MS 36493. Cumberland initially wrote 200, but changed it to 400.
10. BL Add MS 36493.
11. Anon 1834, p. 176.
12. Anon 1834, p. 176.
13. There is no record of a surviving seaman called 'Horn' in the *Royal George* muster book TNA ADM 34/365. He may have been sailing under a false name or was not on board that morning. *Essex Standard* 16 December 1836 says 'Horn's wife and seven other married women were permitted to go out with their husbands to assist the surgeons in case of an engagement'.
14. BL Add MS 36493.
15. BL Add MS 36493.
16. Adkins 2008, pp. 153–64.
17. Vernon 1792, pp. 9–10.
18. Anon 1834, p. 176.
19. *Derby Mercury* 5 September 1782.
20. BL Add MS 36493.
21. Anon 1834, p. 176.
22. Garstin 1925, pp. 60, 62.
23. *Derby Mercury* 26 September 1782.

## CHAPTER ONE: BEGINNINGS

1. From 'The *Contrast* by a Soldier in Gibraltar', BL Add MS 38606.
2. REM 5601.49.1.
3. Drinkwater 1785, p. 45.

4. 346M/F22, with kind permission of Devon Archives and Local Studies Service.
5. Drinkwater 1785, p. 49. War was declared by Spain on 16 June 1779.
6. Drinkwater 1785, p. 51; BL Add MS 50256.
7. Skidmore 2013, pp. 54–6.
8. Ayala 1782, appendix XI.
9. Hills 1974, p. 104. Isabella died in November 1504. Joanna was known as Joan the Mad.
10. Payne 1793, pp. 315–16. Portugal had held Tangier since 1471. Muley Ismail became ruler of Morocco in 1672.
11. Payne 1793, pp. 114–15.
12. The Ceuta siege lasted from 1694 to 1720 and 1721 to 1727.
13. It was reported that mayonnaise was prepared for a banquet in honour of Richelieu (who commanded the French troops).
14. McGuffie 1955, p. 217; Stead 2000, p. 208. Because of peace negotiations in February 1778, it was decided the 72nd should help with fortifications at Gibraltar.
15. Budworth 1795, p. vi.
16. The first action was between the *Belle Poule* and *Arethusa*.
17. Drinkwater 1785, p. 55.
18. Russell 1965; McGuffie 1965.

## CHAPTER TWO: BLOCKADE

1. Tayler 1914, p. 316. The Duffs travelled to Gibraltar in early January 1778; Helen was ill in bed for a week after their arrival.
2. Bell and Ayala 1845, p. 174.
3. Bell and Ayala 1845, pp. 174–5.
4. GNA 1777 census.
5. The Town Range barracks were built 1740 and survived the siege. The South Barracks were built 1730–5.

6. Their son William-Smith was born on Gibraltar in January 1761.

7. Bell and Ayala 1845, p. 173. Green laid out the garden in 1777. See also Garcia 2014, pp. 104, 109–10.

8. REM 5601.49.1a.

9. REM 5601.49.1. Three of Mrs Green's journals are in the Royal Engineers Museum, with overlapping dates. Much was published as Kenyon 1912a and 1912b. We have used the original.

10. 1398 feet.

11. Carter 1777, pp. 230–1. He lived there in 1772.

12. Carter 1777, pp. 250–1.

13. Hills 1974, pp. 222–5. This was Article X.

14. Anon 1782, p. 13.

15. James 1771, p. 382. He lived in Gibraltar 1749–55.

16. BL Add MS 50256.

17. TNA WO 1/286; BL Add MS 45188; TNA PRO 30/85/1.

18. TNA PRO 30/85/1; BL Add MS 45188.

19. 346M/F104, with kind permission of Devon Archives and Local Studies Service. Letter of 26 February 1776, signed 'Bob Boyd'.

20. Cornwallis was a veteran of the Battle of Culloden in 1746.

21. Horsbrugh married Margaret Bell on 29 September 1762; she died at Cupar in August 1782. One daughter was called Christian Arabella Penfold, born 5 February 1776. Boyd Horsbrugh was born in 1770.

22. Conolly 1866, p. 239; Harvey 1961.

23. Charles Ross was from Morangie, Ross-shire, born about 1729. See Harvey 1961.

24. BL Add MS 50260.

25. BL Add MS 50260.

26. Conolly 1866, p. 239.

27. TNA PRO 30 85/1.

28. In *Westminster Magazine* 7 (1779, p. 477), Duff says that the only ships there were the *Childers*, *Panther* and *Enterprize* (also spelled *Enterprise*). Helen Duff was buried at Gibraltar (Tayler 1914, pp. 315, 317).

29. REM 5601.49.1; BL Add MS 50256; BL Add MS 45188 says 'Three Dover Cutter privateers 16 to 20 guns each'. Dover had a reputation for building fine cutters.

30. Drinkwater 1785, pp. 55–6.

31. BL Add MS 50256; REM 5601.49.1.

32. BL Add MS 45188.

33. *Westminster Magazine* 2 (1779), p. 478; BL Add MS 50256.

34. REM 946.8'1799' ('Journal of the Blockade and Siege of Gibraltar which commenced 21st June 1779 and continued until the 2nd February 1783 by C.Lt. RE Holloway'). Only Holloway's first diary is available in REM, but others were seen by Porter when writing a history of the Royal Engineers (Porter 1889).

35. REM 5601.49.1.

36. REM 5601.49.1.

37. Drinkwater 1785, p. 58.

38. TNA PRO 30/85/1. See also Spilsbury 1908, p. 2.

39. Drinkwater 1785, p. 60; Landmann 1852, p. 25. The caricature was set in his library.

40. TNA PRO 30/85/1; Anon 1785, p. 5; REM 946.8'1799'.

41. Drinkwater 1785, p. 61.

42. TNA PRO 30/85/1; BL Add MS 50256.

43. Drinkwater 1785, p. 61.

44. Kendall 2012, pp. 116–17.

45. BL Add MS 50256; BL Add MS 45188.

46. BL Add MS 45188; TNA PRO 30/85/1; GNA 1777 census.

47. BL Add MS 45188.
48. REM 5601.49.1.
49. REM 5601.49.1.
50. REM 5601.49.1.
51. BL Add MS 45188.
52. Drinkwater 1785, p. 63.
53. BL Add MS 45188.
54. REM 946.8'1799'.

## CHAPTER THREE: INVASION

1. Patterson 1960; Syrett 1998.
2. Ellis 1958, pp. 60–77; Patterson 1960, p. 96.
3. BL Add MS 24173.
4. Herbert 1967.
5. McGuffie 1965, p. 58; Macdonald 1906, pp. 35–41.
6. Macdonald 1906, p. 42.
7. *Drewry's Derby Mercury* 27 August 1779.
8. *Hampshire Chronicle* 23 August 1779.
9. Macdonald 1906, pp. 42–3.
10. *Hampshire Chronicle* 23 August 1779.
11. Patterson 1960, p. 89; Syrett 1998, p. 76.
12. *Hampshire Chronicle* 23 August 1779.
13. Rutherford 1941.
14. Eliott-Drake 1911, p. 313.
15. Eliott-Drake 1911, pp. 313–14.
16. Patterson 1960, p. 183–4; Syrett 1998, p. 76. Rear-Admiral Francis William Drake was brother of Sir Francis Henry Drake.
17. Fortescue 1928a, p. 411.
18. Barnes and Owen 1936, pp. 89–90.
19. Vernon 1792, p. 12.
20. Wright 1837, p. 37.
21. Donne 1867, p. 282.
22. Barnes and Owen 1936, pp. 93–4.
23. Barnes and Owen 1936, pp. 94–5.
24. Barnes and Owen 1936, p. 97.
25. *Scots Magazine* 41 (1779), p. 503.

26. D'Arneth and Geffroy 1874, pp. 355, 357.
27. *Annual Register* 1780, p. 15.

## CHAPTER FOUR: FIREPOWER

1. REM 5601.49.1.
2. Spilsbury 1908, p. 4.
3. Stonehouse 1839, p. 387.
4. Carter 1777, pp. 142–3.
5. BL Add MS 50256.
6. REM 5601.49.1.
7. From 1707 to 1711. Roger Elliott (not Eliott) was born 1665, married a sister (Charlotte) of Eliott's mother in 1712 and died in 1714, before Eliott's birth.
8. Eliott was born at Wells House near Stobs Castle, and different sources say he was the 7th, 8th or 9th son; Tancred (1907, p. 35) says he was the 11th and last child, with one girl and ten sons, two dying as infants; DALSS 346M/F103.
9. Eliott-Drake 1911, p. 254.
10. *Caledonian Mercury* 22 July 1790. Anne Eliott died in London in February 1772.
11. Upton 1781, pp. 4, 19. She is cited as Catharine in this publication, but as Catherine elsewhere (e.g. in Upton 1784 and her marriage licence).
12. BL Add MS 50260.
13. Anon 1782, p. 39.
14. REM 946.8'1799'.
15. BL Add MS 45188.
16. REM 5601.49.1.
17. See McConnell 1988 for details of guns.
18. REM 946.8'1799'; Ancell 1784, p. 6. In his 1793 edition, she is identified as Mrs Skinner.
19. Skinner 1891. William Skinner died 25 December 1780.
20. REM 5601.49.1.
21. REM 5601.49.1.

22. BL Add MS 50256.
23. Ancell 1784, p. 6.
24. BL Add MS 50256.
25. Ancell 1784, pp. 6–7.
26. BL Add MS 50256.
27. BL Add MS 50256; BL Add MS 45188; Spilsbury 1908, p. 5.
28. Spilsbury 1908, p. 5; TNA PRO 30/85/1; REM 5601.49.1.
29. TNA PRO 30/85/1.
30. TNA PRO 30/85/1.
31. Drinkwater 1785, p. 69.
32. BL Add MS 45188; Drinkwater 1785, p. 69.
33. Gordon 1784, p. 12.
34. Gordon 1784, p. 12.
35. BL Add MS 45188.
36. BL Add MS 45188; REM 946.8'1799'.
37. Cranfield 1844, p. 11.
38. Anon 1785, pp. 8–9.
39. Spilsbury 1908, p. 7.
40. BL Add MS 50256.
41. REM 5601.49.1; TNA PRO 30/85/1; TNA WO 25/435.
42. BL Add MS 50256.
43. Drinkwater 1785, p. 32.
44. James 1771, p. 351.
45. James 1771, p. 296.
46. Crespo and Galliano 2013, p. 54.
47. Crespo and Galliano 2013, pp. 55–6.
48. Drinkwater 1785, p. 70.
49. Drinkwater 1785, p. 70.
50. BL Add MS 50256.
51. BL Add MS 45188.
52. BL Add MS 45188.
53. Ancell 1784, p. 11.
54. Anon 1782, pp. 2–3.
55. REM 946.8'1799'.
56. TNA PRO 30/85/1.
57. Ancell 1784, p. 12.
58. BL Add MS 45188; Paterson gives the balls as 9 pounds, the powder 1–1½ pounds, elevation 12 degrees and range 450–537 yards.
59. Drinkwater 1785, pp. 71–2.
60. TNA PRO 30/85/1.
61. Drinkwater 1785, p. 72.

## CHAPTER FIVE: SHORTAGES

1. TNA PRO 30/85/1.
2. Drinkwater 1785, p. 75.
3. TNA PRO 30/85/1.
4. TNA PRO 30/85/1.
5. TNA PRO 30/85/1.
6. Drinkwater 1785, p. 75.
7. Spilsbury 1908, p. 7.
8. Macdonald 2004, pp. 21–5.
9. Ancell 1784, p. 24; Spilsbury 1908, p. 8.
10. Drinkwater 1785, p. 40.
11. Twiss 1775, p. 272. He visited in 1773.
12. Based on Spilsbury 1908, opp. p. 1.
13. Ancell 1793, p. 18fn; see Garcia 2016, Lyall 2009.
14. Ancell 1784, pp. 10, 12.
15. Spilsbury 1908, p. 10.
16. Holmes 2002, pp. 281–2; Venning 2005, p. 27.
17. REM 946.8'1799'.
18. REM 946.8'1799'.
19. BL Add MS 45188.
20. TNA PRO 30/85/1.
21. TNA PRO 30/85/1.
22. Crespo and Galliano 2013, p. 53.
23. BL Add MS 45188.
24. REM 5601.49.1.
25. Bell and Ayala 1845, pp. 174–5.
26. Benady 2005, pp. 85–6, 96–7.
27. Benady 2005, pp. 94–5.
28. BL Add MS 45188.
29. TNA PRO 30/85/1.
30. TNA PRO 30/85/1.
31. Spilsbury 1908, p. 10.
32. Drinkwater 1785, p. 76.
33. Ancell 1784, p. 18.
34. BL Add MS 45188.
35. Drinkwater 1785, p. 77.
36. Ancell 1784, p. 18; Drinkwater 1785, p. 77; Anon 1785, p. 15.
37. Drinkwater 1785, p. 79.

38. REM 5601.49.1.
39. REM 5601.49.1.
40. Spilsbury 1908, p. 10 with additions from his manuscript in the Garrison Library.
41. BL Add MS 45188.
42. James 1771, p. 359.
43. Upton 1781, p. 6.
44. Creswell 1863.
45. Upton 1784, p. 11.
46. *Manchester Mercury* 19 March 1771. The family of Joseph Budworth, who would become a lieutenant in the 72nd, most likely owned her school premises.
47. BL Add MS 45188.
48. Drinkwater 1785, p. 80; REM 5601.49.1; GNA 1777 census.
49. Ancell 1784, pp. 14–15.
50. Ancell 1784, p. 20.
51. TNA PRO 30/85/1.
52. Ancell 1784, p. 20.
53. BL Add MS 50256.
54. TNA PRO 30/85/1.
55. TNA PRO 30/85/1.
56. BL Add MS 45188.
57. Drinkwater 1785, p. 82; TNA PRO 30/85/1.
58. *London Courier and Evening Gazette* 31 July 1827. Price married Ann Stewart in 1791 at Clifton, Bristol.
59. BL Add MS 50256.
60. Crespo and Galliano 2013, p. 56; GNA 1777 census.
61. BL Add MS 50256.
62. Spilsbury 1908, p. 13.
63. TNA PRO 30/85/1.
64. REM 5601.49.1.
65. Anon 1785, p. 16.

## CHAPTER SIX: MOONLIGHT BATTLE

1. REM 5601.49.1; Drinkwater 1785, p. 85.
2. REM 5601.49.1; BL Add MS 45188.
3. TNA WO 25/435.
4. BL Add MS 50256; REM 5601.49.1; TNA PRO 30/85/1.
5. BL Add MS 50256.
6. BL Add MS 45188.
7. BL Add MS 45188; TNA PRO 30/85/1.
8. TNA PRO 30/85/1.
9. REM 5601.49.1.
10. Crespo and Galliano 2013, p. 56.
11. GNA 1777 census; GNA History of Inhabitants Houses 1778.
12. TNA PRO 30/85/1.
13. Drinkwater 1785, p. 86.
14. REM 5601.49.1.
15. Skinner 1891, King's Chapel MS 'Baptism in the year 1780'. He was baptised on 13 or 18 July 1780.
16. James 1771, p. 296.
17. Drinkwater 1785, p. 86.
18. Ancell 1793, p. 15.
19. Upton 1781, p. 3; Drinkwater 1785, p. 85.
20. REM 5601.49.1.
21. Evelegh 1965. He married Ann Guest in 1764, became an ensign in 1765, lieutenant in 1771 and captain-lieutenant in 1779. Their oldest daughter, Ann, died in 1781, aged twelve, and was buried at Southport.
22. TNA 25/435.
23. REM 5601.49.1.
24. Baynes is also spelled Baines.
25. Hennen 1830, p. 89; Benady 1994; GNA 1777 census. The apothecaries were William Chapman and Thomas Grand; the midwife was Madalena Manusa.
26. Coad 2013, p. 358.
27. James 1777, p. 343.
28. Ancell 1793, p. 15.
29. See Patterson 1960; Syrett 1998.
30. Mundy 1830, pp. 205–6.
31. Mundy 1830, pp. 211–12.
32. Mundy 1830, p. 213.
33. Macdonald 1906, pp. 43–4.

34. Macdonald 1906, p. 44.
35. Vernon 1792, p. 13.
36. Macdonald 1906, pp. 44–5.
37. Mundy 1830, pp. 218–19; Syrett 1998, p. 85.
38. Mundy 1830, pp. 219–20.
39. Smyth 1795, pp. 36–7.
40. Smyth 1795, p. 225.
41. Mundy 1830, pp. 220–1.
42. Macdonald 1906, p. 46.
43. Vernon 1792, p. 16.
44. Vernon 1792, pp. 16–17.
45. See Syrett 1998.
46. Vernon 1792, p. 17.
47. Vernon 1792, p. 18.
48. Mundy 1830, pp. 222–3.
49. Vernon 1792, pp. 18–19. The ship was driven ashore, the crew saved and the British contingent taken prisoner.
50. Gordon 1784, p. 10. Before joining the 73rd, Gordon was a labourer at Chapel of Garioch, near Aberdeen, in Scotland; TNA WO 120/17.
51. Mundy 1830, p. 223.

CHAPTER SEVEN: RODNEY'S RELIEF

1. Ancell, 1793, p. 15.
2. REM 5601.49.1.
3. REM 5601.49.1.
4. REM 5601.49.1.
5. Syrett and DiNardo 1994, p. 364.
6. Drinkwater 1785, pp. 89–90.
7. Anon 1806, p. 181.
8. BL Add MS 50256.
9. REM 5601.49.1.
10. BL Add MS 45188.
11. TNA PRO 30/85/1.
12. Lawrance 1994, p. 13; Anon 1785, p. 21.
13. Drinkwater 1785, pp. 90–1.
14. REM 5601.49.1.
15. Anon 1785, p. 19; Ancell 1793, p. 26; BL Add MS 50256.

16. BL Add MS 50256; BL Add MS 45188.
17. BL Add MS 45188.
18. Barnes and Owen 1936, p. 194.
19. 346M/F102-161, with kind permission of Devon Archives and Local Studies Service.
20. Drinkwater 1785, p. 121.
21. Upton 1781, p. 3.
22. REM 5601.49.1.
23. REM 5601.49.1.
24. Ancell 1793, pp. 28–9.
25. Drinkwater 1785, p. 97; BL Add MS 50256.
26. Drinkwater 1785, pp. 97, 102.
27. Owen 1933, p. 77 (letter from Hood at Portsmouth Dockyard to Henry Shales, 29 February 1780).
28. Barnes and Owen 1936, p. 195.
29. Barnes and Owen 1936, p. 195.
30. Drinkwater 1785, pp. 93–4.
31. Anon 1784, p. 127.
32. BL Add MS 50256.
33. Crespo and Galliano 2013, p. 57.
34. BL Add MS 50256; TNA PRO 30/20/13 cited in Syrett 2007, p. 326.
35. Macdonald 1906, pp. 47–8.
36. Gordon 1784, p. 10.
37. Macdonald 1906, p. 48.
38. TNA MPHH 1/79 (plan of The Mount).
39. REM 5601.49.1.
40. BL Add MS 50256.
41. Huish 1837, pp. 67–8.
42. REM 5601.49.1.
43. REM 5601.49.1.
44. REM 5601.49.1.
45. Mundy 1830, pp. 235–7.
46. REM 5601.49.1.
47. BL Add MS 50256.
48. TNA PRO 30/20/13 cited in Syrett 2007, pp. 318–19, 335.
49. REM 5601.49.1.
50. Mundy 1830, pp. 257–8.
51. BL Add MS 50256.

## CHAPTER EIGHT: SMALLPOX

1. REM 5601.49.1.
2. REM 5601.49.1.
3. REM 5601.49.1.
4. Many thanks indeed to Dr Jane Richards for the professional analysis of the symptoms.
5. REM 5601.49.1.
6. REM 5601.49.1.
7. BL Add MS 45188. They arrived on 30 January 1780. Mawhood is spelled Maud here, probably reflecting its pronunciation.
8. REM 5601.49.1.
9. Atkinson 1947, p. 111; *Caledonian Mercury* 9 March 1785.
10. REM 5601.49.1.
11. BL Add MS 50256.
12. Macdonald 1906, p. 48.
13. REM 5601.49.1.
14. REM 5601.49.1; Drinkwater 1785, p. 104; Ancell 1793, pp. 36, 38.
15. REM 5601.49.1.
16. REM 5601.49.1.
17. REM 5601.49.1.
18. REM 5601.49.1.
19. Drinkwater 1785, p. 105.
20. Ancell 1793, pp. 36–7.
21. BL Add MS 50256.
22. BL Add MS 50256.
23. Ancell 1793, p. 38.
24. Drinkwater 1785, p. 107.
25. Ancell 1793, p. 38.
26. REM 5601.49.1.
27. REM 5601.49.1.
28. REM 5601.49.1. She was 6 feet tall.
29. REM 5601.49.1.
30. REM 5601.49.1.
31. Ancell 1784, p. 46.
32. REM 5601.49.1.
33. Drinkwater 1785, pp. 82–3; Marshall 1955, p. 54; Pocock 1955.
34. BL Add MS 50256.
35. BL Add MS 50256.
36. Ancell 1784, p. 48.
37. Ancell 1784, p. 49.
38. REM 5601.49.1.
39. Ancell 1784, pp. 48–9.
40. Crespo and Galliano 2013, pp. 57–8.
41. BL Add MS 50256.
42. BL Add MS 50256.
43. TNA PRO 30/85/1.

## CHAPTER NINE: GUNBOATS

1. Ancell 1793, p. 44; BL Add MS 50256.
2. Ancell 1793, p. 44.
3. REM 5601.49.1.
4. REM 5601.49.1.
5. Carter 1777, pp. 237–8.
6. Drinkwater 1785, pp. 36–7.
7. Carter 1777, pp. 231–2.
8. Twiss 1775, p. 269, talking about 1773.
9. Drinkwater 1785, p. 36.
10. Ancell 1793, p. 47.
11. Ancell 1793, pp. 47–8.
12. REM 5601.49.1.
13. Anon 1785, pp. 36–7.
14. GNA 1777 census, which implies that Moubray left Gibraltar with his wife in 1779 and that Mackellar left in 1777, though he was certainly back in 1780; GNA List of Inhabitants Houses 1778; REM 5601.49.1.
15. REM 5601.49.1.
16. TNA PRO 30/85/1; GNA 1777 census; REM 5601.49.1.
17. REM 5601.49.1.
18. GNA/MSP/2a/1780–1783.
19. GNA/MSP/2a/1780–1783.
20. Drinkwater 1785, p. 114.
21. Anon 1785, pp. 37–8.
22. REM 5601.49.1.
23. Ancell 1784, pp. 62–3.
24. REM 5601.49.1.
25. REM 5601.49.1.
26. Landmann 1854, p. 6.
27. Fortescue 1902, p. 201. The battle took place on 3 January 1777.

28. BL Add MS 50256; Spilsbury 1908, p. 20.
29. REM 5601.49.1.
30. REM 5601.49.1.
31. With many thanks to Dr Jane Richards for her professional analysis.
32. REM 5601.03.3.
33. REM 5601.49.1.
34. REM 5601.49.1.
35. REM 5601.49.1.
36. REM 5601.49.1.
37. REM 5601.49.1.
38. REM 5601.49.1.
39. REM 5601.49.1.
40. REM 5601.49.1; BL Add MS 50256.
41. Ancell 1784, pp. 86–7.

## CHAPTER TEN: SCURVY

1. Drinkwater 1785, p. 115.
2. *Stamford Mercury* 21 September 1780.
3. Drinkwater 1785, p. 118.
4. Drinkwater 1785, pp. 119–20.
5. Upton 1781, p. 5.
6. REM 5601.49.1.
7. One daughter was stillborn, Susanna lived three days and Albert four months. Source: familyhistorybyclaytontalbot. weebly.com/george-gledstanes. html
8. REM 5601.49.1; they were probably Ensign George Gregory and Lieutenant Nathaniel Cooke.
9. REM 5601.49.1.
10. REM 5601.49.1; Anon 1785, p. 44; Ancell 1793, p. 56.
11. Ancell 1793, pp. 57, 59; Spilsbury 1908, p. 22.
12. Upton 1781, pp. 4–5; REM 5601.49.1.
13. REM 5601.49.1.
14. GNA/MSP/2a/1780-1783.
15. Drinkwater 1785, p. 119.
16. Drinkwater 1785, pp. 119–20.

17. Drinkwater 1785, p. 115.
18. Ancell 1793, pp. 54–5; Spilsbury 1908, p. 21.
19. Drinkwater 1785, p. 117.
20. Drinkwater 1785, p. 117.
21. Ancell 1793, pp. 55, 56.
22. Ancell 1793, pp. 67–8.
23. BL Add MS 50257.
24. Ancell 1793, p. 34; Drinkwater 1785, p. 126.
25. REM 5601.49.1. Also spelled Montagu's bastion.
26. Anon 1785, pp. 58–9.
27. TNA PRO 30/85/2.
28. Ancell 1793, pp. 62–3.
29. REM 5601.49.1.
30. Ancell 1793, pp. 63–4.
31. BL Add MS 50257.
32. BL Add MS 50257; Ancell 1793, p. 66.
33. Ancell 1793, p. 66.
34. BL Add MS 50257.
35. BL Add MS 50257; REM 5601.49.1.
36. Ancell 1793, p. 57.
37. BL Add MS 50257, REM 5601.49.1.
38. REM 5601.49.1.
39. Ancell 1793, p. 70.
40. REM 5601.49.1.
41. REM 5601.49.1
42. Conn 1942, pp. 190–8; Hills 1974, pp. 320–5.
43. BL Add MS 50257; REM 5601.49.1.
44. Anon 1785, p. 68.

## CHAPTER ELEVEN: DARBY'S CONVOY

1. BL Add MS 50257, REM 5601.49.1. The settee was captured about 29 December 1780.
2. REM 5601.49.1.
3. REM 5601.49.1.
4. Upton 1781, pp. 18, 19.
5. Upton 1781, pp. vi–vii, 2–3.
6. Anon 1785, p. 76.
7. Gordon 1781, pp. 13–14.

8. Drinkwater 1785, pp. 141–2; Ancell 1793, p. 80.
9. GNA/MSP/2c/1781.
10. GNA/MSP/2c/1781.
11. GNA/MSP/2c/1781.
12. BL Add MS 50257.
13. Drinkwater 1785, p. 137.
14. BL Add MS 50257.
15. Ancell 1793, pp. 81–2.
16. BL Add MS 50257; REM 5601.49.1.
17. Atkinson 1919.
18. BL Add MS 50260 (letter to his brother-in-law Charles Bell in Cupar, Scotland). The Hanoverians arrived in 1775.
19. TNA PRO 30/85/1; Anon 1785, p. 71; REM 5601.49.1.
20. REM 5601.49.1; BL Add MS 50257.
21. Drinkwater 1785, p. 139; TNA WO 1/286.
22. Spilsbury 1908, pp. 21, 28.
23. REM 5601.49.1.
24. REM 5601.49.1.
25. Spilsbury 1908, p. 28.
26. Ancell 1784, p. 107.
27. Upton 1781, p. 5.
28. Cranfield 1844, pp. 18, 183.
29. Upton 1781, pp. 5–6.
30. Ancell 1793, p. 84.
31. Ancell 1793, pp. 84–5.
32. Ancell 1793, p. 85.
33. REM 5601.49.1.
34. Anon 1785, p. 80.
35. Ancell 1793, p. 86.
36. GNA/MSP/2c/1781.
37. Barnes and Owen 1938, p. 34.
38. Drinkwater 1785, pp. 145–6.
39. Drinkwater 1785, p. 146.
40. Crespo and Galliano 2013, p. 59.
41. Ancell 1793, p. 87.

## CHAPTER TWELVE: BOMBARDMENT

1. Drinkwater 1785, p. 147.
2. Ancell 1784, p. 112.
3. Crespo and Galliano 2013, p. 59.
4. Upton 1781, pp. 9–10.
5. BL Add MS 50257.
6. TNA PRO 30/85/1.
7. Cranfield 1844, p. 12.
8. 346M/F161, with kind permission of Devon Archives and Local Studies Service.
9. Crespo and Galliano 2013, p. 59; GNA List of Inhabitants Houses 1778.
10. Crespo and Galliano 2013, p. 59.
11. Crespo and Galliano 2013, p. 60.
12. Crespo and Galliano 2013, p. 60.
13. Crespo and Galliano 2013, p. 60.
14. Upton 1781, pp. 10–11.
15. Upton 1781, p. 11.
16. Ancell 1793, pp. 92, 95.
17. Drinkwater 1785, p. 150; Gordon 1784, pp. 14–15.
18. Drinkwater 1785, pp. 150–1.
19. Upton 1781, p. 12; Drinkwater 1785, p. 150.
20. Upton 1781, p. 12.
21. Spilsbury 1908, p. 135; TNA PRO 30/85/1.
22. BL Add MS 38605.
23. The British Library has two journals, Add MS 38605 and 38606. If they were not written by Boyd himself, it was somebody very close and admiring of him, most likely his aide-de-camp Captain William Wilson of the 39th Regiment. The handwriting is probably not Boyd's, though clerks often did copies of letters and journals.
24. BL Add MS 38605.
25. BL Add MS 50257; BL Add MS 38605.
26. Ancell 1784, pp. 114–15.
27. Ancell 1784, pp. 121–2.
28. Ancell 1784, p. 122.
29. Vaughan 1839, pp. 115–18.
30. TNA C 12/1538/16; Benady 2005, pp. 100, 104.
31. TNA C 12/1538/16; Benady 2005, p. 104.

32. Serfaty 2005, p. 34.
33. Crespo and Galliano 2013, p. 61.
34. Maria Raymundo was a sixty-three-year-old widow, and her surname is also spelled Reymundo
35. Ancell 1784, p. 120.
36. BL Add MS 38605.
37. Drinkwater 1785, p. 153; Upton 1781, pp. 12–13.
38. TNA PRO 30/85/1.
39. Ancell 1784, p. 114.
40. GNA/MSP/2c/1781.
41. GNA/MSP/2c/1781.
42. *Naval Chronicle* 6 (1801), pp. 19–20.
43. Ancell 1793, p. 100.
44. Crespo and Galliano 2013, p. 62.
45. BL Add MS 50257.
46. Crespo and Galliano 2013, pp. 63–4.
47. BL Add MS 50257.
48. Drinkwater 1785, p. 154; Upton 1781, p. 15.
49. Ancell 1793, p. 98.
50. Upton 1781, pp. 14–15.
51. GNA/MSP/2c/1781.
52. BL Add MS 50257; Drinkwater 1785, p. 155–6.
53. TNA C 12/1538/16.
54. GNA/D&P/1/1781-1782; TNA C 12/1538/16.
55. BL Add MS 38605.
56. TNA PRO 30/85/1.
57. Barnes and Owen 1938, p. 35.
58. Barnes and Owen 1938, pp. 35–6.
59. Barnes and Owen 1938, pp. 34–5 fn.

## CHAPTER THIRTEEN: DEVASTATION

1. Drinkwater 1785, p. 157.
2. BL Add MS 50257. The *St Firmin* was delayed by an accident and was later captured.
3. Ancell 1793, pp. 101–2; REM 5601.49.1; *Journal Historique et Litteraire* 159 (1781), p. 193.
4. Drinkwater 1785, p. 158.
5. BL Add MS 50257; Drinkwater 1785, p. 158.
6. Upton 1781, p. 16; see Bell and Ayala 1845, p. 171 for the 1766 storm.
7. Drinkwater 1785, p. 149.
8. Ancell 1784, p. 131.
9. TNA C 12/1538/16.
10. Drinkwater 1785, pp. 161–2.
11. Drinkwater 1785, pp. 160, 162; TNA PRO 30/85/1. He died 7 May 1781.
12. GNA/D&P/1/1781-1782.
13. Crespo and Galliano 2013, p. 64.
14. GNA/D&P/1/1781-1782.
15. BL Add MS 38605.
16. Anon 1782, p. 39; Drinkwater 1785, p. 162.
17. BL Add MS 38605.
18. Diary quoted by Sir John Fortescue in *The Times* 19 August 1929.
19. Drinkwater 1785, p. 180.
20. Upton 1781, p. 17.
21. BL Add MS 38605.
22. Benady 2005, p. 111; Howes 1951, p. 172.
23. Drinkwater 1785, p. 165.
24. TNA PRO 30/85/1.
25. BL Add MS 38605; Ancell 1784, p. 117.
26. Upton 1781, p. 18.
27. Benady 2005, p. 112. They were Esther and Sarah Benider.
28. TNA WO 34/133.
29. Anon 1785, p. 82.
30. TNA WO 34/133.
31. TNA WO 34/133; Spilsbury 1908, p. 33; Ancell 1793, p. 107.
32. GNA/D&P/1/1781-1782; Upton 1781, pp. 6–7, 13.
33. Spilsbury 1908, p. 33; TNA WO 25/435; GNA/D&P/1/1781-1782; Ancell 1793, p. 107.
34. Drinkwater 1785, pp. 166–7; BL Add MS 38605.

35. GNA/D&P/1/1781-1782.
36. BL Add MS 38605.
37. Ancell 1793, pp. 102, 107; TNA PRO 30/85/1.
38. BL Add MS 38605.
39. REM 5601.49.1.
40. REM 5601.49.1.
41. REM 5601.49.1.
42. REM 5601.49.1.
43. REM 5601.49.1.
44. GNA/D&P/1/1781-1782.
45. REM 5601.49.1.
46. BL Add MS 50257.
47. BL Add MS 50257.
48. TNA PRO 30/85/1.
49. BL Add MS 50257.
50. Hogg and Batchelor 1978, p. 25.
51. BL Add MS 50257.
52. BL Add MS 38605.

## CHAPTER FOURTEEN: SURRENDER

1. BL Add MS 38605.
2. TNA PRO 30/85/2.
3. BL Add MS 50257.
4. BL Add MS 38605.
5. REM 940'1781/82' ('Journal of the Blockade of St Philips Castle in the island of Minorca 1781 and 1782', anonymous unpublished manuscript).
6. *Stamford Mercury* 6 September 1781.
7. *Stamford Mercury* 6 September 1781.
8. Drinkwater 1785, pp. 178–9.
9. BL Add MS 38605.
10. Drinkwater 1785, pp. 181–2.
11. BL Add MS 38605.
12. Spilsbury 1908, p. 44.
13. Cairncross 1783, pp. 296–7.
14. Cairncross 1783, p. 298.
15. Cairncross 1783, p. 302.
16. Cairncross 1783, p. 304.
17. Cairncross 1783, pp. 302–3, 304.
18. TNA WO 120/17.

19. 346M/016, with kind permission of Devon Archives and Local Studies Service.
20. Spilsbury 1908, p. 45.
21. TNA PRO 30/85/2.
22. TNA PRO 30/85/2.
23. Spilsbury 1908, p. 44–5.
24. Drinkwater 1785, p. 190.
25. TNA PRO 30/85/2.
26. Drinkwater 1785, p. 191.
27. Ancell 1793, p. 125.
28. BL Add MS 50257.
29. BL Add MS 50257.
30. TNA PRO 30/85/2.
31. BL Add MS 50257.
32. BL Add MS 50257.
33. Drinkwater 1785, p. 200.
34. Wheatley 1884, p. 138.

## CHAPTER FIFTEEN: COUNTERSIGN STEADY

1. Drinkwater 1785, pp. 202–3; Ancell 1793, p. 135.
2. Gordon 1784, p. 16; TNA WO 10/169.
3. Drinkwater 1785, pp. 200–1.
4. Gordon 1784, pp. 16–17.
5. Spilsbury 1908, p. 50.
6. Ancell 1793, p. 135.
7. BL Add MS 50257.
8. BL Add MS 50257.
9. Gordon 1784, p. 17.
10. Drinkwater 1785, p. 206.
11. BL Add MS 50257.
12. BL Add MS 50257.
13. Baldry 1936, p. 149. The article contains a contemporary report by an anonymous artillery officer.
14. Baldry 1936, p. 150.
15. Baldry 1936, pp. 150–1; Drinkwater (1785, p. 209) says there were eight 13-inch mortars.
16. Baldry 1936, pp. 149–50.
17. Ancell 1793, p. 157.
18. Heriot 1792, pp. 82–3.
19. Heriot 1792, p. 83.

20. Heriot 1792, pp. 80–1.
21. Ancell 1793, p. 137.
22. BL Add MS 50257.
23. Ancell 1784, p. 173; BL Add MS 38605; Anon 1782, p. 35.
24. Heriot 1792, p. 73; Baldry 1936, p. 149.
25. Drinkwater 1785, p. 209.
26. Baldry 1936, p. 149.
27. *London Gazette* 25 December 1781.
28. BL Add MS 50257.
29. Heriot 1792, pp. 83–4. Freire's name is also given as Don Vincente (or Vicente) Freese (or Friza).
30. Heriot 1792, p. 84.
31. Heriot 1792, p. 75
32. Duncan 1872, p. 284.
33. BL Add MS 38605; GNA/D&P/1/1781–1782. Lindsay divorced his wife in 1807 on the grounds of adultery.
34. BL Add MS 38605.
35. BL Add MS 50257.
36. BL Add MS 38605.
37. TNA PRO 30/85/2.
38. BL Add MS 50257.
39. BL Add MS 50257.
40. Anon 1785, p. 105; Ancell 1793, p. 138; Heriot 1792, pp. 79–80.
41. Baldry 1936, pp. 148–9.
42. 346M/F161, with kind permission of Devon Archives and Local Studies Service.

## CHAPTER SIXTEEN: MINORCA FALLS

1. Heriot 1792, p. 85.
2. Bell 1795, p. 23 of part 3. He was not an army surgeon; not to be confused with John Bell, an army surgeon in the West Indies.
3. Anon 1785, p. 107.
4. BL Add MS 38605.
5. Heriot 1792, p. 89.
6. BL Add MS 38605.
7. TNA PRO 30/85/2.
8. Gordon 1784, pp. 17–18.
9. Fortescue 1902, p. 410.
10. *Carnet de la Sabretache* 1907, p. 278. He was writing to his close companion, Prince Salm-Salm.
11. BL Add MS 50257.
12. BL Add MS 38605.
13. BL Add MS 38605.
14. Cranfield 1844, p. 17.
15. Drinkwater 1785, p. 222.
16. Drinkwater 1785, p. 224; Spilsbury 1908, p. 57.
17. BL Add MS 38605.
18. Ancell 1784, p. 193.
19. Drinkwater 1785, pp. 226–7.
20. Drinkwater 1785, p. 227.
21. REM 940'1781/82' ('Journal of the Blockade of St Philips Castle in the island of Minorca 1781 and 1782', anonymous unpublished manuscript).
22. REM 940'1781/82'.
23. REM 940'1781/82'.
24. Duncan 1872, p. 294.
25. Duncan 1872, pp. 294–5.
26. Duncan 1872, p. 295.
27. *London Gazette* 23 March 1782.
28. *London Gazette* 23 March 1782.
29. *London Gazette* 23 March 1782; Benady 2005, p. 109.
30. Drinkwater 1785, p. 230.
31. 346M/016, with kind permission of Devon Archives and Local Studies Service.
32. BL Add MS 50257.
33. 346M/016, with kind permission of Devon Archives and Local Studies Service.
34. Spilsbury 1908, p. 61.
35. BL Add MS 38605.
36. Drinkwater 1785, p. 231.
37. Drinkwater 1785, pp. 232–3.
38. Connolly 1855, pp. 30–3.
39. Ancell 1793, p. 167.
40. Drinkwater 1785, p. 235.
41. Drinkwater 1785, p. 228.
42. BL Add MS 50258.

43. BL Add MS 38605.
44. Anon 1785, p. 124.
45. Drinkwater 1786, p. 232.

## CHAPTER SEVENTEEN:
## FRENCH INGENUITY

1. *Kentish Gazette* 3 April 1782.
2. Hills 1974, p. 312; Patterson 1960.
3. BL Add MS 50258.
4. *Kentish Gazette* 3 April 1782.
5. Anon 1785, p. 123.
6. Anon 1785, p. 123.
7. Ancell 1793, p. 173.
8. BL Add MS 50258.
9. Anon 1785, p. 127.
10. Ancell 1793, p. 175.
11. Drinkwater 1785, p. 163.
12. Connolly 1855, p. 13.
13. 346M/016, with kind permission of Devon Archives and Local Studies Service.
14. 346M/016, with kind permission of Devon Archives and Local Studies Service.
15. BL Add MS 38605.
16. Rose and Rosenbaum 1991, p. 84.
17. Anon 1785, pp. 127–8.
18. BL Add MS 50258.
19. BL Add MS 38605.
20. Spilsbury 1908, p. 62; GNA 1777 census says the family was Palerano; Horsbrugh calls her Maria Periano (BL Add MS 50258).
21. BL Add MS 38605.
22. Ancell 1793, pp. 177–8.
23. BL Add MS 38605.
24. BL Add MS 50256.
25. REM 946.8'1799'; BL Add MS 45188.
26. Drinkwater 1785, p. 242.
27. BL Add MS 50258.
28. BL Add MS 38605.
29. BL Add MS 38605.
30. BL Add MS 50258; Ancell 1793, p. 181; Drinkwater 1785, p. 246.
31. Drinkwater 1785, p. 246.

## CHAPTER EIGHTEEN:
## TUNNELS

1. Spilsbury 1908, p. 67.
2. *Newcastle Journal* 6 July 1782.
3. 346M/016, with kind permission of Devon Archives and Local Studies Service.
4. BL Add MS 38605.
5. Spilsbury 1908, p. 68.
6. BL Add MS 50258.
7. Drinkwater 1785, p. 250.
8. Drinkwater 1785, pp. 250–1; BL Add MS 38605; TNA WO 10/169.
9. Drinkwater 1785, p. 252; Ancell 1793, p. 188.
10. Drinkwater 1785, pp. 252–3.
11. Spilsbury 1908, pp. 68, 69.
12. Ancell 1793, pp. 186–7.
13. Barnes and Owen 1938, p. 257.
14. Gordon 1784, p. 19.
15. REM 5601.49.1b.
16. Drinkwater 1785, p. 254; BL Add MS 50258; GNA/MSP/2b/1782.
17. Drinkwater 1785, p. 256; 346M/016, with kind permission of Devon Archives and Local Studies Service.
18. Drinkwater 1785, p. 254.
19. Drinkwater 1785, pp. 254–5.
20. *Belfast News-Letter* 21 September 1882.
21. Drinkwater 1785, p. 258.
22. Anon 1783, pp. 14–15 (actually by F.-S.-D. Houdan-Deslandes, though formerly attributed to d'Arçon).
23. Dumont 1819, p. 5.
24. TNA PRO 30/11/271.
25. Anon 1783, p. 16.
26. TNA WO 25/435; GNA/MSP/2c/1781; TNA CO 91/42 Memorial of Mrs Hannah Hassan, who also claimed that her son joined at 'the first commencement of the attack', referring to the assault by the floating batteries.
27. Spilsbury 1908, p. 71.

28. 346M/017, with kind permission of Devon Archives and Local Studies Service.
29. Drinkwater 1785, p. 260.
30. Adams 1840, p. 171.
31. Anon 1793, pp. 18–19.
32. Anon 1783, pp. 18–19.
33. Drinkwater 1785, p. 261.
34. Drinkwater 1785, p. 262.
35. Drinkwater 1785, p. 263.
36. Drinkwater 1785, p. 264.
37. Ancell 1793, p. 193.
38. BL Add MS 38605. Thanks to Sam Benady for the aubergine suggestion.
39. Ancell 1793, p. 193.
40. Anon 1783, p. 21.
41. Drinkwater 1785, p. 265.
42. Anon 1783, p. 23.
43. Anon 1783, p. 24.
44. Drinkwater 1785, p. 265; Ancell 1793, p. 193.

CHAPTER NINETEEN: WAITING

1. *Newcastle Courant* 20 April 1782.
2. Fortescue 1928b, p. 93.
3. *Kentish Gazette* 10 August 1782.
4. *Notes and Queries Sixth Series* 6 (1882), p. 244.
5. BL Add MS 36493.
6. Falconer 1946.
7. Marsden 1838, p. 51; he would later become secretary to the Admiralty.
8. Marsden 1838, p. 52.
9. Ancell 1793, p. 201.
10. Ancell 1793, p. 196.
11. Ancell 1784, pp. 252–3.
12. Anon 1783, pp. 26, 27.
13. Anon 1783, pp. 27, 28.
14. Ancell 1793, p. 201.
15. Drinkwater 1785, p. 273; Ancell 1793, p. 202.
16. Anon 1783, pp. 28–9.
17. Anon 1783, pp. 29, 49.
18. TNA PRO 30/11/271.

19. *Carnet de la Sabretache* 1907, p. 539.
20. Ancell 1793, p. 203.
21. Drinkwater 1785, p. 278.
22. Anon 1783, pp. 34–5.
23. BL Add MS 38605.
24. Ancell 1793, pp. 203–4.
25. Ancell 1793, p. 203.
26. Drinkwater 1785, pp. 279–80. He died in 1821.
27. Ancell 1793, p. 204.
28. Anon 1783, pp. 37–8.
29. BL Add MS 38605.
30. Drinkwater 1785, p. 283.
31. Drinkwater 1785, p. 271.
32. BL Add MS 38605; DALSS 346M/016.
33. Anon 1783, p. 40.
34. Drinkwater 1785, p. 284.
35. *Newcastle Journal* 17 August 1782.
36. Anon 1783, p. 44.
37. Ancell 1793, p. 206.
38. Ancell 1793, p. 207.
39. REM 5601.03.2.
40. Lindsay 1793, p. 491.
41. REM 5601.03.2.
42. Drinkwater 1785, p. 286.
43. Anon 1783, p. 47.
44. Drinkwater 1785, p. 287.

CHAPTER TWENTY: MASS ATTACK

1. Drinkwater 1785, p. 288.
2. Drinkwater 1785, pp. 288–9.
3. Ancell 1793, p. 208.
4. Anon 1783, pp. 47–8.
5. Langle 1785, p. 71.
6. D'Arçon 1783, p. 14 fn.
7. REM 5601.03.2.
8. Lindsay 1793, p. 493.
9. *Universal Magazine* 71 (1782), p. 273.
10. Anon 1783, p. 45; d'Arçon 1783, p. 12.
11. Drinkwater 1785, p. 295 fn.
12. REM 5601.03.2.
13. Drinkwater 1785, p. 289.
14. Gordon 1784, p. 25.
15. Lindsay 1793, pp. 493, 502.

16. Ancell 1793, p. 209.
17. Anon 1783, pp. 48–9.
18. Anon 1783, p. 49.
19. Anon 1783, p. 49.
20. BL Add MS 38605.
21. Lindsay 1793, p. 494.
22. BL Add MS 38605.
23. Lindsay 1793, p. 503.
24. Ancell 1793, p. 221.
25. Drinkwater 1785, p. 301.
26. Ancell 1793, p. 211.
27. Lindsay 1793, p. 504.
28. Drinkwater 1785, pp. 290, 291.
29. REM 5601.03.2.
30. Anon 1783, pp. 49, 50.
31. Ancell 1793, p. 211.
32. Lindsay 1793, pp. 494–5.
33. BL Add MS 38605; Ancell 1793, p. 221.
34. D'Arçon 1783, pp. 24–5.
35. Anon 1783, p. 51.
36. Lindsay 1793, p. 495.
37. Anon 1783, p. 51.
38. Gordon 1784, p. 23.
39. Lindsay 1793, p. 496.

## CHAPTER TWENTY-ONE: EXPLOSION

1. Anon 1783, p. 52.
2. Crillon 1791, p. 360.
3. D'Arçon 1783, p. 32.
4. Lindsay 1793, p. 497.
5. Lindsay 1793, p. 497.
6. BL Add MS 38605.
7. Anon 1783, p. 52.
8. Drinkwater 1785, p. 292.
9. TNA PRO 30/11/271.
10. Anon 1785, p. 152.
11. Lindsay 1793, p. 498.
12. Anon 1783, pp. 52–3.
13. Drinkwater 1785, p. 292.
14. Gordon 1784, p. 47.
15. *Universal Magazine of Knowledge* 71 (1782), p. 271.
16. *Universal Magazine of Knowledge* 71 (1782), p. 271.

17. Anon 1783, p. 53.
18. Lindsay 1793, p. 499.
19. *London Gazette* 16 November 1782.
20. Ancell 1793, p. 214.
21. Spilsbury 1908, p. 78.
22. Lindsay 1793, p. 501.
23. TNA PRO 30/11/271; Picton wrongly claimed this was the *Pastora*, which did not explode.
24. TNA PRO 30/11/271.
25. DALSS 346M/017.
26. Ancell 1793, p. 215.
27. Ancell 1793, p. 217.
28. Drinkwater 1785, p. 302.
29. Ancell 1784, p. 267.
30. 346M/016, with kind permission of Devon Archives and Local Studies Service.
31. 346M/F160, with kind permission of Devon Archives and Local Studies Service.
32. Gordon 1784, p. 26.
33. Anon 1783, p. 59.
34. BL Add MS 38605.
35. Gordon 1784, p. 28.
36. Drinkwater 1785, pp. 302–3.
37. Lindsay 1793, p. 504.
38. BL Add MS 38605.
39. Anon 1783, p. 56.
40. Anon 1783, p. 57.
41. Lindsay 1793, pp. 503–4.
42. Anon 1783, pp. 57–8.
43. *Aberdeen Journal* 25 November 1782; *Manchester Mercury* 15 October 1782.

## CHAPTER TWENTY-TWO: HURRICANE

1. Drinkwater 1785, p. 300.
2. Anon 1783, p. 65.
3. Drinkwater 1785, p. 301.
4. BL Add MS 38605.
5. Drinkwater 1785, p. 308.
6. Anon 1783, p. 76.
7. Drinkwater 1785, pp. 309–10.
8. Anon 1783, pp. 65–6.

9. Laughton. 1902, p. 217.
10. *New Lloyd's List* 24 September 1782; *Hampshire Chronicle* 30 September 1782.
11. *New Lloyd's List* 8 October 1782.
12. Laughton 1902, p. 217; Beatson 1804, pp. 647–8.
13. Drinkwater 1785, pp. 314, 316; Anon 1783, p. 78.
14. Anon 1783, p. 79.
15. 346M/017, with kind permission of Devon Archives and Local Studies Service.
16. 346M/017, with kind permission of Devon Archives and Local Studies Service.
17. *Political Magazine* December 1782, p. 721.
18. Drinkwater 1785, pp. 319–20.
19. Anon 1783, pp. 81–2.
20. Drinkwater. 1785, pp. 320–1.
21. Macdonald 1906, p. 59.
22. Drinkwater 1785, p. 320.
23. *Political Magazine* December 1782, p. 721.
24. BL Add MS 38605.
25. Drinkwater 1785, p. 323.
26. Wale 1883, p. 224.
27. Laughton 1902, pp. 218–19.
28. Historical Manuscripts Commission 1894, p. 65.
29. Laughton 1902, p. 219.
30. Laughton 1902, p. 219.
31. *Kentish Gazette* 14 September 1782.
32. Historical Manuscripts Commission 1894, p. 65.
33. *Kentish Gazette* 30 November 1782.
34. *Newcastle Chronicle* 30 November 1782.
35. *Carnet de la Sabretache* 1907, p. 548.

## CHAPTER TWENTY-THREE: PEACE AND PLENTY

1. BL Add MS 38606.
2. Drinkwater 1785, p. 329.
3. Drinkwater 1785, p. 331.

4. *Parliamentary History of England* 23 (1814), p. 239.
5. *Parliamentary History of England* 23 (1814), pp. 239–40.
6. *Scots Magazine* 44 (1782), p. 681.
7. *Scots Magazine* 44 (1782), p. 682.
8. Spilsbury 1908, p. 107.
9. Spilsbury 1908, p. 90; BL Add MS 38606.
10. Drinkwater 1785, p. 332.
11. Connolly 1855, p. 24.
12. BL Add MS 38606.
13. Drinkwater 1785, p. 333.
14. BL Add MS 38606.
15. TNA WO 25/435.
16. Drinkwater 1785, p. 334.
17. BL Add MS 38606; Spilsbury 1908, p. 91.
18. Drinkwater 1785, pp. 337, 338.
19. Adams 1840, p. 176.
20. BL Add MS 38605.
21. Gordon 1784, p. 33.
22. Drinkwater 1785, p. 337.
23. Spilsbury 1908, p. 93; Drinkwater 1785, p. 339.
24. Spilsbury 1908, pp. 94, 95 and manuscript in the Garrison Library. *Cross Purposes* was a farce and *True Blue* (or *The Press Gang*) a musical interlude.
25. BL Add MS 38606.
26. 346M/016, with kind permission of Devon Archives and Local Studies Service; BL Add MS 38606.
27. 346M/016, with kind permission of Devon Archives and Local Studies Service.
28. Ancell 1793, p. 228; BL Add MS 38606.
29. BL Add·MS 38606.
30. Drinkwater 1785, p. 343; BL Add MS 38606.
31. Ancell 1793, p. 235.
32. BL Add MS 38606.
33. Drinkwater 1785, p. 345.
34. Gordon 1784, p. 33.
35. Ancell 1793, pp. 235–6.

36. Ancell 1784, p. 285.
37. BL Add MS 38606.
38. Drinkwater 1785, p. 345.
39. Drinkwater 1785, pp. 344, 345.
40. Spilsbury 1908, p. 98.
41. Drinkwater 1785, p. 346.
42. Drinkwater 1785, p. 347.
43. Spilsbury 1908, p. 101; BL Add MS 38606.
44. Drinkwater 1786, p. 343.
45. Drinkwater 1786, p. 343; Heriot 1792, p. 135; BL Add MS 38606.
46. Heriot 1792, p. 135.
47. Drinkwater 1785, p. 346.
48. Drinkwater 1785, p. 351.
49. Drinkwater 1785, p. 351.
50. Spilsbury 1908, p. 104.

## CHAPTER TWENTY-FOUR: AFTERMATH

1. BL Add MS 38606, from 'The Contrast' by a Soldier in Gibraltar'.
2. Vernon 1792, pp. 99–100. Vernon became lieutenant in 1793 and died three years later, aged thirty-one.
3. Lovell 1879, p. 16.
4. Drewry's Derby Mercury 17 July 1783.
5. Johnson 1971.
6. Essex Standard 16 December 1836. Her husband John had already died, and she died in 1837.
7. 346M/017, with kind permission of Devon Archives and Local Studies Service.
8. Cockburn 1815, pp. 17–18.
9. Cockburn 1815, p. 17.
10. Cockburn 1815, p. 16.
11. Cockburn 1815, p. 18.
12. Gibraltar Chronicle 28 December 1811.
13. Gibraltar Chronicle 28 December 1811.
14. 346M/017, with kind permission of Devon Archives and Local Studies Service; GNA 1777 census.
15. Annual Register 1806 (1808) p. 511.
16. Biographie Universelle, ancienne et moderne, supplément, vol. 67 (1840), p. 364.
17. Cranfield 1844, pp. 23–4; King's Chapel MS 'Marriages for the year 1783'.
18. Cranfield 1844, pp. 26–7.
19. 21 Charles Street; Adkins 2003, p. 349.
20. Macdonald 1906, pp. 67–8.
21. Macdonald 1906, p. 68; Landmann 1852, pp. 21, 24.
22. Landmann 1852, pp. 22–3.
23. Landmann 1852, pp. 24–5.
24. Landmann 1852, p. 27; Macdonald 1906, pp. 70–1.
25. Gentleman's Magazine 60 (1790), p. 671.
26. The Times 17 July 1790.
27. Landmann 1852, p. 28; TNA PROB 11/1194/187.
28. Chester Chronicle 6 August 1790.
29. Rosado 2002, pp. 8–9.
30. Upton 1784, p. viii.
31. Upton 1784, p. 6.
32. Sinclair 1783, pp. v–vi, 12; he admits he was the author in Sinclair 1831, p. xxix.
33. Sinclair 1783, p. 32.
34. Tancred 1907, p. 23.
35. Annual Register 1783 (1784), pp. 217–18.
36. Atkinson (1919) says they were not the same regiments as the Hanoverians, but that the Kaiser in 1901 awarded them the Gibraltar honour for prestige.
37. Tancred 1907, pp. 23–4.
38. Fortescue 1928b, p. 192.
39. Glueckstein 2013–14.
40. Churchill 1953, p. 607.
41. Adkins 2004, pp. 275–7.
42. NMM MDT/3.
43. NMM MDT/23.
44. Smith 1866, p. 183.
45. Drinkwater 1797.
46. Manchester Courier and Lancashire General Advertiser 20 January 1844.

# BIBLIOGRAPHY

———— ◆ ————

Adams, Mrs 1840 (2nd edn) *Letters of Mrs. Adams, The Wife of John Adams, with an introductory memoir by her grandson, Charles Francis Adams vol. 1* (Boston)

Adkins, L. 2003 *Empires of the Plain* (London)

Adkins, R. 2004 *Trafalgar: The Biography of a Battle* (London)

Adkins, R. and L. 2008 *Jack Tar: Life in Nelson's Navy* (London)

Ancell, S. 1784 *A circumstantial journal of the long and tedious blockade and siege of Gibraltar* (Liverpool)

Ancell, S. 1793 (4th edn) *A journal of the blockade and siege of Gibraltar* (Cork)

Anon 1782 *An accurate description of Gibraltar: interspersed with a pathetic account of the progress of the siege* (London)

Anon 1783 *Histoire du siège de Gibraltar* (Cadiz)

Anon 1784 *Nachrichten von Gibraltar in Auszügen aus Original-Briefen eines hannöverischen Offiziers aus Gibraltar, vor und während der letzen Belagerung* (Frankfurt, Leipzig)

Anon 1785 *An authentic and accurate journal of the late siege of Gibraltar* (London)

Anon 1806 'Biographical Memoir of Sir Thomas Louis, Bart K.M.T. and K.S.F. Rear-Admiral of the White Squadron' *Naval Chronicle* 16, pp. 177–93

Anon 1834 'The loss of the Royal George' *Penny Magazine* 3, pp. 174–6

D'Arçon, M. 1783 *Mémoire pour servir à l'histoire du siège de Gibraltar* (Cadiz)

D'Arneth, A. and Geffroy, M. A. 1874 (2nd edn) *Marie-Antoinette. Correspondance Secrète entre Marie-Thérèse et le Cte de Mercy-Argenteau avec les lettres de Marie-Thérèse et de Marie-Antoinette vol. 3* (Paris)

Atkinson, C.T. 1919 'The Hanoverians at Gibraltar' *United Service Magazine* 59, pp. 25–41

Atkinson, C.T. 1947 *The Dorsetshire Regiment vol. 1* (Oxford)

Ayala, I.L. de 1782 *Historia de Gibraltar* (Madrid)

Baldry, W.Y. 1936 'The sortie from Gibraltar, 27th November, 1781' *Journal of the Society of Army Historical Research* 15, pp. 144–51

Barnes, G.A. and Owen, J.H. (eds) 1936 *The Private Papers of John, Earl of Sandwich, First Lord of the Admiralty 1771–1782 vol. 3* (Navy Records Society)

Barnes, G.A. and Owen, J.H. (eds) 1938 *The Private Papers of John, Earl of Sandwich, First Lord of the Admiralty 1771–1782 vol. 4* (Navy Records Society)

Beatson, R. 1804 *Naval and Military Memoirs of Great Britain from 1727 to 1783 vol. 5* (London)

Bell, J. 1795 *Discourses on the Nature and Cure of Wounds* (Edinburgh)

Bell, J. and Ayala, I.L. 1845 *The History of Gibraltar (translated from the Spanish of Don Ignacio Lopez de Ayala)* (London)

Benady, S. 1994 *Civil Hospital and Epidemics in Gibraltar* (Grendon)

Benady, T. 2005 'The Settlement of Jews in Gibraltar, 1704–1783' *Gibraltar Heritage Journal* special edn, pp. 71–117 (a reprinted and updated article from *Transactions of the Jewish Historical Society of England* 26, 1979, pp. 87–110)

Budworth, J. 1795 *The Siege of Gibraltar: A Poem* (London)

Cairncross, A. 1783 'A curious case of a very remarkable and surprising recovery in a private soldier of the second battalion, 73d Regiment, serving in Gibraltar, 1781' *Medical Commentaries for the years 1781–82* (ed. A. Duncan), pp. 296–304

Carter, F. 1777 *A Journey from Gibraltar to Malaga vol. 1* (London)

Churchill, W. 1953 *The Second World War Volume VI Triumph and Tragedy* (Boston)

Coad, J. 2013 *Support for the Fleet: Architecture and engineering of the Royal Navy's Bases 1700–1914* (Swindon)

Cockburn, G. 1815 *A Voyage to Cadiz and Gibraltar vol. 1* (London)

Conn, S. 1942 *Gibraltar in British Diplomacy in the Eighteenth Century* (New Haven, London)

Connolly, T.W.J. 1855 *The History of the Royal Sappers and Miners vol. 1* (London)

Conolly, M.F. 1866 *Biographical Dictionary of Eminent Men of Fife* (Cupar, Edinburgh)

Cranfield, T. 1844 *The Useful Christian: A Memoir* (London)

Crespo, M. and Galliano, M. 2013 'The Great Siege – with a Minorcan Emphasis' *Gibraltar Heritage Journal* 20, pp. 50–69

Creswell, S.F. 1863 *Collections towards the History of Printing in Nottinghamshire* (London)

Crillon, Duc de 1791 *Mémoires Militaires de Louis de Berton des Balbes de Quiers* (Paris)

Donne, W.B. 1867 *The Correspondence of King George The Third with Lord North From 1768 to 1783 vol. 2* (London)

Drinkwater, J. 1785 *A History of the Late Siege of Gibraltar* (London)

Drinkwater, J. 1786 (2nd edn) *A History of the Siege of Gibraltar* (Edinburgh)

Drinkwater, J. 1797 *Narrative of the Proceedings of the British Fleet commanded by Admiral Sir John Jervis, KB, in the late action with the Spanish fleet* (London)

Dumont, P.-J. 1819 *Narrative of thirty-four years slavery and travels in Africa, collected from the account delivered by himself by J.S. Quesne* (London)

Duncan, F. 1872 *History of the Royal Regiment of Artillery vol. 1* (London)

Eliott-Drake, E. 1911 *The Family and Heirs of Sir Francis Drake vol. 2* (London)

Ellis, K. 1958 *The Post Office in the Eighteenth Century: A Study in Administrative History* (London)

Evelegh, A. 1965 *Some Notes on the Evelegh Family* (Southsea)

Falconer, A.F. 1946 'The loss of the Royal George' *Mariner's Mirror* 32, p. 188

Fortescue, J.W. 1902 *A History of the British Army vol. III 1763–1793* (London, New York)

Fortescue, J. (ed.) 1928a *The Correspondence of King George the Third from 1760 to December 1783 vol. 4* (London)

Fortescue, J. (ed.) 1928b *The Correspondence of King George the Third from 1760 to December 1783 vol. 6* (London)

Garcia, R.J.M. 2014 *A Mighty Fortress set in the Silver Sea* (Gibraltar)

Garcia, R.J.M. 2016 *The Currency and Coinage of Gibraltar, 1704–2014* (Gibraltar)

Garstin, C. 1925 *Samuel Kelly: An Eighteenth Century Seaman* (London)

Glueckstein, F. 2013–14 'Churchill and the Barbary Macaques: A visit to Gibraltar's Fabled Rock' *Finest Hour* 161, pp. 53–5

Gordon, W. 1784 *The History of the Blockade and Siege of Gibraltar. To which are added, memoirs of the life and military services of General Elliot* (Aberdeen)

Harvey, P.D.A. 1961 'An account of the Siege of Gibraltar, 1779–83' *The British Museum Quarterly* 23, pp. 93–5

Hennen, J. 1830 *Sketches of the Medical Topography of the Mediterranean* (London)

Herbert, C. 1967 'Coxheath Camp, 1778–1779' *Journal for the Society of Army Historical Research* 45, pp. 129–48

Heriot, J. 1792 *An historical sketch of Gibraltar, with an account of the siege* (London)

Hills, G. 1974 *Rock of Contention: A History of Gibraltar* (London)

Historical Manuscripts Commission 1894 *The Manuscripts of his Grace the Duke of Rutland, K.G. preserved at Belvoir Castle vol. III* (London)

Hogg, I. and Batchelor, J. 1978 *Naval Gun* (Poole)

Holmes, R. 2002 *Redcoat: The British Soldier in the Age of Horse and Musket* (London)

Howes, H. 1951 *The Gibraltarian: The origin and evolution of the people of Gibraltar* (Gibraltar)

Huish, R. 1837 *The History of the Life and Reign of William the Fourth* (London)

James T. 1771 *The History of the Herculean Straits, now called the Straits of Gibraltar vol. 2* (London)

Johnson, R.F. 1971 *The Royal George* (London)

Kendall, P. 2012 *The Royal Engineers at Chatham 1750–2012* (Swindon)

Kenyon, E.R. (ed.) 1912a 'A Lady's Experience in the Great Siege of Gibraltar (1779–83)' *Royal Engineers Journal* 15, pp. 37–44, 107–18, 163–82, 245–62, 309–26, 383–400

Kenyon, E.R. (ed.) 1912b 'A Lady's Experience in the Great Siege of Gibraltar (1779–83)' *Royal Engineers Journal* 16, pp. 31–50

Landmann, T. 1854 *Recollections of my military life vol. 1* (London)

Langle, M. de 1785 *Voyage en Espagne vol. 2* (Neuchatel) (attributed to J.C. Fleuriau)

Laughton, J.K. 1902 'Journals of Henry Duncan Captain, Royal Navy 1776–1782' *The Naval Miscellany vol. 1*, pp. 105–219 (Navy Records Society)

Lawrance, C. 1994 *The History of the Old Naval Hospital Gibraltar 1741 to 1922* (Lymington)

Lindsay, C. 1793 *Extracts from Colonel Tempelhoffe's History of the Seven Years War vol. 2* (London)

Lovell, W.S. 1879 (2nd edn) *Personal Narrative of Events, from 1799 to 1815, with anecdotes* (London)

Lyall, B. 2009 'Gibraltar's Heart Cut Coinage' *Gibraltar Heritage Journal* 16, pp. 55–60

McConnell, D. 1988 *British Smooth-Bore Artillery: A Technological Study to Support Identification, Acquisition, Restoration, Reproduction, and Interpretation of Artillery at National Historic Parks in Canada* (Ottawa)

Macdonald, J. 1906 *Autobiographical Journal of John Macdonald Schoolmaster and Soldier 1770–1830* (Edinburgh)

Macdonald, J. 2004 *Feeding Nelson's Navy* (London)

McGuffie, T.H. 1955 'The Royal Manchester Volunteers' *Manchester Review* (summer 1955) pp. 209–22

McGuffie, T.H. 1965 *The Siege of Gibraltar 1779–1783* (London)

Marsden, W. 1838 *A brief memoir of the life and writings of the late William Marsden* (London)

Marshall, M.A.N. 1955 'The armed ships of Folkestone' *Mariner's Mirror* 41, pp. 53–9

Mundy, G.B. 1830 *The Life and Correspondence of the Late Admiral Lord Rodney vol. 1* (London)

Owen, J.H. 1933 'Letters from Sir Samuel Hood 1780–1782' *Mariner's Mirror* 19, pp. 75–87

Patterson, A.T. 1960 *The Other Armada* (Manchester)

Payn, J. 1885 *Peril and Privation: Stories of Marine Disaster Retold* (London)

Payne, J. 1793 *The Naval Commercial, and General History of Great Britain* vol. 2 (London)

Pocock, T.A.G. 1955 'Captain Fagg of Folkestone' *Mariner's Mirror* 41, pp. 242–4

Porter, W. 1889 *History of the Corps of Royal Engineers vol. 1* (London and New York)

Rosado, P. 2002 *The Convent Gibraltar* (Gibraltar)

Rose, E.P.F. and Rosenbaum, M.S. 1991 *A Field Guide to the Geology of Gibraltar* (Gibraltar)

Russell, J. 1965 *Gibraltar Besieged 1779–1783* (London)

Rutherford, G. 1941 'The capture of the Ardent' *Mariner's Mirror* 27, pp. 106–31

Serfaty, A.B.M. 2005 'The Jews of Gibraltar under British Rule' *Gibraltar Heritage Journal* special edn, pp. 5–34 (a reprinted 1958 study)

Sinclair, J. 1783 *The Propriety of Retaining Gibraltar Impartially Considered* (London)

Sinclair, J. 1831 *The Correspondence of the Right Honourable Sir John Sinclair, Bart. vol. 1* (London)

Skidmore, C. 2013 *Bosworth: The Birth of the Tudors* (London)

Skinner, T. 1891 (ed. A. Skinner) *Fifty Years in Ceylon: An Autobiography* (reprinted in 1974 from *Ceylon Historical Journal* 21) (Sri Lanka)

Smith, J.F. 1866 *The Admission Register of the Manchester School* (Chetham Society)

Smyth, J.C. 1795 *A Description of the Jail Distemper, as it appeared amongst the Spanish Prisoners, At Winchester, in the Year 1780* (London)

Spilsbury, J. 1908 *A Journal of the Siege of Gibraltar 1779–1783* (ed. B.H.T. Frere) (Gibraltar)

Stead, B.L.M. 2000 '"Poor Distress'd Weavers": conflicting interpretations of the raising of the 72nd Regiment, Royal Manchester Volunteers' *British Journal for Eighteenth-Century Studies* 23, pp. 203–31

Stonehouse, W.B. 1839 *The History and Topography of the Isle of Axholme* (London)

Syrett, D. 1998 *The Royal Navy in European Waters During the American Revolutionary War* (Columbia)

Syrett, D. (ed.) 2007 *The Rodney Papers. Selections from the Correspondence of Admiral Lord Rodney vol. 2* (Aldershot)

Syrett, D. and DiNardo, R.L. 1994 *The Commissioned Sea Officers of the Royal Navy 1660–1815* (Aldershot)

Tancred, G. 1907 *Rulewater and its People* (Edinburgh)

Tayler, A. and H. 1914 *The Book of the Duffs* vol. 2 (Edinburgh)

Twiss, R. 1775 *Travels through Portugal and Spain in 1772 and 1773* (London)

Upton, C. 1781 *The Siege of Gibraltar from the Twelfth of April to the Twenty-Seventh of May, 1781* (London)

Upton, C. 1784 *Miscellaneous Pieces in Prose and Verse* (London)

Vaughan, W. 1839 *Memoir of William Vaughan, F.R.S. with miscellaneous pieces relative to docks, commerce, etc* (London)

Venning, A. 2005 *Following the Drum: The Lives of Army Wives and Daughters Past and Present* (London)

Vernon, F.V. 1792 *Voyages and Travels of a Sea Officer* (London)

Wale, H.J. 1883 *My Grandfather's Pocket-Book* (London)

Wheatley, H.B. 1884 *The Historical and the Posthumous memoirs of Sir Nathaniel William Wraxall 1771–1784 vol. 2* (London)

Wright, G.N. 1837 *The Life and Reign of William the Fourth vol. I* (London)

# LIST OF MAPS

# LIST OF ILLUSTRATIONS

———— ·◆· ————

## BLACK-AND-WHITE PLATES

The capsizing of the *Royal George* at Spithead on 29 August 1782 (J. Sleight 1844 *A Narrative of the Loss of the Royal George* (Portsea))

Typical Mediterranean vessels – a tartan, settee and xebec (after Spilsbury 1908)

The *Pastora* floating battery ('junk ship'); Spanish gunboats and a mortar boat; Royal Navy prames and a gunboat; a Moorish galley; and a smaller floating battery (two views) (Spilsbury 1908)

George Augustus Eliott, Governor of Gibraltar, from a painting by G.F. Koehler of the Royal Artillery (Authors' collection)

Captain John Drinkwater, depicted with writing materials and plans and holding his published book on the siege (J. Drinkwater 1905 *A History of the Siege of Gibraltar 1779–1783* (London))

Admiral Sir George Brydges Rodney (G.B. Mundy 1830 *The Life and Correspondence of the Late Admiral Lord Rodney vol. 2* (London))

Admiral Lord Richard Howe (J. Allen 1852 *Battles of the British Navy vol. 1* (London))

Port Mahon and Fort St Philip, Minorca (after *Carnet de la Sabretache* (1907))

Comte de Crillon (*Carnet de la Sabretache* (1907))

The British surrendering to the combined French and Spanish forces at Fort St Philip, Minorca (*Illustrated History of England* vol. 5 (*c.* 1860))

The quadrangular naval hospital, surrounded by a wall, with Parson's Lodge battery behind (Spilsbury 1908)

Koehler's depressing gun carriage (Spilsbury 1908)

Gun carriage elevated at 45 degrees, developed by Lieutenant-Colonel Williams of the Royal Artillery (Spilsbury 1908)

The Strait of Gibraltar viewed from the Line Wall. Much of the coastline is that of Barbary, and on the far right is Cabrita Point. Illustration by Captain John Drinkwater (Authors' collection)

Gibraltar viewed from across part of the isthmus, with the typical cloud caused by easterly winds, shrouding the site of the Rock Gun (Authors' collection)

The ruins of the Spanish Fort St Barbara, looking south towards the eastern and northern sides of Gibraltar (Authors' collection)

Looking from the hills above Algeciras to Gibraltar in a print of 1840. The town of Algeciras is just beyond the aqueduct and the Green Island lies to the right (Authors' collection)

San Roque viewed from the Governor's Palace. In the distance, on the left, is Gibraltar and on the right is the Spanish coast with Cabrita Point and Algeciras. Ape's Hill in Barbary rises above the layer of mist. The chimneys of an oil refinery (right) mark the site of the Carteia Roman ruins (Authors' collection)

The Governor's Palace at San Roque, the headquarters of the Spanish military campaign during the siege (Authors' collection)

A view northwards to Spain from Signal Hill towards Middle Hill and the site of the Rock Gun. On the right is the sheer eastern side and the Mediterranean (Authors' collection)

Barbary macaques largely inhabited the inaccessible eastern side of Gibraltar during the siege (Authors' collection)

Looking from Willis's battery (now with World War Two structures) towards the north front of the Rock. The protruding rock on the left is 'the Notch', towards which Ince was mining a tunnel in 1782 (Authors' collection)

The Landport gate and tunnel through which the soldiers passed during the sortie of November 1781. The stone bridge was demolished a few months later, and the sally port in the ditch (bottom left) was used instead (Authors' collection)

Looking through the original Southport Gate from the town (Authors' collection)

One of the larger floating batteries moving into position (*Carnet de la Sabretache* (1907))

A brass cannon on a wooden gun carriage, made by Bowen in 1758, now in the Alameda Gardens, in front of the Wellington monument (Authors' collection)

A brass howitzer, made by the Verbruggens at Woolwich in 1778, looking at the muzzle down which gunpowder and ammunition were loaded. It now forms part of a large monument in the Alameda Gardens dedicated to Eliott (Authors' collection)

British officers, one with a telescope, watching the floating batteries burn. In the distance are white tents of the French and Spanish camp (Authors' collection)

Obverse of a halfpenny token showing the head of General Eliott (spelled Elliot here). The reverse has a fleur-de-lys with the words 'Birmingham Halfpenny 1792' (Authors' collection)

A Dutch medal commemorating the sinking of the *Royal George*, the loss of Admiral Kempenfelt and the floating batteries attacking Gibraltar (Authors' collection)

# ACKNOWLEDGEMENTS

During our research, we have been generously assisted by a range of libraries, archives and other institutions, and we are especially grateful for permission to use quotations from manuscripts. We would like to extend our appreciation to Danielle Sellers and her colleagues at the Royal Engineers Museum, Library and Archive; the British Library; the London Library; the National Archives at Kew; Devon Archives and Local Studies Service; the Archives and Local Studies at Manchester Central Library; Exeter University's Library; Portsmouth History Centre and Records Office; Gibraltar's Garrison Library, with thanks to Dr Jennifer Ballantine Perera and Chris Tavares; the Gibraltar National Archives, with thanks to Anthony Pitaluga; the King's Chapel archives; the Gibraltar Tourist Board; the Gibraltar Museum; and Turismo San Roque.

We have benefited greatly from the professional expertise of Dr Jane Richards, who allowed us to bombard her with medical ailments. Peter N. Lockyer of Gosport generously rooted out information and documents in the Portsmouth area, all for the promise of a pint, while Simon Fowler was an invaluable asset at The National Archives. We would also like to thank Beth Torgerson, Patrick Ray and members of the Martineau Society for assistance, Dr Bonnie Huskins for sharing her research on the Royal Engineer William Booth, Scott McCracken for his expertise on military medals, Sam and Eleanor Simmons at Folklife Quarterly for constant support, Chris Mortimer of Blacksnow Web Design for his expertise in keeping us online, David Vassallo, Marguerite Galloway and many others on Gibraltar. In particular, we would like to mention the immense help given to us by Charlie Rosado, Pepe Rosado, Sam Benady and Richard Garcia.

As ever, friends and family have been sorely neglected while writing this book, and we are grateful for their understanding.

We owe particular thanks to Richard Beswick at Little, Brown (UK) and to Rick Kot at Viking Penguin (US) for steering us towards this book. We are also indebted to all those at Little, Brown involved in the various publishing processes, including Zoë Gullen (for her brilliant work), John Gilkes (for his maps), Richard Collins (for the copyediting) and Steve Cox (for proofreading); while at Viking Penguin we are also indebted to Tricia Conley, Alyson D'Amato, Caitlin Noonan, Ryan Boyle, Jason Ramirez, Colin Webber, Diego Núñez and Tony Forde.

# INDEX

———— •◆• ————

Ship names are in italics. Army units of soldiers and officers are given in brackets after their name, such as (58th) or (engineers). 'Gibraltar' is not specified for places and structures located on the Rock.

# ALSO AVAILABLE

### GIBRALTAR
The Greatest Siege in British History

### JANE AUSTEN'S ENGLAND
Daily Life in the Georgian and Regency Periods

### THE WAR FOR ALL THE OCEANS
From Nelson at the Nile to Napoleon at Waterloo

### NELSON'S TRAFALGAR
The Battle That Changed the World

PENGUIN BOOKS

Ready to find your next great read? Let us help. Visit prh.com/nextread